Causal Case Study Methods

In this comprehensive reconstruction of causal case study methods, Derek Beach, Rasmus Brun Pedersen, and their coauthors delineate the ontological and epistemological differences among these methods, offer suggestions for determining the appropriate methods for a given research project, and explain the step-by-step application of selected methods.

The authors begin with developing cohesive, logical foundations for small-N comparative methods, congruence methods, and process-tracing, and they delineate the distinctive types of causal relationships for which each method is appropriate. Next, the authors provide practical instruction for deploying each of the methods individually and in combination. They walk the researcher through each stage of the research process, starting with issues of concept formation and the formulation of causal claims in ways that are compatible with case-based research. They then develop guidelines for making causal inferences using Bayesian logic in an informal, nontechnical fashion as a set of practical questions for translating empirical data into evidence that may or may not confirm causal relationships.

Widely acclaimed instructors, the authors draw upon their extensive experience at the graduate level in university classrooms, summer and winter school courses, and professional workshops, literally all over the globe.

Derek Beach is Professor of Political Science at Aarhus University.

Rasmus Brun Pedersen is Associate Professor of Political Science at Aarhus University.

Jørgen Møller is Professor of Political Science at Aarhus University.

Svend-Erik Skaaning is Professor of Political Science at Aarhus University.

Causal Case Study Methods

Foundations and Guidelines for Comparing, Matching, and Tracing

Derek Beach *and* Rasmus Brun Pedersen

University of Michigan Press
Ann Arbor

Published in the United States of America by
The University of Michigan Press
Manufactured in the United States of America
⊗ Printed on acid-free paper

2019   2018   2017   2016   4   3   2   1

A CIP catalog record for this book is available from the British Library.

Library of Congress Cataloging-in-Publication Data

Names: Beach, Derek, author. | Pedersen, Rasmus Brun, 1978– author.
Title: Causal case study methods : foundations and guidelines for comparing, matching and tracing / Derek Beach and Rasmus Brun Pedersen.
Description: Ann Arbor : University of Michigan Press, 2016. | Includes bibliographical references and index.
Identifiers: LCCN 2015049565 | ISBN 9780472073221 (hardcover : alk. paper) | ISBN 9780472053223 (pbk. : alk. paper) | ISBN 9780472122318 (e-book)
Subjects: LCSH: Case method. | Research—Methodology. | Causation—Research.
Classification: LCC LB1029.C37 B43   2016 | DDC 371.39—dc23
LC record available at http://lccn.loc.gov/2015049565

Contents

Acknowledgments

This book would not have been possible without the extensive feedback supplied by participants in numerous doctorate-level methods training courses held by the authors throughout the world. In these intensive, multiday courses, we challenge participants to apply the developing standards for case-based designs in their own research. Through a long process of trial and error, we have developed a set of guidelines for the design of within-case and small-N comparative research that match the underlying ontological foundations of case-based research, but more important, that also actually work in practice, giving researchers a set of hands-on tools to define concepts and theories and study them empirically. We are greatly in debt to the participants in these courses on case study methods, including, but by no means limited to, the participants at the ECPR Summer School (2011–15) and Winter Schools (2012–16), IPSA Summer Schools in Sao Paulo (2012–16) and Singapore (2012), the Berlin Graduate School for Transnational Studies (2012–14, 2016), two APSA short courses in 2013 and 2014, and in the Concordia Workshops for Social Science Research (2013–15). We would particularly like to thank our teaching assistants in courses at the ECPR and IPSA schools in the past three years as vital interlocutors and sparring partners in developing our ideas for this book. We would like to thank Terra Budini, Hilde van Meegdenburg, Kim Sass Mikkelsen, Camila Rocha, and Yf Reykers.

We have also benefited from interaction and feedback from a number of colleagues at workshops and conferences. In no particular order we would like to thank in particular Robert Adcock, Andrew Bennett, Colin Elman, Guillaume Fontaine, Patrick Jackson, Markus Kreuzer, Craig Parsons, Ingo Rohlfing, and David Waldner for feedback on our ideas. In this book, we have also more extensively drawn on the considerable expertise of our colleagues Jørgen Møller and Svend-Erik Skaaning on topics related to conceptualization (chapter 4), operationalization and measurement (chapter 5), and comparative analysis (chapter 7). Any and all mistakes in this book are solely our responsibility, however.

We hope that this book will prove useful to a new generation of case-based scholars who want to go beyond the tired quantitative versus qualitative debate, building on the work of past generations of great scholars like Skocpol, George, and Sartori to develop a comprehensive set of methodological guidelines that are appropriate for case-based research. We have only scratched the surface in this book.

Derek Beach and Rasmus Brun Pedersen
Aarhus, Denmark
May 2016

CHAPTER I

Causal Case Studies

I thought that if you had an acoustic guitar, then it meant that you were a protest singer. Oh, I can smile about it now but at the time it was terrible.

The Smiths

1.1. Introduction

Raising teenagers can be a trying experience. The crux of the challenge is that one of the ways in which teenagers develop their identity is through opposition to their parents. Parents often let out a sigh of relief when their children reach a level of maturity at which their identity formation is no longer dependent on this opposition, instead being created and re-created through their own activities and achievements.

We can see a similar trajectory in the scholarly debates within qualitative causal case study methodology.[1] Two decades ago, the 1994 publication of King, Keohane, and Verba's (KKV) *Designing Social Inquiry* started a heated debate about whether qualitative and quantitative methods for doing causal research really differ. Numerous articles and books were published in response, making the case for the distinctive (but often complementary) nature of qualitative causal case study methods in relation to quantitative methods (e.g., Brady and Collier 2011; George and Bennett 2005; Geortz and Mahoney 2012; Brady, Collier, and Seawright 2006; Mahoney 2000, 2001).

We believe that the debate on causal case study methods has now reached a level of maturity at which it is no longer necessary for us to define foundations and principles merely by how they differ from variance-based (quantitative) methods. We now know that process-tracing methods focus on different types of causal relationships than variance-based analyses do, using a different type of empirical evidence from difference-making. We know that analyzing necessary conditions using comparative methods involves analyzing asymmetric causal relationships that are fundamentally different from the symmetric relationships assumed in variance-based analyses.

What we now want to know is *how* causal case study methods themselves are similar and different to each other as regards both their ontological and epistemological foundations, as well as the research situations in which they can be utilized and the guidelines and best practices for their use. A new post-KKV generation of scholars has begun asking the question, "And now what?" shifting the focus of methodological work toward defining the nature and uses of different causal case study methods on their own terms.

George and Bennett started this process with the publication of their 2005 book *Case Studies and Theory Development in the Social Sciences*, show-ing, for example, that comparative case studies and within-case methods like process-tracing have very different ontological and epistemological foundations. However, while they made an important first step, George and Bennett did not clearly delineate the commonalities and differences in the logical foundations of the different causal case study methods, nor did they provide guidelines that are clear enough to enable researchers to actually utilize the book's methods. Other recent contributions have developed the foundations and guidelines of *particular* causal case study methods, but by treating each method in isolation, they do not enable scholars to be able to choose which causal case study method offers more bang for the buck in a particular research situation, nor do they enable scholars to combine different methods together in a nested analysis (e.g., Beach and Pedersen 2013; Schneider and Wagemann 2012). Finally, several works have developed multiple case-based methods (e.g., Blatter and Haverland 2012). However, Blatter and Haverland (2012), for example, do not develop the ontological foundations upon which case-based research rest, and their work on com-bining case studies with cross-case methods is too cursory to offer real guid-ance in how this can be achieved.

Our ambition in this book is to consolidate and build on the past two decades of methodological work on causal case study methods, attempting to provide a more comprehensive answer to the question, "And now what?" Our goal is twofold: (1) to provide causal case study methods with more cohesive logical foundations by taking seriously the distinctive nature of the types of causal relationships that each method aims to analyze and (2) to provide a set of practical guidelines that will enable scholars to utilize each of the causal case study methods in their own research. The three methods that are developed in this book are the three most important and widely used in causal case study research: *small-N comparative methods, congruence methods,* and *process-tracing methods.*

This consolidation involves both clearing the brush by removing vestiges of variance-based thinking, such as the use of terms like "independent and dependent variables" and "most-likely/least-likely cases" that are not in alignment with the underlying ontological assumptions of case-based research.

At the same time, by gaming through each of the methods to ensure methodological alignment with these foundations, we have uncovered a number of overlooked methodological implications that have major impacts on how to design case-based research. These include the following:

- Case-based research shares the common ontological assumptions of asymmetry and determinism but *differs* according to whether causation is viewed in counterfactual or mechanistic terms, and whether causation is singular or implies regularity.
- The widespread use of *most-likely/least-likely cases* does not match the deterministic ontological assumption that is required if case-based research is to make any sense.
- *Causal homogeneity* is much more important for case-based research than is often recognized, especially when working with theories of causal mechanisms in process-tracing.
- Causal concepts in case-based research should *define only the positive pole* of concepts.
- *Differences of degree* in causal concepts are at best irrelevant, and at worst produce flawed generalizations in case-based research.
- *Strong causal inferences* are possible using either evidence of difference-making gained from experiments in variance-based research or *within-case mechanistic evidence* gained from congruence or process-tracing case studies.
- *Comparative case-based methods* can be used only to make disconfirming causal inferences. However, they are very useful for finding causes and for mapping populations of cases into causally similar bounded populations.
- *Congruence and process-tracing* case studies both produce mechanistic evidence, but they *differ* in the *depth of evidence* produced because congruence studies do not explicitly unpack causal mechanisms.
- We do not need to "control for other causes" when selecting cases,

where we select a case in which other factors are not present. Instead, control can be achieved at the empirical level by evaluating the uniqueness of the evidence of the workings of mechanisms within cases.

It is important to note that our book has a *pluralist interpretation* of methodology. We believe that there are fundamental differences both in the logical foundations of different causal case study methods and in the guidelines for their proper use. This pluralist understanding stands in marked contrast to the unifying ambitions that scholars like King, Keohane, and Verba, as well as John Gerring and others, have for social science methodology (see King, Keohane, and Verba 1994: 3–5; Gerring 2011: 7–11). The consequence of a unified logic is, in our opinion, that scholars elevate one methodological position above others, relegating other positions to second-best status.

However, pluralism is not the same as an "anything goes" position. For example, we provide arguments in chapter 2 for why determinism at the ontological level is the only logical assumption possible when we take individual cases as our analytical point of departure. Our understanding of the term "pluralism" means that we acknowledge that there are fundamental differences between case-based and variance-based designs, and also within case-based research between designs aimed at tracing mechanisms and comparative designs that build on counterfactuals. But within each of these methods we contend that there is only one set of assumptions regarding causality coupled with the methodology that is appropriate for studying it. For instance, it makes little sense to claim that cross-case comparative methods build on a mechanism understanding of causation.

We respect differences in this book by showing that different case-based methods provide distinct comparative advantages when used in appropriate research situations. For example, process-tracing methods focus on the causal mechanisms that lie in between a given condition and outcome, building on a mechanism-as-systems understanding of causal relationships. This makes process-tracing a very strong analytical tool for detecting *how* a given cause contributes to produce an outcome in a single case. However, process-tracing methods cannot be used to make cross-case inferences; this requires using comparative methods to nest the single case study in the broader population of the phenomenon. Crucially, the cross-case inferences are made using comparative methods, not process-tracing.

Despite delving into the logical foundations of causal case study methods, this book is not intended to be a treatise on philosophical questions of ontology and epistemology. Logical foundations of the methods are discussed because we need to understand them in order to tease out their methodological implications for research design. Further, by understanding these logical foundations, researchers will be better able to choose the appropriate method and research designs for a particular research situation.

Before we proceed, note that we do not develop the logic of "constitutive causation" in this book, given that it builds on a reflectivist philosophical position that is not compatible with the methodological precepts of this book. However, we do suggest that if one conceptualizes the construction of interests and identities as outcomes that can be created through processes (Bhaskar 1979: 113–14; Jackson 2011: 101–2; Schwartz-Shea and Yanow 2011), we can investigate the construction of interests and/or identities using the case study methods developed in this book.

1.2. What Is a Case?

In this book, we define a "case" as an instance of a causal process playing out, linking a cause (or set of causes) with an outcome. How we define a case in practical terms of temporal and spatial scope and unit of analysis is then contingent upon the theoretical claim we are making. The scope of a case determines the bounds of what one is making a causal inference about. Therefore, the definition of "case" is the unit in which a given causal relationship plays out, from the occurrence of the cause to the theorized outcome.

What a case is in relation to a causal theory can be better understood by using an analogy to sport games like soccer, baseball, and cricket. The rules of the game that determine how long the game lasts, where it is played, the ball used, how many players participate, and how the game is conducted are analogous to a causal theory. Just as a game of soccer lasts two forty-five-minute periods, whereas cricket matches can last days, some causal theories play out over a short amount of time among only a few participants (e.g., studying the impact of stress on elite decision-making), whereas other theories play out at the level of the international system over an extended period of time (e.g., the impact of power shifts on rivalry dynamics between great powers).

Individual games pitting Corinthians against Santos (soccer), the San Francisco Giants against the Kansas City Royals (baseball), or the Mumbai Indians against the Delhi Daredevils (cricket) are examples of what we would term a "case," although if our theory dealt instead with the impact of money on sporting results, a more appropriate bounds for a case might be a single season of a team.

In the social sciences, a case of a theory should be understood as a single iteration of the workings of a causal theory. There would be many cases of a theory of stress and elite decision-making (e.g., decision-making by the Bush administration in the immediate aftermath of 9/11), but one could argue that the causal dynamics might be different when dealing with cases in crises that could result in nuclear war, as under the Cold War, in comparison to nonnuclear crisis.

The crucial distinction to draw is between the level at which the causal relationship operates (a single case) and the population of cases in which similar causal processes are hypothesized to be operative. The population of cases is then the sum total of all comparable individual cases in which the causal theory plays out in a similar fashion. The population of cases for baseball would be all of the games since professional baseball leagues were created in the late 1800s.

We return to the question of comparable cases in chapters 3 and 7, only alluding to the critical distinction between variance-based, large-N research, and case-based designs here. A key difference is that variance-based research opts for large populations of potentially causally dissimilar cases, in which causal theories play out in different ways because of different contexts, in order to achieve enough cases to engage in meaningful statistical analysis. While they are aware of the potential risk of causal heterogeneity, variance-based researchers would claim that these potential errors, unless systematic, should wash out in a large population.

Case-based researchers opt to keep populations smaller to ensure that the cases being compared are as causally similar as possible, because of the importance of generalizing from the single studied case to a population of causally similar cases. Returning to sports, a variance-based researcher might use statistical trends of team performance over several seasons to understand a particular case. The conclusion might be that the team in the particular game underperformed, but one would expect on average better performance.

In contrast, case-based researchers take the individual case as the analytical point of departure. They would analyze the single game much more closely, and generalize from it only to games played in very similar contexts. For example, if one was analyzing team performance in soccer in a game against a title rival played at home early in the season, one would compare this game only with other home games against title rivals early in the season. The reason for these restrictions is that team performance might be expected to be very different against weaker teams, or later in the season. These would therefore be causally relevant contextual factors that would have to be included when defining the bounds of causally similar cases in the population.

The causal homogeneity of the population enables us to infer from the studied case or cases to the rest of the cases in the population using the argument "we found a relationship in cases A, B, and C, and logically we should expect the same to hold in cases D, E, and F, given that their similarity means that we have no reason to expect different relationships in D, E, and F" (see chapters 2 and 7 for more on causal homogeneity). In variance-based research, this is less of a problem because we are making causal claims about trends at the population level, whereas in case-based research, while we gain within-case evidence about how a causal process played out in a particular case, given the sensitivity of processes to context, it can be very difficult to generalize from the studied case to other, nonstudied cases in even a small, bounded population.

1.3. Plan of the Book

This book deals with research design for case-based methods, walking through different methodological challenges in the research process from conceptualization, measurement, and inferential logics to more practical guidelines for engaging in single case studies and/or comparisons.

The book is organized as follows: In chapter 2 we develop the ontological foundations for case-based research, distinguishing four distinct positions that result in different methods. Readers who want to cut directly to the chase—practical guidelines for the use of each of the three methods—can skip this chapter. However, without a good understanding of the foundational assumptions of the methods, we cannot make informed choices about which method is most appropriate for a given research question based on the relative strengths and weaknesses of different methods, nor can we understand when we can and cannot combine different causal case study methods into a single nested design. For instance, unless we understand the difference between mechanisms and counterfactuals, we cannot understand why process-tracing can make causal inferences within a single case when there is *no variation* in our research design that could produce evidence of difference-making.

Chapter 2 develops the logical building blocks of the three causal case study methods, illustrating which assumptions about causation are shared and which differ across methods. The methodological significance of different logical assumptions about the ontological nature of causation become apparent when we take into account the *principle of methodological alignment*, which states that "the appropriateness of a particular set of methods for a given problem turns on the assumptions about the nature of the causal relations they are meant to discover" (Hall 2003: 374). By making explicit the foundational building blocks of each causal case study method, we enable scholars to provide clear justifications for their choice of a particular variant of causal case study methods, and more important, by understanding the inner workings of the method, scholars can understand why a particular method offers the greatest analytical bang for the buck for a given research situation.

We argue that case-based methods share the assumptions of asymmetry and determinism but differ on the issues of counterfactuals versus mechanisms, how mechanisms are understood, and whether causation can be singular (token) or refers only to regular relationships. We develop four distinct positions as underlying particular case-based methods:

1. Small-N comparative methods: regularity and counterfactuals
2. Single-case counterfactual (comparative) case studies: singular and counterfactual
3. Congruence case studies: minimalist understanding of mechanisms (and either singular or regular)
4. Process-tracing case studies: mechanisms-as-systems understanding of mechanisms (and either singular or regular)

The chapter ends with a discussion of three important methodological implications of the shared ontological assumptions of determinism and asymmetry, including why the logic of most-likely/least-likely cases is not appropriate for case-based designs, why causal homogeneity is so important, and why we should focus only on categorical, difference-of-kind distinctions when defining causal concepts in case-based research.

Chapter 3 provides practical guidance for what different types of causal explanations in case-based research can look like. These include claims about necessity and/or sufficiency, as well as mechanisms understood either in a minimal sense or as systems. The core claim of the chapter is that good causal theoretical explanations make explicit the causal logic that makes a cause a cause and explain why the outcome is expected to be produced. For instance, when theorizing a mechanism as a system, each part of the mechanism that links a cause and outcome together is clearly described in a way that makes explicit what it is about a part that transfers "causal forces" to the next part.

Chapter 4 presents a set of principles for concept formation that are in alignment with the underlying understandings of causation in case-based research. These include concept structure (e.g., focusing only on the positive pole of concepts when causation is asymmetric) and the key differences between understanding theoretical concepts as conditions and as variables. Chapter 5 turns to questions relating to operationalization of causal concepts (measurement procedures), focusing in particular on capturing empirically the causally relevant differences of kind and qualitative thresholds that demarcate real-world cases where a causal relationship is possible from those where it is not.

Chapter 6 develops Bayesian logic as the inferential underpinnings of causal inference in case-based research, showing how it enables inferences in both cross-case and within-case evidence. Instead of a one-size-fits-all claim about cross-case variation in values of X and Y being the only relevant form of empirical evidence (i.e., evidence of difference-making) (King, Keohane, and Verba 1994; Gerring 2005, 2007), the chapter develops a more sophisticated Bayesian-inspired framework in which the types of evidence match the underlying assumptions about the nature of the causal relationships being investigated. In contrast to much recent work that attempts to formalize and quantify Bayesian logic in case studies (e.g., Bennett 2014; Humphreys and Jacobs 2015), we avoid the use of formulas and numbers in order to focus our attention on what actually matters: the careful interpretation of which empirical material potentially can be evidence of in particular contexts. In addition, while the existing literature has focused only on the probative value of individual pieces of evidence, we provide a set of practical guidelines for aggregating evidence in a case study.

The final three chapters of the book develop specific guidelines for each of the three causal case study methods, illustrating the methodological consequences that different ontological assumptions have for research design. Each chapter starts by defining the shared assumptions underlying each method. At the same time, each individual method is actually composed of different *variants* according to the uses to which the methods are put. For instance, process-tracing can be divided into explaining outcome, theory-building, theory-testing, and theory-refining variants, depending on the research situation and the underlying understanding of science itself. We do not distinguish different variants for their own sake, but only because different variants have different research purposes, which then imply quite different research designs.

Chapter 7 develops the different uses of comparative methods, and in particular how they can be combined with within-case studies to enable us to generalize from single cases to the rest of a causally similar population. The core of small-N comparative methods is a focused comparison of a small number of cases using designs such as the method of agreement or a most-similar-system comparison that enable disconfirming inferences to be made about conditions (negative inferences). While there are numerous books and articles on comparative methods, the value this chapter adds is that we develop how to combine comparisons with case studies in a way that takes the distinctive nature of each method seriously. We also develop clear guidelines for using comparative methods to find new causes, building causally homogeneous populations for use when generalizing from single cases, and disconfirming tests of claims of necessity and/or sufficiency. The chapter concludes with a set of practical, step-by-step guidelines for using the most common variants of comparative methods, focusing especially on how they can be combined with within-case studies (either congruence or process-tracing). We conclude with an example of the use of a comparative design that uses a most-similar-systems test.

Chapter 8 reintroduces the congruence case study method, illustrating the many theory-building and testing purposes that it has. George and Bennett (2005) took important first steps toward defining the congruence method, and we build upon those, although we take the cue from Khong (1992) in moving away from the focus on cross-case covariation to discuss how congruence can produce within-case evidence. We believe that congruence case studies actually have more uses than process-tracing, in particular as plausibility probes or when we do not need to flesh out a mechanism in detail. We develop guidelines for four variants of the congruence method: explaining outcome congruence, theory-building (searching for new causes), and two types of theory-testing (plausibility probes and robust tests). We conclude with an extended illustration of the use of congruence case studies.

Chapter 9 presents a set of guidelines for process-tracing case study methods. In comparison to other case study methods, process-tracing involves "attempts to identify the intervening causal process—the causal chain and causal mechanism" (George and Bennett 2005: 206–7) that links a cause (or set of causes) and an outcome. We go beyond existing work by developing clearer guidelines for building theories of mechanisms and case selection, and in using process-tracing to revise existing theories by tracing mechanisms in deviant cases. We differentiate process-tracing into four variants: explaining outcome process-tracing that accounts for particular historical outcomes, as well as theory-building, theory-testing, and theory-refining variants. We conclude with an extended example of the use of process-tracing.

1.4. Three Philosophical Positions and Case-Based Research

The three methods and the underlying ontological foundations might appear to favor particular philosophical positions on deeper issues relating to the nature of science itself (for a good introduction, see Jackson 2011). We believe that while methodological principles being used must be in alignment with the underlying ontological understandings of causation, we do not believe that different philosophical positions are incompatible with the three case-based methods developed in this book, with the exception being a reflectivist position that we believe dictates a different set of methodological tools (e.g., poststructuralist or critical methodologies).

We follow Jackson (2011) in simplifying the philosophical debate on the nature of science into four key positions: neopositivism, critical realism, pragmatism or analyticism, and reflectivism. We contend that the methods developed in this book can be adapted to each of the three first positions.

The neopositivist position is the most widespread in the social sciences; it builds upon the ideas that there is a "mind-independent" world that can be studied empirically by testing whether what we find empirically corresponds to our hypotheses, but also that we should focus only on the directly observable (phenomenalism). If we adopt a neopositivist understanding of science in combination with our methodological guidelines, the focus of research would be on analyzing narrowly conceptualized observable causes and their empirical effects. Parsimony would be favored over more complex causal theories (e.g., about conjunctional causation, where causes work together in complex formations), and the goal would be to generalize to as many cases as reasonably possible. If mechanisms are being studied, they would be construed as more or less directly observable phenomena that are close to being manipulable intervening variables.

The critical realist position differs from neopositivism in terms of whether we can study nonobservable phenomena, in particular regarding causal mechanisms (e.g., Bhaskar 1978).[2] When building on critical realism, case-based research would focus more broadly on sets of causes and causal complexity and would also be interested in studying "deeper" causes such as ideas and beliefs that cannot be measured directly. Singular causal claims would also be made when relevant, but limited generalizations would also be made to small, bounded populations of similar cases.

Finally, what Jackson terms "analyticism" can be understood to have the common denominator that we as observers are part of the social world we are studying, meaning that knowledge separate from our place in it is impossible. Instead, we can learn about the world through practical instruments, such as ideal-types that produce knowledge by grounding theory in the social and cultural world of the research (Jackson 2011: 142). Of most relevance to the methods developed in this book is the *pragmatist* variant of analyticism, where theories are understood to be heuristic tools to capture important aspects of what is going on in particular cases (Humphreys 2010; Friedrichs and Kratochwill 2009; Peirce 1955). Theories are not "tested" per se, but are utilized in a more instrumental fashion to craft comprehensive explanations of particular cases. Cases are here also understood in a more holistic fashion, where the goal is to explain the "big and important" things going on in particular cases. Given this goal, multiple theories are typically combined in an eclectic fashion, as one theory by itself is almost never sufficient (Sil and Katzenstein 2010). Allison's (1971) classic case study of the Cuban Missile Crisis is an example of this type of research, where three different theories are employed to explain different aspects of the crisis in a complementary fashion. We suggest a pragmatist variant of both congruence and process-tracing in chapters 8 and 9, termed "explaining outcome."

To conclude, table 1.1 describes how case-based research can look depending on which overall philosophical position one adopts. However, depending on whether one is working with a neopositivist or more pragmatic understandings of science, there is a distinction in how cases are understood. In the first, we study causation at the case-level to learn something about

TABLE 1.1.   Different philosophical positions and what they look like in case-based research

Neopositivism	• Causes are narrowly conceptualized • Research focuses on effects of particular causes across cases • Parsimonious causal theories are favored • Generalization across cases attempted • Causal conditions in focus, and if mechanisms are theorized, they are viewed as very similar to intervening variables
Critical realism	• Causes are broader and more complex, often working in conjunction with each other • Research focuses on complex causal patterns • Generalization only to small, bounded populations • Singular causation also in focus • Mechanisms are at the core of research
Pragmatism (analyticism)	• Causes are complex, often involving eclectic combinations of different theories to account for the big and important things in cases • Cases are not "cases of" generalizable phenomenon, but instead are understood holistically as proper nouns (e.g., *the* Cuban Missile Crisis)

causal relationships in a broader set of similar cases. For example, we might study a particular case to shed light on the causes of social revolutions in a small bounded population of causally very similar cases (Skocpol 1979). The cross-case generalization would involve using the evidence of a causal relationship in case 1 and a cross-case comparison that tells us that cases 2 and 3 are similar on all causally relevant aspects; then we could infer that the same causal relationship found in case 1 should be present in cases 2 and 3. When more pragmatic understandings of science are used, cases are understood in a more holistic fashion, where the goal is to account more comprehensively for a particular outcome. Causes and outcomes are formulated as proper nouns. For example, we might engage in a detailed case study that investigates the causes of *the* Russian Revolution in 1917 instead of a case study of a generic revolution. The case is no longer narrowly understood as a "case of" social revolutions, but as the big and important things going on that can help us understand why the Russian Revolution occurred.

CHAPTER 2

Understanding Causation in Case-Based Methods

If you don't know where you are going any road can take you there.

Lewis Carroll, *Alice in Wonderland*

2.1. Introduction

An explanation of an event is more than classifying or describing the event as part of a class of a phenomenon. Instead, causal explanations shed light on *why* events take place (Kuhn 1977: 23).[1] Causal explanations and the methods to make inferences about them using empirical evidence is what this book deals with. But what, then, does it mean to claim that a factor is a cause, or a contributing cause, of an outcome? Unfortunately, there is no easy answer to this question, and philosophers of science have debated the question since the birth of philosophy itself.

On the basis of recent debates about causation within the field of the philosophy of science, we now have an appreciation that the term "causal relationship" can refer to many different types of causal relationships between phenomena that are connected to the underlying concept of causation adopted, understood as the ontology of causation (e.g., Brady 2008; Kurki 2008; Waskan 2011; Illari 2011). In this chapter we argue that there is *not* one common set of ontological assumptions about causation underlying all social science methodology, as some scholars otherwise claim (e.g., Gerring 2011; Morgan and Winship 2007; Woodward 2003). We claim that there is not even one shared understanding within the field of case-based research, as suggested by some recent works (e.g., Goertz and Mahoney 2012; Lebow 2014). Instead, in case-based research we can identify four different combinations of ontological assumptions that logically fit together into clusters, all of which build on a common core of asymmetry and deterministic ontological assumptions.

Methodological Alignment and the Nature of Causation

Debates about the nature of causation are important to understand because different conceptions of causation result in different types of causal claims, which then imply that different methodologies are needed to investigate them appropriately. For instance, the most appropriate method for investigating a probabilistic, counterfactual-based causal claim about the mean causal effects of factor X would be an experiment that produces evidence of difference-making across a set of cases chosen using randomization. In contrast, the best method to investigate a deterministic claim about the causal mechanisms that produce outcome O in a given context would be an in-depth process-tracing study of several cases, each of which produces mechanistic evidence of the causal processes as they played out in the individual cases.[2]

It is important to note that while we advocate a pluralist position on methodological issues, in which one accepts and understands ontological and epistemological differences across methods, we do not argue an "anything goes" position. Instead, we argue for the principle of alignment, by which our methods are in alignment with the deeper ontological and epistemological assumptions that we adopt. Misconstrued, one might contend that we are actually methodological monists, wedded to one particular interpretation. However, monism means that there is only one understanding, with other positions subsumed under that umbrella (Reiss 2011). For instance, Gerring's work is arguably monist, as the counterfactual, probabilistic understanding of causation is viewed as the "unified framework" binding all methodologies together (2005, 2011: 11). In contrast, while we believe that using ontological determinism and asymmetry as the core common foundation for case-based methods is the only logical position when taking causation at the case level as the point of departure, we contend that outside of this common core there are (at least) four distinct positions based on different ontological understandings of causation that combine assumptions about counterfactual- versus mechanism-based causation, and regularity versus singular causation. Further, we do not attempt to subsume all methods under this umbrella. For instance, while methodologically very different, we agree that probabilistic, counterfactual-based causal claims based on experiments also can produce compelling evidence of causal relationships (i.e., evidence of difference-making), albeit of a different kind than that produced by case-based methods (i.e., mechanistic, within-case evidence).

Methodological alignment starts with how we understand the nature of causality itself. Understanding causation in terms of counterfactuals leads one down a different methodological path than if one is interested in tracing mechanisms. Counterfactuals, especially when coupled with assumptions of causation as regular association, lead to cross-case designs that investigate invariant patterns of association across cases using comparative methods. In contrast, when causation is understood in mechanism terms, the most appropriate designs for investigating this involve tracing these processes using within-case methods like congruence or process-tracing.

In case-based research, the focus is on making claims about causal relationships at the level at which they operate. A "case" is an instance of a causal process playing out, linking a cause (or set of causes) with an outcome. How we define a case in terms of temporal and spatial scope and unit of analysis is, of course, contingent upon the theoretical claim we are making. Cases can be individual persons making a split-second decision or large macro-processes involving the world economy over an extended time period. The crucial distinction to draw is between the level at which the causal relationship operates (a single case) and the population of cases in which similar causal processes are assumed to be operative (Russo and Williamson 2011; Mahoney 2008). The population of cases, then, is the sum total of all comparable individual cases in which the causal theory plays out in a similar fashion. Case-based research can therefore be thought of as "bottom-up," whereas variance-based designs are more "top-down," taking the population or a sample thereof as the analytical point of departure. Evidence in case-based methods of causal relationships is typically what can be called mechanistic evidence, providing empirical evidence of causal processes at the level at which causes actually operate. In contrast, in variance-based methods, evidence is typically at the level of the population (or samples thereof), with difference-making evidence illustrating the impact that changes in values of a cause (treatment) have on values of an outcome, controlling for other causes, but where our evidence of causal relationships is not at the same level at which the causes actually operate.

Taking cases as the point of analytical departure does not mean that case-based research is always producing causal explanations about why *particular* social outcomes occurred in *single* cases. As was discussed in the introductory chapter, whether we want to craft a comprehensive causal explanation of a particular outcome or to say something about a causal relationship that can travel within a bounded population of similar cases depends on the philosophical position we take on the nature of science itself.

This chapter proceeds in three steps. We first introduce the fundamental debates on the nature of causation and causal relationships that are relevant for understanding the foundations of the three causal case study methods in this book, illustrating how they differ both from the assumptions of variance-based methods and from each other. The next section develops which sets of assumptions logically fit together, where we make the claim that there are four distinct logical combinations that form the ontological foundations of case-based research.

The chapter concludes by discussing three important but overlooked methodological implications that these different combinations of understandings have, focusing on why most-likely/least-likely case selection strategies are not compatible with deterministic understandings of causation, the importance of causal homogeneity when making deterministic and asymmetric claims, and the focus only on differences of kind in case-based research.

2.2. Different Ontological Assumptions in Causal Case Study Methods

When we say that there is a *causal* relationship between a cause (C) and outcome (O), what are we actually claiming? Here it is important to put aside commonsense understandings based on intuitions about what it means to claim that C is the cause of O, as they can play tricks on our mind. And given the numerous challenges related to claiming causation, it is not surprising that the nature of causation has been a topic hotly debated by philosophers of science since Aristotle.

The following develops several core distinctions in the ontological assumptions about causation underlying different methods in case-based research (see figure 2.1). The discussion starts by making the claim that ontological determinism and asymmetry are the shared core assumptions of case-based research, building on the works of Mahoney, Goertz, and Ragin (Mahoney 2008; Goertz and Mahoney 2012; Ragin 2000, 2008). As the name suggests, the basic level of causal relationship in case-based research is the case, with a case defined as the unit in which a given causal relationship plays out. In any given case, either a hypothesized causal relationship has taken place or not; this means that there logically are no within-case

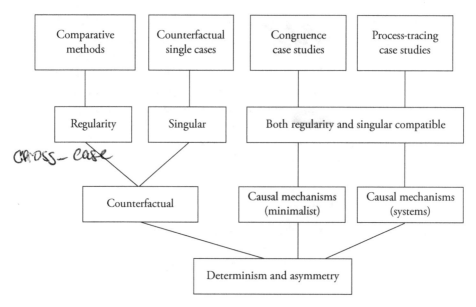

Fig. 2.1. Different ontological assumptions and causal case study methods

probabilities. As will be developed in this chapter, this implies that case-based research should use the ontological assumptions of determinism and asymmetry.

While case-based research takes causation at the case level as its point of departure, this does not mean that we cannot learn anything about causal relationships by studying cross-case patterns, which is what we do in comparative methods that build on counterfactual understandings of causation. However, whether we can learn about causal relationships by studying cross-case or within-case evidence is an *epistemological* discussion that we will return to in later chapters. What we are focusing on in this chapter is the ontological assumptions underlying different case-based methods, all of which share ontological determinism and asymmetry as core assumptions.

The chapter then moves on to discuss the distinction between viewing causation in terms of counterfactuals or mechanisms, depicted as the first branch in figure 2.1. Whereas counterfactuals logically lead one down the path of comparative methods, studying mechanisms in some fashion results in a focus on studying the evidence *actually* produced by causal processes *within* cases, thus leading to in-depth single case studies.

The final distinction is whether causation has to be found across multiple cases (regularity), or whether there is what can be termed "singular causation" (also termed "token-causal claims") (Woodward 2003: 210–20; Russo and Williamson 2011). When coupled with the assumption of causation as counterfactuals, regularity results in designs where cross-case patterns are investigated, whereas if singular causation is viewed as possible, the only logical possibility available is comparison of the single positive case with a hypothetical counterfactual. On the mechanism side, many adherents of mechanisms claim that only regular conjunctions are causal. However, it is also possible to ascribe to a singular understanding when tracing mechanisms, in particular when adopting more pragmatic understandings of science (see chapter 1). Given this, we contend that it is logically possible to hold either assumption. When regularity is assumed, the goal of research becomes to find mechanisms that work across multiple cases within bounded populations, whereas when singular causation is assumed, the focus is on assessing how mechanisms work in particular cases. We refer to the former as theory-centric research, as it aims to generalize beyond the bounds of the single case, and to the latter as case-centric research.

2.3. The Core of Case-Based Research: Determinism and Asymmetry

We now turn to defining in more detail the common ontological core assumptions about causation shared in case-based research, introducing first ontological determinism, followed by asymmetry and why we claim that it is the only logical position when we take individual cases as our analytical point of departure, as we do in case-based research.

Ontological Determinism

The distinction between ontological probabilism and determinism is one of the most misunderstood distinctions in the social sciences, with many scholars conflating *ontological* and *epistemological* probabilism.[3] In this chapter we are discussing the nature of causal claims (ontology), not whether we can be certain about empirical knowledge gained from research (epistemology). Building on the work of Mahoney, we make the claim that only a deterministic ontology is compatible with case-based research (Mahoney 2008; Goertz and Mahoney 2012); anything else makes the study of individual cases a secondary exercise used to substantiate what variance-based researchers perceive as the more important causal trends at the population level.[4] At the same time, we contend that case-based designs should adopt a probabilistic epistemology that tells us that our knowledge of the world will never be certain, but instead that our *degree* of confidence in a causal relationship being valid depends on the quality of the evidence produced (for more on this, see chapter 6). Epistemological determinism would mean that we can gain knowledge about causal relationships that is 100 percent certain, which is naturally an impossibility outside of the realm of trivial facts and conspiracy theories. Surprisingly, the distinctive combination of ontological determinism and epistemological probabilism has not been clearly developed in social science, although it has long existed in the methodological and philosophical literatures.[5]

Given the lack of development of this position, many existing accounts of case-based research adopt a pragmatic middle position as a means of protecting themselves from critiques of epistemological determinism by softening their deterministic ontological (theoretical) claims. For example, many case-based scholars use terms like an "almost deterministic" relationship to refer to a pattern where C might be necessary for O in 19 out of 20 cases (e.g., Ragin 2000; Goertz 2003). In practice this loosening has quite serious implications for the building and testing of theories both within and across cases, given that we never really know whether we have found an exception that proves the rule (the 20th case), or whether there is only a weak relationship or none at all. We develop this argument further in chapter 6.

Ontological probabilism means that we are dealing with a world in which there are random (i.e., stochastic) properties, best seen in the error terms used in regression analysis (see, e.g., King, Keohane, and Verba 1994: 89n11). Probabilistic claims are about trends (e.g., mean causal effects) in the relationship between causes and outcomes, but there can be many reasons the relationship does not hold in individual cases (Williams and Dyer 2009). This randomness can be the product either of an inherent randomness in the world or of complexity of causal patterns across a population of cases, such as omitted variables (Williams and Dyer 2009: 210–11). The argument for a probabilistic ontology based on the inherent randomness of the world is often linked to theories of quantum physics.[6] However, there are at least two reasons to not accept that theories from quantum physics tell us that the social world should also have a degree of inherent randomness. First, the theory of decoherence in physics attempts to explain why nonclassical (probabilistic) quantum behavior at the subatomic level gets suppressed as a result of interactions between objects and systems, thus resulting in the emergence of classical (deterministic) behavior as we move toward the levels of analysis that we as social scientists are interested in (Bacciagaluppi 2012; Joos et al. 2003). Second, at the empirical level, few physicists claim that the theoretical mathematics in quantum theory actually represents the world as it is; rather, it is a conceptual tool to understand the "spooky action" properties of what they observe empirically. And recent applications of Bayesian probability theory have begun to make sense of the seemingly random nature of observations where particles appeared to be in two places at the same time, developing a probabilistic Bayesian epistemology to account for uncertainties in measurement (Von Baeyer 2013; Fuchs 2010).

A more plausible argument for ontological probabilism in the social world than importing lessons from quantum behavior is that when we are making causal claims across a number of cases, we can at best detect trends (e.g., mean causal effects) because of the causal complexity of the social world.[7] For example, many scholars make the probabilistic claim that a strong national economy increases the chances for an incumbent US president to be reelected (Fair 2012; Nadeau and Lewis-Beck 2001). However, these strong mean causal effects of economic factors tell us little about particular cases, given that the population of US presidential elections is quite heterogeneous. Fair (2012), for example, analyzes the relationship in all US elections from 1916 to 2008. In such a heterogeneous population, the effects of economic factors can be stronger, weaker, or even nonexistent in any given case because of contextual factors. For instance, the 1976 election is an example of population-level claims *not* holding in the single case. Despite a poor economy in 1976 that would lead us to expect that this would lead the incumbent president Gerald Ford to lose the election quite badly, challenger Jimmy Carter only narrowly defeated incumbent Ford given a combination of post-Watergate fatigue with politicians in general coupled with an increasingly partisan atmosphere that enabled Ford to do better than Fair's theory leads us to expect (Miller 1978). In contrast, in a case-based design, studying the 1976 would tell us something about the contextual factors required for economic factors to matter.

At the end of the day, whether the stochastic elements of the social world are inherent or the product of causal complexity across cases is irrelevant, as the implications for probabilistic theorization are the same (Marini and Singer 1988; Gerring 2005; King, Keohane, and Verba 1994: 211). The claim is that causal relationships can at most be modeled as probabilistic when we are making claims about a population of cases. The analysis of single cases, understood in King, Keohane, and Verba's terms as one observation of the values of a cause (X) and an outcome (Y), by definition does not enable us to investigate *trends* across cases. More simply put, no evidence of difference-making is produced when there are no differences to account for. Causal claims in probabilistic theories therefore take the form of "Y tends to increase when X increases," which are best assessed by examining trends *across* cases.

For statisticians deterministic causality refers to a theoretical model where there is no error term (i.e., no random component), which basically means that, if properly specified, a deterministic model should explain 100 percent of the variance of a given dependent variable. In contrast, case-based scholars and many philosophers operate with a different take on ontological determinism by contending that events do *not* happen randomly at the level of individual cases (Adcock 2007; Mahoney 2008; Bhaskar 1979: 70–71). Mahoney summarizes this understanding succinctly by stating, "The assumption of an ontologically deterministic world in no way implies that researchers will successfully analyze causal processes in this world. But it does mean that randomness and chance appear only because of limitations in theories, models, measurement and data. The only alternative to ontological determinism is to assume that, at least in part, 'things just happen'; that is, to assume truly stochastic factors . . . randomly produce outcomes" (2008: 420). Further, accepting causation as deterministic does not mean that actor choice, agency, and free will do not exist. Instead, the debate about structure versus agency (also termed the micro-macro debate) is a theoretical one (e.g., Archer 2000; Coleman 1990; Emirbayer and Mische 1998; Giddens 1984; Hedström and Swedberg 1998) rather than a more fundamental one about the nature of causation. This means that ontological determinism is compatible with multiple theoretical positions in the debate on structure versus agency.

Case-based research by definition takes individual cases as the analytical point of departure because this is the level at which causal relationships take place. If we instead were to adopt a probabilistic understanding of causation, case studies would be relegated to a secondary position. Indeed, it can even be argued that studying probabilistic causal relationships at the case level makes little sense, given that we then always can discount a negative finding with the claim that the found relationship in the single case was a chance occurrence—the exception that proves the rule. This is why King, Keohane, and Verba contend that we should never engage in a single case study, but instead transform our research into a comparative design to have enough "variation" to assess trends, either temporally (before and after) or by disaggregating across issues or geographically (1994: 217–28). For more on their strategy of making "one into many," see chapter 6.

In contrast, we believe that ontological determinism results in better theoretical and empirical explanations for real-world phenomena. The reason for this is that when we make ontological deterministic claims, we are forced to tackle head-on any incongruences and anomalies that result from in-depth empirical case-based research instead of discounting them as being exceptions to an overall trend, as we would if we were working with probabilistic theoretical claims. If we do not find a causal relationship in a case for which our theory told us that it should be present, we do not just discount this as an exception to an otherwise strong cross-case trend. Instead, we are forced to reappraise our theory, attempting to figure out why what we expected did not occur in the case (Dion 2003: 106–7; Mahoney 2008; Adcock 2007). These failures of our theories are intensely interesting for case-based researchers, enabling us to build better theories (Andersen 2012). For instance, if we are claiming that C is a sufficient cause, we are theorizing that, if C is present in a case, O will occur if the requisite contextual (scope) conditions are present.[8] If C is present and O does *not* occur in a particular case, we would not be satisfied in case-based designs with concluding that the chosen case was an outlier from an otherwise strong probabilistic mean causal effect. Instead, if our ontological understanding is deterministic, we would want to know what it is about the analyzed deviant case that resulted in the nonoccurrence of O despite the presence of C. After examining both the deviant case itself and comparing it with other positive cases, we might find that there was an omitted cause in the deviant case, with O occurring only when C and C_1 are present together. This finding would enable us to update our empirical theory, resulting in a better theoretical understanding of the causal relationship and the contextual conditions under which it holds. This intense interest in updating our theories by learning from our theoretical mistakes in deviant cases marks a key analytical difference between research designs based on probabilistic and deterministic ontological understandings of causal relationships. The analytical result of grounding case-based research in the assumption of ontological determinism is that our theories are progressively refined in an iterated process of empirical research, thus making our findings less and less wrong as we better understand how causal relationships work and the contextual bounds in which these relationships hold through repeated meetings with empirical evidence.

It is important to reiterate that determinism at the ontological level does not logically imply that we can gain certain empirical knowledge about why things occur. In this book we suggest that at the epistemological level we should adopt a probabilistic, Bayesian-inspired logic. As we develop in chapter 6, while the social world at the ontological level can be claimed to be deterministic (i.e., things do not happen randomly), our empirical knowledge about why things occur will always be imperfect and contingent upon further research.

Case-based scholars typically couple the term "deterministic" with theories of necessary and sufficient causes in individual cases, or combinations of these types of conditions (Mahoney 2008: 417). However, logically we can utilize a deterministic ontological understanding of causal relationships in connection with nonsufficient contributing causes, where we would make the argument that if a cause occurs, it will trigger a mechanism that has an impact on the outcome but will not produce it by itself, but only in conjunction with other contributing causes.

If causation is also understood in cross-case terms (regularity), then the empirical evidence that suggests that a causal relationship is present in a given case is generalized to relationships within small, bounded populations of similar cases. But in these circumstances, case-based research typically operates with smaller bounded populations of causally homogeneous cases when attempting to make cross-case inferences in order to minimize the risks of flawed inferences about deterministic relationships. We return later in this chapter to the importance of causal homogeneity when ontological deterministic assumptions are used.

Case-Based Research Makes Asymmetric Causal Claims

The claims we are making in case-based research are asymmetric, which means that we make claims about the causes (C) of an outcome (O), but at the same time we are making no claims about what causes the absence of an outcome.[9] Claiming that a cause is necessary for an outcome is an asymmetric claim in that we are not making any claims about the causes of the absence of the outcome (depicted using logical not; i.e., ~O). When we trace mechanisms in a case, we are also tracing mechanisms only between a given cause and outcome, meaning that we are making no presumptions about mechanisms in cases where the cause and outcome are not present. In contrast, symmetric theoretical claims would claim that an independent variable (X) has an impact *across* values of the dependent variable (Y). Whether we make symmetric or asymmetric claims has major implications for research design, notably as regards how we conceptualize concepts (chapter 4), how we make causal inferences (chapter 6), and proper case selection (chapters 7–9).

Symmetric causation means that we attribute causal effects to different values of X across cases. This can also be understood as capturing the differences that values of a cause have for values of the outcome Y. For example, a deterministic symmetric claim would be that low values of X result in low

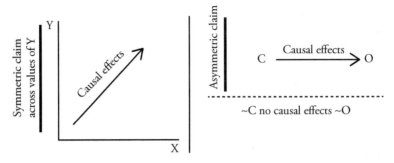

Fig. 2.2. Symmetric versus asymmetric causal claims

values of Y and high values result in high values of Y. A probabilistic symmetric claim would be that as values of X increase, so does the probability of higher values of Y occurring. Symmetric claims are typically made by variance-based scholars who build on constant conjunction (i.e., regularity) and/or counterfactual understandings of causation (e.g., Woodward 2005; Gerring 2011).

A symmetric claim is illustrated on the left side of figure 2.2, where a linear relationship is theorized, with low values of X producing low values of Y, and higher values of X producing higher values of Y. When treated individually, the underlying causal model in symmetric claims is often additive, meaning that (1) the causal effects of individual variables can be isolated, and (2) when more than one cause is present, they will have an additive effect upon values of Y. An asymmetric claim is made in the right-hand side of figure 2.2, where C is theorized to be causally related to O, but no causal claims are made about the effects of ~C or the causes of ~O. As an example, when theorizing asymmetrically we might make the claim that development (C) is a necessary condition for democracy (O), but this makes no claims about what the causes of nondemocracy are (Ragin 2008: 15). Implicitly we are assuming when making asymmetric claims that the causes of a given outcome (O) are usually very different from the causes of its negation (~O).

When making symmetric claims, theoretical concepts are typically treated as variables (see chapter 4 for more on the distinction between variables and conditions). This can take the form either of a dichotomous variable where each pole of the concept is defined (e.g., both war and peace) or of different values being defined on an ordinal or higher scale (e.g., interval-scale per capita gross domestic product). The analytical focus is then on assessing whether differences in values of X produce a difference in values of Y. Both probabilistic and deterministic symmetric claims require evidence of variation and difference-making, typically in the form of ordinal or higher scales of variables, but it can also be dichotomous variation (presence or absence). The population of cases to which symmetric causal claims refer to includes both positive and negative cases of Y (see figure 2.2).

Because of the need for variation, we argue that symmetric causal claims cannot be made about *within-case* causal relationships unless we transform a single case into a set of cases by either disaggregating temporally or spatially, or unless we live in a utopian world in which closed-system experiments are possible in the social sciences (see section 2.4 for more on this). As we expand on in chapter 6, transforming one case into many creates so many sources of potential error that our findings based on within-case variation will be vastly inferior to proper analyses of cross-case variation where the requirements for valid comparison hold.

Returning to asymmetry, all of the claims we are making in case-based research are arguably asymmetric. Asymmetric claims can be made either about cross-case causal relationships, as in Mill's methods (see chapter 7), or within-case causal relationships (e.g., mechanisms). We make asymmetric claims when theorizing about necessary and/or sufficient causes either across or within cases, and within cases when theorizing about causal mechanisms. For example, by tracing causal mechanisms in case 1, we might conclude that it appears that C is a cause of O. This is an asymmetric *within-case* causal claim, in that by claiming that democracy (C) produces peace (O) and tracing the mechanism in a case, we are not making any claims about the causes of war. To generalize our findings, we could compare case 1 with other cases in which C and O are present, concluding that cases 2 and 3 are very similar on a range of causally relevant conditions. We then could infer *across* the cases that if C was a cause of O in case 1, we should also expect the relationship to hold in similar cases 2 and 3. However, in both the within- and cross-case causal claims we are not making any inferences about the causal effects that ~C (cause not present) has, or about the causes of ~O (outcome not present). Therefore, the population of cases in focus when making asymmetric claims includes only the positive cases of the outcome (O).[10]

At the core of asymmetric causal claims is set theory, where concepts are defined by the theoretical characteristics that determine whether a given case is a member of the set of the concept. Set membership is defined by a qualitative threshold that demarcates whether a given case is a member of the set of a given theoretical concept or not. This means that causal concepts in case-based research are *not* variables but instead are defined solely in terms of what causally relevant attributes characterize cases within the set of the population of the phenomenon from those outside it.

2.4. Causality as Counterfactuals versus Mechanisms

Beyond the common core of ontological determinism and asymmetry, we contend that case-based research diverges on whether causation is understood on two dimensions: (1) counterfactuals or mechanisms and (2) whether causation implies regular association across cases or not. This distinction is not the same as the one made by Goertz and Mahoney (2012), where they claim that the "qualitative tradition" builds either on a counterfactual or on a regularity understanding (2012: 78–81). They claim that when building on a counterfactual understanding, scholars make claims about necessity, whereas if one builds on regularity, scholars are making claims about sufficiency. As the position of mechanisms as a distinct understanding of causation is not developed in their book, the result is that Goertz and Mahoney's methodological guidelines ignore the critical distinction between claiming that a cause is either necessary or sufficient for an outcome, and that a cause is causally linked to the outcome through an explicit mechanism.[11] Additionally, we believe that they are incorrect for two reasons when they link claims of sufficiency with regularity causation (Goertz and Mahoney 2012: 79–81). First, a claim of sufficiency can be interpreted as being based on a counterfactual. Woodward for instance writes about sufficiency as being a counterfactual by stating, "If it is possible to manipulate Y by intervening on X, then we may conclude that X causes Y, regardless of whether the relationship between X and Y lacks various other features standardly regarded as necessary for causation" (2003: 49). Second, pragmatic or analyticist scholars tend to make sufficiency claims for single outcomes, which by definition are not regular (see Jackson 2011).

In this section we develop further the distinction between counterfactual- and mechanism-based explanations, returning in the next section to the differences between regularity and singular causation.

The ontological distinction between counterfactuals and mechanisms is not one that can be proved empirically; instead, it belongs to the realm of metaphysical debates where there is not a right or wrong answer. Ontological debates relate to our beliefs about how the world works at the most fundamental level. From our experiences teaching PhD students, we have a hunch that individuals feel more comfortable with *either* counterfactual-based explanations or mechanism-based ones and the evidence associated with them because they are either hardwired from birth to think in a particular fashion or because of formative learning experiences.[12] Some of us are "tinkerers," meaning that we are only comfortable in claiming causation when we are able to understand and observe the *actual process* whereby an event came about. Other individuals are "experimenters," more comfortable with causal claims when we can show the *difference* that a given cause makes on the world. Irrespective of whether our hunch holds up to empirical scrutiny, we suggest that the distinction between counterfactuals and mechanisms is important to understand for adherents of both positions, enabling the recognition that the other position is legitimate and that it has relative methodological advantages and disadvantages in comparison to the position that you hold yourself.

Counterfactuals

The philosopher David Hume, in a reaction to the then prevalent understanding of causation as a necessary connection in the form of a "hook" or "force" between a cause and an outcome, contended that we cannot measure the "secret connection" that links causes and outcomes. He wrote that "we may define a cause to be *an object, followed by another, and where all the objects similar to the first are followed by objects similar to the second* or in other words *where, if the first object had not been, the second never had existed*" (Hume 1927: 157, italics in original). Unpacking this definition, we see that the first part refers to causation as regularity (constant conjunction), whereas the second refers to a counterfactual understanding developed in the following. We explore regularity later in this chapter, focusing here on counterfactuals.

At the core of a counterfactual understanding is the idea of *difference-making*. In the counterfactual understanding, we can claim that a cause produced an outcome on the basis of studying whether the *absence* of the cause results in the *absence* of the outcome, all other things being held equal (Lewis 1986: 160; Woodward 2003). While sometimes treated separately, the basic counterfactual understanding and the manipulation account collapse into a single understanding of counterfactuals, where the only real difference is whether causation claims are situated in the *logical* counterfactual argument that the outcome could have been different if the cause had not occurred (possibility), or in the actual manipulation of the cause, where we investigate whether actively manipulating whether the hypothesized cause occurs or does not occur has a discernible impact on the outcome, usually in the form of an experiment (Brady 2008: 240; Woodward 2003: 10).

In both instances the causal claims relate to the *difference* that the cause makes or potentially makes upon values of the outcome—one grounded in the empirical claim based on the observed difference that the cause actually makes across cases, the other on the logical potential. Designs building on the counterfactual model are therefore often referred to as potential outcomes frameworks. The logical counterfactual involving elaboration of other potential outcomes that a cause could produce enables us to distinguish causal from irrelevant factors by comparing the existing to another alternative possible world, whereas an experiment produces actual empirical evidence of difference-making.

Woodward uses the following example to illustrate the benefits of logical counterfactuals about potential outcomes to distinguish causal factors from irrelevant ones (2003: 352). In his example, if we decided to investigate the effects of birth control pills on a male population, we might in the first instance infer that because there is no difference in the number of pregnancies for the treatment and control groups (both are zero), we might infer incorrectly that birth control pills have no causal effect. However, if we engaged in a logical counterfactual, we would quickly find that the outcome "pregnant man" is a logical impossibility, meaning that the outcome (nonpregnancy of men) is the same irrespective of treatment or control, and therefore that the pills are causally irrelevant in explaining the outcome.

There can be difficulty in establishing the direction of causation when operating with the basic model of counterfactual understanding of causation when we do not have the ability to manipulate causes (Brady 2008: 237). Finding that if a factor occurs the outcome is also present, and that when the factor does not occur the outcome is not present, does not allow us to infer that the factor was the *cause* of the outcome, given that we can just as plausibly contend that the outcome was the cause of the factor, or there can be a common background cause of both. While we can incorporate the role of temporality to solve the first problem, it does not necessarily solve the challenge created by potential shared background causes. This is why many scholars argue that confirmation of causal relationships is possible only when we have the actual manipulation of cause in experiments; everything else is merely evidence of correlations. We agree with this in relation to counterfactuals based on observational data, which is why we argue in this book that comparative methods do not enable us to confirm causal claims.

The counterfactual account of causation does not require constant conjunction (regularity), although in practice they are often coupled together when experiments are undertaken in open systems. In an "ideal" experiment, the treatment is given in a closed system in which there are no other potential causes present and the size of the measurement error is known. Here we would not need to repeat the experiment multiple times, nor would we have to create a control group, because we can use the before-treatment state itself as the counterfactual control, and because we know that because there is no unknown measurement error, any differences before and after can be inferred to be solely due to the treatment. Therefore, in an experiment in a closed system, if the outcome changes after the treatment *and* there are no other potential causes present, we can infer that the treatment caused the outcome based on the manipulation (treatment applied) and the counterfactual before-treatment state. While this type of research situation is not possible in the social sciences, it is in theory possible in disciplines like chemistry.

Experiments in the social sciences are always in more or less open systems, where multiple causes are present. Rubin's classic aspirin example describes an experiment in an open system (1974). In the example, Rubin claims that when he takes an aspirin he would not know whether the outcome of "headache disappears" is produced by the aspirin or some other cause, such as the body over a short amount of time reestablishing chemical imbalances that originally caused the headache, resulting in the headache disappearing irrespective of any effects of the aspirin. Therefore, when multiple causes of the outcome are present, we run into the fundamental problem of causal inference, where we do not know whether an observed effect is due to the treatment or to some other factor (Holland 1986). To solve it in an experiment we would need to compare cases where the treatment has been given with comparable cases where it has not been given. To ensure comparability and control for other potential causes, advocates of experiments suggest random selection of a relatively large number of cases. The combination of randomness and a relatively large number of cases should mean that all significant differences between cases in the treatment and control group wash out. As the only systematic difference across cases should be the treatment itself, we can infer that the treatment was the cause of the difference in values of the outcome because of a counterfactual comparison, assuming that the regularity assumption holds (for more on this, see section 2.5).

Control for other causes at the case level is critical to the counterfactual account of causation to ensure that the other cause(s) did not produce differences in the values of outcomes across cases. In the medical experiment, control is achieved through the use of a treatment and control group of subjects that are randomly selected. Any difference in values of the outcome between the two groups then can have only one cause: the treatment. Therefore, at the core of the counterfactual model is the idea of isolating the effect of causes, controlling for other potential causes.[13]

While the counterfactual account of causation provides a solid logical foundation for causal claims, critics of counterfactuals claim that finding that the manipulation of a hypothetical cause produces differences in values of the outcome still does not tell us much about *how* the cause actually contributes to producing the outcome (Machamer 2004; Waskan 2011; Waldner 2012; Russo and Williamson 2007; Illari 2011; Dowe 2011). And when we lack the ability to engage in active manipulation of causes in experimental designs, we are left with either what are in essence correlational claims based on cross-case evidence that do not enable us to make strong claims about causation, or logical hypotheticals in which we have no real empirical evidence of causation (see chapter 7 for more on this). Mechanism accounts of causation therefore have comparative advantages in assessing causation in case-based research, as they focus on how causes work in actual cases by tracing causal processes, producing mechanistic evidence at the within-case level.

Causal Mechanisms

Viewing causation in mechanism terms means that we explain why something occurred by analyzing *the actual causal processes* whereby an outcome was produced. Despite being categorically rejected by Hume and scholars following in his footsteps for several hundred years, the past forty years has seen the reintroduction by realist philosophers of the notion that to make causal claims we need to examine the evidence of the "connection" between causes and effects, where the core idea is that the analyst should study causal processes in-between a cause and outcome (e.g., Bhaskar 1978; Bunge 1997; Glennan 1996; Machamer, Craver, and Darden 2000; Machamer 2004; Salmon 1998). In the mechanism understanding, causation is seen as *more* than just counterfactual difference-making. Here the analytical focus is on the *actual* causal process in-between C and O, that is, how C contributes to producing O. In contrast, the counterfactual understanding can be perceived as viewing the world "as if" it were a laboratory in which control for other causes is possible. In the mechanism understanding, we step out of the pseudolaboratory, attempting to observe in real-world settings how a cause (or set of causes) is linked with an outcome within a particular case. Here "control" for other causes is achieved not through counterfactual "what ifs" or by selecting cases where only one cause is present, but instead at the level of within-case evidence through the careful evaluation of the theoretical uniqueness of a given piece of evidence. We return to this question of control at the empirical level in chapter 6.

Whereas there is relative agreement among scholars about the nature of

Factors vs variables

counterfactuals, and adherents of mechanisms share the concern with causal processes, there are strong disagreements amongst proponents of mechanisms as to what mechanisms actually are. Simplifying very complex philosophical and methodological debates slightly, we claim that one can identify two overall positions: a minimalist position and a systems understanding of mechanisms.

Before we turn to debates about what mechanisms are, it is important to make clear what causal mechanisms are not. Some scholars view mechanisms as a series of events, or a narrative story, leading to an outcome (e.g., Abell 2004; Mahoney 2012: 571; Roberts 1996: 16; Suganami 1996: 164–68). Yet mechanisms are more than just a series of events. While describing a series of events can provide a plausible descriptive narrative about *what* happened, they do not shed light on *why* things happened in the case. Causal explanation involves more than just tracing temporal sequences (Gryzmala-Busse 2012: 1268–71). Tracing a series of events between C and O is in reality merely crafting a "just so" story of case-specific happenings between C and O, with the theoretical mechanism completely black-boxed. Abell goes a bit further than just tracing events, contending that we need to develop narrative structures with action linkages that build on subjective counterfactuals, where we ask actors who participated in a process whether things could have been different at critical junctures of a process (2004: 295–96). However, this position has two problems. First, logically it collapses onto the counterfactual understanding of causation, thereby defining away the distinctive nature of mechanisms (see below for more on this point). Second, it reduces the scope of research questions significantly to only those that can be assessed by asking actors themselves whether things could have been different.

Mechanisms are also not just intervening variables. Using the term intervening variable implies a research design where we have *variation*, with *multiple* observations of the values of X, the intervening variable (mechanism, CM), and Y that enable us to assess the net effects of X and CM on values of Y (Gerring 2007). King, Keohane, and Verba suggest that to do this we can disaggregate our case, for example, by transforming a single case (national level) into multiple cases by observing values of variables at a lower level (e.g., the state level), or by comparing two similar cases (King, Keohane, and Verba 1994: 219–28). Yet this recommendation in effect transforms the *within-case* study of causal processes into a *cross-case* analysis of patterns of variation at a lower level of aggregation, where we lose focus on the process *between* the cause and outcome (Mahoney 2001: 578; Mayntz 2004: 244–45; Hedström and Ylikoski 2010: 51–52; Waldner 2012: 76–77). The result of transforming a within-case tracing of causal processes into a cross-case assessment of variation is that we gain no information about *how the process actually played out in a case study*. But studying the process *between* a cause and an outcome was the very reason we would want to engage in the analysis of causal mechanisms in the first place. Furthermore, the "tracing mechanisms as intervening variables" designs will always be an analytical second best in relation to both larger-N covariational analysis and experimental designs, given that more cases are (almost) always better (Gerring 2005: 187–88; 2011). For example, when comparing a handful of cases, we are very susceptible to making flawed inferences due to problems created by comparing potentially heterogeneous units. In contrast, in a larger sample these problems tend to wash out as noise that only weakens the strength of found associations. It is for this very reason that we suggest that the analytical workhorse of case-based methods should be detailed, within-case analyses, relegating small-N comparisons to adjunct tools for assisting in finding potential causes and in generalizing from one case study to a small, bounded population.

We now turn to two overall understandings of mechanisms: a minimalist and a systems understanding. In minimalist understandings, the causal arrow between a cause and outcome is not unpacked theoretically in any detail. In contrast, in a systems understanding, the ambition is to unpack explicitly the causal process that occurs in-between a cause (or set of causes) and an outcome. That there are two distinct answers to the question of what mechanisms are has resulted in considerable confusion in the methodological literature about what process-tracing methods are. We contend that it makes analytical sense to refer to case studies that trace only minimalist mechanisms as congruence studies, whereas the term "process-tracing" should be reserved for studies that more explicitly unpack mechanisms and engage in detailed empirical tracing of them. We now develop these two positions on mechanisms in greater detail.

Minimalist Understanding of Mechanisms

We refer to understandings of mechanisms as minimalist when the causal process in between C and O is not unpacked in detail. Advocates of a minimalist position often describe mechanisms as a form of *intervening factors* between C and O, often depicted as C $\rightarrow$ CM $\rightarrow$ O (e.g., George and Bennett 2005: 6; Pearl 2000; Morgan and Winship 2004: 224–30; Gerring 2007; Falleti and Lynch 2009: 1146; Elster 1998; Mahoney 2015).

In a minimalist understanding, causal mechanisms are treated as factors in between the occurrence of a cause (or set of causes) and an outcome. For example, Mahoney writes, "I use the term mechanism to refer to a factor that intervenes between a cause and outcome. I treat mechanisms in the same way as causes and outcomes; they are particular events or specific values on variables. Mechanisms are different from causes and outcomes because of their temporal position: they stand between a cause and outcome in time. Thus, in the expression X → M → Y, the letters refer to events or specific values on variables, with X being treated as the cause, M as the mechanism, and Y as the outcome" (2015: 206). Notice that the causal process that binds the cause, the mechanism and the outcome together is not unpacked theoretically, but instead is "gray-boxed" by being described merely with a causal arrow.[14]

A good example of a minimalist understanding can be seen in Rosato's description of a causal mechanism that links two states being democratic (C) with peaceful relations between them (O) as being as follows: democracy → accountability → group constraint → peace (2003: 585). However, there is precious little information in the article that details the causal process linking C with O. What is it about accountability that binds democracy and peace together in a causal relationship? How does accountability then influence group constraint? While it is possible to see an implicit causal process in the example if one has good knowledge of theories of the democratic peace, the mechanism remains in a form of theoretical gray box. And because the causal process is not theorized explicitly, the resulting empirical analysis does not engage in a detailed, empirical tracing of the causal process. In effect, it becomes what we term a congruence case study, where minimalist mechanisms are assessed empirically solely based on the observable manifestations that M is predicted to have (see chapter 8).

The analytical result of gray-boxing in congruence case studies is that the causal claims about mechanisms linking C to O are based on weaker evidence about the causal process than they would have been if the mechanism had been explicitly unpacked and then studied empirically, as in the systems understanding. In contrast, this type of mechanism-based empirical research requires significantly fewer analytical resources, and it does enable at least some inferences to be made about causation because causal processes are studied to some degree. We return to this question in chapters 8 and 9 when discussing the pros and cons of using congruence versus process-tracing.

Mechanisms as a System

In contrast, there are scholars who contend that we need to unpack the causal process in between C and O in extensive detail, theorizing the causal mechanism(s) in between as a theoretical system composed of a series of interlocking parts that transmit causal forces from C to O. Proponents of the system understanding like Bhaskar, Bunge, and Glennan have contended that Descartes's mechanistic understanding of causal mechanisms, which was prevalent prior to Hume's treatise, should be reintroduced in a more modern fashion (Glennan 1996; Bhaskar 1978; Bunge 1997). Here, "a mechanism explanation for some happening that perplexes us is explanatory precisely in virtue of its capacity to enable us to understand how the parts of some system actually conspire to produce that happening" (Waskan 2011: 393).

The focus in mechanism understandings of causality is the dynamic, interactive influence of causes upon outcomes, and in particular how *causal forces* are *transmitted* through a series of interlocking parts of a causal mechanism to produce an outcome.[15] Philosopher Stuart Glennan, for instance, defines a mechanism as "a complex system, which produces an outcome by the interaction of a number of parts" (1996: 52; 2002). Within social science research, Andrew Bennett has defined causal mechanisms as "processes through which agents with causal capacities operate in specific contexts to transfer energy, information or matter to other entities" (2008b: 207). David Waldner has defined mechanisms as "an agent or entity that has the capacity to alter its environment because it possesses an invariant property that, in specific contexts, transmits either a physical force or information that influences the behavior of other agents or entities" (2012: 75).

Mechanisms in the systems understanding are often described as being comprised of a series of parts composed of entities engaging in activities (Machamer, Darden, and Craver 2000; Machamer 2004; Rohlfing 2012: 35–36; Beach and Pedersen 2013: 29–32). Entities are what engage in activities (the parts of the mechanism that can be understood as the toothed wheels in a machine), where the activities are the producers of change or what transmits causal forces through a mechanism (the movement of the wheels in the machine that transmit forces) (Machamer, Darden, and Craver 2000; Machamer 2004). Parts have no independent existence (they are not considered variables) in relation to producing an outcome; instead, they are integral parts of a system that transmits causal forces to the outcome. We return in chapter 3 to what these parts can look like in practice.

It is important to note that there is disagreement in the literature regarding whether a mechanism refers to both the causal conditions that trigger it and the mechanism itself, or merely to the causal pathway between C and O. We put forward in chapters 3 and 4 the claim that how we define concepts needs to be in alignment with the type of causal claim being made. This means that while the cause and the subsequent mechanism are conceptually distinct, they are also dependent on each other because definitions of causes that trigger mechanisms need to include attributes that can theoretically trigger the mechanism.

It is also important to note that a mechanism linking C and O does not logically have to be sufficient or necessary to produce O. While the assumption that a mechanism is sufficient to produce an outcome is found in the literature (Mahoney 2001: 580; Mayntz 2004: 241–53; Andersen 2012: 416; Waskan 2011: 403), there are no logical reasons that it has to be necessary or sufficient (Hedström and Ylikoski 2010). For instance, if we have theorized that a cause is neither necessary or sufficient, if the cause actually has a productive relationship with the outcome as a contributing cause, there would still be a mechanism linking it with the outcome. But the mechanism (and cause that triggered it) would be neither necessary nor sufficient for the outcome.

In the more permissive understanding of mechanisms in this book, the only requirement for a mechanism to be causal is that it transfers some form of causal forces from C to O, meaning that C has a causal relationship with O through the operation of the mechanism. It can be sufficient, but it can also only be a contributing cause that together with other causal conditions produces the outcome.

By studying mechanisms as systems using in-depth case studies, case-based researchers are arguably able to gain what Salmon refers to as deeper explanatory knowledge of causal relationships, thus enabling stronger claims about causation to be made (1998). We develop this argument further in chapter 9 on process-tracing.

It is important to note that some adherents of the counterfactual understanding contend that mechanisms at the deepest level are just more elaborate forms of counterfactual statements about the links between the parts of the mechanism, best seen in the work of Woodward (2003: 350–58). Woodward claims that adherents to the mechanism understanding cannot logically account for what links each part of a mechanism to the others, and he therefore contends that mechanisms bottom out in the counterfactual claim that if a given part of a mechanism did not exist, the next part of the mechanism would also not have existed.

Although this critique is potentially damaging, it can be countered by the argument that what we are interested in when we study causal mechanisms is what *actually* took place in a case, instead of hypothetical what-ifs about what *could have* happened (Andersen 2012: 430; Machamer 2004; Russo and Williamson 2007; Waskan 2011: 393; Illari and Williamson 2011; Groff 2011). This argument can be referred to as the actualist position, and with it, we are more concerned with what actually took place in the empirical record and develop theories on this basis instead of based on counterfactuals of what might have happened if things had been different (Waskan 2011: 394; Gross 2009; Groff 2011; Machamer 2004). In the words of Bogen, "How can it make any difference to any of this whether certain things that did not happen *would have* or *might have* resulted if other things that did not actually happen *had* happened?" (2005: 415). Machamer contends that counterfactuals are not adequate as explanations for causal processes: "In the case of counterfactuals, the modality of the subjunctive contrast is somehow supposed to warrant the necessity of the actual causal case. But even if this were true, and I am not sure it is, there still would be no explanation, for they would still have forsaken the process of production by which these certain entities and activities produced such and such changes, which was what was to be explained" (2004: 31). Groff claims that mechanisms are real processes that involve the exercise of causal powers in the real world, not in logically possible worlds (2011: 309).

Adherents of the actualist position on mechanisms claim that understanding a mechanism merely as a set of lower-level counterfactual links would result in the theoretical and empirical masking of the critical links in the causal process that led us to study mechanisms in the first place. The argument in the actualist position is that the goal of causal explanation is to gain a better understanding of causal processes, we should focus our analytical attention on the *activities* that link parts of the mechanism together, whereas in the counterfactual understanding these activities are masked when parts are theorized to be manipulable counterfactuals.

At the theoretical level, if the parts of mechanisms are understood as lower-level counterfactuals, they are then depicted as causal arrows linking one part to the next without making explicit what it is about one part that links to the next because it is the counterfactual dependence that enables the theoretical claim of causation (e.g., Woodward 2003; Steel 2008; Pearl 2000). In contrast, in an actualist understanding, the most important aspect of theorization is capturing what is inside these causal arrows—that is, the activities or causal forces that link one part to the next, attempting to develop an overall mechanism where there is productive continuity from the cause to the outcome (see chapter 3 for more). Illari and Williamson refer to the counterfactual-based approach to mechanisms as a "'passive approach, where the mechanism just becomes a set of patterns of regularity in this or other possible worlds" (2011: 834). In contrast, in the actualist understanding mechanisms are viewed in more active terms, elaborating on the activities, capacities and powers that link parts of mechanisms together. The counterfactual understanding therefore results in black-boxing of the causal links in our theory (Groff 2011), which paradoxically was the very reason we wanted to unpack the mechanism in the first place.

Further, in a system understanding of mechanisms, mechanisms are seen in a holistic fashion, where they are more than the sum of their parts. When we theorize a mechanism as a system, there is often a complex inter-relationship between the parts of the mechanisms. This means that the effects of individual parts often manifest themselves fully only when they work together with the effects of other parts—that is, they only function properly when embedded in the whole of the mechanism. In the words of Cartwright, "There are any number of systems whose principals cannot be changed one at a time without either destroying the system or changing it into a system of a different kind" (2007: 239). Therefore, actualists claim that the counterfactual logic of demonstrating the theoretical effect of parts by conceiving of their individual "absence" creates an atomistic theory of trees in which we do not see the broader forest.

Theoretical black-boxing of activities is problematic, but the methodological implications of using counterfactuals are even more serious, because building our understanding on counterfactuals means that, to be in alignment, we have to manipulate causes (either through actual or natural experiments or through the use of logical hypotheticals) to be able infer that a process is actually causal. These implications are clearly seen in Runhardt's 2015 article, where she admonishes existing process-tracing case studies of mechanisms for not attempting to "find an actual intervention variable or establish the counterfactual claim of what would happen if an intervention were made" (1305). Following Woodward, Runhardt claims that to establish that there is a mechanism (Z) linking a cause (X) and outcome (Y), we have to assess empirically the following:

1. Is X a direct cause of Z? In other words, is there a (human, natural, or hypothetical) intervention on X that will change Y or the probability of Y when one holds fixed all other variables in V at some value?
2. Is Z a direct cause of Y? In other words, is there a (human, natural, or hypothetical) intervention on Y that will change Z or the probability of Z when one holds fixed all other variables in V at some value? (Runhardt 2015: 1304)

The claim is basically that without investigating interventions empirically, we can make no causal claims. Runhardt then attempts to show the utility of the counterfactual approach by examining how an existing process-tracing case study could be improved by using interventions as an empirical strategy. She reconstructs Bakke's (2013) article that claims that the presence of transnational insurgents, X, is a contributing cause for the increased use of suicide bombings in Chechnya (Y), via the intervening "mechanism" of watching videos of suicide bombings, Z. Runhardt then suggests that an actual human intervention (manipulation) is probably not possible in the case, and therefore she claims that the researcher should try to use a natural experiment to compare the Chechen case with a "sufficiently similar cause in which the cause is not present, to see what would happen to the effect. In Bakke's case, we would need to find a (set of) conflict(s) that are similar in every other way to the Second Chechen War, but where transnational insurgents are not present" (2015: 1305). Alternatively, Runhardt suggests that Bakke could have engaged in a logical counterfactual, asking, "Could we have prevented the local insurgents from watching suicide bombing videos, in a way that is in no way connected to their use of this radical tactic through a different route? Would they have used suicide bombings less if we had prevented them from watching such videos?" (2015: 1305).

Both strategies face significant empirical challenges. If we take the natural experiment route, if we unpack a mechanism into multiple parts, it would involve trying to find cases in which *all other* factors are present but the part of the mechanism being assessed, which would require strong theoretical assumptions about the modularity of parts of mechanisms and about the lack of impact of contextual conditions on their working (see section 3.4. for more on modularity). We would then have to repeat this for each part of the mechanism. Even more problematic, as Runhardt herself admits, "a similarity comparison in areas like political science is, however, difficult to defend" (2015: 1306), because of the complexity of the social world, meaning that there usually are no cases in which the "all other things equal" assumption required in a natural experiment actually hold (we return to this question in chapter 7).

And even if we could manipulate each of the parts of the mechanism in isolation to assess whether the absence of one results in the mechanism breaking down, this assumes that there is not redundancy embedded in the mechanism. In biological mechanisms there is (luckily) redundancy of key parts of mechanisms, meaning that if we remove one part to see what happens, we will still find that the mechanism worked to produce the outcome, because another previously unknown part with similar capacities became activated instead (Illari and Russo 2014: 158). There are no good logical grounds for not expecting similar redundancy in key parts of important social mechanisms. But based on the counterfactual logic, if we found that removing a part had no real effect on the outcome, we would disconfirm the part as being causally relevant, which would be a flawed inference. Instead, the correct inference would be that the part was one of multiple ways that causal forces could be transferred through the mechanism, but we could not make this inference using the simple counterfactual manipulation.

Logical hypotheticals face the critical challenge of being logical what-ifs without any real empirical evidence backing them. Despite many attempts to build a methodology for logical counterfactuals, there are no objective empirical truth conditions for assessing a nonexistent "possible" alternative world (we return to this question in chapter 7). In the case of Runhardt's 2015 article, although we could speculate about whether the insurgents would have used the tactic if they had not watched the videos, we would never really know, because in the actual case they did.

Actualists contend that instead of engaging in logical parlor games or dirty natural experiments, we should assess the observable evidence of the actual activities of entities to assess how causal processes played out in a real-world case. Using an example from the natural sciences, Waskan illustrates the futility of attempting to engage in logical counterfactuals of actual processes in the real world (2008: 266). He suggests that if we are investigating the question of whether a catastrophic meteor collision 65 million years ago contributed to the extinction of dinosaurs on the Earth, then using the counterfactual approach, we would want to ask ourselves questions like the following:

- If the asteroid had missed the Earth, then the chain of events leading to extinction would not have happened, other things equal.
- If the asteroid had been made out of a soft material (e.g., ice) instead of metal, the chain of events leading to extinction would not have happened, other things equal.

Yet irrespective of whether we are able to manipulate the presence of parts of a mechanism, or whether we are forced to rely on natural experiments or logical reasoning, investigating this "difference-making" of parts still leaves us in the dark regarding the causal process that *actually linked* the posited cause (meteor collision) and the outcome (extinction). An actualist analysis would want to go to the field to observe the traces actually left by the activities that each part of the mechanism is composed of—something that can be referred to as mechanistic evidence (see chapter 6). Inferring causation would be enabled by the collection of observational evidence in the form of the traces left by the parts of the activities of the mechanism and how they played out in the real world. Instead of asking whether things could have been different, causal inferences in the actualist position are enabled by observing the traces of activities that transferred causal forces through a mechanism. In the words of Machamer, "Causality lies in the actual production" (2004: 35).

An actualist would therefore ask whether there is physical evidence of the meteor actually colliding with the Earth (e.g., in the form of a crater, or other observables like rock structures transformed by massive shock waves) and of the resulting ash cloud that would have had worldwide impacts (e.g., in the form of an ash layer in rocks from around the world that are 65 million years old) (Waskan 2008).

Another critique of mechanisms by adherents of counterfactuals is that we sometimes can establish that a causal relationship is valid without providing extensive information about mechanisms (Woodward 2003: 66). However, just because we can claim causation using experimental manipulation does not mean that studying mechanisms is pointless (Russo and Williamson 2007; Illari 2011). Indeed, recent work in the philosophy of science suggest that causal claims can be made either by using difference-making evidence from the experimental manipulation of causes or by using mechanistic evidence gained from tracing causal processes within cases (Russo and Williamson 2007; Illari 2011). Difference-making provides evidence of the cross-case effects of changing values of a posited cause, whereas mechanistic evidence sheds light on causal processes within individual cases.

The point in this book is that different understandings of causation and the methods they entail shed light on different aspects of causal relationships. When embarking on a study of the mechanisms linking a cause and outcome, we often already possess cross-case knowledge about patterns of difference-making between the two factors. The reason we then trace mechanisms using in-depth case studies is to investigate the "how actually" question, shedding more light on whether there is evidence of a mechanism and thereby also informing us how a cause contributes to produce an outcome.

Given that the debate between the counterfactual-based versus actualist positions is, at the end of the day, an ontological debate, there is not one "objective" right answer to the question. We are dealing with a metaphysical issue, meaning that we cannot just go out and empirically "test" the validity of different views. Therefore, in the spirit of pluralism, we suggest that one adopts the understanding one feels most comfortable with. However, it is then important to recognize that choosing counterfactuals as the ontological basis for mechanisms means that one must assess the parts of the mechanism using some form of experimental or logical manipulation instead of the type of observational evidence of activities that we advocate in this book.

2.5. Regularity versus Singular Causation

Can we speak of causation in relation to particular historical events? When we study the end of the Cold War, can we claim that a speech in 1988 by Soviet leader Mikhail Gorbachev that proclaimed that Eastern Europe "could go its own way" was a contributing cause of the peaceful resolution of the Cold War (Evangelista 2014)? Or is an explanation truly causal only when we can determine that an individual event is just an instance of a more general pattern across a set of cases?

Singular causation, or token causation, means that claims about a causal relationship in a particular event can be made, whereas the regularity position holds that causation per definition requires that the individual event is subsumed under a more general relationship between cause and effects. The following discusses this debate, illustrating that regularity as an assumption is required only when engaging in comparative methods, whereas both singular and regular causation are compatible with within-case methods like process-tracing.

In many respects, where one falls in this debate is determined by the foundational assumptions one holds on the nature of science itself (Jackson 2011; Groff 2011). Whereas neopositivism is typically associated with a neo-Humean regularity understanding, pragmatists and analyticists favor singular causation because they believe that real-world events are too complex and multifaceted to compare the causes of events like the start of World War I and World War II. In the critical or philosophical realist school, one finds both adherents to singular and regularity, although regularity tends to come in the form of contingent generalization within very bounded populations (e.g., midrange theories). We now develop the two positions in more detail.

In the regularity understanding, for a relationship to be causal it must occur more than once. In the philosophy of science, this position is associated with David Hume. The neo-Humean understanding of causality as nothing more than patterns of regular empirical association has traditionally been the most prevalent in social science (Brady 2008; Kurki 2008: 33–59; Jackson 2011: 67). Hume's claim can be understood by using the example of a pen falling to the ground. We can observe that the pen falls to the ground, but we cannot observe the gravitational forces that *caused* the object to fall. Given this inability to empirically observe the causal forces that link the cause with the outcome for many phenomena in the natural world at the time, Hume argued that we should merely define causes in terms of constant conjunction (correlations) between factors; any theorization of "undetectable" mechanisms would quickly, in his opinion, degenerate into metaphysics. For causality to be established, Hume argued that three criteria for the relationship between a cause (C) and outcome (O) need to be fulfilled: (1) C and O were contiguous in space and time; (2) C occurred before O (temporal succession); and (3) there is a regular conjunction between C and O (Holland 1986). For example, a regular association across a number of cases between governments that impose austerity measures to cut deficits (C) and their inability to win the subsequent election (O) would in this understanding suggest that there is a causal relationship between C and O, assuming that the three criteria are fulfilled.

Causation is taken to involve the regular association between C and O, controlled for other relevant possible causes (Chalmers 1999: 214; Marini and Singer 1988; Holland 1986). Adherents of regularity deny that causal claims can be made about individual outcomes. This can be seen in King, Keohane, and Verba's definition of mean causal effects, where causation is defined both as a counterfactual and as a regularity when they write, "*The difference between the systematic component of observations made when the explanatory variable takes one value and the systematic component of comparable observations when the explanatory variables takes on another value*" (1994: 81–82, italics in original). Deconstructing this definition, they state that causation is *always* about regularity because they focus on systematic components, defined as factors that are present across cases, coupled with the explicit use of a counterfactual-based comparison to evaluate causality.

Regularity is sometimes referred to in the neopositivist tradition as a covering or general law to be used to subsume the particular as an instance of a more general relationship. A covering law is defined by Hempel as "a regularity of the following type: In every case where an event of a specified kind C occurs at a certain place and time, an event of a specified kind E will occur at a place and time which is related in a specified manner to the place and time of the occurrence of the first event" (1965: 232).

But despite Hume's three criteria holding, there can be other causes that produced the pattern of constant conjunction—for example, a common background condition. And even if we control for other causes, we would still not have any within-case evidence of a relationship, meaning that we cannot make strong inferences about causal relationships solely based on patterns of constant conjunction, therefore the adage "correlation is not the same as causation." This is why the regularity understanding is (almost) never used by itself, but instead is coupled with either a counterfactual or mechanism-based understanding.

In contrast, singular causation refers to explanations of particular events, that is, causal relationships that occur only once. There is both a counterfactual- and mechanism-based position on singular causation. Within the literature on counterfactuals, many claim that constant conjunction (regularity) is not needed when counterfactual *singular* causation claims can be made that enable us to assess difference-making logically (Woodward 2003). As we discuss further in chapter 7, the existing real-world case is "compared" with a hypothetical counterfactual case, where the argument is then made that if C had not occurred, O would not have occurred by comparing the two cases (Goertz and Levy 2007; Tetlock and Belkin 1996; Levy 2014).

In mechanism-based understandings, in the philosophical debate one finds a range of different positions on whether mechanisms are regularly occurring phenomena (e.g., Andersen 2012; Hedström and Ylikoski 2010) (i.e., they are midrange theories that exist within a bounded population of cases), or there also can exist singular causal mechanisms that apply only in a particular case (Bogen 2005; Waskan 2011; Glennan 2011). In the latter instance, it is within-case evidence of what *actually* happened in the case that enables us to make a causal claim, not patterns of regularity across cases.

Where one falls on this question reflects back onto the underlying philosophical understanding of science itself discussed in chapter 1.[16] In neopositivist and many critical realist understandings, the goal is to achieve contingent generalizations about mechanisms, meaning that mechanisms are seen as regular (within a bounded context), whereas in more pragmatic and analyticist understandings, the goal is to use multiple causes and mechanisms to explain why an event occurred in a particular case.

We contend that both positions are logically defensible as long as one is then consistent in the methodology one applies. If one claims to be studying a singular causal mechanism in a particular event, one cannot then claim that the study found a causal relationship that should be found in other typical cases of the phenomenon. What is required is only that C actually produces O through a causal mechanism linking the two in the particular case. Therefore, studying mechanisms can be compatible with single-case causation, which is why we include both singular and regularity understandings of causation as compatible with congruence and process-tracing methods.

2.6. Methodological Implications of Deterministic and Asymmetric Causal Claims

Ontological determinism and asymmetry as assumptions about causation have important downstream methodological implications for case-based methods, three of which are explored in the following. First, the widespread practice of selecting most- or least-likely cases is not compatible with an ontologically deterministic understanding of causation at the case level. Second, making deterministic and asymmetric claims that are intended to be applicable to more than one case implies that we should be intensely concerned about achieving as causal homogeneous population of a given theoretical phenomenon as possible. Third, we contend that asymmetry and a concern with causal homogeneity should result in defining causes and outcomes only in terms of categorical, differences of kind.

Most-Likely/Least-Likely Cases Are Not Compatible with Deterministic Claims at the Case Level

The logic of selecting most-likely/least-likely cases is a long-standing qualitative practice that goes back at least to Eckstein in the mid-1970s.[17] However, while intuitively pleasing, the logic conflates both theoretical and empirical likelihood, and within-case and cross-case likelihoods, in ways that are not compatible with the underlying ontological assumptions about the nature of causality in case-based research. These problems lead us to suggest dropping the distinction between most- and least-likely when selecting cases in case-based research because it is a vestige of variance-based designs. Instead, we should use a logic for case selection that is in alignment with the assumptions about deterministic and asymmetric causation underlying case-based research, where causal relationships are either possible or not in any given case.

Before we proceed, it is important to note that there are a variety of different ways in which most- and least-likely cases have been defined in the literature (see table 2.1). Common to most definitions is the idea that a most-likely case is one where other causal conditions except the C in focus suggest that O should occur but it does not, implying that we can disconfirm C being a cause across the population. A least-likely case is where other causal conditions except C point in the direction of O not occurring but it does, enabling us to infer that, given that it occurred where we least expected it, it should also occur in more probable places. It is vital to note that the likelihood of a causal relationship occurring in a case is based on *theoretical* reasons; that is, contextual conditions that are more or less conducive determine the likelihood of the causal relationship occurring. As can also be seen in table 2.1, there is also a variety of ways in which cases are categorized, either by scores on causal conditions and outcomes (variables) (or changes therein, e.g., Eckstein), or based on the assumptions of theories. We have

TABLE 2.1. Different definitions of most-likely/least-likely cases in the literature

Eckstein (1975: 118–20)	• Cases categorized based on scores of cases on variables, but if marked change in X has occurred and other causes remain constant, the case can also be crucial • Most likely = X_1 strongly predicts Y but X_2 found to matter (disconfirmatory for X_1) • Least likely = X_2 strongly predicts Y but X_1 found to matter (confirmatory for X_1)
King, Keohane, and Verba (1994: 209)	• Cases categorized based on case scores on pertinent variables • Most likely = "if predictions of what appear to be an implausible theory confirm with observations of a most-likely observation, the theory will not have passed a rigorous test but will have survived a 'plausibility probe' and may be worthy of further scrutiny" • Least likely = case that "seems on a priori grounds unlikely to accord with theoretical predictions—a 'least-likely' observation—but the theory turns out to be correct regardless"
George and Bennett (2005)	• Cases categorized based on scores on variables • Most likely = Single variable X at such an extreme value that its underlying causal mechanism, even when considered alone, should strongly determine Y. If the predicted Y does not occur, then hypothesized causal mechanism strongly impugned • Least likely = Case least likely for causal mechanism and alternative hypotheses offer different predictions, but causal mechanism correctly predicts Y
Gerring (2007a: 115)	• Cases categorized based on scores on variables, in particular the outcome • Most likely = "on all dimensions *except* the dimension of theoretical interest, is predicted to achieve a certain outcome, and yet does not" • Least likely = "on all dimensions *except* the dimension of theoretical interest, is predicted not to achieve a certain outcome, and yet does"
Levy (2008: 12)	• Cases categorized based on values of key variables, or theory's assumptions and scope conditions satisfied or not satisfied • Most likely = case is likely to fit a theory but data from case does not fit, strongest if case is least likely for alternative theory • Least likely = case is not likely to fit a theory but data supports theory, strongest if case is most likely for alternative theory
Schneider and Rohlfing (2013: 23)	• Cases categorized based on case membership scores above qualitative threshold • Most typical case = displays maximum set membership scores in the subset and the superset

also included Schneider and Rohlfing's definition of a "most typical" case, given that is similar to a most-likely case but is understood in more set-theoretic terms.

The most serious problem with the likelihood logic and case selection strategies is that they conflate theoretical (ontological) and empirical (epistemological) likelihood. In this book we argue for ontological determinism but a Bayesian-inspired probabilistic epistemological position about using empirical evidence to update the degree of confidence we have about causal relationships. Note that ontological probabilism is not the same thing as epistemological probabilism as incorporated into Bayesian logic, a distinction we develop in greater detail in chapter 6. Priors and posteriors in Bayesian logic relate to the degree of *empirical* confidence in a relationship being actually present in a case or a population that we can reasonably hold before and after empirical evidence is collected. In case-based research, the types of *theoretical* causal claims we are making about relationships in particular cases are deterministic. Things do not just happen randomly; they happen for a reason. At the same time, Bayesian logic tells us that it might be difficult empirically to detect why things happen, and we will never be 100 percent certain empirically.

Bayesian logic makes no assumptions about the underlying theoretical nature of causality (ontology), and Bayesian reasoning is utilized when making inferences about both deterministic and probabilistic causal relationships (Howson and Urbach 2006). Instead, Bayesian logic deals with *epistemology*, relating to how empirical evidence updates the degree of confidence we have in a given causal theory, irrespective of it being deterministic or probabilistic. However, most-likely/least-likely logic conflates the two, resulting in philosophically incoherent arguments.

The use of the term "likelihood" in relation to causation requires a probabilistic ontological understanding of causation, where "a cause raises the probability of an event occurring" (Gerring 2005: 167). Causal relationships are more likely in more conducive circumstances (contextual conditions strongly present) and less likely in less conducive (contextual conditions mostly absent). Claiming that a relationship is likely in a case (e.g., 75 percent likelihood) is also claiming that the relationship will be present in three out of four studied cases. However, if we accept ontological probabilism as an assumption, there is basically no reason to study any given case, because if we do not find the relationship in the case, we do not know whether it is because there is no causal relationship or because we just selected one of the 25 percent of cases where the relationship is not present. Therefore, ontological probabilism is simply not compatible with a research approach that takes individual cases as the point of departure for causal explanations (Mahoney 2008: 415–16).

In case-based research we want to produce explanations that can account for what happened in particular cases instead of just producing theoretical odds for whether something might occur across a range of cases. In a deterministic understanding of causation, if a sufficient cause is present along with the requisite contextual conditions, the outcome *will* occur. Any case that fulfills these conditions should demonstrate the relationship, meaning that logically the relationship is not more or less likely in any particular case. Understood in deterministic and asymmetric causal terms, the relevant distinction is simply possible and not possible. If an outcome occurs when we did not theoretically expect it (a least-likely case), this should result in revision of the theory about the context in which the relationship holds instead of enabling us to make a strong cross-case inference that the relationship should also work in other more typical cases! For example, when studying elite decision-making, we might have selected a least-likely case for the relationship between efficient presidential leadership (C) and rational decision-making (O), where in a severe crisis situation, conditions like the extreme stakes involved and the short time frame for decisions would be expected to trump efficient presidential leadership (C), thereby resulting in poor decision-making processes (~O). If we then found in a least-likely case study that the outcome was actually rational decision-making (O), we would not make a strong cross-case inference that C matters across the population of more typical cases because it mattered when we least expected it. Instead, in case-based research we would want to delve into the case to understand why our theoretical expectations about the impact of the adverse context were confounded, probing which factors enabled presidential leadership to matter that would enable us to delineate the contextual conditions required for presidential leadership more accurately.

Second, and related, case studies produce within-case mechanistic evidence, updating our posterior confidence in a causal relationship being present within a single case.[18] Inferring *beyond* the single case to the rest of the population requires that it is causally similar to the studied case. However, given the large differences in the contextual conditions present in least-likely, most-likely cases, and more "normal" typical cases, and given the sensitivity of causal processes to contextual conditions that are typically assumed in case-based research, we should expect the different types of cases to exhibit high degrees of causal heterogeneity. This means that we cannot just infer that because we found confirming evidence of a causal mechanism in a least-likely case that it should also be present in other, potentially causally *dissimilar* cases throughout the population (e.g., in most-likely cases). This point is particularly salient when discussing causal mechanisms in process-tracing, where finding within-case evidence of particular mechanisms linking C to O in a chosen case requires a strong assumption of causal homogeneity across cases to be able to infer from the studied cases to other similar cases. Therefore, the "Sinatra inference" that states that if "you can make it there, you can make it everywhere" (Levy 2008: 12) does not hold for case-based research. Irrespective of the musical virtues of the song, a case-based scholar would rebut that Sinatra was basically wrong in claiming that just because you "make it" as a crooner in a major venue in New York you would "make it" everywhere. The reason for this is that he ignores the importance of context for causal relationships. For example, the style of music might matter, leading us to expect that Sinatra probably would not "make it" in a bluegrass club in Nashville or in a Chinese opera in Beijing. The type of audience would probably matter also, meaning that just because Sinatra made it at a nightclub in New York and Las Vegas, we should not infer that he would also rock an audience that is hard of hearing in a nursing home in Albuquerque. Case-based scholars claim that context matters, meaning that we should be very cautious in inferring across causally heterogeneous sets of cases.

Schneider and Rohlfing (2013) have developed a definition of most-likely cases that is more compatible with asymmetric causation. They suggest that causal relationships are easier to study when both C and O are strongly present (high set-membership scores). Yet this assumes a "more is better" logic in the theory we are studying in relation to whether it is empirically observable, and it assumes that degree differences matter theoretically. Empirically, using an analogy, if the outcome is fire, the outcome would have higher scores on O the more fuel is present, and given that more fire is more observable, other things equal, it would also be easier to study empirically up to the point that the fire gets so big that you would be scorched. Yet for most of the types of causal claims being assessed in case-based research, these differences of degrees are causally and empirically irrelevant. At the theoretical level, if C is theorized to be necessary, it is necessary in a case when the cause and requisite contextual conditions are present in the case; a cause cannot be "more" or "less" necessary. At the empirical level, a case that has maximum scores of both C and O would in this logic be a type of "perfect storm" that would best enable us to study it empirically. However, this conflates theoretical concerns and empirical accessibility. If we are studying the relationship between the resources possessed by interest groups (C) and influence over US foreign policy (O), the case of the Israel lobby might be a most typical case that we could select, given that it has relatively high levels of economic and political resources in comparison to other interest groups, and scholars have made it plausible that they have had large influence over US foreign policy. However, given the sensitivity of the politics surrounding this most typical case, it is also very difficult to empirically assess in a systematic fashion, which is also the reason that Mearsheimer and Walt's case study of the Israeli lobby has been criticized for building on poor, anecdotal evidence that does little to update confidence in the causal claims made in the book (2007; for critique, see Goldberg 2007; Lieberman 2009).

Concluding, most-likely/least-likely logic conflates ontological and epistemological probabilism, and within-case and cross-case evidence, in ways that are impossible to untangle. We therefore recommend the use of the term typical case without any qualifications about likelihood, referring to cases where the theorized causal relationship is possible because C, O, and the requisite contextual conditions for the relationship to occur are present. We also recommend thinking about whether one has access to empirical material or not when selecting cases, and whether the theory is predicted to leave empirical fingerprints that can be observed in a particular case. For example, choosing to studying bureaucratic politics by selecting a case from an organizational setting where most deliberations are not recorded in written form would be very difficult, as the theory would leave few empirical fingerprints that could be assessed. Additionally, accessibility concerns are paramount when selecting cases. There is a reason historians typically study only cases where there is a rich documentary record that is accessible after archives are opened after thirty or more years. Unfortunately, many of the research questions we want to investigate are too contemporary for archives to be opened and/or are so politically sensitive that we can have difficulties gaining access to impartial sources. Given that good case-based research is data-demanding, selecting typical cases where we expect to be able to access as much information as possible is a wise case selection strategy.

Causal Homogeneity Is Vital When Generalizing Deterministic Claims to Other Cases

A causally homogenous population is one in which a given cause can be expected to have the *same* causal relationship with the outcome across cases in the population,[19] whereas a causally heterogeneous population is one where a given cause might have many different effects across different cases, in terms of either the same cause producing a different outcome or the same cause being linked to the same outcome through different causal mechanisms.[20]

The *causal* inferences we make in case-based research are mostly based on the in-depth, *within-case* analysis of the evidence left by the operation of causal mechanisms (i.e., mechanistic evidence; see chapter 6). This implies that the assumption of a causally homogeneous population is vital if we want to generalize from the single, studied case to other cases in the population when making deterministic causal claims. Basically, we need to be able to claim that what we found in the studied case (or small set of cases) should also be found in the rest of the population based on the logic "we found mechanistic evidence of the relationship in case 1. Cases 2 and 3 are similar on a range of causally relevant factors, ergo we should expect the relationship to also be present in cases 2 and 3."

Causal heterogeneity is not as large a problem for variance-based designs because they are making probabilistic claims based on patterns of difference-making across cases. In large-N, variance-based designs, a causally heterogeneous population would typically result in weaker correlations being found, meaning that we might falsely reject a hypothesis in the worst-case situation (false negative) (Rhodes 2010). And one of the reasons variance-based designs make probabilistic claims about trends across cases is that they make inferences within relatively causally heterogeneous populations, a natural consequence of including a large enough number of cases to engage in statistical assessment of mean causal effects. However, if we are studying a single or small number of cases and want to generalize from the studied to the rest of the bounded population, if we have selected from a causally heterogeneous population we risk concluding that there is a relationship in the population, when there in reality is a relationship only within a subpopulation that is causally similar to the selected case (false positive) (Geddes 1990; King, Keohane, and Verba 1994; Mahoney 2007).

In case-based research the goal is therefore to achieve homogeneous populations of theoretical phenomena that enable us to compare what is going on in causally similar cases and contrast, where relevant, causally dissimilar cases (Collier and Mahoney 1996: 68–69; Goertz 2006: 29; Mahoney 2007; Ragin 2000). This is achieved by operating with smaller bounded populations of cases, a point we return to in chapter 7. The types of causal claims we are operating with are therefore typically "middle-range theories" (Merton 1967), bounded in time and space by concerns about causal homogeneity.

A causally heterogeneous population of cases can be the product of ignoring important contextual factors that result in the same cause having different effects, or the same outcome being produced by different causes depending on context, or ignoring causally important differences between cases by lumping them together using excessively broad definitions of concepts.

As an example of the importance of context, in international relations scholarship we see that Alexander Wendt claims that there are three "cultures" of anarchy, a term to describe the nature of the relations between states (conflictual, competitive, or cooperative) (1999). In a time period and region where there is little interdependence between states and few international institutions binding them together (e.g., in Europe in the years after the French Revolution), Wendt claims that conflicts between states will produce interstate wars (O_1) (1999: 270). In contrast, in contemporary Western Europe, the ties in terms of interdependence and institutions that bind states together has resulted in a situation where conflicts are dealt with amicably between friends, with peace the result (O_2) (1999: 297–99). The methodological point is that depending on the context, the same causes can produce very different outcomes (O_1 or O_2). Therefore, comparing the effects of conflicts between states in two cases that span these two contexts that demarcate a kind difference would be comparing two very causally dissimilar cases.

An example of causal heterogeneity produced by lumping cases together can be found in the literature on inequality and intrastate conflict (civil war). Bartusevičius (2014) has made the argument that existing theorization has neglected two causally important differences of kind when conceptualizing the outcome that result in a causally heterogeneous population (O = intrastate conflict): (1) what the conflict is being fought over, either governmental control or territory, and (2) whether the conflict is ethnic or nonethnic. By focusing relentlessly on plausible causal relations between inequality and conflict, he theorizes that we should expect that the causal relationship of inequality with *ethnic* territorial conflict is very different from what we should expect in *nonethnic* governmental conflicts. There is a difference of kind between ethnic and nonethnic conflicts, with the first produced by inequality (C_1), whereas the latter tend to have very different causes (e.g., C_2, elite-related factors like military dissatisfaction with the country's leadership because of a lost war). The resulting causally heterogeneous population is depicted in figure 2.3, where in cases 1, 2, and 3, O_1 is produced by C_1 (inequality) (C_2 has no impact), whereas C_2 produces O_2 in the other three cases (nonethnic conflicts) and C_1 has no causal impact.

If we were testing the relationship between inequality (C_1) and intrastate conflict (O), we would have very different findings depending on which case we selected within this heterogeneous population. Therefore, inferring from the single case to the rest of the causally heterogeneous population of cases

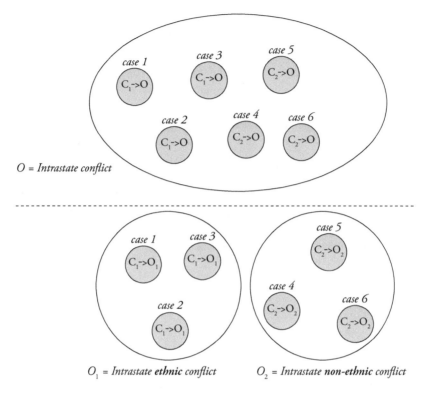

Fig. 2.3. A causally heterogeneous population turned into two homogeneous populations

of interstate conflict would result in flawed inferences, either claiming that there was a relationship across cases whereas in reality there was only a relationship in a subset (false positive), or inferring no relationship in a situation where it was actually present in a subset (false negative). What we should do here would be to include the difference of kind present in the outcome to be explained (depicted in the lower half of figure 2.3), resulting in bounded populations of more causally homogeneous cases (cases 1, 2, and 3 = O_1 (ethnic conflicts) and cases 4, 5, and 6 = O_2 (nonethnic territorial conflicts). In the first population, C_1 matters, whereas in the latter, C_2 matters.

Unfortunately, full causal homogeneity of a set of cases is an unattainable ideal. No matter how carefully we define our concepts, there will always be differences across cases that will be masked by treating them as causally similar cases within a bounded population. For instance, if we categorized cases like World War I and World War II as a subclass of war defined as post-1815, systemic conflict between great powers, one could still argue that the causes of conflict were very different between the two cases. Therefore, even in a population of two cases, causal heterogeneity can be present. This is why scholars working in the analyticist and pragmatic traditions tend to avoid generalizations across cases because they believe interesting, real-world cases are too complex to meaningfully compare with each other; views they share with many historians (see chapter 1 for more on this tradition).

Yet if one has the goal of generalizing beyond the single case, we should think of causal homogeneity as a goal to strive for in case-based research, acknowledging at the same time that there always will be a trade-off between the ambition to generalize across cases, thereby creating greater risks of heterogeneity, and the desire to craft causally homogeneous populations that result in bounded generalizations across a very small number of cases. We now turn to the question of why case-based research should operate only with concepts measured using differences of kind.

Case-Based Research Should Operate Only with Differences of Kind in Concepts

Case-based research designs will always include some form of within-case tracing of mechanisms in order to make confirming inferences about causal relationships, because cross-case comparative methods enable only disconfirming inferences (see chapter 6 and 7 for more on this). However, when we couple mechanism-based research with the assumption of asymmetry, degree differences in causal concepts become irrelevant at best and at worst risk producing flawed causal inferences when we attempt to generalize from a within-case tracing of mechanisms in one case to other cases in a bounded population because of the importance of causal homogeneity when studying mechanisms. Differences of degree often mask differences across cases that change the character of a causal relationship. Therefore, utilizing degree differences in a bounded population within which we attempt to generalize from a single case to the rest of the population risks producing flawed inferences. We argue that in case-based research causal concepts should be understood only in categorical terms, focusing on key theoretically relevant differences of kind.

Differences of kind refer to differences in values of case scores on causal concepts that change the *character* of a causal relationship. These are often termed qualitative differences. In contrast, differences of degree are *variations* in scores of causal concepts *within* these kind-differences, often termed quantitative measures. Kind differences are typically captured using a categorical, crisp-set measure of a given causal concept, whereas degree differences are measured using measurement scales from ordinal to ratio, or fuzzy-set, scores.

Differences of kind in causal concepts are a natural product of operating with *asymmetric* causal claims, where a discontinuous causal relationship is theorized across scores of a concept. When a case is *below* the causally relevant threshold on a cause or set of causes (C or multiple causes that work in conjunction), either there are no causal effects, the causal effects are very different (a different outcome might be produced), or the same cause might be linked to the same outcome through different causal mechanisms.[21] Above the threshold the theorized causal relationship is possible, contingent upon the contextual (scope) conditions for the relationship also being present. For an outcome, a case above the threshold is one where the theorized cause (or set of causes) can potentially have been the cause of the outcome, whereas cases below the threshold are ones where the outcome has not occurred.

The classic example of the distinction between kind and degree differences is being pregnant, where the argument is that one cannot be a little bit pregnant, meaning there is a difference of kind between persons who are pregnant and everyone else. This does not mean that once a person is in the set of pregnant persons that she cannot be more or less pregnant (six weeks in comparison to six months—a degree difference). And Coppedge correctly points out that the dichotomous nature of the concept pregnancy depends on *how* one defines it (2012: 42). He then discusses several possible exceptions to a crisp-set distinction of pregnancy, including having delivered one of two twins. However, here the woman would still technically be "pregnant" because there is still a fertilized fetus in the woman. And if we are interested in understanding the causal process whereby an outcome like pregnancy is produced, these technical distinctions are irrelevant.

There are some methodologists who question the distinction between degrees and kind (Munck 2005; Coppedge 2012). For example, Munck (2005) has claimed that all measurement involves both categorical dichotomies and degree differences. He claims that "measurement is quantification because it consists of assigning numbers to objects according to rules. Yet measurement is also necessarily qualitative, because each number, inasmuch as it is theoretically interpretable, can always be linked to a class of phenomena. Thus, the proper distinction to draw among scales concerns not whether the scales are qualitative (i.e., 'of kind') or quantitative (i.e., 'of degree'), but rather the mathematical properties of the relationship among the numbers. Indeed, efforts to distinguish between qualitative and quantitative scales lack meaning and are based on arbitrary choices. . . . [H]igher level measures are always preferable because they offer more information than lower level measures" (Munck 2005: 4–5). While Munck is correct to state that both quantitative degree differences and qualitative differences of kind can be modeled mathematically (Michell 2011: 245), his argument that measurement always involves both is only correct when we are operating with difference-making evidence (see chapter 6 for more on this). As we will develop in the following, degree differences are at best irrelevant when operating with both mechanism- and counterfactual-based claims in case-based research.

Why, then are, degree differences irrelevant in case-based research? When we are working with mechanism-based asymmetric causal claims, we engage in the within-case tracing of mechanisms to produce so-called mechanistic evidence upon which we base our causal inferences (see chapter 6 for more). When using mechanistic evidence, we are focusing on what is actually going on *within* the studied case—that is, we are tracing causal mechanisms as they actually played out in a real case. Mechanistic evidence is not produced by negative cases; without smoking, there will be no mechanisms linking smoking to the production of lung cancer, meaning that observing the lungs of a nonsmoker will not produce any mechanistic evidence because the mechanism is not present. One could argue that a negative case plays the role of a counterfactual, providing evidence that without C (and the requisite contextual conditions), the mechanism does not occur. But this is a *logical* hypothetical, whereas what mechanistic evidence provides is empirical material that shows how a mechanism actually played out in a particular case.

In any given selected case for tracing mechanisms, the scores of the case on C and O are fixed; indeed, within-case variation would prejudice mechanistic evidence because we could no longer be certain that we are studying the same causal processes in the case. For example, if we are engaging in process-tracing of a causal process linking the dependence of politicians upon the expertise of interest groups (C_1) with interest-group influence over enacted policies (O), we would want to trace the process in a case where C_1 and O both were present and did not vary to see whether there was mechanistic, within-case evidence of the process actually working as hypothesized. If the dependence of a set of key politicians on the information provided by a central interest group in the policy area decreased in the course of the case being studied because the politicians gained access to bureaucratic resources that lessened informational dependence, we would expect different causal processes to start working. The same outcome might have occurred, but instead it might have been because the interest group was then able to mobilize significant outside constituents in support of their cause (C_2), re-

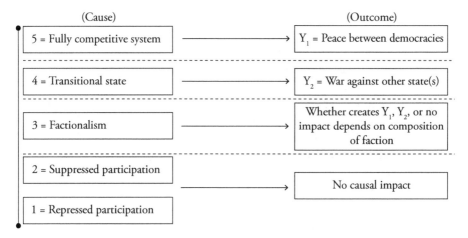

Fig. 2.4. An example of an ordinal scale that includes multiple differences of kind

sulting in a very different mechanism playing out than the one linking C_1 to O. The methodological point here is that "variation" captured by differences of degree in values of C is at best irrelevant when tracing causal mechanisms in cases.

Degree differences are not only irrelevant in mechanism-based research, but utilizing this type of measure often introduces unwanted causal heterogeneity into the populations of the causal relationship that we are attempting to generalize to. Most ordinal and higher scale measures usually include hidden differences of kind (Michell 2011). We argue that many, if not most, existing definitions of social science concepts that utilize ordinal or higher scales to model concept structure conflate degree and kind differences, resulting in causally heterogeneous populations that are inappropriate when we want to generalize in case-based research.

For example, in the Polity IV democracy data set, a five-point ordinal scale is used to model different degrees of political competition. But as illustrated in figure 2.4, if we utilize the defined concept in a process-tracing case study of the effects of political participation (X) on peace or war between states (Y_1 or Y_2), there would in reality be up to three distinct kind differences between cases with different values on the cause. We use the notation X and Y here because we are talking about variables as causes or outcomes.

The first kind difference is arguably between values of 1 and 2 of X, reflecting either repressed or suppressed levels of political competition, and the rest of the scale. When competition is repressed or suppressed, we would theoretically not expect there to be causal effects between X and to either peace (Y_1) or war (Y_2). The next kind difference is between value 3 (faction-alism) and the rest of the scale, where we could expect that war-proneness would depend on which faction is influential at a given time (a contingent causal relationship). Another kind difference is between value 4 (system in transition) and the rest of the scale, where we could theorize that transitional systems are more war-prone than both more suppressed and more competi-tive systems, where X at this value produces Y_2 and not Y_1 (Mansfield and Snyder 2002). Finally, there is a potential kind difference between the causal relationship of cases with value 5 (fully competitive) upon peace (Y_1) and the rest of the scale.

If we utilized this scale to model the causal effects of political partici-pation upon peace, given the very different causal properties of different values of the ordinal scale (kind differences), the analytical result would be a causally heterogeneous population where our cross-case inferences based on case studies would be flawed if we generalized our positive findings in a case where X = 4 to cases where X has other values. Therefore, an appropriate use of this ordinal scale in case-based research would be first to dichotomize it to capture the causally relevant difference of kind in relation to the causal theory one is testing. In this example, if we are testing whether democracy (a fully competitive system) produces peace between states, we would in-troduce a qualitative kind threshold at score 5, meaning that all cases with X = 5 would be in the set of cases in our population, and all cases with lower scores would be outside. Yet this means that we have transformed a degree difference into a kind difference, with the "extra" information about cases included in the ordinal scale being irrelevant for our analysis.

Some scholars have argued that fuzzy-set measures are a good way to avoid problems with including degree differences in case-based research (Goertz and Mahoney 2012; Ragin 2000: 149–58; 2008; Schneider and Wa-german 2012). In a fuzzy-set concept structure, full membership in the con-cept is given a score of 1, full nonmembership a score of 0, and the scores between 0 and 1 are degrees, with the midpoint of 0.5 a cross-over point marking cases that are more in than out of the set (Ragin 2000: 154).[22] How-ever, fuzzy-set structures run into the same problems of masking potential kind differences *within* the scale. But before we present this argument, we need to clear up exactly what degrees of membership in fuzzy-sets actually refer to, given that scholars often conflate empirical uncertainty with theo-retical questions relating to concept structure in the literature.

In Ragin's own presentation, he fluctuates between seeing scores as degrees of empirical confidence about membership of particular cases and degrees as scores on a scale that represent more or less of a concept being present. In the former, uncertainty is due to differences in the quality of empirical evidence that determine degrees of membership (e.g., Ragin 2008: 90). In his 2000 book he uses the example of membership in the set "nonprofit organization being a major actor," defining the fuzzy-set as follows: 0 = definitely a major actor, 0.75 = probably a major actor, 0.5 = may be or may not be a major actor, 0.25 = probably not a major actor, and 0 = definitely not a major actor (157). This relates to assessments about the *ambiguity of the evidence* enabling us to classify cases. But used in this fashion, fuzzy-set scores do not tell us anything about the underlying *theoretical* concept structure.

At other points, Ragin describes fuzzy-set scores as points on an underlying continuous scale that map onto the theorized concept structure. Values of 0 and 1 are given to cases below and above which variation is irrelevant (Ragin 2000: 158–59). Fuzzy-set scores in this usage describe actual characteristics of cases (e.g., levels of GDP per capita) instead of the empirical certainty of membership based on the quality of the evidence. However, fuzzy-set scores run into the same risk of conflating kind and degree differences when defining concepts as conventional ordinal and higher-level scales.

Using Ragin's definition of economic development (2008: 90), where $20,000 income per capita denotes full membership, under $2,500 is full nonmembership, and a cross-over point of $5,000, the resulting fuzzy-set potentially conflates kind differences into a single scale. For sake of example, let us assume that we theorize that economic development is sufficient to produce democracy. In fuzzy-set QCA (qualitative comparative analysis), we would then expect a cross-case pattern of cases as in figure 2.5, where case scores of C are less than scores of O. However, there might plausibly be a kind difference between higher scores of C and midrange scores of C, with scores above $10,000 producing democracy through CM_1 ($C \rightarrow CM_1 \rightarrow O$), whereas in the range of $10,000 to $4,000 the same C and O are linked through a different mechanism (CM_2). This could be because middle-income cases are causally different from higher-income countries, resulting in a different mechanism linking C and O. Below the qualitative threshold of C and O, no relationship is possible. But the analytical result of using fuzzy-sets would be a population of positive cases in which there is ample potential for selecting cases that would result in false positives or false negatives.

In figure 2.5, the distribution of cases would support a fuzzy-set QCA claim of C being sufficient for O (scores of O are greater than scores of C, marked by the dotted line in the figure). Yet if we then chose case 2 as a positive case to investigate whether there is within-case mechanistic evidence that the theorized causal mechanism 1 links C with O, we would not find

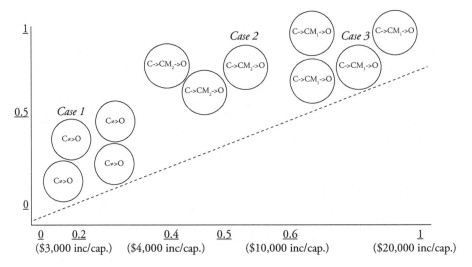

Fig. 2.5. A hypothetical example illustrating potential causal heterogeneity in fuzzy-sets

the expected relationship. In contrast, selecting case 3 would result in a false positive about CM_1 for the whole population of positive cases, in that the found relationship is only present in the cases above the 0.6 threshold of C.

This does not mean that fuzzy-set scores are irrelevant for our analysis, only that they do not solve the problem of causal heterogeneity and the risks it raises for making flawed inferences within a population of positive cases. In the example in figure 2.5, we can use fuzzy-set scores to divide the population of positive cases into two subpopulations, attempting to find the difference of kind that demarcates middle-income from higher-income cases because two different causal mechanisms link C with O in the two subpopulations. We would want to compare cases within these two subpopulations to see which causally relevant attributes that each set shares among themselves but differentiates them from those in the other set. We might, for instance, find that the middle-income countries all have higher levels of economic inequality, which might account for the different mechanism operating. But by doing this, we would have transformed the fuzzy-set degree differences into two distinct kind differences.

A recent methodological innovation is the introduction of what Skaaning, Gerring, and Bartusevičius (2015) refer to as a lexical scale. They claim that it is an ordinal scale, but where each of the category levels are determined by necessary and sufficient attributes that have to be present for a case to be a member of the set of that level, resulting in each category in the scale

0 = No elections

1 = No party or one-party elections (only regular elections present)

2 = Multi-party elections for legislatures (regular elections * opposition parties participate in legislative elections and to take office)

3 = Multi-party elections for executive (regular elections * opposition parties participate in legislative * executive chosen directly/indirectly by elected legislature through multi-party elections)

4 = Minimally competitive elections (all of above * important seats directly or indirectly filled by elections characterized by uncertainty)

5 = Male or female suffrage (all of above * virtually all adult male or female citizens allowed to vote)

6 = Universal suffrage (all of above * virtually all adult citizens allowed to vote)

Fig. 2.6. Lexical index of electoral democracy

demarcating a kind difference. For example, figure 2.6 shows how a lexical scale of electoral democracy can be defined.

Lexical scales are, however, not the solution to the problem unless we treat them as if they are dichotomous kind differences scales when delineating a population of causally homogeneous cases. For instance, in the example in figure 2.6, if we are focusing on studying the mechanisms linking competitive electoral systems with economic growth, all of the cases with values of 4 or more would be included in the population, contingent on their not being important contextual conditions that might alter the nature of the causal relationship within these cases. In other words, while the lexical scale might provide more information, in relation to mechanistic evidence of causal relationships at they play out in particular cases, we would have to transform a lexical scale into a dichotomous difference of kind anyway before we could craft a causally homogeneous set of cases that could be inferred using comparative methods.

CHAPTER 3

Types of Causal Explanations in Case-Based Research

No, no! The adventures first, explanations take such a dreadful time.

Lewis Carroll, *Alice in Wonderland*

3.1. Introduction

Causal case study methods make different types of causal claims depending on the ontological assumptions upon which they rest. In this chapter we first develop the commonalities of theorization about causal relationship in case-based designs that derive from the core assumptions of ontological determinism and asymmetry.

We then discuss what causal explanations look like in case-based research, developing what claims of necessity or sufficiency look like, and how they differ from the claim that C is causally related to O in a minimalist-mechanism understanding, or that C is linked to O through an explicitly theorized mechanism (systems understanding of mechanisms). We conclude with a discussion of the importance of theorizing the context in which a given theory is expected to function.

3.2. The Types of Causal Claims Being Made in Different Methods

As discussed in chapter 2, the ontological assumptions underlying case-based research differ from variance-based research. But we also contend that these different ontological assumptions about causation result in different types of causal explanations than typically made in variable-based designs.

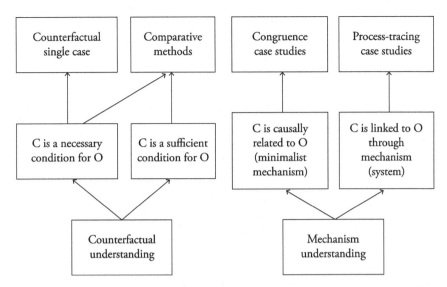

Fig. 3.1. Different kinds of causal explanations and the associated case-based methods

Figure 3.1 illustrates the four different kinds of causal explanations we make in case-based research, along with the associated method for investigating them, which are developed in chapters 7–9.

If causation is understood in counterfactual terms, then one is making claims about necessity and/or sufficiency. If causation is understood as mechanisms, but mechanisms are viewed in minimalist terms, then one is basically claiming that there is a discernible within-case causal relationship between C and O. The relationship is neither necessary nor sufficient, nor is it based on an in-depth tracing of a causal mechanism. In contrast, in the systems understanding, the causal claim is that C is linked to O through an explicit causal mechanism. Claims about necessity, sufficiency, and/or mechanisms can all be either singular (e.g., cognitive misperceptions (C) influenced the US decision to escalate the conflict in Vietnam in 1965 (O)), or cross-case regularity-based claims about causal relationships within a small, bounded population (e.g., economic development (C) was necessary for democratization (O) in Southeast Asia in the 1980s).

The differences between these four types of causal explanations are developed in the following, illustrated with examples from published work. For each type of causal explanation, we provide practical guidance for how causal relationships can be formulated in alignment with the different underlying understandings of causation. In particular, given the lack of practical guidance in the literature on theorizing mechanisms as systems, we develop the ideal of what productive continuity can look like in social science theories, including what it is that we want to capture in theoretical terms when conceptualizing mechanisms.

The Importance of Ontological Determinism When Formulating Causal Theories

When theorizing causal relationships between conditions and outcomes in case-based research, relationships should *not* be formulated in probabilistic terms, as in variance-based research, where, for instance, increases in the value of X tend to increase the value of Y. We should make clear that, in case-based research, our causal claims should match the deterministic ontological understanding underlying case-based research (see chapter 2).[1] Basically, theories should be formulated clearly enough that we can be wrong in a case, thus enabling us to update our theoretical knowledge based on empirical case studies.

For example, when claiming C is a sufficient cause, we are theorizing that if C is present in a case, O *should* occur if the requisite contextual conditions are also present. If C is present and we find that O does not occur in a particular case, we would not be satisfied with concluding that the chosen case was an outlier from an otherwise strong probabilistic correlation. Instead, if our ontological understanding is deterministic, we would want to know what it is about the analyzed case that resulted in the nonoccurrence of the outcome despite the cause being present. One explanation that we might find by examining both the case itself and comparing it with other positive cases is that there might be an omitted cause, with O occurring only when C_1 and C_2 are present together. This intense interrogation of deviant cases marks a key analytical difference between research designs based on probabilistic and deterministic ontological understandings of causal relationships. Concluding, then, it is important to make clear the logic of the deterministic nature of the causal claim when developing causal theories in case-based research.

The Importance of Asymmetry When Formulating Causal Theories

As discussed in chapter 2, the types of causal claims we are making in case-based research are all asymmetric, meaning that we are making claims about the effects of C, the causes of O, or the mechanisms linking a given C and O together. When we make a claim about necessity, we claim that all instances of the outcome (O) also have the cause present, but we are not theorizing about the causes of ~O. When making sufficiency claims, we are making no claims about what happens if a given cause is not present. When we are making claims about mechanisms linking C and O, we make no claims about what happens when C is not present. This means that our asymmetric causal theories are invariant causal claims that assign causal properties only to the positive pole of concepts. Therefore, we do not need to theorize explicitly what causal relationships occur in the absence of C, O, or both. If, for example, you are theorizing that conflict of interest is a necessary condition for war to occur, you do not need to also theorize explicitly what the causes of peace are.

3.3. Necessary and Sufficient Conditions

Claims of necessity and sufficiency can be expressed in set theoretical terms as subset relations, where cases that are members of the outcome constitute a subset of cases that are members of the cause. This is depicted in figure 3.2. In a claim of necessity, all of the cases of O are within the set of C, but there are also cases where C is present but O does not occur. When claiming sufficiency, if C is present O will occur, but there are often also other causes of O besides those in the set of C.

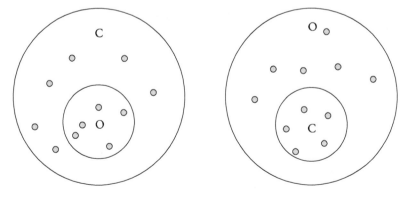

C is a necessary cause of O (O subset of C)   C is a sufficient cause of O (C subset of O)

Fig. 3.2. Subset relationships and necessity and sufficiency

Sufficient Causes

Sufficiency claims occur when C is by itself enough to produce O, contingent upon a set of contextual conditions being present.[2] Claims of sufficiency build on the counterfactual understanding of causation (Woodward 2003: 45). That is, C does not have to be present for O to occur, but when C is present, O will *always* occur. In set theoretic terms, a sufficient causal explanation is where cases that are members of C are a subset of cases that are members of O (depicted in figure 3.2). But just because C is sufficient for O does not mean that there are not other pathways to an outcome; this is illustrated by the cases that are not in the set of C but are in the set of O.

There are few examples of theories of *individual* causes being sufficient for nontrivial outcomes, with the democratic peace theory one notable exception (see Owen 1994, 1997). In contrast, there are numerous examples of theories of conjunctions of causes that together are sufficient.

How, then, can we understand conjunctions of conditions? Conjunctional causation means that causes work only as part of a whole (Ragin 2000, 2008). This also means that when they are isolated, individual causes that are part of a conjunction might not have a discernible causal impact by themselves. We contend that whether one operates with conjunctional causal claims depends on one's overall philosophical position (see chapter 1). Neopositivists typically assess the causal impact of individual causes, meaning that they would feel more comfortable with assessing the necessity of an individual cause than with a conjunction of causes that is sufficient for an outcome to occur. In contrast, critical realists and pragmatists tend to assume conjunctional causation, especially as regards explaining outcomes in single cases.

The simplest form of conjunctional causation is an INUS cause, where INUS stands for an individually necessary part of an unnecessary but sufficient condition (Mackie 1965: 246). An INUS cause is a condition that is an individually necessary part of an unnecessary but sufficient condition. Each INUS condition has no effect by itself, but together with the other INUS conditions they are sufficient to produce an outcome. This can be illustrated as $C_1 * C_2 + C_3 * C_4 \rightarrow O$ (read: either C_1 and C_2 or C_3 and C_4 produce O).[3] Here C_1 is an INUS condition, and if only C_1 is present in a case, O will not occur. It is only when a case is a member of the set of either C_1 and C_2 or C_3 and C_4 that O occurs. In contrast, SUIN explanations are causes that are a sufficient but unnecessary part of a factor that is insufficient but necessary (Mahoney, Kimball, and Koivu 2007). A SUIN cause would be C_3

or C_4 in the example of $C_1 * C_2 \rightarrow O$, where $C_2 = C_3 + C_4$. Here the two SUIN causes are substitutable sufficient conditions for a necessary but not sufficient condition (C_2) to be present.

What can claims about sufficiency look like in practice? Below are three examples, all of which make claims about conjunctions of conditions that together are sufficient for the outcome.

- "When liberals run the government, relations with fellow democracies are harmonious. When illiberals govern, relations may be rockier. Even then, if war is threatened with a state that the liberal opposition considers a fellow democracy, liberals agitate to prevent hostilities using the free speech allowed them by law. Illiberal leaders are unable to rally the public to fight, and fear that an unpopular war would lead to their ouster at the next election" (Owen 1994: 89).
- "I have analyzed the decision of the EU to expand to Central and Eastern Europe [O]. Both theoretical perspectives were found wanting in their 'pure' form: Although rationalism [C_1] can explain most actor preferences and much of the bargaining behavior [parts of O], it fails to account for the collective decision for enlargement. Sociological institutionalism [C_2], in turn, can explain the outcome but not the input [other parts of O]. To provide the missing link between egoistic preferences and a norm-conforming outcome [the final parts of O], I introduced 'rhetorical action,' the strategic use of norm-based arguments [C_3]" (Schimmelfennig 2001: 76, bracketed text inserted).
- "In each case, social revolution [O] was a conjuncture of three developments: (1) the collapse or incapacitation of central administrative and military machineries; (2) widespread peasant rebellions; and (3) marginal elite political movements" (Skocpol 1975: 178, bracketed text inserted).

It is vital that one makes the causal logic behind the sufficiency claim explicit in one's theorization. Basically, why should we expect C (or a set of causes) to be sufficient for the outcome? In other words, we need to develop plausible theoretical arguments for why C (or a set of causes) is enough to produce the outcome. When theorizing multiple causes that together are sufficient, it is important to theorize how the causes interact, and why each of them are individually necessary parts of the overall sufficient cause. And as with necessity, claims of sufficiency are also deterministic because if C (or a set of causes) is present in a case together with the requisite contextual conditions (see later in this chapter on contextual (i.e., scope) conditions), the outcome will occur.

If a sufficient cause (either an individual or conjunction) is present in a case, other causes are theorized to *not* be causally relevant. When dealing with multiple sufficient causes in a case, they are logically *theoretically exclusive* of each other.[4] This relates to the question of overdetermination, defined as a situation where multiple sufficient causes are present in a case. The classic example of overdetermination from the philosophy of science is a person found dead after wandering in the desert (Brady 2008). It is found that there was poison in the person's canteen, but there was also a hole in the canteen. In this instance, both poison (C_1) and thirst (C_2) are potentially sufficient causes, but only one can actually have had a causal relationship with the outcome at the theoretical level; that is, he died either of poisoning or of dehydration, because one cannot die from poison and dehydration at the same time. This means that C_1 and C_2 are both individually sufficient but theoretically exclusive of each other. However, overdetermination at the theoretical level does not mean that we cannot figure out why the man in the desert died in the actual case in hand. This is because we can distinguish at the *empirical evidence level* between the fingerprints that causes C_1 and C_2 would leave. For example, we would expect to find poor skin turgor, tinting of skin, sunken eyes, and/or dry galea and organ surfaces if the man died of dehydration (Madea and Lachenmeier 2005), whereas poisoning—for example, by cyanide—could be detected as increased levels of cyanide in the blood if the autopsy is conducted relatively quickly after death (Musshoff et al. 2002). We return to this question of distinguishing between the empirical fingerprints of different theories in chapter 6.

Necessary Causes

Necessary causal explanations are intimately linked to the counterfactual understanding of causation (Goertz 2003; Goertz and Levy 2007). If a cause is necessary, it has to be present in a case for the outcome to occur. Without C, O will not occur. Necessary causal explanations are based on set-theoretical relations between causes and outcomes.[5] Cases are generally categorized as either being in the set of members of a causal concept or not.

When theorizing necessary condition causal relationships, there are many different ways that a necessary relationship between C and O can be expressed; examples include formulations such as C "must be there," C "is necessary" for O, and C is a "precondition" or "prerequisite" for O to occur (Goertz 2003: 49). Examples of necessary causal theories include the following (for more examples, see Goertz 2003: 76–94):

- "Only when a group of policy-makers is moderately or highly cohesive can we expect the groupthink syndrome to emerge as the members are working collectively on one or another of their important policy decisions" (Janis 1982: 176).
- "Two key *requisites* for cooperation to thrive [O] are that the cooperation be based on reciprocity [C_1], and that the shadow of the future is important enough to make this reciprocity stable [C_2]" (Axelrod 1984: 173, italics and bracketed text inserted).
- "Three *prerequisites*—hegemony [C_1], liberal ideology [C_2], and common interests [C_3]—must exist for the emergence and expansion of the liberal market system [O]" (Gilpin 1987: 73, italics and bracketed text inserted).
- "The primary regulative effect of the taboo [norm against using nuclear weapons] is the injunction against using nuclear weapons first. It constrains a behavior (nuclear use) that would exist whether or not there were any rules about it. . . . Thus, although the taboo is not the sole explanation for non-use (non-use has occurred for other reasons), it is *essential* to explaining the overall pattern of non-use" (Tannenwald 1999: 439–40, italics and bracketed text inserted).

In these examples, the full causal logic behind the counterfactual claim of necessity is not developed. Unfortunately, much existing work does not go much further than a postulate that a cause is necessary. We suggest that it is not enough to postulate that C is necessary; one has to provide more detailed theoretical logic for why C is plausibly necessary, requiring that the *logical counterfactual is made explicit* in one's theorization. In the Axelrod example, this requires developing logical arguments for why we should expect cooperation to breakdown in the absence of reciprocity (C_1) and a long shadow of the future (C_2), something he does in the book where he discusses the counterfactual situation of noncooperation using the prisoner's dilemma as a theoretical explanation for why the absence of C_1 and C_2 results in non-cooperation ($\sim$O) (Axelrod 1983: 9–10).

Additionally, it is important to be very clear about whether one is only talking about individual causes being necessary, as in the Tannenwald example, or more complex causal explanations like each individual cause is a necessary part of a sufficient cause of the outcome (i.e., an INUS conjunction) (as appears to be the claim in the Axelrod quote).

Common to all formulations of necessity is that it is a deterministic, asymmetric, and counterfactual-based causal claim; if no C, no O will occur. While many scholars have attempted to make necessity compatible with probabilistic claims, at the case level necessary causes are either necessary or not in the individual case—they can logically not be just a little bit necessary in the case.

In contrast to sufficiency claims, necessity claims usually have no logical implications for other causes. This means that causal theories typically are not theoretically exclusive of each other. This can be explicitly seen in Tannenwald's theorization, where she makes clear that other causes besides norms (the nuclear "taboo") also matter, writing, "Clearly, any sufficient explanation must synthesize material and normative factors, and a full account details all three explanations: deterrence, 'nondeterrence' material factors, and the taboo—though not, of course, equally or necessarily in all cases. . . . Thus, although the taboo is not the sole explanation for non-use (non-use has occurred for other reasons), it is essential to explaining the overall pattern of non-use" (1999: 439–40). Therefore, the "gladiator"-style competitive theoretical test that we often find used in the social sciences is usually *not* relevant when we are assessing claims about necessity.

Differences between Single-Case and Cross-Case Claims of Necessity and Sufficiency

There is a difference in formulating claims of necessity or sufficiency about a single case (singular causation) and in a bounded population of cases. As will be explored in more detail in chapter 7 (comparative methods), making a claim about necessity within a single case requires using a hypothetical counterfactual to compare the actual with what could have happened hypothetically in a parallel possible world, whereas claims across cases are assessed using classical comparative methods.

As an example of what singular case claims can look like, in assessing necessary and sufficient conditions for different critical points in the outbreak of the World War I, Jack Levy claims that "the German decision to support Austria-Hungary was a necessary condition for a local war and thus for any larger war; Russian intervention was a necessary and sufficient condition for a continental war, but not sufficient for a world war" (2007: 59). Note that he is very careful about the scope of different singular causal claims of both necessity and sufficiency—for example, that the German decision was necessary for a local war (which could result in a larger war or not), whereas the Russian intervention was necessary and sufficient for continental war but not sufficient for a world war.

Beyond single-case counterfactuals, claims about sufficiency in a single case tend to be made when operating with a more pragmatic/analyticist understanding of science (see chapter 1). For example, in his classic study of the Cuban Missile Crisis, Allison crafted a sufficient explanation of the big and important things in the case by combining three different analytical frameworks together (1971; Allison and Zellikow 1999).

3.4. Causal Mechanisms—Minimalist and Systems Understandings

When we are theorizing about causal mechanisms, we are turning our attention away from causes and outcomes to focus analytically on what is going on *in between* them if the relationship is causal. On the basis of the mechanism understanding of causation, if the relationship between C and O is causal, we should be able both to theoretically unpack the causal process in between in some detail and to produce empirical (mechanistic) evidence of the process acting in an actual case.

It is important to be aware of the problem of "masking" when working with mechanisms (Steel 2008: 68). In some situations, a given cause might be linked to an outcome through multiple mechanisms that have different effects on the outcome. Steel uses the example of exercise (C) and weight loss (O). Exercise triggers a mechanism relating to the burning of calories (CM_1) that starts a process leading to weight loss (O), but at the same time, exercise also triggers an increase-in-appetite "mechanism" (CM_2) that produces weight gains ($\sim O$) (Steel 2008: 68). Here the operation of one mechanism would "mask" the operation of the other in terms of overall net effects on the outcome. It is therefore vital to be very clear when theorizing a mechanism that one is not making claims about the *overall net effects* of a cause on an outcome, but instead is digging down into a *specific* causal process linking C with a particular O. If we are dealing with causes that have multiple effects, each of these effects would be linked to outcomes through different mechanisms that we would theorize independently of each other unless they work in combinations. Additionally, at the empirical level the operation of one mechanism would not "mask" the other because we should be able to discern unique empirical fingerprints of each of the mechanisms (for more on uniqueness and evidence, see chapter 6).

While theorizing causal relationships in C → O terms is (relatively) straightforward, it is much more difficult to conceptualize causal mechanisms, a challenge made even greater by the existence of two distinct understandings of mechanisms in the literature (minimalist versus systems). As discussed in chapter 2, in the minimalist understanding mechanisms are not unpacked in any detail, but instead are treated as intervening factors that can be depicted as C → CM → O. In the systems understanding, the causal process is unpacked in greater detail in an attempt to theorize a mechanism that achieves what Machamer, Craver, and Darden (2000) term "productive continuity," where the mechanism composed of entities engaging in activities is theorized to transmit causal forces in an uninterrupted process that links cause(s) and outcome. In the systems understanding, a three-part mechanism can be depicted as $C \rightarrow [E_1 \rightarrow E_2 \rightarrow E_3] \rightarrow O$, where, for instance, in part 1 both the entity E_1 and the activity associated with it (depicted as an arrow) are explicitly theorized.

We contend that stronger mechanistic evidence is produced when we theorize mechanisms based on the systems understanding because we are forced to use process-tracing to trace in detail the actual operation of each of the parts after we have theorized them explicitly in terms of entities engaging in activities. In contrast, in the minimalist understanding, mechanisms remain theoretically in a form of being gray-boxed, resulting in empirical analysis that does not explicitly study the causal links of the mechanism (Bunge 1997). However, despite not being able to provide as strong mechanistic evidence about the existence (or nonexistence) of causal mechanisms, this does not mean that adopting a minimalist understanding is always an analytical second best. On the contrary, using a minimalist understanding is a deliberate choice that reflects the type of research situation one is in. For example, in situations where we are not very confident in a causal relationship being present, we can use a congruence case study based on the minimalist understanding as a "plausibility probe," where even relatively weak confirming mechanistic evidence enables updating to take place. In contrast, when there is extensive research that has demonstrated that there is a causal relationship, a systems understanding is more relevant because it adds to our knowledge by answering the *how* question, that is, how a given cause (or set of causes) produces an outcome through a causal mechanism or mechanisms. We return to these differences in chapters 8 and 9.

Before we develop the two understandings of mechanisms and the differences in the types of causal explanations they enable, it is important to first illustrate what theories of mechanisms in practice definitely are not. Here we utilize Blatter's 2009 case study of cross-border environmental regulation in the case of the Bodensee in Germany as an example of a scholar who claims to be studying mechanisms, but in fact is only producing a descriptive narrative of events in a case.

Why Descriptive Narratives Are Not Causal Mechanisms

In the article, Blatter claims he is building a new theorized mechanism using process-tracing, putting forward the argument that changes in a discursive context allowed actors in cross-border communities and intergovernmental networks to make a name for themselves as successful problem-solvers (C) by pursuing cross-border regulation, with the outcome (O) being "unique standards in the highly symbolic field of water policy" (2009: 96).

But despite all of its other merits, the subsequent empirical case study is a descriptive tracing of events from the early 1970s to the 1990s, where negotiations were concluded successfully. The article leaves the reader in the dark regarding the causal mechanism whereby actors striving for an attractive image connect themselves to cultural and communicative trends in their social environment, thereby producing the outcome. In the text section that follows, we see a series of events that happened. However, no effort is made to explain *why* things happened, meaning that it is a purely descriptive narrative. Yet any given event can happen for many different reasons. In order to be a part of a causal explanation, events need to be placed into an explicit explanatory framework in the form of a theorized mechanism that links cause with the outcome. Midway through the article, we find the following section that is an accurate representative of the empirical "analysis," where it is claimed that mechanisms are being traced:

1. "Already in the early 1980s, the environmental policy debate on boats on the lake
2. reached a new peak. The IGKB [water conservation commission] prepared a report on the 'Limnological effects of
3. motorized boating on Lake Constance.' This report focused on the harm caused by
4. pollutants, and confirmed a threat to water quality. Although the report made
5. large political waves at Lake Constance, and governmental representatives in the
6. IBK [Internationale Bodenseekonferenz] immediately responded by proposing restrictive regulations, at this time a

7. transborder agreement was not reached. During a time when there was much talk
8. about 'Euro-sclerosis,' the idea of the Euregio Bodensee had also lost its appeal to
9. politicians, and in 1984 the government of the Canton of Thurgau could afford to
10. withdraw its agreement on strict regulation of boats at the last moment within the
11. IBK." (Blatter 2009: 98)

Analyzing the selected text in more detail, there are a number of questions that we would want to have answered if the analysis was actually tracing a theorized causal mechanism. First, at no point are we told about what parts of the causal mechanism are being probed in relation to the events discussed. Indeed, the actual causal mechanism is never made explicit in the article, not in the purely descriptive "case study" or in the subsequent section, "Abstract Formulation of the Causal Mechanism and Its Scope Conditions" (Blatter 2009: 100–104).

For example, in line 2, how does the production of a report by a group relate to the proposed causal theory? In lines 4–5, the author writes that the report (published in 1982) made "large political waves." But why did it produce controversy, and among which actors? How does this relate to the proposed causal relationship? Further, why was a transborder agreement not reached? Was it due solely to the broader context of "Euro-sclerosis," as seems to be implied in lines 7–8, or solely to the withdrawal of support from the Canton of Thurgau in 1984 within the IBK? Finally, on an empirical note, there is no evidence offered in support of postulates such as "the idea of the Euregio Bodensee had also lost its appeal."

The purely descriptive narrative is followed by a section that discusses the theoretical concept of performance as something that can link actors with regulation, but at no point does the article detail the actual causal process whereby actors, through their performances, agree to new policies as "side-effects of political performances primarily motivated by a search for attention and recognition" (Blatter 2009: 101). This short quote is actually the closest the article comes to detailing the abstract causal process (i.e., mechanism) whereby C is linked with O.

When we couple the lack of theorization of the causal process (mechanism) linking C to O with the purely descriptive case study preceding it, we can conclude that the article leaves us in the dark regarding the mechanism or mechanisms that link actors engaging in performance with regulatory outcomes. While the article does trace a series of events, the actual causal mechanism linking C and O is completely left in the black box.

Minimalist Understandings—Talking about Mechanisms without Explicitly Unpacking Them

Fortunately, there are articles and books that go beyond mere description of what happens between C and O, attempting to theorize the mechanisms linking causes and outcomes. However, many of these do not unpack causal mechanisms in any detail, with the result that mechanisms are gray-boxed—what we termed a minimalist understanding of mechanisms in chapter 2. The minimalist understanding of mechanisms stands in contrast to the systems understanding, in which mechanisms are unpacked into entities engaging in activities. These different understandings of mechanisms are also what differentiates congruence from process-tracing as methods, a difference we explore in greater detail in chapters 8 and 9.

It is important to note again that this is a deliberate choice, given that in many research situations it makes sense to not flesh out a causal mechanism as a system because once a mechanism is explicitly theorized as a multipart causal process, the analyst should then study each of the parts and their interaction with each other in an in-depth case study, something that requires considerable analytical resources but that is not necessary when engaging in a "plausibility probe" study, or is not possible when a larger number of cases are being investigated.

In the minimalist understanding, mechanisms are typically formulated as intervening factors in the form of C $\rightarrow$ CM $\rightarrow$ O, where some information about what is going on in between C and O is offered, but not enough to warrant the claim that a detailed causal process has been developed. One good example of this is Waldner's proposed use of causal graphs as a technique for depicting causal mechanisms. He depicts a causal graph as X $\rightarrow$ $M_1 \rightarrow$ M_2 $\rightarrow$ Y, writing, "Nodes or vertices of the graph represent random variables; for simplicity, we can treat these random variables as binary variables that are either true or false. Directed edges, or arrows, refer to relations of conditional dependence. *Arrows therefore represent causal mechanisms.* Mechanisms should not be confused with intervening variables or mediators; M_1 and M_2 are random variables that are contingently located in non-initial and non-terminal nodes; they are not mechanisms. . . . For each realization of the causal graph in a particular case study, process tracing requires the specification of a set of events that correspond to each node in the causal graph" (2014: 134, 135, italics added). However, in his understanding the actual mechanism *never is fleshed out in any detail*, meaning that he utilizes a minimalist understanding where it is the empirical correspondence between what empirical events were predicted to occur between the nodes in the graph and what we find, enabling inferences about a parent node (here M_1) and the value of its descendant node (here M_2).

When the minimalist understanding of mechanisms is adopted, the scholar is only able to make the claim that there is within-case evidence that C is causally related to O, termed "diagnostic evidence" by Bennett and Checkel (2014). We prefer the term "mechanistic evidence," but it relates to the same thing: within-case evidence that sheds light on a causal process in between C and O to some extent. But by not explicitly theorizing the parts of a causal mechanism in detail, we are left unable to answer basic questions about the underlying causal logic linking C and O together, making it difficult to evaluate whether the theorized causal process is logically consistent; and even more problematic, it is very difficult to trace empirically whether there is mechanistic evidence of the process when we are not told what the process is that is being traced.

First, given that the causal processes are not explicitly theorized, we cannot logically make claims about mechanisms linking C and O because they remain in an analytical gray box. Second, because the causal mechanism is not explicitly theorized, the subsequent empirical analysis does not trace the causal process in any detail empirically, reducing our ability to make strong causal inferences about mechanisms on the basis of empirical mechanistic evidence. Basically, how can we have claimed to have a traced a causal process (a.k.a. mechanism) when we do not know what the process looks like?

The following illustrates what minimalist claims look like with in-depth analyses of two published articles, showing that despite the authors using the term "mechanism," the causal process is only minimally theorized, with the result that the analysis is only justified in claiming that C is causally related to O. In both studies, the gray-boxing of mechanisms is a *deliberate choice* because they were in research situations where there was low prior confidence in the posited causal relationship.[6] In Tannenwald's case, existing research suggested that it was not very plausible that the posited relationship existed, whereas Ziblatt needed some within-case evidence to back up his cross-case evidence from variance-based analysis.

Nina Tannenwald's 1999 article on the impact of norms on US decision-making is often cited as an example of good process-tracing.[7] However, while the study has many merits, the causal mechanism whereby norms against the nonuse of A-weapons (C) (a nuclear "taboo") contributed to US decision-makers avoidance of using them (O) remains firmly within a theoretical gray box, with the result that the empirical analysis tells us precious little about the causal processes that links C with O.

In the theoretical section of the article, Tannenwald does not detail the causal processes whereby norms can lead to nonuse. The closest she gets to unwrapping causal mechanisms in the theory section is when she describes two causal processes with a few sentences: "The primary regulative effect of the taboo is the injunction against using nuclear weapons first. It constrains a behavior (nuclear use) that would exist whether or not there were any rules about it. . . . [T]he taboo also exhibits several constitutive effects: on the categories actors use to understand weapons and on the identity of a 'civilized' state. Categories provide important boundaries with implications for both behavior and identity. The taboo helps to define a category of unacceptable 'weapons of mass destruction,' distinguished from unproblematic 'conventional' weapons that are, in contrast, viewed as legitimate and usable" (1999: 437).

The "mechanism" is therefore minimalist because we are left in the dark about the details of the theoretical causal process whereby injunctions against nonuse constrain behavior, or how norms come to constitute actor understandings of acceptable behavior. At the end of the article she claims to have found evidence for three causal mechanisms based on her case studies, but again the causal processes are not developed beyond a minimalist, C → CM → O depiction. In a section titled "Norms and Causal Mechanisms," she writes that "norms work through three pathways: force, self-interest, and legitimacy. In this story, the taboo operated both by appearing as a constraint on self-interested decision makers—entirely consistent with a rationalist conception of the instrumental operation of a norm as a 'cost'—and in a more substantive or principled fashion as reflected in beliefs about the growing illegitimacy of nuclear use" (1999: 462). Yet these brief descriptions do not describe actual causal processes with productive continuity between a cause and an outcome; they can be depicted as norms → constraint on self-interest → nonuse. For instance, what is the causal process whereby norms operate as a constraint on decision-making? In a systems understanding, we would flesh out the causal arrows linking norms with constraint, ideally detailing a multipart causal "story" that theoretically explains how norms might matter for nonuse without any gaping holes in the "story." However, this gray-boxing of mechanisms is justified in a research situation where there is low prior confidence in the existence of a causal relationship. The natural follow-up would of course be to probe mechanisms in more detail by unpacking them as theoretical systems.

Another example of a minimalist understanding can be seen in Ziblatt's 2009 article on electoral fraud, an article where he claims to be assessing a "capture" causal mechanism that links landholding inequality (C) to electoral fraud (O), describing how local officials becoming captured by landed elites to perpetrate electoral fraud (2009: 12–18). However the actual causal mechanism linking with C and O is never fleshed out in sufficient detail to allow us to either evaluate the underlying causal logic or to assess using a case study whether there is empirical evidence supporting the "capture" mechanism. The closest we get to a theoretical description of the causal mechanism is where he writes, "They [landed elites] exert influence *indirectly* via the capture of rural public officials such as mayors, county commissioners, police officials, and election officials, who in turn are the actors that interfere with free and fair elections. In its most acute form, capture occurs as socioeconomic interests infiltrate the state by using their *own* personnel to staff the state" (2009: 14).

While telling us something about the process between C and O—that is, it goes through local officials—he does not detail a causal mechanism that exhibits productive continuity as in the systems understanding (see page 80). In particular, he sheds little theoretical light on the causal process whereby landed elites are able to capture local officials. For instance, what types of power resources do landed elites deploy to capture officials? Does capture occur through the use of material resources such as the power to control revenue or through control of appointment processes? Or perhaps by deploying more discursive resources? Do landed elites have to *actively* intervene to capture officials, or do officials *anticipate* what local officials want? When and why should local officials be responsive? And once captured, what is the process whereby local officials actually engage in electoral fraud? What types of actions do they use? Removal of voters from electoral rolls, pressuring poll officers, and so on? By not explicitly theorizing a causal mechanism, we do not know what aspects of the causal process we should be studying empirically.

Ziblatt's subsequent empirical case study does illustrate that both C and O are present, and that there is some anecdotal evidence suggesting that the link is through something like a capture process. However, given that the mechanism is not explicitly theorized, the actual analysis produces small empirical vignettes that merely insinuate the existence of an underlying mechanism without providing strong mechanistic evidence. Indeed, it is difficult to determine whether the presented empirical material confirms the underlying mechanism, given that we are left guessing about what the actual underlying mechanism is.

The anecdotal nature of the evidence is clear in the following quote that is representative of the types of empirical material presented. Ziblatt writes, "As one Landrat from Posen reported in his memoirs in 1894, 'I had to join the local branch of the Agrarian League, because everyone I interact with socially—and everyone I hunt with—is a member!'" (2009: 16). It is obvious that this piece of empirical material relates in some fashion to an underlying part of mechanism whereby landed elites can pressure local officials. But by not detailing the underlying causal mechanism, we are left unsure about basic questions such as whether social pressure is the only means whereby local officials are captured. Further, by not telling us what empirical fingerprints (predicted evidence) each of the parts of the mechanism can be expected to leave in a case, the presentation of empirical material seems very unsystematic. A scholar critical of case study methodology might go so far as to state that it is just cherry-picking empirical observations instead of being a systematic analysis of whether there is empirical evidence that confirms or disconfirms the theoretical mechanism being present in the case. The analytical result is that Ziblatt is justified in claiming that there is some form of causal relationship, but he cannot make any claims about the actual causal mechanism linking C and O.

Concluding, in the minimalist understanding of mechanisms, the causal process in between C and O is not unpacked in any detail. Because a causal process is not explicitly theorized, one cannot claim that one is actually tracing causal mechanisms. But this is a deliberate trade-off, given that in many research situations there is no need to go into often excruciating detail about the causal process.

Systems Understanding of Mechanisms

In the systems understanding of mechanisms, a causal mechanism is defined as a theory of a system of interlocking parts that transmits causal forces between a cause or a set of causes to an outcome (Glennan 1996, 2002; Bunge 1997, 2004; Bhaskar 1978). Hernes has helpfully defined a mechanism as "a set of interacting parts—an assembly of elements producing an effect not inherent in any one of them. A mechanism is not so much about 'nuts and bolts' as about 'cogs and wheels'—the wheelwork or agency by which an effect is produced" (1998: 78). Here mechanisms can for heuristic purposes be understood using a machine analogy. Each part of the theoretical mechanism can be thought of as a toothed wheel that transmits the dynamic causal energy of the causal mechanism to the next toothed wheel, ultimately contributing to producing outcome O.

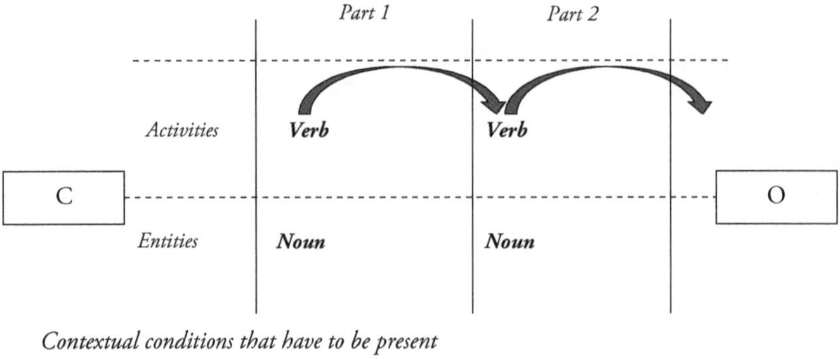

Fig. 3.3. A simple template for a two-part causal mechanism

In the systems understanding, causal mechanisms can be defined in terms of entities that engage in activities that transfer causal forces from C to O (Machamer, Darden, and Craver 2000; Machamer 2004; Beach and Pedersen 2013; Rohlfing 2012). Entities are the factors (actors, organizations, or structures) engaging in activities (the parts of the mechanism, i.e., toothed wheels), where the activities are the producers of change or what transmits causal forces through a mechanism (the movement of the wheels). What the entities and activities more precisely are will be dependent on the type of causal explanation, along with the level at which the mechanism works and the time span of its operation (see below for more). The activities that entities engage in move the mechanism from an initial or start condition through different parts to an outcome. In the following we depict entities as E_1, E_2, E_3 and activities using arrows ($\rightarrow$). A part of the mechanism is therefore the combination of entity and activity (e.g., $E_1 \rightarrow$).

When theorizing the parts of a causal mechanism, the parts should exhibit some form of *productive continuity*, meaning that each of the parts logically leads to the next part, with no large logical holes in the causal story linking C and O together (Machamer, Darden, and Craver 2000: 3; Darden 2002: 283). If a mechanism is represented schematically by C$\rightarrow$ [$E_1 \rightarrow$ $E_2 \rightarrow E_3$] $\rightarrow$ O, then the continuity lies in the arrows and their transferal of causal forces from one part of a mechanism to the next. A missing arrow, namely, the inability to specify an activity connecting E_1 and E_2, leaves an explanatory gap in the productive continuity of the mechanism (Machamer, Darden, and Craver 2000: 3). The overall mechanism can be depicted as in figure 3.3, where each part of the mechanism in between C and O is detailed in terms of entities engaging in activities. The entities are defined as nouns, whereas the activities are depicted as verbs.

When conceptualizing a causal mechanism in the systems understanding, we should be able to identify clearly the different parts and how they are related through the nature of the activities. However, the distinction between minimalist and systems mechanisms is better understood as a continuum, with some theorized mechanisms closer to one or the other pole. The key distinction is whether the mechanism is disaggregated in terms of parts where we can clearly see the productive relationship between a cause (or set of causes) and the outcome. It is of course always possible to go further in depth when theorizing mechanisms, disaggregating individual parts into subparts that could then be further disaggregated in an infinite regress. Kincaid puts it well when he states that if we want to study the mechanism linking two macro-level factors, "Do we need it at the small-group level or the individual level? If the latter, why stop there? We can, for example, always ask what mechanism brings about individual behavior. So we are off to find neurological mechanisms, then biochemical, and so on" (1996: 179). If we go down this path the logical result would be that no causal claims can be established without absurd amounts of information (Steel 2004). Additionally, depending on our theory, we might claim that macro-level factors have "emergence," which is understood as properties at the macro-level that are not just the sum of micro-level interactions.

In most research situations a mechanism "sketch" that captures the key causal components of the process is more than adequate, providing us with theoretical guidelines for what we should be tracing in a case study (Machamer 2004). In other words, instead of a detailed, theorized causal story, we often capture the most important highlights of a causal process. How complicated the mechanism is also depends on whether one is developing a case-specific mechanism or a more abstract mechanism expected to be able to be applicable in multiple cases in a bounded population. Mechanisms can also be composed of many parts, depending on what is required to model the causal process. Therefore, the formulation of any given mechanism depends on the complexity of the given causal process being studied.

Note that figure 3.3 shows a very simple, linear mechanism. There is nothing in the logic of theorizing mechanisms that tells us that they cannot include more complicated forms. For instance, we might expect a mechanism to split into two parallel mechanisms for part of the causal process, or there might be feedback loops and other forms of nonlinear relationships. Mechanisms can also operate at multiple levels, for example, going from the micro-level of individual actors to societal-level processes and back again, depending on which theory one is operating with. There can also be redundancy in critical parts—for instance, where the connection between E_1 and E_3 is bridged by either $E_{2a} \rightarrow$ or $E_{2b} \rightarrow$.

It is important to reiterate that, in the systems understanding, a mechanism that links C and O does not logically have to be sufficient or necessary to produce the outcome. If the cause and requisite contextual conditions are present, the mechanism will always be triggered (see below on contextual conditions). But the mechanism linking C with O in a causal relationship cannot logically be more causally important than the initial causal condition triggering it. If we theorize that C is neither necessary nor sufficient but only has a causal impact on O, the mechanism linking C with O cannot logically be either necessary or sufficient. The mechanism is merely the link, and therefore cannot be causally more important than the condition that triggers it.

Some scholars have even made demanding claims about how we should conceptualize mechanisms. For example, Goertz and Mahoney write that when studying mechanisms, we "inevitably carry out an over-time, processual analysis of the case. . . . The analyst will normally identify historical junctures where key events directed the case toward certain outcomes and not others. She or he may well pause to consider how small changes during these junctures might have led the case to follow a different path. . . . The overall explanation likely will be rich with details about specific events, conjunctures, and contingencies" (2012: 89). All of this has a close resemblance to historical institutionalist (HI) theory. Blatter and Haverland (2012) discuss mechanisms as a way to capture causal complexity, which also links to HI theory or types of constructivist theorization. Other (rational choice–inspired (RC)) scholars have claimed that we always need to theorize multiple mechanisms when studying macro-level phenomena, describing mechanisms linking the macro-level to the micro-level (situational mechanisms), micro-micro (action-based mechanisms), and micro-level to macro-level (transformational mechanisms) (e.g., Hedström and Swedberg 2008). Yet in all of these instances, scholars have imported theories into their description of methodologies, biasing the method towards specific theories. However, there is no logical reason a mechanism has to look like an integrative, macro-micro-macro RC theory, or a highly contingent, HI theory with path dependencies and critical junctures. A theory is *not* a research methodology, and vice versa. Our theory should tell us what type of causal mechanism to expect, but theory should not dictate our understanding of mechanisms themselves.

Given the difficulty in defining causal relationships as mechanisms, and the great amount of confusion in the literature about what causal mechanisms actually look like, the following provides two examples of defined mechanisms that are more in line with a systems understanding, where mechanisms are disaggregated into parts that enable us to trace the workings of a mechanism empirically in considerable detail.

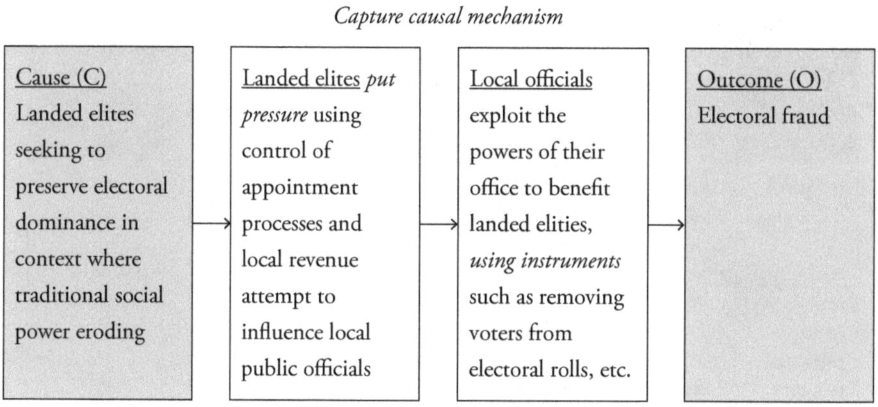

Capture causal mechanism

Cause (C) Landed elites seeking to preserve electoral dominance in context where traditional social power eroding	Landed elites *put pressure* using control of appointment processes and local revenue attempt to influence local public officials	Local officials exploit the powers of their office to benefit landed elities, *using instruments* such as removing voters from electoral rolls, etc.	Outcome (O) Electoral fraud

Fig. 3.4. A "capture" causal mechanism linking landed elites with electoral fraud

Returning to the example of Ziblatt, if we were going to make the mechanisms more explicit, as in the systems understanding, we would first want to disaggregate the mechanism into an interlocking series of parts linking landed elites with electoral fraud. A suggested mechanism that is more explicitly described is depicted in figure 3.4, composed of two parts linking C and O; this is theorized on the basis of the empirical insights drawn from the case study.

The core difference between the minimalist mechanism used by Ziblatt in his article and the "capture" mechanism described in figure 3.4 is that the latter *explicitly* theorizes each part of the causal mechanism, telling us more about how and why capture is theorized to happen. The first part of the mechanism details the how and why process whereby local officials are captured, followed by theorizations on the process whereby captured officials influence elections, resulting in electoral fraud.

As we develop in chapters 6 and 9, the subsequent empirical analysis would then systematically trace whether there is evidence suggesting that the observable implications of the two parts of this simple mechanism were present instead of the empirical anecdotes used by Ziblatt, anecdotes that shed some light on the workings of the mechanism but in an ad hoc fashion. By tracing an explicit mechanism, we would be more justified in making the claim that C is linked to O through a causal mechanism.

Another example of what an explicitly theorized causal mechanism can look like is shown in figure 3.5. While the mechanism could be fleshed out even more, we recommend keeping the theorized mechanism as simple as meaningful in relation to the research question. Tracing a mechanism with

Cause	Informal delegation causal mechanism				Outcome
	Part 1 "identifying problems"	Part 2 "crafting proposals"	Part 3 "tabling proposals"	Part 4 "building support"	
Informal delegation of leadership functions from principals to agent	Agent identifies zone-of-possible-agreement by collecting information on "problem" and principal's preferences	Using information gained, agent crafts a proposal (or set of proposals) that maximizes own gains	Agent tables proposal either directly or through proxy	Agent manages process by building support for proposal, brokering compromises, etc.	Agent proposal(s) accepted but with delegation costs

Fig. 3.5. A "facilitating leadership" causal mechanism linking delegation and agency costs

thirty parts empirically would be a daunting task, and there is the serious question of whether we could formulate a generalizable mechanism that is so complex.

A principal-agent (PA) theory is chosen as an example for what mechanisms-as-systems theories might look like because most formulations of PA theory tell us almost nothing about the process in between delegation and agency, that is, about *how* C (delegation) can cause O (agency costs). Most uses of principal-agent theories focus instead merely on input and output. Yet just because there is a correlation between an act of delegation by principals and achieved outcomes that are close to what an agent wanted does not mean that delegation produced agency costs. Tracing an explicitly theorized mechanism empirically enables us to make stronger claims about a causal relationship between C and O.

The mechanism depicted in figure 3.5 describes a linear process composed of four parts linking informal delegation of leadership functions to an agent with agency costs (Tallberg 2006; Hawkins et al. 2006; Kiewiet and McCubbins 1991). The mechanism is triggered by an act of informal delegation, with principals asking the agent to assist their negotiations by drafting texts and performing other leadership functions. We would then need to describe the causal process whereby C can produce O.

In the first part of the mechanism, the agent identifies a zone of possible agreement by gathering information on principal preferences and their distribution, along with detailed information about the problem under discussion. This information is used by the agent to craft a proposal, or set of proposals, which is then tabled by either the agent or a proxy (a willing principal). In parallel with tabling the proposal, we would expect the agent to engage in a range of different activities to secure adoption of the proposal, building coalitions supporting it, brokering compromises, and so on. Finally, we should expect that because of these actions the final outcome in the issue is more efficient than it would have been in the absence of agent leadership, and that this leadership has resulted in delegation costs that are proportional to the amount of leadership provided.

The analytical value-added of adopting the systems understanding of mechanisms is that we gain a greater understanding of the causal process between C and O, shedding both theoretical and empirical light on *how* causes, through a mechanism, contribute to produce an outcome. Theorizing the mechanisms in terms of parts that transfer causal forces, with each being composed of entities engaging in activities, provides a more compelling theoretical logic because we have to explicitly answer the question of how we get from one part to the next. Empirically, tracing each of the parts of the mechanism in an in-depth process-tracing case study then results in the production of stronger mechanistic evidence than if we do not unpack the mechanism.

The downside is that even in a single case study, research is extremely labor-intensive because empirical evidence for each part of the mechanism has to be analyzed. This challenge is made even greater by the fact that even if we find strong evidence of the theorized mechanism in a single case study, we cannot infer that the *same* mechanism links C and O in other cases within the population (Gerring 2010), what can be termed "equifinality at the level of mechanisms" (Beach and Rohlfing 2016). This means that we ideally need to trace mechanisms in several typical cases before we can infer that C is linked to O through a given theorized mechanism. We return to this point in chapter 9 on process-tracing.

Levels of Mechanisms

There is considerable debate in the philosophy of social science on whether mechanisms always have to be reducible to the micro-level (Hedström and Swedberg 1998; Little 1996: 35) or whether there are also macro-level

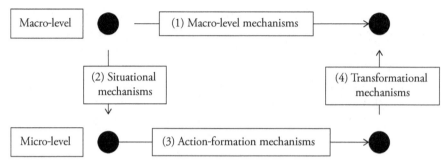

Fig. 3.6. Levels of causal mechanisms

mechanisms that cannot be reduced to the micro-level (Mayntz 2004; Bunge 2004; McAdam, Tarrow, and Tilly 2001). The question is basically whether we should reduce every causal mechanism to the micro-level, investigating the actions of individuals, or whether there are causal mechanisms that have macro-level properties.

To introduce the debate on the level of causal mechanism, Hedström and Swedberg have a helpful figure that illustrates how the level debate relates to the study of causal mechanisms (1998: 22) (see figure 3.6). However, they take an extreme position that there are no purely macro-level mechanisms. George and Bennett take a similar position when they state that mechanisms are "processes through which agents with causal capacities operate" (2005: 137). They go on to define mechanisms as the microfoundations of a causal relationship that involve the "irreducibly smallest link between one entity and another" (2005: 142).

In our view, this unnecessarily requires us to always engage in some form of micro-level examination when using process-tracing, usually at the level of individual actors and their behavior in specific decision-making processes. Yet there is no logical reason that a mechanism should be theorized at the micro-level. These are theoretical claims that should be dealt with as such— there is no logical reason to wed our methodologies to particular theories. If one is working with a macro-level theory, and the mechanisms linking two macro-level phenomena have empirical manifestations at the macro-level, there is no logical reason to do injustice to the macro-level theory by lowering the level of analysis to the micro-level of interaction between individuals (Wight 2004: 292; Sawyer 2004: 260). Unfortunately, many accounts of mechanisms in the social sciences have been wedded to particular theoretical positions, biasing methods towards studying particular theories (e.g., rational choice, historical institutionalism). A method is not a theory, nor is a theory a method.

Many of the most interesting social phenomena we want to study, such as democratization, cannot meaningfully be reduced solely to the actor level, but in certain situations they can be better analyzed empirically at the macro-level (McAdam, Tarrow, and Tilly 2001). Given that this conundrum is in essence the classic debate between agent and structure, we argue in the following for an agnostic and pragmatic middle-ground position, where the choice of level that is theorized is related to the level at which the implications of the existence of a theorized causal mechanism are best studied. Mechanisms may occur or operate at different levels of analysis, and we should not see one level as more fundamental than another (Falleti and Lynch 2009: 1149; George and Bennett 2005: 142ff.; McAdam, Tarrow, and Tilly 2001: 25–26; Mahoney 2003: 5).

Macro-level mechanisms are therefore structural theories that cannot always be reduced to the actions of individuals (type 1 in figure 3.6). Many sociologists claim that the search for the micro-level foundations of behavior is futile, and that much of the capacity of human agents derives from their position in society (structure) (Wight 2004; McAdam, Tarrow, and Tilly 2001; Mahoney 2001). Many of the important causal mechanisms in the social world are arguably macro-level phenomena that are "collaboratively created by individuals yet are not reducible to individual" action (Sawyer 2004: 266). Here we are dealing with emergence, which means that macro-level mechanisms have their own existence and have properties that cannot be reduced to the micro-level. Institutional roles, norms, and relational structures can play a significant role for actor behavior, and there are structural properties of mechanisms that cannot be defined solely by reference to the atomistic attributes of individual agents (Sawyer 2004). For example, system-level theories in international relations include neo-realism, where the balancing mechanism is theorized by Waltz to be solely the product of macro-level factors (1979).

There are three different types of mechanisms that are related to the micro-level actions of agents, two of which combine macro-level properties with micro-level actions. At the micro-level are action-formation mechanisms (type 3), or what Hedström and Ylikoski term "structural individualism," where all social facts, their structure, and change are in principle explicable in terms of individuals, their properties, actions, and relations to one another (2010: 59). Purely micro-level theories relate to how the interests and beliefs of interests of individuals impact their actions, and how individuals interact with each other (type 3). However, this does not mean that actors are necessarily individual humans. Social science operates with many forms of collective actors that are treated "as if" they were individuals, most bravely captured by Wendt's contention that "states are people too" (1999: 194). One example of a purely micro-level theory is Coleman's rational choice–based theory of social action, where even actions like altruism are reduced solely to individual self-interested motivations (desire for reciprocity in a long-term iterated game) (1990).

Situational mechanisms link the macro-level to the micro-level (type 2). Situational mechanisms describe how social structures constrain individuals' action and how cultural environments shape their desires and beliefs (Hedström and Swedberg 1998). Examples of a macro-micro mechanism include constructivist theories of actor compliance with norms that are embedded at the macro-level (structural).

Transformational mechanisms describe processes whereby individuals, through their actions and interactions, generate various intended and unintended social outcomes at the macro-level (type 4) (Hedström and Swedberg 1998). An example of this type of micro-macro mechanism could be socialization processes, whereby actors through their interaction create new norms at the macro-level. Another example is from game theory, where individual actions in situations like the prisoner's dilemma create macro-level phenomena like the tragedy of the commons.

There is no single correct answer to the question of which level a causal mechanism should be theorized. There are social mechanisms whose observable implications can best be theorized and measured at the macro-level. Therefore we agree with Stinchcombe's conclusions:

> Where there is rich information on variations at the collective or structural level, while individual-level reasoning (a) has no substantial independent empirical support and (b) adds no new predictions at the structural level that can be independently verified, theorizing at the level of [individual-level] mechanisms is a waste of time. (1991: 380)

The position on levels of mechanisms advocated in this book is that they can hypothetically exist at both the macro-level and the micro-level, along with mechanisms spanning the two levels (situational and transformative mechanisms). The choice of level for our theorization of causal mechanisms depends, in our view, on pragmatic concerns, such as the level at which the empirical manifestations of a given causal mechanism are best studied, and/ or on the level used in the theoretical approach one is working with. If the strongest tests of a given mechanism are possible at the macro-level, then it should be theorized and studied empirically at that level, whereas if the empirical manifestations are better observed at the micro-level, then we should conceptualize and operationalize our study at this level.

Contextual Conditions and Causal Homogeneity

Contextual conditions can be understood as factors that determine whether a causal relationship functions as theorized, be it an C → O relationship or a mechanism in between linking C and O (Falleti and Lynch 2009: 1152; Kurki 2008: 231). They are often termed "scope" conditions in the literature, but we prefer the term "contextual" because it better captures the bounded nature of theoretical phenomena in case-based research.

Contextual conditions can be difficult to distinguish from causal conditions. It is relatively easy to distinguish the two when we are operating with causal theories where C and O are linked together with a causal mechanism. When operating with mechanism-based understandings of causation, a cause is defined as something that triggers a mechanism that is in a productive relationship with the outcome. Here a cause "does something," whereas a contextual condition is merely an enabler; it does not do anything active. For example, if we conceptualize a car as being a mechanism that transfers causal forces from a cause (the burning of fuel) to the outcome (forward movement), we might theorize that the contextual conditions in which the car mechanism can be expected to operate include the presence of oxygen and relatively level ground. If we throw the car mechanism in a lake, even though the mechanism might be in perfect shape, it will still not work, as it is outside of the contextual conditions in which it will run. But the presence of oxygen or ground does not actually do anything in a causal sense; it is only the absence of these contextual conditions that prevent C from producing O.

In contrast, when working with the counterfactual understanding, it can be more difficult to distinguish contextual from causal conditions because we lack conceptual tools for distinguishing between them. If a contextual condition like oxygen is required for a relationship to function, it is necessary, which then implies it actually plays a *causal* role as a counterfactual despite lacking any "productive" relationship with the outcome. But as absence of oxygen results in no forward movement of the car, we would term it a necessary condition for the relationship between C and O to function. If we are in this situation, we can attempt to theorize a plausible mechanism linking the condition with the outcome even though we might not be studying the mechanism empirically. If we cannot develop a plausible mechanism, the condition is probably a contextual condition that is necessary but has no productive relationship with the outcome (Beach forthcoming).

Contextual conditions are closely linked with the question of equifinality, which refers to the idea that depending on context, there can be multiple causes linked to a given outcome (*equifinality at the level of causes*), or that the same cause is linked to the same outcome through different mechanisms (*equifinality at the level of mechanisms*) (Beach and Rohlfing 2016). War, for example, can be theorized as caused by both conflicts of interest (rationalist theory) and by severe misunderstandings (cognitive theories), depending on the context. Equifinality in a given population means that there is causal heterogeneity, suggesting that the population should be divided into more homogenous subpopulations (see chapter 2).

Equifinality at the level of causes is at the core of many comparative research designs, where scholars analyze how different causes, or conjunctions of causes, can produce the same outcome. In contrast, equifinality can pose severe challenges for designs that analyze the individual net effects of particular causes, given that we might not find a significant relationship across the population.

Equifinality can also be present at the level of mechanisms linking a given C with O. Gerring makes the point that for any given C → O relationship there can in theory be multiple plausible causal mechanisms in-between the same C and O. As Gerring puts it, "For each [theoretical causal relationship] . . . one finds a litany of theoretically plausible causal mechanisms, most of which have been extensively debated in the literature. . . . The difficulty of testing empirical mechanisms begins with the difficulty of articulating all the possible (theoretically plausible) causal mechanisms for a given X–Y relationship" (2010: 1510). The same mechanism in a different context can produce a different outcome (Falleti and Lynch 2009). "Formally similar inputs, mediated by the same mechanisms, can lead to different outcomes if the contexts are not analytically equivalent" (Falleti and Lynch 2009: 1160). Equifinality at the level of mechanisms has implications for our ability to infer from a studied case to other cases in the bounded population. However, just because we have found evidence in a case that CM_1 links C and O, we cannot assume that CM_1 also links C with O in other cases.

Therefore, when conceptualizing causal relationships and mechanisms we need to clearly define the contextual conditions in which the causal relationship is expected to work.

The Building Blocks of Causal Mechanisms—Modularity and Social Science Mechanisms

When theorizing about mechanisms in the systems understanding, we are not necessarily reinventing the wheel each time. Instead, we can think of mechanisms in building-block terms, with certain elements that are common to similar types of causal explanations (Steel 2008: 49–53). This can also be termed "modularity," where certain parts of a causal mechanism are "modules" that can travel across classes of theories. Similar types of theoretical explanations can share certain conceptual commonalities that can be thought in terms of modules composed of a part or parts of a mechanism. For instance, the mechanism that binds causes and outcomes together in an institutional theory will have certain common elements irrespective of context that deal with how institutions create opportunity structures for individual actors and/or groups. In the systems understanding, while the parts of the mechanism are intrinsically linked to each other in a productive relationship, this does not mean that certain parts might be more "general." As we discuss in chapter 9, this also means that there can be research situations where we can "import" or "export" a particular module from a particular mechanism to other mechanisms.

Structural causal theories focus on the exogenous constraints and opportunities for political action created by the material surroundings of actors (Parsons 2007: 49–52). Common building blocks for structural theories include how certain preferences and a given material structure dictate observed behavior (or in a looser sense, create a pattern of structural constraints and incentives) (Parsons 2007: 65). Another building block of structural theories that might be shared across structural theories is a part that describes action as being a rational process (Parsons 2007: 52). For structure to have any impact, actors have to react in predictable (rational) ways to their structural positions (Parsons 2007: 52). An example is found in the theorization on electoral realignment in the US context, where realignments at the congressional and local level are theorized to be the product of changes in demographic factors and other slow-moving structural mechanisms (Miller and Schofield 2008).

Institutional theories are distinct from structural ones in that institutions are man-made, and thereby manipulable, structures. Institutions can be defined as "formal or informal rules, conventions or practices, together with the organizational manifestations these patterns of group behavior sometimes take on" (Parsons 2007: 70). Typical institutional explanations deal with how certain intersubjectively present institutions channel actors unintentionally in a certain direction. The exact content of institutional explanations is determined by which of the different subtypes of institutional theory is being utilized, ranging from sociological institutionalist explanations that have norms and institutional cultures as common building blocks, over rationalists who share a focus on institution-induced equilibria, to historical institutionalists where causal mechanisms are conceptualized in ways that capture the unforeseen consequences of earlier institutional choices, prioritizing the building blocks of path dependency and temporal effects. An example of an institutional explanation is Streeck and Thelen's layering theory, where progressive amendments and revisions slowly change existing political institutions (2005: 22–23).

Ideational theories share the argument that outcomes are (at least partially) the product of how actors interpret their world through certain ideational elements (Parsons 2007: 96). Here the focus is not on how structures or institutions constrain behavior, but on how ideas matter in ways that cannot be reduced to the objective position of an actor. Common theoretical building blocks include how actions reflect certain elements of ideas and the fact that elements arose with a degree of autonomy from preexisting objective conditions (ideas are not just manifestations of structures). An example is Khong's theory that explains how historical analogies impact upon how actors interpret the world, making certain foreign policy choices more likely than they otherwise would have been (1992).

Finally, psychological theories deal with mental rules that are hardwired into the human brain, resulting in behavioral regularities. Common building blocks include theorization about how and how much internal psychological dispositions interacted with other factors to produce action. An example is Janis's groupthink causal mechanism, where the innate social needs of individuals are theorized to produce a mechanism that results in poor decision-making processes that are dominated by premature consensus (1982).

3.5. Are Causal Theories and Mechanisms Observable?

On a final point, we need to briefly touch on the question of whether causal conditions and mechanisms can be observed directly, or whether we only can infer their existence indirectly through their "observable manifestations"? How one answers this question depends on one's understanding of science, and in particular whether one believes that we can only study phenomena that can be directly measured (phenomenalism), or whether we can

study "nonobservables" more indirectly through their empirical manifestations (realism) (Jackson 2011: 59–69, 78–92; Kurki 2008: 205; Bhaskar 1978:
13; Patomäki 2002: 70–95).

This debate is particularly relevant when speaking of mechanisms. Many
scholars hold the realist view that causal mechanisms are unobservable
but can be studied anyway. For example, George and Bennett posit that
mechanisms are "ultimately unobservable physical, social, or psychological
processes through which agents with causal capacities operate" (2005: 137).
Hedström and Swedberg argue that causal mechanisms are merely analytical
constructs that do not have a real-world existence (1998).

In contrast, other scholars contend that the parts of a mechanism should
be understood as having a "kind of robustness and reality apart from their
place within that mechanism" (Glennan 1996: 53). In the words of Bunge,
"Mechanisms are not pieces of reasoning but pieces of the furniture of the
real world" (1997: 414). Reskin suggests that we only can answer the question of how an outcome was produced by investigating observable causal
mechanisms, thereby excluding many cognitive and macro-level mechanisms (2003).

As with the question of the level of analysis of mechanisms, a full answer
to this question would involve a lengthy philosophical discussion that is
outside of the scope of this book. In this book we take a pragmatic position,
where we agree with scholars such as Bunge and Glennan that our ambition
should be to attempt to get as "close as possible" to measuring the actual,
underlying causal mechanism, but that there can be theoretical and methodological reasons for why this ideal cannot be achieved.

In our opinion there are some types of causal mechanisms that can be
conceptualized and operationalized in a manner that permits quite close observation of the actual mechanism, and where plentiful evidence exists that
enable us to measure the workings of the mechanism quite closely. Other
types of causal mechanisms, such as group-think mechanisms that deal with
conformity pressures in small-group decision-making, are so complex and
involve such difficult measurement issues relating to access to confidential
documents and problems relating to measurement of socio-psychological
factors that we can only measure the mechanism in an indirect fashion
through proxies (indicators) of the observable implications (e.g., Janis 1982).

What are the methodological implications of the choice between adopting an understanding of causal mechanisms as observable or unobservable?
If we believe that mechanisms can be observed quite directly, when we operationalize a mechanism we are aiming to examine the empirical fingerprints
that the mechanism should have left in the empirical record. In contrast, if

we believe that mechanisms are ultimately unobservable, we should instead think in terms of the observable implications that a mechanism should leave. In practice, the two positions result in similar forms of empirical evidence.

3.6. Conclusions; or, How Do I Know a Good Causal Theory When I See It?

This chapter has developed guidelines for what different types of causal relationships can look like in practice in case-based research. How, then, do we know a good theory when we see it?

- A good case-based causal theory is formulated in a way that is in alignment with the underlying understanding of causation employed.
- For all causal theories, the *contextual conditions* under which the theorized relationship is expected to hold are made as explicit as possible.
- A theory of necessity or sufficiency provides *clear justifications for why* the cause (or conjunction of causes) is *theorized to be necessary or sufficient* for the outcome.
- If theorizing minimalist mechanisms, the theory should *shed some light on the causal process* linking C with O.
- If theorizing mechanisms as systems, the theory needs to develop all of the important *parts of the mechanism* that link C with O, with a *clear causal explanation for what takes us from one part to another* to ensure "productive continuity" through the mechanism. Each of the parts should be defined clearly in terms of *entities engaging in activities*.

CHAPTER 4

Defining the Attributes of Causal Concepts

with Jørgen Møller and Svend-Erik Skaaning

Quantitative analysis may well provide more misinformation
than qualitative analysis, especially on account of the aggravating
circumstances that quantitative misinformation can be used without
any substantive knowledge of the phenomena under consideration.

Sartori 1970: 1039

4.1. Introduction

Building on the insights about the types of causal relationships and the
understandings of causation that underpin them, this chapter explores the
implications this has for how we define which attributes causal concepts
include. Figure 4.1 illustrates the process whereby abstract causal concepts
are translated into actual measures of individual cases (inspired by Adcock
and Collier 2001: 531). This chapter deals with the first step in the process
(conceptualization), where the result is a defined causal concept that clearly
describes the causally relevant attributes that define the positive pole of the
concept. Chapter 5 deals with the operationalization and measurement of
causal concepts.

Abstract concepts are intrinsically vague and ambiguous, which means
that debates about what an abstract concept actually means are important
theoretical disputes, but also debates where there is no empirically "correct"
answer (Adcock and Collier 2001: 533).[1] In contrast, defined concepts are the
basic components of any scientific claim about causal relationships, where a
good defined concept meaningfully captures the essence of what is theorized
to be causally relevant about a concept in the real world. In causal case study

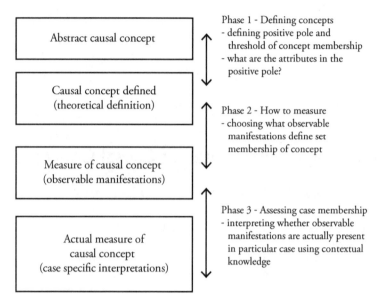

Fig. 4.1. The conceptualization and operationalization of theoretical concepts

research, the goal is to capture the attributes of theoretical concepts that are relevant to the specific types of causal claims we are making, exploiting the case-specific knowledge that comes from the closeness we have to our cases in order to avoid excessively broad definitions that would result in studying causally dissimilar cases. In the following we contend that when conceptualizing concepts we need to think causation all the way down, only including those attributes that are actually causally relevant.

This chapter first explores two of the overlooked implications of the ontological assumptions underlying case-based research. First, asymmetric, deterministic claims are invariant, meaning that causes should be defined as causal conditions instead of as "variables." For example, making the claim that C is sufficient for O implies that we are making no claims about what ~C does, meaning that C is not a variable per se. Second, the assumption of asymmetry means that only the positive pole of causal concepts needs to be defined.

The chapter then discusses different forms of concept structure that are relevant in case-based research, detailing differences between AND, OR, and AND/OR relationships between attributes, along with the disaggregation of concepts using these relations into different variants of concept subtypes. The chapter concludes with a set of practical guidelines for conceptualizing causal concepts in a manner that is in alignment with the underlying ontology of causation used in case-based research. We develop a three-step procedure for defining the attributes that make up the content of causal concepts, illustrated using the concept of feudalism.

While there are a number of works on conceptualization and operationalization, we believe that existing guidelines for conceptualization and operationalization gloss over key differences between case-based and variance-based research. For instance, Goertz's (2006) otherwise excellent book on concepts does not differentiate significantly between defining causes in variance-based and case-based research, resulting in definitions of concepts that focus on variation.[2] However, variation of this type is only relevant when we are using difference-making evidence to make causal inferences about *symmetric* causal relationships, something that is arguably only possible when working with experimental designs. In contrast, our guidelines are compatible with the asymmetric and deterministic assumptions underlying case-based research, resulting in concepts that are defined and measured in a way that, for example, enables us to collect mechanistic evidence upon which to make within-case causal inferences.

At first glance, conceptualizing and operationalizing concepts appears easy. When working with concepts such as democracy or economic development, there exist well-established definitions that can be taken off the shelf, often with quantitative data sets measuring them right at hand. For example, if we are interested in studying the causal impacts of *electoral* political participation of voters on economic redistribution (e.g., Gradstein and Milanovic 2004: 518; Przeworski 2007), we could then select an existing quantitative index measuring democracy, such as the widely used Polity IV measure (Marshall and Jaggers 2004). However, the Polity IV definition of democracy *excludes* the electoral dimension of political participation, focusing only on political competition between political groups, meaning that cases like the United States in 1850 are given the same score as 2000, despite blacks and women not having the franchise in 1850 (Munck and Verkuilen 2002: 11). Utilizing the Polity IV index as a measure of democracy would create the risk that we select cases for intensive study where the electoral dimensions of political participation that we want to study are simply not present. Depending on the case we select, we might then wrongly conclude that political participation did not have the hypothesized causal impact.

In contrast, given that we are not dependent on defining our concepts in a way that can capture a large number of cases across time and space, case-based researchers have the luxury of tailor-making definitions of concepts that fit more closely with the types of causal claims we are making. We can focus our attention on strategically selecting precisely the attributes of concepts that enable us to capture the causally relevant aspects of them in relation to our research question. And as we are also closer to our cases, we can fully deploy our case expertise and contextual knowledge when conceptualizing and operationalizing causal conditions and relationships in order to capture subtle but causally important differences in conceptual content across different contexts.

Defining concepts is of course different when engaging in more holistic, *case-centric* research, where the goal is not to explain the relationship between generalizable causes and outcomes, but to understand why a *particular* historical outcome occurred. The outcome in case-centric research is therefore not a "case of" something, but instead is holistically understood as the "big and important things" going on in a historical outcome (for a good example of this type of research applied to the Cuban Missile Crisis, see Allison 1971; Allison and Zellikow 1999). But even here it can be a good idea to speculate about what the Cuban Missile Crisis can potentially be a "case of" in order to be inspired about which existing theories might be used to gain explanatory traction in accounting for the outcome. In Allison's study of the Cuban Missile Crisis, the case is viewed holistically as a case of many different things, including rational decision-making, crisis bargaining, *and* foreign policy implementation. Therefore, thinking about what the case might be a "case of" can be relevant when engaging in case-centric research in order to identify potential explanations from existing theoretical literature.

4.2. The Implications of Determinism and Asymmetry for Conceptualization

There are two overlooked implications of the ontological assumptions of case-based research that need to be taken into consideration in order for our methods to be in alignment with the underlying assumptions.

Causal Concepts in Case-Based Research Are Not Variables

First, the term "variable" is used throughout the case study literature to refer to causes (Goertz 2006; Coppedge 2012; Gerring 2007; for a notable exception, see Goertz and Mahoney 2012). We argue that using the terms "independent variable" for causes and "dependent variable" for outcomes does not fit with the underlying assumptions of determinism and asymmetry in case-based research. Critical here are the methodological implications of taking individual cases as our analytical point of departure.

Variation is relevant when making inferences based on evidence of difference-making *across* cases when we can manipulate values of X in a controlled experiment. Here it is the variation in either giving the treatment or not that has causal properties because we manipulate the presence/absence of the purported cause. But why, then, is the term "variable" inappropriate in case-based research? The core reason is that using the term "variable" in causal terminology means that it is variation on case scores across cases that is analyzed as the cause of an outcome. However, variation does *not* have causal properties in both mechanism-based and counterfactual-based case study research. When we are tracing a mechanism in case-based research, what enables us to make a causal inference is not variation, but instead the match between what empirical evidence we would hypothesize that the mechanism should leave and what we actually find in the case (see chapter 6). Evidence of the mechanism is therefore *solely* within case; variation here would mean that we no longer trace the operation of the mechanism within a case, but instead are assessing difference-making evidence across cases. This means that variation does not "do" anything in a causal sense in relation to the operation of a mechanism. What we want to capture theoretically when defining a cause that triggers a mechanism is the attributes of the cause that are actually productive in relation to a mechanism in a case or bounded population of cases. Using an analogy to a trial, using variation to make inferences would be like assessing whether person A was guilty in a case by comparing the motives and opportunities of the suspect in the case with values of these across a range of cases with similar and dissimilar scores on the cause and the outcome, inferring guilt if there was a strong correlation in the data. Variation is therefore completely irrelevant when assessing within-case evidence.

Variation is also irrelevant when operating with a counterfactual-based understanding in case-based research. When claiming necessity and/or sufficiency, we are making *invariant*, asymmetric claims where only one of the poles of the concept has causal properties (see the following section, on positive poles). If C is necessary, only the absence of C actually "does" something, whereas if C is sufficient the presence of C "does" something. Both are "invariant" theoretical claims where variation is irrelevant.

Given this, we strongly suggest using the more appropriate terms *causal conditions* for causes (symbolized by C), and *outcomes* for the product of a causal process (O) instead of using the term *variables* (either independent (X) and dependent (Y)).

Define Only the Positive Pole of Concepts in Case-Based Research

Existing treatments of causal concepts suggest that we should define both the positive and negative poles of concepts, along with the continuum between them (Goertz 2006; Coppedge 2012). The positive pole of our concept is defined as the attributes that are included in the definition of our concept for a case to be a member of the concept. The negative pole of a concept is often understood as being the conceptual opposite of a concept; for example, democracy and autocracy are commonly treated as conceptual opposites. The positive pole would develop what attributes define democracy, whereas the negative pole would be what attributes define an autocratic system. The continuum in between could be either a dichotomy or a continuous scale (e.g., ordinal scale). The two poles should then be mutually exclusive (cases cannot be both democratic and autocratic).

Capturing the bipolarity of concepts is important when defining variables, given that we typically are interested in capturing the impact that differences in values of independent variables have across the full range of values of the dependent variable across a set of cases. If we are defining democracy as a variable, we will therefore also define what it means to be the negative pole to assess the difference that values of X have on values of Y across a range of comparable cases.

What is often overlooked when conceptualizing in case-based research is that the negative pole of the concept is analytically irrelevant when making asymmetric claims. Given that the causal case study designs developed in this book build on asymmetric notions of causality—implied in both necessity-sufficiency and mechanism-related causal claims—we only need to define the positive pole of a concept and the threshold defining set membership. Cases that are not members of the positive pole are just "everything else but the concept." The negative pole would only need to be defined when we want to explain its causes distinctly from those of the positive pole.

The argument for excluding the negative pole in case-based designs is simple: when making asymmetric causal claims we are *only* ascribing causal powers to the positive pole of a concept. Claiming that democracy is necessary for economic development makes no claims about autocracy having any causal impact on levels of economic development. In other words, we are not studying whether the conceptual opposite (autocracy as a negative pole of democracy) has a causal relationship with economic development. Similarly, claiming that a causal mechanism links democracy with peace makes no claims about whether there is a causal relationship between autocracy and war. If democracy is the cause in our research, we would only define the positive pole and qualitative threshold of the concept, with cases clearly outside of this set merely being defined as "anything but" democracy.

Therefore, when working with asymmetric causal claims, we need to define what attributes have to be present in a case for it to be a member of the given causal concept, along with the qualitative threshold that defines whether a given case is a member of the set of the concept.[3] Naturally there have to be cases that do not qualify for membership; otherwise the concept is so broad that it becomes a trivial cause.

Goertz (2006) contends that concepts should be understood as being continuous, with both the positive and the negative poles defined clearly. He writes, "If one's ontology specifically allows for the existence of borderline cases then one is ready to see them in reality. If one starts with dichotomous concepts then the tendency is to downplay, if not ignore, the problems—theoretical and empirical—of the gray zone" (2006: 34). He then uses countries in democratic transitions as being in the gray zone between democracy and autocracy. However, if we take causal homogeneity seriously, cases of democratic transition would be better understood as another class of political system with distinct causal properties (e.g., there are a number of theories about democracies in transition being particularly war-prone; Mansfield and Snyder 2002). They would therefore be defined as a different set of cases that would be analytically distinct from democracy or autocracy given that they have different causal properties.

Additionally, even if the cases in the gray zone are causally similar to the positive and negative pole, we contend that it is a measurement issue that can be resolved with transparent measurement procedures (see chapter 5). If we focus our attention squarely on potentially ambiguous cases by forcing ourselves to assess the probability of our measures of C and O being accurate in terms of "how confident are we that a given case A is in the set of C and/or O," we would have to justify with empirical evidence why we believe particular cases are members or not of the defined causal concept. Goertz's suggestion about continuous measures offers no way to deal effectively with gray zone cases, whereas we provide concrete suggestions in chapter 5 to deal with the challenges.

4.3. What Does a "Good" Defined Causal Concept Look Like in Case-Based Research?

We adopt what is sometimes called an *essentialist position* on conceptualization,[4] where the goal is for our definitions to capture the essence of what the concept means as a cause or outcome instead of thinking of conceptualization in terms of choosing indicators (Sartori 1984). This can also be termed a "concept-driven" approach, in contrast to the "data-driven" approaches found in variance-based research (Gerring, Pemstein, and Skaaning 2015; Gerring 1999).

Using democracy as an example, Goertz writes that "competitive elections are not indicators of democracy but what it means to be a democracy" (2006: 15). We also agree with Goertz that we should go a step further than Sartori by also taking into account the *causal* nature of concepts explicitly in our definitions (Goertz 2006: 28). However, we take this argument to its logical conclusion by contending that the *type* of causal relationship we are theorizing should actually be incorporated into the definition of what attributes constitute a concept. Our understanding of causation underlying our design therefore makes a difference in conceptualizing causes and outcomes, in that we need to include the attributes that fit with the type of causal relationship being theorized.

In defining concepts, one is theorizing about the causally relevant dimensions of the concept and how they relate to each other. We utilize the term "attributes" to refer to these dimensions. For example, the concept of societal corporatism (the abstract concept) could be defined by the presence of two attributes: organizational centralization and associational monopoly (Schmitter 1979).

How, then, do we know a good defined concept when we see it in case-based research? There are four guiding principles that should be ever-present when defining concepts in case-based research:

1. Concepts are defined thickly, attempting to create as causally homogeneous a population as possible by creating contextually specific defined concepts.
2. At the same time, only the most causally relevant attributes should be included in the definition.
3. Defined concepts should be compatible with the type of causal claim being made.
4. Defined concepts should only focus on the positive pole.

The starting point in case-based research is that we typically choose to create what can be called "thick" definitions of concepts that include a number of causally relevant attributes that result in smaller, bounded populations of relatively causally homogeneous cases (Coppedge 1999, 2012; Collier and Mahoney 1996). The connotation describes the attributes of a defined concept that determine what the words used apply to, whereas the denotation describes the referents, or real-world cases out there. Thick definitions of concepts include more attributes and/or define them more narrowly (more extensive connotation), resulting in fewer cases being a member of the concept (narrower denotation) (Sartori 1970; Coppedge 2012).

In case-based research we want to avoid conceptual stretching, where concepts are defined too broadly, resulting in a causally heterogeneous population, as too many cases that have different causal properties are allowed to enter the population (Collier and Mahoney 1996; Adcock and Collier 2001). Defining interstate conflict (war) as a militarized conflict that results in at least one thousand battle deaths would arguably produce a very causally heterogeneous population, with everything from World War I to the Football War of 1969 categorized as a war, but where we might have very good reasons to expect that the causes of major systemic wars would be very different from minor border skirmishes.[5] In case-based research, we would want to narrow our definition to craft a more causally homogenous population of cases in which our deterministic causal claims are theorized to hold.

Second, only causally relevant attributes should be included in the defined concept. Defining concepts is deeply embedded in thinking about causal relationships (Adcock and Collier 2001: 532). But it makes little sense to define democracy before one knows whether it is a cause or an outcome, and what it is theorized to cause or be produced by. There can, though, be exploratory research situations where we do not know what democracy is a cause of, or what potentially produced it if it is treated as an outcome to be explained. In this type of exploratory situation, we would therefore merely speculate about the causal properties that democracy might have when defining the concept instead of embedding it into an C $\rightarrow$ O causal claim. However, overall the focus should be on only including the causally relevant attributes of concepts.

Third, our defined concept should be compatible with the type of causal claim being made. If we are making a claim about necessity, we are theorizing that C has to be present for O to occur. This means that our conceptualization of a necessary cause would need to capture the attribute(s) whose *absence* would prevent the outcome from occurring. In other words, we would want to think carefully about what it is about particular attributes that make them necessary for an outcome to occur, and only include those that are causally relevant to this claim. If we are theorizing mechanisms in between C and O, we would conceptualize the cause as including attributes that can actually trigger the start of the mechanism theorized to link it with the outcome.

Fourth, as discussed earlier, defined concepts in case-based research should be categorical with a focus only on the positive pole, defining the attributes whose presence demarcates cases where a given causal relationship is possible from those where it is not.

4.4. Defining the Attributes That Make Up Causal Concepts—Concept Structure

Before we present the three-step framework for defining concepts, we first need to present the basics of concept structure that are relevant for case-based research, and in particular different logical ways in which attributes can relate to each other, distinguishing between whether they are used in a logical AND fashion, or logical OR fashion, or a combination. The section concludes by discussing how attributes can be used to express concept subtypes.

There are three logical forms of theorized relationships between attributes of a concept that are relevant in case-based research.[6] These relationships utilize the logical AND, OR, and a combination of the two (AND/OR). These three relationships have also been termed a "necessary and sufficient" relationship between attributes (AND), a family resemblance relationship (OR), and a radial relationship (AND for several of the conditions, OR for the rest) (e.g., Goertz 2006).[7] The relationships are depicted in figure 4.2. In all three relationships, all the included attributes should be tapping into the same overarching concept (either a cause or an outcome).

It is vital that the relationship between attributes fits with the broader causal claim being made (Munck and Verkuilen 2002: 24). This is especially relevant in the OR and AND/OR relationships, where it is critical that the different combinations of attributes that result in a case being covered as a member of the set of the concept all have similar causal properties. For example, Goertz offers an OR definition of the concept of a welfare state (2006: 74–75). For a case to qualify as a welfare state, at least two of four attributes must be present (workers' compensation, unemployment compensation, pension system, and health care). However, if we are using this definition as an outcome, there might be different causes of a welfare state composed of pensions and health care than one offering workers compensation and pensions, meaning that the population is potentially not causally homogenous (i.e., depending on which attributes are present, outcomes would be produced by different causes). This highlights the need to think

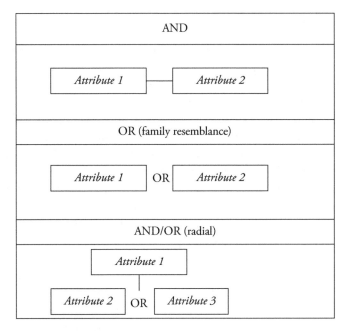

Fig. 4.2. AND, OR, and AND/OR relationships between concept attributes

carefully about causal relationships and causal homogeneity all the way through the conceptualization process.

When we theorize a logical AND relationship between attributes, the inclusion of more attributes increases concept intension, thereby decreasing concept extension (fewer cases are included in the population).[8] The attributes are nonsubstitutable when theorized to be in an AND relationship, which can be seen in many definitions of democracy (Goertz 2006; Munck 2009: 51). Attributes in an AND relationship can, depending on the theory, be theorized to interact with each other in complex ways, such as by boosting each other's causal effects.

In contrast, when theorizing an OR relationship (family resemblance), including more attributes increases the number of ways in which a case can qualify for being a member of the set, resulting in an increase in the number of cases in the population (increased extension) (Goertz 2006: 72–74). The AND/OR combination (radial) can result in both a reduction and an increase in the number of cases in the set. More attributes in the hub that are related to each other by the logical AND results in a decrease in the set of cases that are members of the concept, whereas more attributes in the spokes (logical OR) results in an increase in the set.

Concept Subtypes

Additionally, we have to ask ourselves whether the concept we are defining can be seen as a stand-alone concept or whether it is part of a broader concept that can be divided into subtypes. The reason we would theorize subtypes of a broader concept is because we theorize that the subtypes have different causal properties; otherwise, the distinctions are analytically irrelevant and we should just utilize the broader concept. As an example, if democracy is the broader, overarching concept, we might have theoretical reasons to expect that parliamentary democracy is a necessary condition for democratic stability, whereas presidential democracy is not expected to be necessary given that we might have theorized that it has different causal properties. Here we would have theoretical reasons for dividing the broader concept democracy into two causally distinct subtypes: parliamentary and presidential democracy.

There are two primary ways to theorize concept subtypes and their causal significance, commonly termed (1) "concept PLUS attributes" and (2) "concept MINUS attributes." In the first, we put an adjective such as "parliamentary" or "presidential" in front of the concept to mark the addition of one or more attributes that divides cases into two distinct subpopulations with different causal properties. In the concept MINUS relationship, we remove attributes from the broader defined concept. This can result either in the creation of diminished subtypes, where cases included do *not* overlap with the broader concept (Collier and Levitsky 1997), or in the broadening of the set of the concept itself. An example of a diminished subtype could be theorizing that states that do not protect civil liberties (e.g., termed illiberal democracies) have different causal properties than fully democratic systems (Collier and Levitsky 1997). This is illustrated in figure 4.3. The dots in the figure depict individual cases (countries), with cases within a set of a concept having all the theorized constitutive attributes. As can be seen in the right-hand side of the figure, the diminished subtype depicts the illiberal democratic cases outside of the set of fully democratic countries because they are theorized to have different causal properties.

In contrast, if reducing the number of attributes results in a broader defined concept, we are creating not a concept subtype but instead a new, broader theoretical concept. For example, if we remove constitutive attributes of democracy such as elections, we could argue that the new broader concept—electoral regime—has different causal properties than the original concept. Therefore we would not be creating subtypes here but instead a new, broader concept.

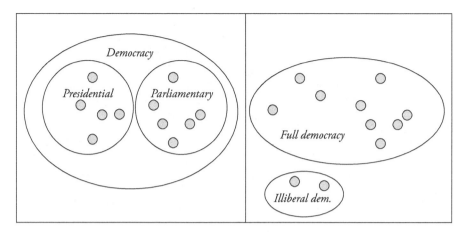

Fig. 4.3. Concept PLUS and MINUS subtypes and the number of cases included (extension)

Concept PLUS and diminished subtype relationships have different implications for the number of cases included in the population of the subtypes. The concept PLUS subtype relates directly to what Sartori talks about as the "ladder of abstraction" (1970: 1041), where the number of cases included in a concept definition (extension) *decreases* as the number of attributes of a concept *increases* (intension). This is illustrated in the left-hand side of figure 4.3, where the introduction of the attributes that demarcate parliamentary from presidential democracies reduces the number of cases in each subtype. It is important to note that the subtypes should be mutually exclusive, with no cases being included in the set of two subtypes simultaneously. In figure 4.3, the presidential-parliamentary distinction is mutually exclusive. The concept MINUS relationship that results in diminished subtypes reduces the size of the population in relation to the broader concept, but in a manner in which they do not overlap. Here a *decrease* in concept intension by removing attributes results in a *decrease* of concept extension, the opposite of what happens in the concept PLUS subtype structure. This is illustrated in the right-hand side of figure 4.3, where the diminished subtype of illiberal democracy is a distinct population outside of the set of the concept of full democracy.

When concept MINUS attributes result in a broadening of the concept, the *decrease* in the number of attributes results in an *increase* in the number of cases included in the population of the new, broader concept. This is illustrated in figure 4.4, where the removal of attributes such as civil liberties and full contestation of elections produces a much larger set of cases in the

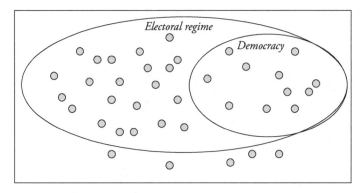

Fig. 4.4. Concept MINUS and broadening of the concept

population. The broader concept of electoral regime includes both the cases within the smaller set of democracy and other cases that do not have these two attributes.

When using concept PLUS subtypes, if we fuse together two or more distinct dimensions, this results in typological subtypes dividing the broader concept into mutually exclusive categories (Collier, LaPorte, and Seawright 2012). For example, if we theorize that there are two dimensions with two categories each that are causally important, this would result in four distinct subtypes. These can be portrayed in a four-cell table (see table 4.1), where each of the four individual cells is a distinct subtype of the basic concept (Collier, LaPorte, and Seawright 2012).[9] When understood as causal concepts, each of the four cells should therefore be treated as a causally distinct subtype of the concept, given that we have theorized that each of the dimensions has different expected causal properties. If the dimensions have no causal importance, they should not be included in the first place. For example, if we are theorizing about regime competence as the basic concept, we might formulate two distinct dimensions: governmental capacity and regime type (Collier, LaPorte, and Seawright 2012: 223). This would result, as illustrated in table 4.1, in four subconcepts, each with different expected causal properties.

TABLE 4.1. A typology of regime competence—four subconcepts

		Regime type	
		Autocratic	Democratic
Government capacity	High	High-capacity autocratic	High-capacity democratic
	Low	Low-capacity autocratic	Low-capacity democratic

Source: Collier, LaPorte, and Seawright 2012.

4.5. Defining Concepts—A Three-Step Procedure

While specific guidance for what to include in the definition of a causal concept will be contingent upon the theoretical debates and substantive knowledge in the field in which one is working, there are also a range of steps that we have to take, irrespective of this, that are shared when conceptualizing causes, mechanisms, and outcomes in case-based research and that differ from how we define concepts as causes and effects in variance-based designs.

Throughout the conceptualization process, choices need to be made transparently, with all decisions and trade-offs explicitly justified in either the main text or in some form of appendix to the research. We need to justify why we believe our definition captures what is causally important about the concept and why the populations of cases thereby created are expected to be causally homogeneous. Justifying requires both that we think hard about causation in relation to the research question and, in particular, that we focus on which attributes of a concept can be a cause of a given outcome and which attributes define an outcome as something that could have been caused by a given cause (or set of causes). Concept definition is a back-and-forth process, as illustrated in figure 4.1. While some scholars argue that we never should look at cases at the empirical level when defining concepts (Goertz 2006), we agree with Ragin that defining concepts is a back-and-forth process between empirical research and theoretical revision (2008: 78–81). Often we find that our definition did not capture what we actually wanted to capture when we start exploring real-world cases, thus resulting in theoretical revisions.

Conceptualizing the positive pole of causal concepts involves translating an abstract concept with multiple meanings into a clearly defined, unambiguous concept that can then be empirically measured. The three-step procedure for defining concepts includes the following steps:

1. Map existing definitions.
2. Brainstorm about which attributes are causally relevant for the research question.
3. Choose the attributes that are causally relevant and develop how they relate to each other (concept structure).

Mapping Existing Definitions

We suggest starting the conceptualization process by mapping how others have defined the causal concept that one is defining, describing the semantic and conceptual field in which one is operating (Sartori 1984; Munck and Verkuilen 2004; Gerring, Pemstein, and Skaaning 2015). It is important that this mapping is only used as an inspiration, because it is important not to be trapped by existing definitions and measures. Instead, one should relentlessly focus on what it is about concepts that can be causes and outcomes in relation to our own research question.

At the same time, concepts like power and democracy have a long theoretical and linguistic history, meaning it is not just "anything goes." Adcock and Collier write, "In any field of inquiry, scholars commonly associate a matrix of potential meanings with the background concept. This matrix limits the range of plausible options, and the researcher who strays outside it runs the risk of being dismissed or misunderstood. . . . At any given time, however, the background concept usually provides a relatively stable matrix. It is essential to recognize that a real choice is being made, but it is no less essential to recognize that this is a limited choice" (2001: 532).

One needs to think carefully about what the abstract theoretical concept means in the field, and in particular the different things that might be implied in addition to the literal meaning of a concept (Collier, LaPorte, and Seawright 2012; Gerring 1999). When working with concepts with a long history, it is important to map the different definitions utilized within the field. This also means that any significant deviations from well-established understandings of a concept should be clearly justified with empirical and theoretical arguments. Gerring talks about this in terms of "familiarity," where a good defined concept either is familiar to an academic audience or there are clear justifications for why the definition departs significantly from the established understandings (Gerring 1999: 368–70).

However, it is also important not to be trapped by existing definitions, as they might not be capturing the attributes of the concept that we theorize are causally important. The only attributes of the concept that should be included are those that are expected to be causally important. Here we basically ask ourselves questions like, "What attributes are causally relevant to include if we are theorizing that C is necessary to produce O?"

Turning to the practical example of conceptualizing the concept of feudalism, there is a large body of literature that argues that feudalism was a necessary condition for explaining outcomes related to modernization in Europe, including the advent of capitalism, the modern state, and modern democracy.[10] Most recently, Blaydes and Chaney (2013) have revisited the concept of feudalism to account for the medieval development of European institutions of constraints in the form of representative institutions (see

Stasavage 2010, 2011, 2014; Van Zanden et al. 2012). However, as can be seen in the review of the literature, not all of the concepts or their attributes are causally relevant for this theorized relationship.

Overall, we can identify three different approaches to defining feudalism in the literature: the Marxist definition of feudalism as a mode of production, the Weberian definition of feudalism as a method of government, and a broader definition in terms of a feudal society, associated with scholars such as Otto Hintze and Marc Bloch (see Møller 2015a). Table 4.2 reviews a selection of different definitions of feudalism, along with the attributes defined in the literature.

Brainstorm about Which Attributes Might Be Causally Relevant

The next step is to brainstorm about which attributes might define one's concept, using existing definitions as a source of inspiration. Brainstorming about attributes is closely linked to the type of causal claim being made. If we only know a cause and want to explore what effects it might have, we would speculate about what aspects of C could produce something. If our research is using an existing causal claim as its point of departure, we would want to think about what aspects of C can be a cause of O. We ask ourselves, "What is it about the concept that can be a cause or outcome?" For instance, what are the causally relevant attributes of democracy that might produce peace between two democratic states in a situation where they otherwise could have gone to war?

When dealing with contextually specific, bounded concepts, multiple attributes are usually required to capture the causally relevant aspects of the concept. In variance-based designs, concepts can have multiple dimensions, seen as different types of continuous scales that are captured by different attributes (Blalock 1982; Goertz 2006). For example, democracy might have both electoral and liberal, rights-based attributes, making the concept a two-dimensional concept. Given that when assessing asymmetric causal claims the negative pole need not be defined, concepts do not have a continuous underlying structure. Therefore, we only utilize the term "attributes" to denote aspects of the positive pole of concepts, without assuming any underlying dimensionality of concepts. If there are multiple theoretical dimensions in the attributes one wants to include that would result in cases in the set of the concept having different causal properties, then one should either drop the offending attribute or refine the definition by formulating the concept in a more restrictive fashion by adding an attribute in a concept PLUS attribute

TABLE 4.2. A selection of existing definitions of feudalism in the literature

Author	Definition of feudalism
	Feudalism as a form of society
Bloch (1971b [1939]: 446) Other authors with similar definitions: Hintze 1975 [1931]	*"A subject peasantry; widespread use of the service tenement (i.e., the fief) instead of a salary, which was out of the question; the supremacy of a class of specialized warriors; ties of obedience and protection which bind man to man and, within the warrior class, assume the distinctive form called vassalage; fragmentation of authority—leading inevitably to disorder; and, in the midst of all this, the survival of other forms of association, family and State, of which the latter, during the second feudal age, was to acquire renewed strength—such then seem to be the fundamental features of European feudalism."* • Attribute 1: Subject peasantry • Attribute 2: Ties of dependence • Attribute 3: Feudal military organization • Attribute 4: Fragmentation of public authority
	Feudalism as a mode of production
Mann (1986: 375) Other authors with similar definitions: Wickham (1984: 6)	*"[T]he extraction of surplus labor through ground rent by a class of landlords from a dependent peasantry."* • Attribute 1: Subject peasantry • Attribute 2: Rents and labor service predominate
	Feudalism as a method of government
Strayer (1975: 13) Other authors with similar definitions: Strayer and Coulborn (1956: 4–6)	*"It is possession of rights of government by feudal lords and the performance of most functions of government through feudal lords which clearly distinguishes feudalism from other types of organization. This means that Western European feudalism is essentially political—it is a form of government. It is a form of government in which political authority is monopolized by a small group of military leaders, but is rather evenly distributed among members of the group."* • Attribute 1: Fragmentation of public authority
Stephenson (1941, 1942) Other authors with similar definitions: Poggi (1978)	*"'By 'feudalism,' in other words, we properly refer to the peculiar association of vassalage with fief-holding that was developed in the Carolingian Empire and thence spread to other parts of Europe. Insofar as this association was effected for governmental purposes, feudalism was essentially political"* (1942: 14). *"The vassal's obligation, being military, was ipso facto political; so, according to Carolingian standards, it was proper for him to receive political privilege in return. The truth should never be overlooked that a fief brought to the holder not merely the rights of a landlord but also those of an immunist"* (1941: 807). • Attribute 1: Fragmentation of public authority • Attribute 2: Immunities and privileges

fashion (e.g., moving from democracy to electoral democracy) (Skaaning, Gerring, and Bartusevicius 2015: 6).

However, this does not mean that case-based concepts need to be simple, one-attribute concepts, as critics of categorical concepts have decried (e.g., Blalock 1982: 109–20). Instead, we can build more complex, contextually specific concepts composed of dichotomous attributes that are linked together in different ways (e.g., AND, OR, AND/OR) (Coppedge 2012: 46–47). Where we depart company with Coppedge is in the recommendation to develop quantitative measures of these multiattribute "thick" concepts. He suggests that we group attributes together into dimensions and then combine them into single quantitative indices for each dimension in order to capture differences of degree (Coppedge 2012: 46–48). However, as we have already argued, when we are evaluating asymmetric causal claims, the negative pole is analytically irrelevant in most circumstances. This means that a large amount of the "extra" information included in the quantitative indices is irrelevant. Further, we risk masking kind differences within concepts by utilizing degree differences, as we discussed in chapter 2, with the risk that we unwittingly create more causally heterogeneous populations of cases.

When defining attributes, the terms utilized should be as unambiguous as possible, thereby avoiding the risk that different scholars will understand the defined concept in very different ways. This is particularly relevant when there is not much existing theorization in a research field.

Returning to the example of feudalism, of the three major approaches depicted in table 4.2, when we evaluate the definitions in terms of what it is about feudalism that could be a cause of the emergence of representative institutions, only feudalism as a method of government can plausibly be causally linked to this outcome. For instance, what in table 4.2 is referred to as feudalism as a "mode of production" is much too broad an occurrence to be theoretically relevant. Such "manorial systems" or "landlordism" (aka *seigneurie, Grundherschafft*) occurred not only "in the feudal society of Western Europe" but "in many other societies as well, both before and after the Middle Ages" (Strayer 1987 [1965]: 13; see also P. Anderson 1974: 402). This definition therefore cannot help us account for the development of representative institutions that only occurred in the medieval West.

On the contrary, there is a large literature that argues that feudalism as a form of rule paved the way for the advent of representative institutions. Various versions of the argument exist, but the core idea is that the privileged feudal groups came to make up the "estate pole" of parliament, which confronted the monarchical pole of the crown in the medieval regime form (e.g., Hintze 1975 [1931]; Poggi 1991: 88–89; Ganshof 1952 [1944]: 154; Strayer 1987 [1965]: 29; Moore 1991 [1966]: 415). The trigger for this development is normally identified as the onset of generalized geopolitical competition in the late Middle Ages (A.D. 1200 onwards) (Hintze 1975 [1931]; Møller 2014). It is in this literature that we should explore which attributes of feudalism might be causally relevant for the rise of representative institutions. But this does not solve the conceptual conundrum. As we expand on later, it is only one of the attributes of feudalism as a form of government that can be causally linked to representative institutions, namely "immunities for estate groups."

Choosing the Attributes and Defining How They Relate to Each Other (Concept Structure)

When selecting which of the brainstormed attributes to use, there should be an informative connection between the terms used and the meanings of the attributes that are causally relevant in relation to our research. In simple terms, the attributes of a concept should coherently fit together (Gerring 1999: 374). When thinking in causal terms, it is important to be cognizant of whether different attributes have different causal properties. If different attributes have contrasting causal effects, then we should disaggregate the defined concept into subtypes. We should select as many attributes as are required to capture what is causally relevant about a given concept. There is naturally a limit to how many attributes to include, both in terms of working within the matrix of existing definitions and in terms of avoiding excessively complex definitions that include so many attributes that only one or two cases would qualify as members.

We also need to make sure that the attributes of the outcome are not also included in the definition of the cause (Munck and Verkuilen 2002: 9). If we theorize that a free market (C) is causally related to democratization (O), we would not want to include market-based attributes in our definition of democratization (Munck and Verkuilen 2002).

Finally, following on the preceding discussion of concept structure, we need to think carefully about how the different chosen attributes relate to each other. The chosen structure should fit with the type of causal claim being made.

There is a clear trade-off between developing custom-fit definitions for the causal relationships we are engaging with in our own research and knowledge accumulation. Very specific definitions risk creating a form of compart-mentalized knowledge, where we learn a lot about a very narrow part of the overall concept (e.g., about the causes of democratization in Latin America during the 1980s instead of causes of democracy more broadly). However, as discussed in the introductory chapter, learning a lot about a little is the reason we engage in case-based research in the first place. And one can also explicitly tackle this question in the conclusions of a work by evaluating the extent the findings can travel to broader definitions of the causal concepts being investigated.

As an example of choosing attributes and developing how they relate to each other, we discuss the existing definitions of crisis in the foreign policy decision-making literature, where it is theorized that a perceived crisis (C) is causally linked with faulty decision-making (O) through stress among decision-makers (the causal mechanism) (Brecher 1980; Hermann 1969; Oneal 1988). Here we focus on the debates about defining the causal condi-tion (crisis). Note that noncrisis is not defined explicitly; it is merely a situ-ation where the defining attributes are not present.

Hermann (1969: 414) originally defined crisis as being composed of three attributes that were all necessary (AND). He contended that a crisis that can produce faulty decision-making occurs when a state is facing the following:

1. Threat to high-priority goals
2. A short amount of time for a response
3. The event is a surprise to the members of the decision-making group

Hermann theorized that there is an AND relationship between the at-tributes, as he believed that all must be present to produce faulty decision-making processes. If states face a threat to high-priority goals, but have extensive time that would enable them to engage in a far-reaching inter-nal deliberation process, this would enable them to approximate a fully ra-tional, synoptic decision-making process (~O) instead of faulty decision-making (O).

Brecher (1980) contended that surprise is not necessary for a crisis atmo-sphere to exist. He suggested that by including surprise as a defining attri-bute, important crises would be excluded from the coverage of the concept, such as the US-Soviet crisis over Berlin in 1961, where US decision-makers faced severe stress in making decisions that could have resulted in war. He then suggested that instead of surprise we should include the high probability of military hostilities in an AND relationship with the other attributes, as this risk is particularly stress-inducing and can produce faulty decision-making when coupled with other attributes. He thereby reduced the scope of Hermann's first attribute, changing it from goals that can shift across different decision-makers and over time to more fundamental core values of the state itself. He also amended Hermann's second attribute, suggesting that it is merely the need to make a decision, instead of the short time period involved, that can induce stress. In the Berlin crisis in 1961, the crisis lasted several months, but this does not mean, in Brecher's opinion, that it was not a crisis. Therefore, the content of his definition of crisis included three refined attributes in an AND relationship with each other:

1. A threat to basic values of the polity
2. The high probability of involvement in military hostilities
3. A finite period in which decisions must be made

These definitional decisions matter, in that they define the population under investigation and the type of causal relationship being theorized.

Returning to the example of feudalism, in the past two generations historians have argued that feudalism as a political regime form never characterized medieval Europe (e.g., Brown 1974; Ward 1985; Reynolds 1994; Bisson 2010). For instance, according to this literature both vassalage and the fief are theoretical constructs that were developed much later, and therefore are not actual institutions found "on the ground" in medieval Europe (see particularly Reynolds 1994). This speaks in favor of refocusing our conceptual interest towards the existence of strong autonomous groups with corporate rights, one of the attributes of the broader definitions of feudalism as a political regime form (Møller 2014). In other words, rather than working with the thicker concept with multiple attributes, it is actually necessary here to narrow the focus to one set of attributes when we relentlessly focus on what it is about feudalism that could actually be a cause. The attribute that therefore appears to be causally relevant is the existence of multiple privileged estate groups—the nobility, the clergy, and the urban estate—with their corporate rights often sanctioned by charters (Finer 1997a; Hui 2005, 202–3; Sabetti 2004). It was this that created "a competitive social environment where powerful social groups could balance off rulers' power; this environment existed in Europe but not elsewhere" (Vu 2010: 159).

4.6. Concluding Guidelines for How to Define the Content of Causal Concepts

This chapter has discussed how to conceptualize causal concepts in a manner that is compatible with the underlying ontological assumptions of case-based research. We summarize in the following the core takeaway ideas.

Defining the Content of Concepts

Underlying assumptions about causation that match case-based research, including deterministic and asymmetric ontological understandings, have important implications for how we define causal concepts. First, causes and outcomes are not variables when we are dealing with asymmetric causal relations. Instead, we focus our analytical attention on the positive poles of concepts.

We identified four guiding principles that should be ever-present when defining concepts in case-based research:

1. Concepts are defined thickly, in an attempt to create as causally homogeneous a population as possible by creating contextually specific defined concepts.
2. At the same time, only the most causally relevant attributes should be included in the definition.
3. Defined concepts should be compatible with the type of causal claim being made.
4. Defined concepts should only focus on the positive pole.

When defining concepts, we suggested a three-step procedure that involved the following:

1. Mapping existing definitions
2. Brainstorming about which attributes are causally relevant for your research question
3. Choosing the attributes that are causally relevant and developing how they relate to each other (concept structure)

The overall goal is to define causes in linguistic terms that capture what it is about a concept that can be a cause of the theorized type of causal relationship and what it is about the outcome that can be the product of this relationship. If economic development is theorized to be a cause of democratization, merely defining economic development in terms of a country with GDP per capita wealth of US$10,000 tells us little, if anything, about what it is about economic development that could actually trigger a theorized causal process that could in turn spur democratization. Teasing out the causally relevant attributes of concepts is by no means an easy task, but thinking creatively and drawing on existing theoretical debates, we believe that by relentlessly focusing on which attributes are causally relevant, we can define concepts in terms that make it clear what it is about them that can be a cause or an outcome.

CHAPTER 5

Measuring Causal Concepts

with Jørgen Møller and Svend-Erik Skaaning

Just 'cause you feel it doesn't mean it's there.

Radiohead, "There There," *Hail to the Chief*

5.1. Introduction

After a concept is defined, the next steps are to develop transparent procedures for how we can measure whether it is present in real-world cases, and then actually measure cases to determine whether they are in or out of the set of the cause or outcome. The measurement process is depicted in figure 5.1 as phase 2 and 3.

When we speak of measuring concepts, what we are doing is describing a set of transparent procedures for deciding whether an actual case is a member of the set of a causal concept. Defining observables of concepts is different from defining which theoretical attributes make up a given concept; defining attributes does not identify the objects in the real world but only spells out the connotation, that is, the causally relevant attributes of the concept and how they relate to each other. Operationalization of concepts in phase 2 of figure 5.1 is also different from the empirical process of assessing whether individual cases are *actually* members of the set of the causal concepts being measured, interpreting using case-specific knowledge whether the predicted observable manifestations were actually present, and assessing the degree of empirical ambiguity of whether a given case is in the set of the concept or not (phase 3 in figure 5.1).

While treated in this and the previous chapter as a somewhat linear process, the translation of abstract concepts into actual case membership is

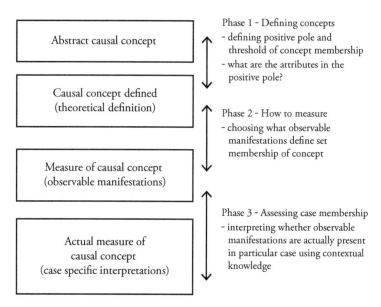

Fig. 5.1. The conceptualization and operationalization of theoretical concepts

usually a back-and-forth between real-world cases and theoretical discussions. In this chapter, we start with developing observable manifestations that we have theoretical justifications for believing are valid, but when applied to actual cases we might find that they are actually measuring something other than what we intended, thus leading us to revise the measure until we are satisfied that our chosen observable manifestations reasonably capture what we intended to measure (Adcock and Collier 2001: 530; Ragin 2000).[1]

While measurement has been dealt with extensively in the methodological literature, many of the existing guidelines and procedures are not compatible with the assumptions underlying case-based research, in particular because of the focus on differences of kind in concepts and the importance of the qualitative threshold defining set membership, the lack of quantification of our measures, and because we are typically making causal claims within small, bounded populations of causally similar cases, which enables us to develop more tailored measures. A particular innovation of this chapter is the fleshing out of ideas about how we can define qualitative thresholds in causal concepts. Existing work has shed some light on how this can actually be done, but has not advanced much beyond recommendations to employ theoretical and empirical knowledge when developing thresholds (e.g., Ragin 2008; Munck 2005; Bogaards 2012). In the following we flesh out a procedure for developing thresholds that are appropriate for measuring causes and outcomes in case-based research.

Good measures of concepts produce maximized discrimination across cases, enabling us to categorize them based on similarities and differences across causally important conditions and outcomes. At the same time, operationalization is always going to be a process of "impoverishment" of theoretical concepts. Working with theories is often rewarding because it is quite abstract and vague, whereas empirical research is difficult and painful. Despite one's best efforts, the choices one makes when deciding how to measure concepts will always be open to critique about the proper assessment of membership of the concept of particular cases, the appropriate choice of observable manifestations, and so on. But this is the whole point of transparency, strengthening our empirical research because other scholars can openly see the cards we are playing with (Moravcsik 2014a, 2014b).

An additional challenge is created by the fact that many of the concepts we are studying in the social sciences, like power and democracy, are analytical constructs, meaning that observable manifestations are only indirectly measuring a theorized concept that does not actually exist. For instance, the concept of middle class does not actually exist because it is a macro-level theoretical concept that can be used to categorize a set of persons with similar socioeconomic attributes. While it is not the time or place to go into the larger epistemological debate between positivists and critical realists on the point of observability, here it is sufficient to conclude that studying causal concepts that are analytical abstractions implies that there is not just one objective measure that we can take down off the shelf. Instead, the measurement process involves difficult choices about the observable manifestations a given causal concept might have if it is present in a population of cases. The core metric for assessing good measures is whether they enable us to capture causally relevant distinctions across cases.

This chapter provides practical guidance as to how the content and measurement of causal concepts can be defined in a manner that is in alignment with the underlying ontology of causation used in case-based research. We first discuss the issues of measurement reliability and validity, followed by a discussion of how measurement in case-based research differs from variance-based designs. We then turn to the presentation of a five-step procedure for developing which observable manifestations the attributes of causal concepts are expected to leave, enabling us to answer the question, "How can I know a concept when I see it in a case?" The chapter concludes with a discussion of the challenges when attempting to evaluate empirically whether real-world cases are actually members of the set of a given causal concept.

5.2. Measurement Reliability and Validity

Irrespective of whether we are measuring variables or causal conditions, a shared concern is to develop reliable measures that are actually measuring what we intend to measure. Given the small number of cases we tend to work with in case-based research, measurement error potentially has huge impacts on analytical results, a reason many quantitative critics have rejected small-N case-based designs as being inherently flawed (Lieberson 1991). While cognizant of this challenge, we contend that being closer to our small number of cases also creates opportunities to develop more valid measures of concepts instead of having to rely on often crude, indirect proxies in large-N research, where the need to measure the same concept across a large number of cases, often across many different contexts (e.g., levels of democracy across the world over a long time span) can produce very causally heterogeneous populations of cases (George and Bennett 2005: 220).

Reliability refers to the extent to which other people using the same operational definitions produce the same results when assessing case membership. Basically, is the measurement procedure robust across different researchers? This is a critical concern in case-based research given that scholars often develop very context-specific measures that require extensive case-specific knowledge coupled with researcher judgments when assessing whether particular cases are in or outside of the set of the concept. To minimize the risks associated with this, we recommend being as transparent as possible when developing measures and assessing cases in order to ensure interresearcher reliability of measurement, providing clear descriptions of procedures and sources used that would enable other researchers to scrutinize and/or replicate one's measures.

Measurement validity in case-based research refers to the extent to which the operationalized measure actually represents the causally relevant aspects of a given causal concept. It can be thought of as concept-measure consistency, where high consistency means that the structure of the measure corresponds to the structure of the causal concept, and the measure captures the semantic meaning of the defined causal concept (Goertz 2006: 110–11; Adcock and Collier 2001; Munck and Verkuilen 2002: 15–17). Measurement validity does *not* involve conceptual issues relating to theoretical debates about how we should understand complex theoretical concepts like democracy or influence and power. Instead, it focuses on the congruence between an already-defined concept and the empirical measure of it.

It is important to investigate using theoretical and substantive case-specific knowledge whether the measure actually is measuring what we intended, something we return to in our five-step procedure later in the chapter. For instance, an increase in the reporting of corruption in the media in a country could mean that corruption has actually increased, but it might just as plausibly be the result of an increase in media freedom to report about corruption, meaning that the chosen observable might be measuring media freedom instead of corruption as intended (Munck and Verkuilen 2002: 16).

When referring to causal concepts, the core goal is to ensure that our measure captures what is causally important in the defined concept. There are numerous examples in the study of the effects of democracy of research where this does not occur. For example, Choi (2004) theorizes that democracies tend to win interstate wars because they are viewed as better allies. Other states view them as better allies because the transparency of democratic systems ensures increased trust among partners, and the constraints in democratic systems make it more difficult for democracies to renege on their promises. However, Choi measures democracy using the composite Polity democracy indicator that does *not* measure the transparency of political systems, and only captures constraints upon the executive using a measure that has little to do with democracy (e.g., Japan in the 1930s and 1940s is given the top score on the attribute executive constraints). In other words, what is causally relevant for her theory of democratic victory is not really captured empirically in the measure that she uses.

The challenges of developing valid measures are arguably less for case-based researchers, given our close proximity to our cases and the fact that our concepts do not have to travel across a large number of cases. In contrast to large-N, variance-based research, we can develop measures that are more contextually specific because we are operating with smaller bounded populations. For instance, if we are only comparing cases within a bounded population, we can utilize measures of democratization that use very different observable manifestations for one context (e.g., Latin American in the 1970s and 1980s) in comparison to another (e.g., Central and Eastern Europe post-1989). In contrast, if we want to compare cases across two or more different contexts, we then have to demonstrate observational equivalence of the different measures, just as in variance-based research.

Despite our best efforts, there will always be a degree of subjectivity in the measurement process (Munck and Verkuilen 2002: 15; Schedler 2012). But by describing transparently our choices during the process of developing and refining observable manifestations (phase 2 in figure 5.1) and the empirical sources we utilized and how we interpreted them in context (phase 3), we lay our cards on the table for other researchers to see. Measuring complex concepts in the real empirical world involves numerous trade-offs; it is important that we are cognizant about these and clearly explain why we made particular choices in light of the research goals we have. Transparency is vital to immunize ourselves against the common quantitative critique that case-based researchers skew measures toward what they want to find (Moravcsik 2014a, 2014b).

5.3. Differences in Measurement in Variance-Based and Case-Based Research

In developing guidelines for the two stages of the measurement process, we focus on making them appropriate for concepts understood as causal conditions in case-based research. In the existing literature on measurement in the social sciences, most attention has been placed on measuring variables, usually for variance-based statistical analysis (Blalock 1982; Bollen 1989). One reason for this is that measurement of concepts is often defined merely as the same thing as quantification. In the words of one of the founders of measurement theory, measurement is "the assignment of numerals to objects or events according to rules" (Stevens 1946: 667). However, while we argue against quantification, we do follow a core tenet of measurement theory that states that the structure of our measures of concepts should be in alignment with the underlying theorized structure of the concept (Borsboom 2005; Michell 1999, 2008; Skaaning, Gerring, and Bartusevičius 2015).

As discussed in chapter 2, given that the types of causal claims we are investigating deal with difference-of-kind distinctions, either in terms of counterfactual presence or absence or in terms of causes being present to trigger a mechanism, our underlying theoretical concepts have a categorical and asymmetric structure that our measures of them should reflect. There is here a basic mathematical structure underlying the measurement of our causal concepts in case study, but this is a set-theoretical one instead of the additive structure typically used in quantitative variance-based research. As a consequence, our measures in case-based research capture qualitative differences of kind, enabling us to differentiate between causally similar and dissimilar cases (Sartori 1970).

While both case-based and variance-based measures share concerns regarding appropriate selection of observable manifestations (i.e., indicators in variance-based research), they differ on several core aspects. At the most basic level, the two types of research differ in their ontological views about the relationship between a measure and the concept itself. Variance-based research builds on a latent factor understanding of the relationship between concepts and measures (Blalock 1982; Bollen 1989; Borsboom 2008). Here measures are viewed as "indicators" that are ontologically separate from concepts (Goertz 2006: 59), with the relationship between indicators and concepts understood in causal terms either as the "causes" or "effects" of latent variables. To capture the latent variable, scholars recommend using multiple indicators (Munck and Verkuilen 2002: 15).

Case-based designs build on an essentialist, or ontological, understanding of concepts (see chapter 4). In alignment with this understanding, measures should not be understood as something analytically distinct or separate from the concept. When we understand concepts in a more qualitative sense, the measure should be seen as being part of the concept itself, that is, as having a constitutive relationship with the concept (Goertz 2006: 13–19). This does not necessarily mean that our measures are directly observing underlying causal concepts, especially when we are speaking about macro-level phenomena such as democracy or class structures. However, using a term like "indicator" implies an analytical distinction. Therefore, we prefer to use the term "observable manifestations" for measures of causal concepts, thereby signaling that we are getting as close as possible to the concept itself instead of a proxy associated with it.

Some scholars have termed this "concept-driven" measurement, in contrast to "data-driven" measurement in variance-based research (Gerring, Pemstein, and Skaaning 2015). In case-based research, concepts and theoretical concerns come before actual empirical data, whereas in the latter, our measures are viewed as the causes of a concept, with empirical data driving measurement. The latter is best seen when developing quantitative measures using tools like factor analysis, where it is the structure of the empirical data that determines concept measures. While the concept- or data-driven measurement distinction does capture a core difference between case-based and variance-based research, we follow Ragin in contending that measurement in case-based research is actually more back and forth than either-or.

When measuring variables, key challenges relate to choosing an appropriate scale of measurement (nominal, ordinal, interval, ratio), along with procedures for aggregation of multiple indicators. In contrast, when defining concepts in case-based research, for us to be in alignment with the underlying asymmetric understanding of causation that implies categorical distinctions (presence or absence), the most challenging decisions we face relate to defining qualitative thresholds that demarcate set membership of individual cases (Sartori 1970: 1038; Ragin 2008: 80–81).

Despite this, many case-based scholars still prefer to measure at the highest scale level possible (e.g., Leuffen, Shikano, and Walter 2013). The reason for this is that many scholars believe that we can only make inferences based on difference-making evidence, where the covariation of values of variables between cases enables causal inferences. However, as is made clear in chapter 6, strong confirmatory within-case inferences can be made without assessing patterns of variation across cases by utilizing "mechanistic" within-case evidence.

A false distinction is that qualitative measures involve extensive subjective assessments by researchers, whereas quantitative measures are more "objective." Irrespective of whether we are using quantitative or qualitative measures, a degree of interpretation is involved in both constructing valid measures and then assessing case scores and membership in a set (Schedler 2012; Beck 2006; Freedman 1991; Wagenaar 2011). While some scholars contend that using simple, objective measures is better than more complicated measures based on subjective judgments (Vanhanen 1997: 37), Beck correctly notes that all quantitative measures involve a significant amount of interpretation, writing that it is only "in conjunction with theory and knowledge of the cases, that allow us to obtain quantitative results that we believe" (2006: 352). Therefore, King, Keohane, and Verba are simply mistaken when they write that qualitative measures are generally less precise because they do not use numbers (1994: 151). Indeed, in good quantitative research, widely used "objective" indicators (e.g., GDP per capita, Gini index) *always* have to be interpreted in relation to causal concepts, providing justifications for why we believe that the chosen indicator actually represents the concept that we intend to measure (Adcock and Collier 2001; Munck and Verkuilen 2002: 15–16; Schedler 2012). The key is to provide transparent justifications that hopefully result in intersubjective knowledge being produced.

5.4. Defining the Observable Manifestations of Concepts

This section deals with the development of observable manifestations of the attributes of causal concepts, and in particular how we can set appropriate empirical thresholds for concepts that map onto the underlying causal structure of the concepts. We utilize the example of measuring the attribute of inclusive political participation as a running example in the following.

Observable manifestations can be contextually sensitive, even differing between cases where relevant (van Deth 2013). In such circumstances, the use of different observables that are functionally equivalent is correct, but explicit justifications for different measures of the same concept across different cases have to be provided, enabling the reader to evaluate whether claims of equivalence across contexts and cases for measures are legitimate (Adcock and Collier 2001: 536; Przeworski and Teune 1970; Teune 1990). For example, the observable manifestations of corruption of politicians might look very different in northern Germany than in southern Italy, but the underlying causal concept might be the same. While many of the procedures in the literature are statistical (e.g., using different factor-analytical techniques), in case-based research equivalence of different observables across cases can be established using construct validation (see section 5.5 for more on validation).

For each attribute of a defined concept, we need to describe transparently the observable manifestation(s) it is predicted it will have that will enable us to determine whether an attribute is present or not in any given case. These need to be clear and precise enough to enable us to distinguish empirical referents from each other. In other words, they should tell us how to recognize the presence or absence of attribute A in a case when we see it in the empirical world. Descriptions of observable manifestations should utilize unambiguous terms and be as simple as is meaningfully possible (Sartori 2009; King, Keohane, and Verba 1994: 152).

Developing multiple manifestations for each attribute might enable us to create more robust measures, but at the same time the use of multiple manifestations raises problems of how they relate to each other (e.g., do all have to be present?). Furthermore, it increases the risk that we do not measure what we intended (lower validity). Whereas variance-based researchers often utilize multiple indicators that are then assessed using confirmatory factor analysis or similar tools in order to be sure that they capture the "latent," unobservable variation of a given concept (Munck and Verkuilen 2002), case-based researchers would counter that this is like shooting a shotgun at a target instead of a more precise arrow. With a shotgun we can be quite sure that we will actually hit something, with the downside that most of the discharge will actually bypass the target. Given that case-based researchers want to develop measures that are not proxy indicators, we should instead focus our efforts on developing single measures that are as close as possible to the concept in a given context.

If we have to utilize multiple manifestations, we then need to think carefully about the relationship between different observable manifestations, and between these manifestations and the attributes of the concept being measured. Are the measures substitutable (OR relationship with each other), or do they all have to be present (AND relationship) (Goertz 2006: 63). If there is an AND relationship between manifestations, do they count equally, or should we weigh some more than others?

Defining and Measuring Qualitative Thresholds

The most important but also most challenging aspect of defining observable manifestations of causal conditions is setting a clear empirical threshold at which causal relationships are theorized to be triggered. That is, the level of presence of concepts at which they have causal properties. The following fleshes out Ragin's and Munck's suggestions for using theoretical and empirical knowledge to define thresholds (Ragin 2008: 82; Munck 2005). Ragin, for example, states that we can use external criteria for thresholds, such as established standards of social knowledge (e.g., that twelve years of education in the US context is an important threshold), collective social scientific knowledge (e.g., established conventions regarding what it takes to be defined as an economic developed country), and the researcher's own knowledge from studying specific cases. Munck more explicitly links the setting of thresholds to the underlying structure of the causal claims being investigated.

Thresholds should be clear enough that they enable us to differentiate cases into classes of mutually exclusive categories of presence or absence of the causal concept. The following will first discuss how we can define thresholds, after which we discuss the importance of assessing the degree of empirical ambiguity of case membership of actual cases.

Because we want to capture causally relevant similarities and differences across cases, we need to avoid arbitrary cutoff points (Verkuilen 2005: 467). We cannot just set a threshold using the justification that we are following conventional practice, or by setting it at the median or mean of an interval scale (for examples of these practices, see Bogaards 2012). Instead, we need to provide clear justifications for why the threshold should be set where we claim it is and why we believe it captures the critical causal distinction across a set of cases. In other words, the empirical threshold is a representation of an underlying pattern of asymmetric causation.

How precisely we understand thresholds links with the discussion of the underlying understandings of causation discussed in chapter 2. For instance, when building on counterfactual understandings of causation, the attributes of concepts are understood as aspects of the causal concept whose absence either individually or as part of a number of attributes will result in the absence of the outcome occurring. In contrast, in the mechanism understanding, when attributes of concepts are present they should be expected to have causal effects on the outcome. When we then discuss observable manifestations, in the counterfactual understanding we are trying to capture the level at which the absence of the observable manifestations of the attribute(s) can be expected to result in the absence of the outcome, whereas when building on the mechanism understanding, defining observable manifestations involves defining empirically the level at which the causal properties of a mechanism are hypothesized to kick in. There will almost always be a degree of uncertainty about the exact empirical threshold in relation to when causal relationships are triggered, a point we return to in the following.

As discussed in chapter 2, the understanding of thresholds as the point at which causal relationships kick in reflects a crisp-set understanding of sets and the causal theories linking sets. In our understanding, the primary focus of measurement should therefore be on determining empirically the threshold of the observable manifestations of attributes at which a causal relationship manifests itself, that is, the minimal level of presence of certain factors that result in a causal relationship being possible. Using an analogy to smoking and lung cancer, this would involve defining the bare minimum level of smoking we would expect could result in cancer. Smoking one cigarette at the age of sixteen is not going to produce lung cancer by itself, but repeated exposure over a certain amount of time (that should be defined more precisely) will under specified conditions produce cancer.

While setting the threshold should in principle be based solely on a theoretical and empirical assessment of when the causal relationships is possible, we need to avoid setting excessively restrictive or permissive thresholds that result in either almost no positive cases included or an anything-goes inclusion of too many causally dissimilar cases. The goal is to develop thresholds that capture causally relevant similarities and differences across cases, clustering cases into the same kind categories.

Figure 5.2 illustrates the implications of setting either too restrictive or too permissive thresholds, using an example of a theorized causal relationship between democracy and economic development. Building on an example from Munck (2005: 8–9), let us assume we are working with a concept of democracy focusing on electoral participation, where our theorization of participation as a cause deals with the impact that the inclusion or exclusion from the political process of the views of groups likely to have conflicting interests might have (e.g., Dahl 1971: 28–29, 246–47; 1998: 76–78; Valenzuela 1985: 28–35; 2001: 251–56). We would want our threshold to capture this causally relevant distinction empirically, but often thresholds are set quite

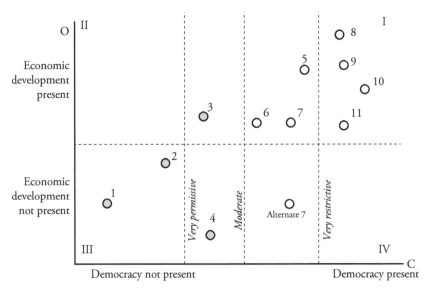

Fig. 5.2. The risks of either excluding similar cases or including dissimilar cases

arbitrarily in the literature, with little or no discussion of how they capture the underlying theorized causal relationship.

For example, we could have arbitrarily set a very permissive threshold of 25 percent of the adult population, meaning that when the proportion of adult males with the right to vote reaches 50 percent, a country is categorized as democratic (Huntington 1991: 16, Boix 2003: 766). A very restrictive arbitrary threshold could be 90 percent of all adults (Dahl 1971: 232–33, 246–48). Given that both are arbitrary, with no real relation to the underlying theorized causal impacts of participation, there would be the strong risk of creating causally heterogeneous populations. In figure 5.2, cases are either depicted as pure white (referring to cases where electoral participation (democracy) has causal effects) or shaded gray (cases where participation does not have causal effects).

The very permissive threshold for measuring democracy would include cases 3 and 4 in the set, both cases where democracy would not have causal effects but that would mistakenly be included in the population. With a very restrictive threshold there is the risk of excluding cases that are causally similar to the rest of the positive cases of X (cases 5–7 are mistakenly excluded). In both instances, flawed cross-case inferences can be the result. If we set an excessively permissive threshold, we would thereby be including causally dissimilar cases into the population of what we assume are similar cases, with the result being flawed inferences if we infer from case 8 that the relationship is also present in cases 3 and 4. For example, we might downgrade our confidence in democracy (C) being necessary for economic development (O) to occur with a cross-case comparative test, or because we did not find evidence of mechanisms in case 3 linking C and O. Yet the correct inference here should be that case 3 is not in the set of C and O. In contrast, an excessively restrictive threshold might exclude cases 5–7. While this would only result in a smaller scope for our inferences in the distribution described in figure 5.2, if case 7 was actually below the threshold of O (depicted as alternate 7 in the figure), our excessively restrictive thresholds would result in the flawed inference that C is potentially sufficient for O, whereas in reality given the presence of alternate 7, we should disconfirm that C by itself is sufficient.

A more appropriate threshold that represents the above-described theorized effects of participation could be when voting rights are extended to two groups, one of which must be a mass, nonelite group (Munck 2005: 8). This measure would arguably result in a more causally homogeneous set of cases. If we then find that the theoretical relationship does not hold when investigated empirically within a more causally homogeneous population, we will be able to infer with more confidence that our theories need to be revised, for example by revisiting the core theoretical claims about the causal effects of participation. Note also that actually measuring the proposed threshold requires a considerable degree of case-specific interpretation for a particular case because the term "one of which must be a mass, nonelite group" can look very different in different cases.

Despite our best efforts, there will always be some residual uncertainty about where we should place a threshold. This means that we need to avoid artificial precision that might lead to flawed inferences. And when applied in practice, if there are many cases close to the threshold, or if small changes in the threshold result in large changes in the number of cases in and out of the set, we should be very cautious about choosing cases close to the threshold for within-case analysis. While we want to avoid vague thresholds, we also have to accept that our thresholds will typically not be razor thin. Instead, there is typically a gray zone of ambiguous cases that can be wider or narrower depending on the precision of our measure and the level of empirical uncertainty. We should attempt to assess the degree of uncertainty of the location of the threshold by exploring the analytical implications that minor adjustments in the threshold have for set membership, enabling us to develop an idea about the width of the gray zone.

There can also be empirical uncertainty about whether particular cases are members of a causal concept or not. Here it is not the theoretical placement but empirical uncertainty about set membership because of empirical

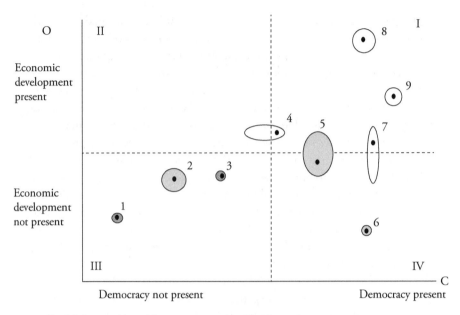

Fig. 5.3. Cases with ambiguous set membership due to inaccurate measures

Note: Black dots depict "true" case membership. The size of circles represents the degree of empirical uncertainty about correct categorization of cases. White circles = causal relationship C > O possible; shaded circles = relationship not possible because either C or O not present.

ambiguity that can produce flawed inferences. Figure 5.3 depicts a set of nine cases, some of which we are more uncertain about membership than others because of the poor quality of the empirical material. For each case, we depict a black dot as the "true" (but unknowable) placement in the sets of democracy (C) and economic development (O). The circles around the black dots depict what can be thought of as the degree of empirical uncertainty about case placement. As can be seen from the figure, only cases 4, 7, 8, and 9 are actually in the set of both C and O—that is, are positive or typical cases of the posited causal relationship. Because of empirical uncertainty, while case 4 is actually a positive case in quadrant I, due to the ambiguous empirical material that we have available for case 4, we cannot be sure whether the case actually is a democracy or not (the circle reaches into both quadrants I and II). The circles where the posited C → O causal relationship are not possible are shaded, whereas the white circles are cases where the relationship is possible (they are positive cases).

Most cases in figure 5.3 are empirically unambiguous about whether they are in or out of the set, meaning that despite degrees of empirical uncertainty we are reasonably confident they are either out or in sets. Cases 1 and 2 are clearly outside of both C and O, whereas cases 8 and 9 are clearly members despite empirical uncertainty. More problematic are the cases like 4, 5, and 7, where we are empirically uncertain whether they are really in or out of the sets of C and O. If we (mistakenly) scored case 5 as economically developed, a case study would suggest there was no causal relationship within the population, which in this instance would be a flawed generalization.

Irrespective of whether the uncertainty about case membership of borderline cases derives from the ambiguity about the measure itself or poor empirical material, the methodological implications are the same. Unless we can document with a reasonable degree of confidence that a case is a member of a causal concept, we should exclude it from our analysis.[2] For example, when selecting individual cases we might mistakenly select a case that we think is in but it is actually out of the sets of C and/or O. In cross-case comparative tests, if there is a large gray zone, we might want to exclude all the cases within the zone of ambiguity, thereby only comparing cases that we are quite sure are causally similar and/or dissimilar. The existence of this gray zone is why case-based scholars tend to be more comfortable with selecting cases that are obviously either in or out of sets (e.g., Goertz and Mahoney 2012; Ragin 2000: 226), meaning that their membership is robust across different definitions of the threshold of the concept.

If we are assessing cross-case patterns using comparative methods, including ambiguous borderline cases would potentially prejudice our results. For instance, if we are assessing whether C is necessary for O and we (mistakenly) scored case 4 as being in quadrant II, we would disconfirm the cross-case relationship because O occurs without C being present in case 4. Similarly, using case 5 for within-case analysis would produce flawed inferences if we believed it was in quadrant I. Analysis of borderline cases is though very relevant in later stages of a research project, where we are much more confident about whether a causal relationship is present or not in the bounded population of nonambiguous cases. For instance, after a series of within-case studies of cases like 8 and 9 that demonstrate a causal relationship, we can turn to more ambiguous cases, using the presence or absence of evidence of the causal relationship as a tool to determine whether the case actually is in or out of the set of the causal concepts.

5.5. Measuring the Attributes of Causal Concepts

We now describe a five-step procedure for developing the observable manifestations of attributes of defined concepts and applying them to categorize actual cases, using the concept of inclusive political participation as a running example. While the procedure is presented here in a linear fashion, in practice it involves numerous iterations and moves back and forth between different steps.

Good measures of causal concepts in case-based research describe an operational definition of a causal concept that identifies empirical referents (cases) in a way that reliably and validly captures the causally relevant attributes of the concept empirically. The result is an operational definition that provides clear guidance in identifying cases that are members of the set of the causal concept in the empirical record. Using this five-step procedure, we are basically answering the question, "How can I know a case of a concept when I see it"?

We propose the following steps when developing a measure of a causal attribute:

1. Engage in a creative brainstorm for potential observable manifestations, describing as many potential empirical fingerprints it could leave as possible.
2. Evaluate the pros and cons of different potential observable manifestation in a systematic fashion, choosing the observable manifestation(s) that can be justified as best capturing the causally relevant aspects of the concept as closely as possible.
3. If working with multiattribute concepts, compile the manifestations of each attribute and develop the relationship between them in a way that is consistent with the underlying concept structure.
4. Validate the chosen measure, for example, by comparing it with existing measures or evaluating how it performs when assessing "ideal-typical" cases for membership in the set of the concept.
5. Categorize actual cases using the measure (case membership assessed).

While the validation of measures should be seen as a continual process of refinement of measures to better capture the structure and semantic meaning of causal attributes, we propose concentrating this in steps 2 and 4 (Adcock and Collier 2001: 538–40). In content validation, for example, we ask ourselves a set of questions relating to whether the content of the causal concept is represented in our measure. While often kept at the conceptual level, we follow Adcock and Collier and Ragin (Adcock and Collier 2001: 539; Ragin 2000: 190–91) in arguing that validation can also include assessing how a proposed measure works for particular cases.

Note also that we suggest that existing measures for a given concept are only brought in late in the process, whereas most variance-based scholars suggest that one starts with existing measures (e.g., King, Keohane, and Verba 1994: 157). The reason to start with a clean slate as regards measurement is that we thereby avoid the risk of becoming trapped by how other researchers have measured something, thereby missing or giving less weight to the empirical observables that are vital to capture the causally relevant distinctions between cases in and out of the set of the causal concept. Even in existing case-based accounts one finds suggestions to start with existing measures (e.g., Ragin 2008: 86). However, these existing measures are typically interval-scale, variance-based measures that are then translated (calibrated) into qualitative set-based measures (Ragin 2008). We contend that the need to focus relentlessly on what is causally relevant in relation to the theories we are studying means that we should not be preoccupied with how others have measured the concept, paying attention to this only later in the measurement process.

The exception to this rule is when there is an existing measure that taps into the causally relevant distinctions one is theorizing and with only minor modifications can be used as a categorical measure with a clear qualitative threshold. For instance, if working with theories about the causes or effects of democratic institutions, the V-DEM (Varieties of Democracy) data set includes a series of dichotomous (and ordinal-scale) measures of a wide range of attributes that can be adapted to one's own research by assessing whether the content and threshold of the V-DEM attribute captures the causally relevant properties of the attributes in one's own research. For instance, if one is studying the relationship between electoral fraud and economic growth (or lack thereof), there is a V-DEM attribute that measures this by asking, "Did fraud compromise the results of this election?" which includes a clear qualitative threshold. The attribute is coded yes (or in the terms of this book, present) if there is strong evidence in a case suggesting that the results of the election might have been different had it not been for the use of nonviolent election fraud by one or more actors (Coppedge 2014).

It is also given that the measure of what is causally relevant about a cause should not tap into the same or similar observable manifestations that the outcome has. Further, there will always be some aspects of our defined concepts that cannot be empirically observed; that is, they are true nonobservables (Sartori 2009: 115). Finally, while we should always strive to improve the validity and reliability of our measures through theoretical and empirical refinement, we also should be clear that there comes a point in the research process where the gains of further refinement are outweighed by the analytical costs.

Before one begins to operationalize concepts in terms of observable manifestations, it is important to recall the analytical level at which the concept is theorized to function at and the theorized scope of the population of causally homogeneous objects. First, at what level is the unit of analysis of the concept? Is it at the country or subnational level, or is the concept at the level of individuals or small groups? If we are measuring democracy, we should expect the observable manifestations to be very different at the country level than within small groups. Second, what is the spatial and temporal scope of the population of causally homogeneous objects? Common delineations that bound populations of countries could be spatially (e.g., regions like Latin America, Western Europe), or temporal (e.g., post–World War II, pre–World War II), although remember that these delineations need to be justified transparently in relation to whether and why they result in a causally homogeneous population of cases.

Step 1—Brainstorming about What Attribute A Would Look Like When You See It

When developing measures that represent the causally relevant aspects of concepts, a good starting point is to brainstorm freely about what types of observable manifestations a given causal attribute could have if present in a case. The brainstorming should be relentlessly focused on the empirical observables that the causally relevant parts of the attribute could potentially leave in a complete empirical record, explicitly discussing the empirical threshold at which these effects are theorized to kick in. Basically one asks the question, "How could I know the causally relevant aspects of attribute A when I see it in a case?" The process of brainstorming should first produce a series of rough ideas of potential empirical fingerprints that are then gradually developed into a small number of promising potential observables that are further refined in the following steps.

Here it is helpful to think about the data-generating processes in relation to causal attributes of the concept being analyzed. If we want to measure "inclusive political participation" as a causal attribute that forms one part of a multiattribute definition of electoral democracy (see, e.g., Bowman, Lehoucq, and Mahoney 2005), we might game through a variety of different empirical fingerprints it might leave if it is present in a hypothetical case (see figure 5.4). For sake of example, these could include (1) no major group is excluded from voting, (2) voter turnout is greater than 50 percent, and (3) suffrage laws are actually enforced.

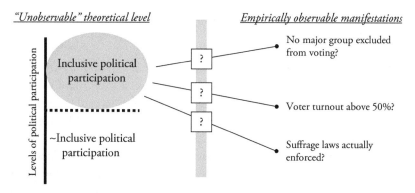

Fig. 5.4. The relationship between unobserved causal attributes and empirically observable manifestations

As depicted in figure 5.4, we do not actually observe a causal attribute directly;[3] instead, it is an analytical construct whose existence we infer from the empirical fingerprints it is hypothesized to leave in the empirical record in cases that are above the theorized qualitative threshold at which causal effects kick in. Note further that in the figure there are only observables connecting the positive pole of the causal concept (inclusive political participation). As discussed in chapter 4, when assessing asymmetric causal claims as in case-based research, we only are interested in the positive poles of concepts; everything else is just "absence of." In contrast, measuring a symmetric cause would involve developing observables that capture both the positive and the negative poles. Note additionally that we do not use arrows to depict the connection, as we would in latent variable theory (where observables are either causes or outcomes—symptoms—of the unobserved latent variable).

We need to speculate about what observable manifestations a causal attribute could have that would best enable us to infer that the attribute actually was present in a case. The inference being made here is *not* causal, but instead involves inferring from the observed empirical fingerprints that an unobserved causal attribute was present in the case with a reasonable degree of confidence.

While each of these potential observables depicted in figure 5.4 arguably measures the underlying causal attribute of inclusive political participation, they have comparative strengths and weaknesses in terms of measurement reliability and validity that then should be systematically evaluated before a choice is made. This occurs in step 2.

Step 2—Evaluating the Pros and Cons of Different Potential Observables in a Systematic Fashion

Evaluating measures requires a set of standards that can help us determine what a good valid and reliable measure is. Here we suggest that four questions be answered: (1) Are vague terms used to define observables? (2) Does the proposed measure match the underlying causal structure? (3) Does the measure capture the semantic meaning of the attribute? and (4) Are the sources of data clearly described? In order to ensure that the evaluation is systematic and transparent, we suggest that the following template developed in table 5.1 can be utilized to evaluate each potential observable on these four questions. As can be seen from the table, both measures a and c are relatively good measures but would require much further specification before they could be employed. By being transparent the evaluation will also illustrate clearly that any operationalization involves difficult trade-offs.

What, then, are the properties that a good measure of a causal attribute possesses? First, observables should be defined in clear terms that enable the analyst to distinguish (relatively) easily cases that are in and out of the set of the attribute(s) of a causal concept, thereby limiting the amount of discretion that the analyst has when assessing case membership of particular cases, thereby also increasing reliability. However, the terms used to describe an observable will never be to such a fine level of detail that there is no interpretation involved.

There is a trade-off between using simple measures that are very clear and more complex measures that require a larger degree of interpretation. In the example of measuring the causal concept of inclusive political participation, the proposed measure "voter turnout above 50 percent" is very clear and simple to implement. However, it arguably also does not map onto the underlying causal structure of the attribute very well, given that the threshold set is arbitrary and probably varies across different case contexts. In contrast, the measure "no major group excluded" arguably captures quite well both the structure and the semantic meaning of the attribute, but it is quite vague. Terms such as "major group" and "excluded" have to be further defined before the measure could be utilized in practice. How do we know a major group when we see it empirically in a case? To what extent does exclusion have to be de jure (e.g., through electoral rules), or can it be de facto exclusion through forms of voter intimidation? Both terms would have to be specified in more detail to avoid leaving too large a degree of discretion to the individual researcher, thereby resulting in unreliable measures.

Second, a good measure achieves concept-measure consistency by *match-*

TABLE 5.1. A template for evaluating potential observable manifestations applied to concept of inclusive political participation

Proposed observable	Vague terms?	Match underlying causal structure?	Captures the semantic meaning of attribute?	Are the sources of data clearly described?
(a) No major group excluded from franchise	• Vague—terms "major group" and "exclusion" need to be further specified.	• Depends on how measure further specified.	• Clearly captures meaning of attribute.	• Not specified.
(b) Voter turnout above 50%	• Very clear terms.	• Arbitrary threshold set that does not necessarily match underlying causal structure.	• Turnout does not necessarily have anything to do with the inclusiveness of participation.	• Yes—official records of turnout would be used in cases where they can be trusted. In other cases reports from international observers would be used.
(c) suffrage laws are enforced	• Term "enforced" is still very vague, and needs to be further specified.	• Depends on how measure further specified.	• Clearly captures meaning of attribute.	• Not specified.

ing the underlying structure of the causal attribute(s). If one is working with causes as counterfactuals, one wants to capture the fingerprints that would signal the presence of the cause, but also whose absence would also mean the cause is not present (the counterfactual). In contrast, if one is working with causal mechanisms, the cause is something whose presence triggers the mechanism. This means that for mechanisms, it is only presence of observables that is relevant when measuring them.

Critical here is the development of the empirical threshold that defines when causal relations are expected to be present in a case. What we want our measure to capture empirically is cases that are above the threshold at which causal effects kick in. This requires a careful reading of the actual causal theory we are working with, developing in detail what it is about the attribute that can be causal (either producing effects or being the outcome of causal effects). Arbitrary "objective" criteria like those proposed by Ragin, including established conventions (e.g., high school graduation as a threshold for education) or established social science "knowledge" (e.g., economically developed threshold at GDP per capita of US$10,000), usually do not map nicely onto the causal thresholds of the attributes we are studying. Instead, we should be more relentlessly focused on developing and refining our ideas about concrete empirical thresholds at which causal relations are possible instead of arbitrary cutoffs.

Returning to the example of inclusive political participation, there is a widespread expectation in the literature that democratization leads to economic redistribution (Gradstein and Milanovic 2004, 518; Przeworski 2007). This claim is based on the intuitive mechanism that the poor, via voting rights, will use political power to redistribute goods. The link has been formalized with reference to median voter theory, which states that extensions of suffrage change the position of the decisive (median) voter in the income distribution, meaning that an increase in the average income relative income of the decisive voter increases redistribution (Meltzer and Richards 1981; see Przeworski 2007; Acemoglu and Robinson 2000). Consequently, we would expect that lifting suffrage restrictions based on property, tax payment, landowning, and education—which are biased against the poor—would be followed by more redistribution.

The relationship is based on a number of assumptions. On the one hand, lifting the types of suffrage restrictions mentioned here only matter if the elections are contested and determine who possesses executive and legislative power. Hence, it is not enough to measure suffrage extensions; we also have to consider if elections are competitive and effective in determining government power. On the other hand, several contextual conditions also have to be present. First, the poor are expected to employ their voting rights. Second, they are expected to vote for candidates and parties prioritizing redistribution from the rich to the poor instead of mobilizing along ethnic lines. Third, the parties should turn their preferences for redistribution into legislation that reflects this preference. Fourth, the redistributive measures need to be effectively implemented, and they should have the intended, redistributive consequences.

Evaluating the three different proposed measures included in table 5.1 in relation to whether they map onto the causal structure of the attribute, "voter turnout above 50 percent" is very arbitrary. It is difficult to see the causal logic in why it is set at this specific threshold and not at 40 percent or 60 percent. The "no major group excluded" measure has to be further specified before we can evaluate whether it maps onto the causal structure of the attribute, although arguably it is the most promising in terms of capturing the critical level at which causal effects kick in.

Third, as discussed earlier, a good measure captures the semantic meaning of the defined attribute(s) of the causal concept as closely as possible. Does the measure exclude important elements relating to the terms used to describe the causal attribute or include elements that are causally irrelevant? In the example in table 5.1, we would discuss what the terms "inclusive" and "political participation" actually mean in light of what we know from theorization on democracy and using case knowledge.

In the example, one could argue that the observable manifestation that best captures the meaning of the attribute is arguably "no major group excluded," although we would then want to define in more detail exactly what a major group actually is. In contrast, we could argue that "levels of turnout above 50 percent" can potentially be quite far from the meaning of inclusive participation, in that turnout might be very low but participation is still inclusive as long as no major groups are systematically excluded from voting.

Fourth, a good measure describes the types of sources that will form evidence of the existence or absence of the predicted observable manifestations to determine whether it is present or not in a case. This increases the reliability of a measure, other things equal.

For some observables, the sources are obvious. In the example in table 5.1, levels of turnout could be from official country statistics, with the provision that if there are good reasons to question the motives that governmental officials might have in exaggerating or downplaying turnout figures, other sources such as international observers might be relevant. Other observables require detailed assessment of primary and/or secondary sources to determine whether they are present. Both the first and the third observables would require much further specification of sources. For example, which types of sources would enable you to determine that no major group was excluded from an election? Would you interview governmental officials or representatives of minority groups? Would you utilize exit polls to determine ethnicity or socioeconomic status of who voted, or even official registers of the ethnicity of individual voters in countries where this is recorded?

Step 3—Compile Observables of an Attribute into Single Measure if Using Multiple Observable Manifestations

If we have multiple observable measures to measure a single underlying causal attribute, we then need to think of how we compile them together into a measure of the attribute. This is not the same thing as having many pieces of evidence of the existence of a single observable manifestation in a case; here we are talking about having multiple measuring instruments for a single causal attribute.

Ideally, one relatively simple and precise measure will be enough to measure an attribute in a valid fashion. However, the more typical situation in case-based research is that it is necessary to develop multiple observables of a single attribute to measure validly what is causally relevant. There can be several situations where it is appropriate to utilize multiple observables to capture an attribute. First, when dealing with complex concepts that are very difficult to measure directly (e.g., power or democratic institutions), it can be necessary to utilize multiple observable manifestations because any single measure will not be enough to determine whether the attribute itself is present in a case. For instance, if we are analyzing actor influence in a political negotiation as an outcome, there would probably not be one definitive measure that would enable us to know that actor A had influence or not. Instead, we could utilize a set of more indirect observables, such as whether actor A had the means, motives, and opportunities to have influence and whether they exploited the opportunities in the negotiations. Only after assessing evidence for all of these observables could we declare in a given case that actor A actually had influence. Second, there can be practical considerations that force us to utilize multiple observables, for instance, when we are not able to gain access to empirical material that would enable us more directly to measure a given concept.

At the same time, it is important that observables all tap into mutually exclusive aspects of the particular attribute. In a latent variable model, multiple measures that yield redundant information enable statistical testing for scale properties and assumptions. In contrast, in case-based research, unless redundant observables are combined in an OR fashion (substitutable), including redundant observables increases the risks of excluding cases that should be in the set of the concept. Even more problematic is when measures of attributes contradict one another. Kreuzer gives a good example of this in discussion of a composite measure of labor market organization by Cusack, Iversen, and Soskice (CIS) (Kruezer 2010). He writes, "Two of CIS' five measures seem to contradict one another. They use craft unions as an indicator of uncoordinated labor markets. This makes sense if the goal is to measure the organizational capacity of unions. Craft unions tended to be local and firm specific and, thus, incapable of cooperating with business at the sectoral or national level. Yet, their operationalization makes less sense if the goal is to measure co-specific labor assets. The members of craft unions tended to have nontradable, firm-specific, formation-intensive skills that are characteristic of coordinated labor markets. After all, craft unions evolved historically from guilds, suggesting continuities in co-specific skill assets. Given this historical continuity, it makes little sense to use craft unions to measure absence of coordination/skill formation while using strength of guilds to do the opposite" (Kruezer 2010: 373).

When combining measures of the same attribute, the default option in the social sciences has been to treat them as having an AND relationship with each other, most often seen in index construction. However, unless this additive relationship maps onto the underlying causal structure of our causal concept, it would result in invalid measurement.

Instead, in case-based research we more often operate with the idea that measures can be substitutable (OR relationship) when we have good reasons to expect that a causal attribute will leave very different empirical fingerprints in different cases, especially when we are operating with a relatively large population of cases. If measures are substitutable, we need to establish equivalence across contexts (Adcock and Collier 2001: 535; van Deth 2013). Utilizing the same measure for a concept like political participation across a range of different contexts (e.g., across regions and time) could result in a measure that validly measures only what is intended in particular contexts. For instance, while "inclusive" political participation in most democracies in the world in the 1800s only involved white men, by the mid-twentieth century the franchise was extended to most major groups in most countries categorized otherwise as democratic. However, if multiple substitutable measures are utilized, we need to provide clear guidance for which measure applies to which set of cases and justifications for why different measures are used in different cases. These different observables should be validated, if possible, using the techniques discussed in this chapter.

Step 4—Checking the Validity of Our Empirical Measures

Concerns about validity are central when evaluating potential observables, asking whether a measure captures empirically what is hypothesized to be causally relevant. There is a large literature on measurement validation, but much of this is only applicable to concepts understood as latent variables. The following adapts three techniques to validating measuring procedures developed for defined causal concepts, focusing in particular on content validation, but also discussing convergent and construct validation. In contrast to variance-based designs, in case-based research the assessment of membership of individual cases is also a useful tool for validation (Sartori 1970; Ragin 1994; Adcock and Collier 2001).

Content validation in case-based research involves exploiting the case-specific expertise we have, thinking through whether there might be any case-specific reasons a given measure might not be valid in a given case or set of cases (Adcock and Collier 2001: 539; Ragin 2000). Are there any reasons a measure that on the surface appears to be appropriate actually might be capturing something very different from what was intended? Actual cases are therefore used to determine whether the measuring procedure is valid. We can start our assessment of a measure of a causal concept by analyzing whether cases that blatantly *have to be* members for the measure to be meaningful; for example, a valid measure of the concept of welfare state would have to include Sweden in the set or the measure would be meaningless. Adcock and Collier write, "Attention to specific cases can spur recognition of dilemmas in the adequacy of the content" of the measure (2001: 539). The goal of content validation is to improve the measuring procedure so that it sorts cases in more conceptually meaningful ways (Adcock and Collier 2001).

Good examples of content validation can be found in Bowman, Lehoucq, and Mahoney (2005) (BLM), where they discuss how broad democracy measures fare when applied to particular cases in Central America. For instance, they engage in content validation of Vanhanen's (2000) measure, which when applied to Costa Rica prior to 1914 scores democracy as absent (~O). But BLM contend that until 1913 elections in Costa Rica were indirect, using electors as in US presidential elections (2005: 947). They note that Vanhanen's measure when applied to the United States "does not punish the United States for having an electoral college[;] we can conclude only that this is also inappropriate for Costa Rica, where the number of electors was erroneously entered into the data set. Factual errors such as these in Vanhanen's 'objective' index likely apply to a number of cases within Latin America" (2005: 947).

Content validation can result in the refinement of our measures, for example, by adopting more case-specific or context-specific measures, using different types of empirical sources to determine case membership in two or more different cases (Adcock and Collier 2001: 535–36). Adcock and Collier cite the example of Nie, Powell, and Prewitt (1969), who in a five-country analysis of political participation find that the attribute of membership in a political party is present in four cases, but that it does not have the same form or meaning in the US case, resulting in their use of a different measure of the attribute in the United States, captured by assessing involvement in a US electoral campaign instead of actual party membership. If we choose to do this, a clear justification is required when describing the measurement procedure.

Another validation technique is to evaluate a measure in relation to what would be found with another measurement instrument—termed *convergent validation* in the literature (Adcock and Collier 2001: 540). Here two (or more) different measures of the same defined concept are compared, assessing whether their placements of cases as members of a set of a concept converge (Kaplan 1964: 203). Returning to the BLM article, the authors utilize convergent validation to demonstrate that their measurement procedure results in a more accurate representation of the empirical evidence. Comparing their measure to that of Mainwaring, Brinks, and Pérez-Liñán (MBP) (2001) for particular years in Costa Rica, they write, "Comparing discrepant years between BLM and MBP, however, reveals some obvious and some not-so-obvious coding errors. For example, MBP code Costa Rica semi democratic from 1945 to 1948 and fully democratic from 1949 to 1999. . . . [A]rchival research and other primary source research establish that electoral fraud, political violence, political persecution, and restrictions were much higher from 1953 to 1958" (2005: 960). Thus they assert that their measure is a more valid measure of democracy than the competing MBP measure.

Comparisons between measures can start by cataloging how the existing literature has operationalized the relevant attribute, after which this can be compared with the measure developed in your research. How does your measure compare? What is the level of agreement between observables in your measure and existing measures? Could you incorporate elements from existing measures to capture even better the causally relevant aspects of at-tributes? If not, you need to provide justifications for why you believe your measure better captures what you intend to measure. Examples of this form of comparison can be found in Munck and Verkuilen (2002: 28), Bowman and colleagues (2005: 959–61), and Skaaning, Gerring, and Bartusevičius (2015). The Bowman and colleagues' example focuses on convergent vali-dation by comparing the correlation in actual case scores of their measure with an existing data set. In contrast, the Munck and Verkuilen piece comes closest to the procedures we recommend, although their discussion focuses on relatively ill-defined "strengths" and "weaknesses" of alternative measures instead of being focused more explicitly on evaluating how well a measure in relative terms captures the causal structure and semantic meaning of the same causal attribute.

Returning to the example of inclusive political participation, if we had chosen a further specified version of the measure "no major group excluded," we would want to compare it to existing measures of political participation to see whether they better captured the causal structure and semantic mean-ing of the causal concept. For the sake of example we limit this search to two existing measures: the Polity IV measure (Marshall and Jaggers 2001) and the V-DEM measure of political participation (Coppedge et al. 2014). We illustrate this comparison in table 5.2, where we find that the Polity IV measure does not validly capture empirically what we want to measure, whereas the V-DEM and the "no major groups excluded" measures have relative strengths and weaknesses relative to each other.

However, there are several problems with utilizing convergent validation in case-based research. First, the measures of causal concepts in case-based research are typically defined in contextually sensitive ways, making them not readily comparable with variance-based measures designed to measure much larger numbers of cases. It is naturally not surprising that a contex-tually specific measure of democracy outperforms a global measure when applied. Second, comparing a case-based, contextually specific measure with an existing variance-based measure can also be problematic, given that meaningfully comparing degree differences with kind differences is difficult. Here recent trends like the V-DEM project—at the core based on categori-cal distinctions that are then aggregated into higher-scale measures of dif-ferent attributes of democracy—make it easier to compare case-based and variance-based measures (Coppedge 2014).

The third validation form is arguably the least relevant for case-based re-search. Adcock and Collier (2001) define construct validation as a procedure that assesses how a measure performs in relation to a well-established causal

TABLE 5.2. A template for comparing the content validity of different measures of inclusive political electoral participation

Observable	Vague terms?	Match underlying causal structure?	Captures the semantic meaning of attribute?
Chosen measure: • "No major group excluded from franchise"	Vague—terms "major group" and "exclusion" need to be further specified.	Yes, but it depends on how measure further specified.	Clearly captures meaning of attribute.
Polity IV measure of political participation: • Competitiveness of Participation measured using an ordinal scale ranging from: (1) Repressed (no significant oppositional activity is permitted outside the ranks of the regime and ruling party) (2) Suppressed (substantial groups representing more than 20% of the population excluded) (3) Factional (polities with parochial or ethnic-based political factions that regularly compete for political influence in order to promote particularist agendas and favor group members to the detriment of common, secular, or cross-cutting agendas (4) Transitional (transitional arrangement from restricted, suppressed, or factional patterns to fully competitive patterns, or vice versa) (5) Competitive (relatively stable and enduring, secular political groups which regularly compete for political influence at the national level; ruling groups and coalitions regularly, voluntarily transfer central power to competing groups. Competition among groups seldom involves coercion or disruption. Small parties or political groups may be restricted in the competitive pattern)	Not very clear terms. For example, what is significant oppositional activity or a particularist agenda?	Arbitrary thresholds set (e.g. more than 20%) that do not necessarily match underlying causal structure. More problematic is the causal heterogeneity in the ordinal scale. In particular, scores 3 and 4 will have very different causal effects than scores 1–2 and 5, suggesting there actually are two overall qualitative thresholds (between 1–2/5 that excludes 3–4, and between 3–4 and the other values)	Does not capture meaning of concept because it only focuses on political groups, not on the ability of citizens to vote. Distinction between scores 1–2 and 5 captures the meaning of inclusive political participation, values 3 and 4 have little to do with the causal effects of inclusive political participation, but instead map onto different theories about different forms of cleavages and their impact on democratic stability

TABLE 5.2. A template for comparing the content validity of different measures of inclusive political electoral participation (*continued*)

Observable	Vague terms?	Match underlying causal structure?	Captures the semantic meaning of attribute?
V-DEM measure of political participation: • Are there suffrage restrictions, referring to conditions such as literacy, land ownership, fortune, income, or tax payment, that constrain the political participation (voting in national elections) of the poor? (yes or no)	Generally it is clear what is meant by the terms, although key terms such as "the poor" could be specified, along with indications of how large the restrictions have to be to count.	Yes if dealing with impact of suffrage restrictions for disadvantaged groups.	Potential problem that the measure reflects legal (de jure) restrictions and thereby not all restrictions that may be operative in practice (de facto).

hypothesis that we are confident about. In other words, we know that we should find evidence of a relationship between C and O based on existing research. If our new measure of C does not relate to an existing measure of O in a case, because we already know there is a relationship between C and O, we would conclude that our new measure did not perform very well and should be revised. Adcock and Collier discuss Lijphart's (1996) study of democracy in India, validating his measure of consociational democracy in the Indian case by showing that a number of factors that have been shown in previous research to be associated with consociational democracy are present (2001: 542). He claims his classification of India as a consociational democracy is validated because it is consistent with well-established causal relationships.

We are more skeptical about the utility of construct validation in case-based research, with the exception of using it to establish equivalence of different observables for the same defined concept in different cases. The reason we are engaging in case-based research is typically dissatisfaction with the existing evidence of the difference-making of causal relationships derived from large-N, variance-based research, especially if it is based on observational data. We choose to expend the considerable analytical resources necessary to produce valid case studies because we want to improve our knowledge about specific causal relationships beyond existing covariational-based claims by engaging in detailed within-case tracing of mechanisms, resulting in the production of mechanistic evidence. But we cannot utilize construct validation if existing research has studied difference-making across cases when what we intend to focus on is mechanistic evidence of causal processes operating within cases.

Concluding, validation of our measurement procedures is a helpful tool for refining our measures and increasing our confidence in the overall accuracy of the measure, other things equal. In particular, content and convergent validation are useful tools but have to be applied in ways that are consistent with case-based research and the types of causal claims we are assessing. The most useful tool for validation in case-based research is the use of "ideal-typical" cases that have to be members of the set for the measurement to be meaningful.

Step 5—Categorizing Actual Cases as Members of the Concept

We now turn to the task of assessing whether particular cases are members of defined concepts, evaluating both the content of the found evidence of the existence of the observable manifestations of the defined concepts and the degree of confidence we can hold in our actual measures of case membership being accurate.

If we possess only ambiguous evidence of a given case being a member of the concept, we should exclude a case from analysis. But categorizing particular cases as members of causal concepts is a difficult task because it involves (1) deploying as much empirical evidence as possible, (2) interpreting on the basis of extensive case-specific knowledge what empirical measures of the concept mean in the given context, (3) providing clear justifications for how confident we can be in membership categorizations for the particular case based on the strength of the documentary evidence, and (4) meticulously documenting one's sources and analysis of them in a transparent fashion, preferably in an online appendix. And even with the most systematic application, there will always be some residual uncertainty in the categorization of all but the most ideal-typical cases. It is therefore important to recognize that measurement is a never-ending process of continual updating of our knowledge of case membership or nonmembership. At the same time, case-based researchers need to aspire to the degree of transparency and systematic documentation found in the best quantitative data sets (Bowman, Lehoucq, and Mahoney 2005; Moravcsik 2014a). The following briefly discusses each of the four tasks in categorizing particular cases.

First, categorization is easier in a data-rich environment. However, the Bayesian framework suggests that more is not always better (see chapter 6). One piece of evidence that we can document as relatively accurate has more inferential weight than a slew of pieces of questionable accuracy. More pieces of evidence are particularly useful as a way of adjudicating between sources with competing interpretations, such as when determining whether nongovernmental international human rights organizations or governmental authorities should be trusted regarding the respect of political rights in a country.

Second, the "facts" do not speak for themselves. Instead, we need to assess the content of particular sources, interpreting them in context. Deployment of extensive contextual knowledge is therefore important for understanding what sources mean in the context of a particular case. Bowman, Lehoucq, and Mahoney (2005), for example, claim that many Central American countries are miscategorized because analysts did not have the requisite case knowledge to interpret sources correctly.

Third, we need to evaluate in a transparent and systematic fashion whether we can trust particular sources of evidence for categorizing cases membership. To do so, we ask source-critical questions for each source of evidence (see chapter 6). We can understand this as providing "uncertainty estimates" of membership of particular cases in the set of the concept (Verkuilen 2005: 483–84), or in Bayesian terms, the degree of confidence we can have in each piece of evidence being accurate that can be thought of as the size of the circles in figure 5.3. The degree of confidence that can be documented determines the confidence we can have in the case membership of each case when engaging in cross-case comparative tests (see chapters 6 and 7).

Finally, professional scientific norms dictate that we should aspire to record our sources of information for measures in a systematic and transparent fashion (Schedler 2012; Lupia and Elman 2014). It is therefore not enough to write, "Some of the more important primary and secondary sources used to generate these codes are available as country bibliographies at the same Web site" (Bowman, Lehoucq, and Mahoney 2005: 956). Here we have no way to evaluate the sources of the claims made about categorization of particular cases.

To make the process of categorizing particular cases systematic and transparent, we need to document the following using procedures adapted from the steps suggested by Moravcsik (2014b: 671). First, we can include an excerpt from the source itself (fifty to one hundred words long). Second, we need to discuss the content of the source and what it means in context, documenting why the source is claimed as evidence upon which a descriptive inference about case membership is based. Third, the degree of accuracy of the source should be evaluated openly (e.g., showing that it has been cross-checked with other trusted sources). Finally, if necessary a full-source citation can be included, and if possible a link to or scan of the full source to enable other scholars to evaluate your interpretation of the source and to utilize the information as a source of evidence for other research. The procedure is depicted in table 5.3.

5.6. Concluding Guidelines for Measurement of Causal Concepts

This chapter has discussed how to operationalize and measure causal concepts in a manner that is compatible with the underlying ontological assumptions of case-based research. We summarize in the following the core takeaway ideas for conceptualization and operationalization.

Defining the Observables of Causal Concepts

In contrast to variance-based designs, measurement in case-based research attempts to capture the causal essence of concepts, focusing in particular on

TABLE 5.3. Documentation table for categorization of particular cases (template)

Case 1—Case categorized as "democratic" based on following sources:	
Source 1	• Excerpt from source • What does source tell us? What is it evidence of? • Can we trust it? Degree of measurement accuracy • Full-source citation (if needed)
Source 2	• Excerpt from source • What does source tell us? What is it evidence of? • Can we trust it? Degree of measurement accuracy • Full-source citation (if needed)

crucial differences of kind that demarcate cases where a given causal relationship can be present from those where it is not possible. Finally, we suggest that there will always be some degree of empirical uncertainty about the placement of the qualitative threshold, meaning that there will be some gray-zone cases that we are unsure are cases where a given causal relationship can be present or not. We suggest that when selecting cases (see chapters 7–9), one avoids the empirically ambiguous cases, at least until one is quite confident about causal relations within the cases that are definitely a member of the set of the concept.

The chapter then developed the following five step procedure for developing a measure of a causal attribute:

1. Engage in a creative brainstorm for potential observable manifestations, describing as many potential empirical fingerprints it could leave as possible.
2. Evaluate the pros and cons of different measures, choosing the observable manifestation that you believe best captures the causally relevant aspects of the concept.

TABLE 5.4. Template for evaluating observable manifestations of causal concepts

Proposed observable	Vague terms?	Match underlying causal structure?	Captures the semantic meaning of attribute?	Are the sources of data clearly described?
Clear description of proposed observable and what theoretical attribute it is measuring	• Evaluation here	• Evaluation here	• Does it capture meaning?	• Degree to which it is specified

3. If working with multiattribute concepts, compile the manifestations of each attribute and develop the relationship between them in a way that is consistent with the underlying concept structure.
4. Validate the chosen measure.
5. Use the measure to categorize actual cases.

In relation to initially validating the measure in step 2, we suggested the template described in table 5.4 to evaluate each proposed observable manifestation in a transparent fashion. These can be helpfully included in an appendix (in print or online) in one's research.

CHAPTER 6

Making Inferences in Case-Based Research

Having gathered these facts, Watson, I smoked several pipes over
them, trying to separate those which were crucial from others which
were merely incidental.

Sherlock Holmes, *The Crooked Man*

6.1. Introduction

This chapter presents a Bayesian-inspired inferential framework for how we
can make causal inferences using empirical evidence in case-based research.
Instead of a one-size-fits-all approach, where frequentist inferential logic is
coupled with difference-making evidence of cross-case variation in values of
X and Y and that is then viewed as the *only* way to make causal inferences
(e.g., King, Keohane, and Verba 1994 [KKV]; Gerring 2005), this chapter
develops a framework where the types of evidence that are relevant for making inferences match the underlying assumptions about the nature of the
causal relationships being investigated.

Our framework uses Bayesian logic in an informal fashion, acting as the
logical foundations for the questions we need to ask of empirical material in
order to transform it into evidence of causal relationships. Our nonquanti-
fied, folk Bayesian framework stands in contrast to recent attempts to quantify and formalize its use in case-based research (Bennett 2014; Humphreys
and Jacobs 2015; Charman and Fairfield 2015).[1] In our view, the informal
use of Bayesian logic enables scholars to focus on what matters most in
case studies—learning about how a causal relationship works (or does not
work) by understanding what particular pieces of empirical material mean
in the context of a particular case, or what an invariant distribution of cases
means within a bounded population. Instead of unnecessarily complicated

techniques that divert attention away from this contextual interpretation, we develop a set of straightforward guidelines that analysts can use to ask the right questions when assessing what their collected empirical material can act as evidence of in a given context, thus enabling them to interrogate their empirical material in a more robust and transparent fashion, which results in the production of stronger confirming or disconfirming causal inferences.

The existing case-based literature has made great strides in answering the question of how the types of empirical material we use in case studies differ from those used in large-N, variance-based designs, but despite these advances we still lack a comprehensive answer to the *how* question; that is, how can we convert raw empirical material into evidence upon which causal inferences can be made using case studies (Elman and Kapiszewski 2014; Moravcsik 2014a, 2014b)? The result is that case study researchers often go where no historian would dare to tread, making strong inferences based on weak empirical evidence because they have not engaged in a robust and transparent assessment of what empirical material actually is evidence of (Moravcsik 2010, 2014a, 2014b). This chapter therefore provides a comprehensive, step-by-step guide for how we can translate empirical material into evidence upon which causal inferences can be made in case-based research.

The chapter proceeds in the following steps. We start by distinguishing between two overall categories of evidence that can be used to make causal inferences: difference-making and mechanistic evidence. The chapter then develops why the existing methodological literature on inferential logics in case studies is inadequate, focusing on (1) the frequentist framework for making inferences in case studies developed by KKV (1994) and (2) the guidelines that were developed by qualitative scholars in reaction to KKV's pronouncements, in particular the widespread term "causal process observations" (CPOs). We argue first that KKV's guidelines send us down the wrong path, where we attempt to design quasi experiments using evidence of difference-making when what we should be focusing on is designing our case studies so we can focus on within-case, mechanistic evidence. While the introduction of the term *CPOs* was an improvement that brought us closer to a clear focus on mechanistic, within-case evidence, the existing non-Bayesian methodological case study literature tells us little about how we can make inferences using evidence; indeed, it cannot even answer the question, "How do I know a CPO when I see it?"

The chapter then presents the core elements of informal Bayesian logic that form the inferential underpinnings of how we can make within-case and cross-case inferences about causal relationships using evidence of either mechanisms or difference-making. It is important to note that this logic has been widely utilized as the logical underpinning for making evidence-based inferences in fields such as law and intelligence analysis, both fields in which inferences are not made by utilizing experiments or assessing patterns of covariation between variables (e.g., Good 1991; Walker 2007; Paté-Cornell 2002; McGrayne 2011). Instead, inferences within cases are made by updating our confidence in theories based upon the correspondence between the mechanistic evidence our theories predict and what we actually find.

We present our Bayesian framework for case-based research in four steps, focusing on (1) the importance of prior confidence in theories, (2) the theoretical evaluation of what might be evidence and what it hypothetically can tell us about a causal relationship, (3) the empirical assessment of the evidence we actually found (or did not find) and the probability that we can trust it, and (4) the evaluation of the collective body of evidence in order to determine our posterior confidence in a hypothesis based on the new gathered evidence.

While we build upon recent advances in the literature on Bayesian logic in case studies,[2] Van Evera's test types,[3] and CPOs,[4] we go further in four respects. First, we develop guidelines that are compatible with both theory-first and empirics-first case studies, whereas existing guidelines are applicable only for theory-first applications. Second, as the existing literature on CPOs is unclear about which types of empirical material can actually act as within-case evidence, we systematize what the potential empirical fingerprints of theories by differentiating mechanistic evidence into four different types: pattern, sequence, trace, and account evidence.

Third, while existing Bayesian-inspired frameworks only discuss the relation between theory and empirical "tests," we show that there are actually two distinct steps when evaluating what empirical material can actually be evidence of. These two steps are (1) the logical link between a causal hypothesis and observable empirical fingerprints in the abstract that tell us what causal inferences are possible upon finding or not finding the observables, and (2) the link between propositions that describe potential evidence in the abstract and actual pieces of empirical material that might be measuring the proposition. In the step between theory and propositions we have to evaluate the theoretical certainty and/or uniqueness of the proposition in relation to the causal hypothesis, whereas in the latter step we evaluate whether a given piece of empirical evidence actually matches the proposition about observables and whether we can trust the found evidence.

Finally, existing treatments of Bayesian logic have focused on the probative value of individual pieces of evidence. What is missing in existing treatments of Bayesian logic in case study research is how we go from *indi-*

vidual pieces of evidence to conclusions about whether the *collective body* of evidence points in a transparent fashion toward a causal relationship being present or not in a given case.

Unfortunately, there are no simple formulas for evaluating what raw empirical data can potentially be evidence of. Instead, making evidence-based inferences in case-based research requires (1) the mapping of the structure of the argument in relation to a given causal hypothesis and developing predictions about the evidence the relationship should leave in the form of proposition and supporting propositions about evidence, resulting in a road map of the structure of the arguments about the relations between empirical material and the underlying causal relationship being assessed, enabling the identification of what evidence supports which parts of the argument; (2) the careful deployment of case-specific expertise to interpret what empirical material means in a given context to determine whether the material is evidence that confirms or disconfirms to some degree a given proposition or supporting proposition (certainty and uniqueness); (3) the careful assessment of whether we can trust found evidence for each proposition or supporting proposition by engaging in thorough evaluations of potential sources of measurement error and by attempting to increase our confidence in measurement accuracy by corroborating with other sources; and (4) the aggregation of evidence through the use of the argument road map and the relationship of individual pieces of evidence to the structure of the argument.

Evaluating and Aggregating Mechanistic Evidence Happens Every Day in Courts

The process of evaluating and aggregating evidence in social science case studies can be meaningfully compared to how evidence is admitted and evaluated in relation to causal theories about the relation between a suspect and a crime in criminal courts of law.[5] In both of these, we do not engage in experiments or quasi experiments, nor do we utilize cross-case variation of values of X and Y to make inferences in a case. Instead, inferences about causal relationships *within* a single case are possible because we evaluate what the collected body of mechanistic evidence tells us about the veracity of a causal hypothesis that explains the case at hand.

In a court proceeding, prosecutors and defenders together put forward competing theories about the crime and propositions that explain why empirical material is evidence of their theory. Before empirical material can be used as evidence the judge and/or jury must evaluate the material put forward by the prosecution and defense by (1) evaluating the structure of the arguments put forward by the prosecution and defense and the postulated relations with evidence for each proposition and/or supporting proposition, (2) deciding whether the particular piece of empirical material can act as evidence in favor of a proposition or supporting proposition, (3) evaluating whether the court can trust the found evidence or not, and (4) deciding how the individual pieces of evidence fit together to produce a body of evidence based on the structure of the argument put forward. Taken together, the judge and/or jury then decides, on the basis of the material presented and interpreted by the defense and prosecutor and his or her evaluation of the material, whether the collected body of evidence admitted points in the direction of guilt or innocence (Good 1991; Walker 2007).

This means that a prosecutor cannot just show up in court with a gun and postulate that it is a smoking gun that proves that the suspect is guilty. The so-called smoking gun is, by itself, only a piece of metal that does not enable us to assess whether the suspect committed the murder. Several things need to occur before the smoking gun can be admitted by the judge as evidence of the suspect having committed the crime using the gun (the theory being tested). First, a plausible proposition has to be developed in which the postulated smoking gun is situated as potentially relevant evidence of the crime. If it is claimed that the suspect killed her husband using the gun, what data-generating process would link the found gun at the scene of the crime with the suspect? That is, what types of empirical fingerprints might the theory leave in the case? Here we would actually need to disaggregate the proposition "smoking gun" into multiple supporting propositions, for example, "the found gun was the same as that used to kill the victim," and "the suspect used the gun." The proposition that a smoking gun links the suspect to the murder is therefore actually a set of propositions, each of which then needs to be assessed empirically. For each of these supporting propositions there might be multiple sources of evidence—some more trustworthy than others. Forensic material like autopsy reports and ballistic tests would be expected to be relatively accurate unless the defense can substantiate that major procedural errors took place. More problematic would be sources like eyewitness accounts placing the suspect at the scene of the crime, especially if the source has potential motives for not telling the truth (e.g., if the source is the daughter of the victim). Notice that evaluating evidence for its probative value in relation to a causal hypothesis has a two-step structure. In a theory-first analysis, the causal hypothesis is first operationalized in the form of predictions about evidence that the relationship should leave. We refer to these predictions about observables as propositions. Propositions about evidence need to describe clearly both what observables are expected to be found and why the observables could in theory be evidence of the causal hypothesis being assessed. Second, actual evidence is then sought for each proposition and evaluated for whether it actually is what we predicted to find and whether we can trust it. In an empirics-first analysis, these steps are reversed.

And even if each of the individual pieces of evidence has probative value and can be trusted, the aggregation of evidence into a collective is not a simple task. Here the legal analogy of a scale is particularly useful, providing a nice heuristic for concluding whether the body of evidence points toward confirmation or disconfirmation. Here the structure of the argument has to be followed when aggregating. When multilevel propositions are put forward, we move from individual pieces of evidence for each supporting proposition to overall propositions in a stepwise fashion. When there are contradictory pieces of evidence (some disconfirmatory, some confirmatory), they are summed together in relation to the direction they point and the weight of the individual pieces for each supporting proposition and then proposition. In using the road map and clear justifications for the relationship between evidence and propositions at each level of the argument, it becomes possible to aggregate evidence in a more systematic fashion. In closing arguments of court trials the prosecution (and defense) do actually put forward their argument road maps of propositions, supporting propositions, and the evidence supporting each proposition, enabling the judge and/or jury to evaluate the direction in which the collective body of evidence points. We suggest that we can use similar road maps to make the aggregation of evidence in social science case studies more transparent and systematic.

6.2. Two Categories of Evidence: Difference-Making and Mechanistic

Strong causal inferences in the social sciences are possible only when we engage in the actual manipulation of causes using experimental methods (Morton and Williams 2010) or through the detailed within-case tracing of causal mechanisms using congruence or process-tracing methods (George and Bennett 2005; Beach and Pedersen 2013; Rohlfing 2012; Bennett and Checkel 2014). Experiments enable causal inference because they provide empirical evidence in the form of what can be referred to as difference-making evidence, which shows that differences in values of X produce differences in values of Y across a set of comparable cases, where all other potential causes of differences are kept constant. In within-case research that traces mechanisms (congruence or process-tracing), mechanistic evidence is utilized, where the empirical fingerprints of hypothesized causal mechanisms are assessed using an in-depth within-case analysis to shed light on unobserved, underlying causal processes operating in the chosen case.[6]

While there is considerable debate relating to whether evidence-based causal explanations require both types of evidence (e.g., Russo and Williamson 2007; Illari 2011; Groff 2011), this question is a more philosophical one that does not concern us here. Instead, what is important here are the implications of the philosophical claim that confirmatory causal inferences are possible only when using either mechanistic evidence gained through in-depth within-case analysis or difference-making evidence from experiments.

This means that when using variance-based methods, we are really only able to make claims about correlations unless we use experimentally manipulated data. This has the implication that when using case-based methods that use evidence of difference-making, like classic Millian comparison, small-N most similar or most different systems designs, and qualitative comparative analysis (QCA), we are only assessing correlations, with the exception that when deterministic hypotheses about necessity and/or sufficiency are tested empirically, we can disconfirm the relationship if we find exceptions to the expected empirical distribution of cases (see section 6.6, also chapter 7). This means that in case-based research we are heavily dependent on mechanistic evidence to make confirming causal inferences.

The key difference between the two types of evidence that is relevant for the argument in this book is that difference-making evidence requires cross-case comparison of values of X and Y, whereas mechanistic evidence involves tracing actually operating causal processes at the level at which they occur—that is, within individual cases. The two types of evidence are depicted in figure 6.1, where the circles illustrate that what we are empirically assessing with evidence of difference-making are values of X and Y across cases, whereas mechanistic evidence focuses on what is actually happening in between the occurrence of a cause and an outcome within a case.

Mechanistic evidence is empirical material that sheds light on actual causal processes operating in a particular case. What we want to capture empirically are the activities that entities are engaging in that transmit causal forces from one part of a causal mechanism to the next (Waskan 2008, 2011; Illari and Williamson 2011; Machamer 2004).

When discussing within-case versus cross-case evidence, it is important to be clear about what a "case" actually is. As discussed in chapter 2, a case is an instance of a causal process (i.e., mechanism) playing out, linking a cause

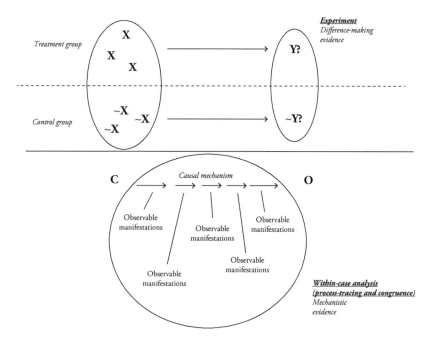

Fig. 6.1. Difference-making evidence versus mechanistic evidence

(or set of causes) with an outcome. How we define a case in terms of temporal and spatial scope and unit of analysis is contingent upon the theoretical claim we are making. The scope of a case determines the bounds of what one is making a causal inference about and the bounds within which empirical material can act as relevant evidence. The crucial distinction to draw is between the level at which the causal relationship operates (a single case) and the population of cases in which similar causal processes are assumed to be operative. The population of cases is then the sum total of all comparable individual cases in which the causal theory plays out in a similar fashion.

6.3. Problems with Existing Inferential Frameworks in Case Study Research

This section first discusses the problems of applying the covariational approach to making within-case inferences, focusing on KKV's 1994 guidelines. We then discuss problems with the existing literature on CPOs, showing that the literature does not tell us what CPOs actually are or the inferential logic that enables us to use them as evidence of causal processes.

Why Difference-Making Is Not Relevant Evidence for Within-Case Causal Claims

Variance-based methodologists have put forward guidelines for case study research that are more or less the same for making inferences in large-N research using difference-making evidence. Gerring, for instance, states categorically, "Empirical evidence of causal relationships is covariational in nature" (2005: 187). KKV speak of assessing the mean effect of causes based on evidence of covariation between values of X and Y across a range of cases, attempting to assess whether increases or decreases in values of X have a measurable effect on values of Y (1994: 129). They state that unless we have difference-making evidence in the form of variation of values of variables, no inferences can be made. They famously write, "Nothing whatsoever can be learned about the causes of the dependent variable *without taking into account other instances* when the dependent variable takes on other values" (1994: 129, italics added).

But how can we then achieve meaningful variation when we are studying a *single* case? KKV recommend that we never study a single case, but instead transform "one-into-many" cases (1994: 217–28). They suggest several different options[7] for disaggregating cases,[8] including splitting a case up into its subunits or temporally. For example, one can split a case temporally by studying a single negotiation as a series of phases (t_0 = prenegotiation, t_1 = agenda-setting, t_2 = bargaining phase, and t_3 = negotiation end game), or one can split the single negotiation into subissues. In both, we transform the single case into a set of cases that can be potentially compared to detect patterns of cross-case variation.

The most fundamental problem with the recommendation to transform one case into many is that we move away from the level at which causal relationships play out. When studying mechanisms using within-case studies, we use mechanistic evidence that is produced by tracing how a given causal process plays out in a particular case. However, if we transformed the case from one to many, we would no longer have evidence at the same unit level as the causal relationship is theorized to operate. For example, if we are studying group dynamics, disaggregation into individuals would move the focus of the research away from the very level at which the causal relationship is theorized to play out, producing "cross-case" evidence of difference-making among individuals that does not match the level of the causal relationship we were intending to study.

Additionally, meaningful comparison across cases requires that they are causally similar (unit homogeneity) and that they are independent of each other (King, Keohane, and Verba 1994: 91–95).[9] Yet almost any one-into-many transformation of cases (1) will result in a set of cases that are not causally similar (e.g., dynamics early in a negotiation are different from in the end game), and (2) there will also be serious violations of case independence where values of X in one case will be affected by values of Y in preceding "cases" (also termed "endogeneity"). For example, in a negotiation what happens at the start (t_0) naturally affects events later in the negotiation, meaning that values of Y in case t_0 will influence values of X in subsequent cases (periods of the negotiation). If the negotiation is disaggregated into issues, we should expect that deals or deadlock with respect to one issue will affect what is going on in other important issues, especially in a setting where package deals are typical forms of resolving negotiations. Therefore, given that within-case variation cannot be created unless we split cases up into nonindependent and causally heterogeneous subcases, we contend that transforming one case into many results in so many sources of error that our "within-case" findings will be vastly inferior to large-N analyses of cross-case variation and/or studies that use experiments, where the requirements for using difference-making evidence to make inferences hold.

Interestingly, KKV actually admit that this is a problem, concluding, "When dealing with partially dependent observations, we should be careful not to overstate the certainty of the conclusions" (1994: 222). We suggest that it might have been more productive for them to develop methodological tools that are appropriate for case-based research instead of importing variance-based ideas of assessing difference-making that result in a set of guidelines in which case studies are always inferior to large-N comparative research or experiments. We expand on in the following, we can utilize a different type of empirical evidence in case-based research to make causal inferences: mechanistic evidence, which is the evidence left by a causal process in a given case (George and Bennett 2005; Collier 2011; Rohlfing 2012; Beach and Pedersen 2013).

Why CPOs Are Not the Solution

Many case study methodologists have accepted the claim that evidence in case-based research is different than KKV's suggested difference-making evidence. Collier, Brady, and Seawright (2010: 184–88) introduced a helpful distinction between the forms of evidence used in variance-based and case-based designs. In variance-based designs, the ambition is to gather cross-case evidence of differences in values of X and Y in the form of data-set observations (DSOs), enabling the assessment of mean causal effects of causes across cases. This is equivalent to the phrase "difference-making evidence" as used in this book.

In contrast, Collier, Brady, and Seawright suggest that in most qualitative research another type of empirical material is gathered: causal process observations (CPOs). These are defined as "an insight or piece of data that provides information about the context or mechanism and contributes a different kind of leverage in causal inference. It does not necessarily do so as part of a larger, systematized array of observations. . . . [A] causal-process observation may be like a 'smoking gun.' It gives insight into causal mechanisms, insight that is essential to causal assessment and is an indispensable alternative and/or supplement to correlation-based causal inference" (2010: 184–85).

Yet there is little guidance in the literature on CPOs for which types of empirical material can act as relevant evidence, and for how a CPO enables an inference to be made. In response to this Nathaniel Beck has critiqued the term "CPOs" as vacuous, stating, "I do not know what it means to directly observe a causal process or how I know when a researcher observes such a process" (2006: 350). He contends that the term does not tell us anything about how we make inferences in research situations where variation across cases is irrelevant (Beck 2010: 500). Here we basically agree with Beck, and we do not believe that case study methodologists have satisfactorily answered Beck's critical question: What exactly does a CPO look like? And more important, how do CPOs enable causal inferences to be made in case studies? We expand on these two problems now. The rest of the chapter then attempts to provide answers to Beck's critique, providing scholars with a framework for asking the right questions when interpreting which inferences mechanistic, within-case evidence can enable in a fashion that lives up to developing standards for transparency in qualitative research (see Moravcsik 2014b).

How Do I Know a CPO When I See It?

First, which type or types of empirical material can act as CPOs in case studies? The first work on CPOs was vague, basically positing that anything can potentially act as a CPO, but it did not offer any answer to the question of how CPOs enable inferences to be made (see Brady and Collier 2004). Subsequent work has attempted to define in more detail what CPOs are, but then defined them in a very narrow fashion, often closely linked to the types of theories they work with.

Mahoney, for instance, describes CPOs as "diagnostic pieces of evidence—usually understood as part of a temporal sequence of events—that have probative value in supporting or overturning conclusions" (2012: 571). Collier describes CPOs as "diagnostic pieces of evidence—often understood as a part of a temporal sequence of events or phenomena" (2011: 824). Blatter and Haverland define CPOs as "a cluster of information that is used (a) to determine the temporal order in which causal factors work together to produce the outcome of interest, (b) to determine the status of these causal factors as individually necessary and jointly sufficient for the outcomes in the cases under investigation, and/or (c) to identify and to specify the social mechanisms that form the basis for mechanism-based explanations" (2012: 23).[10] Later in their book they discuss CPOs in more detail, stating that they can be "information that allows for plotting the historical development of structural factors, such as economic growth, strength of interest groups," but also "information that reveals the perceptions and motivations of individual, collective, or corporate actors" (2012: 106). They conclude, "When the empirical bits and pieces form a coherent picture, they can provide a high level of certainty that a causal-process has occurred as described. . . . Crucially important for 'dense' descriptions are 'smoking guns'—core observations within a coherent cluster of observations that closely link cause and effect in time and space. 'Deeper' insights into the perceptions, motivations, and anticipations of important actors in crucial moments are gained through 'observations' that we call 'confessionals'" (Blatter and Haverland 2012: 110).

However, why should within-case evidence just be in the form of temporal sequences or confessionals from participants? For instance, confessionals have serious problems as sources of evidence, especially for the type of sensitive political events that many social scientists study. Temporal sequences can of course be a relevant form of evidence, but their probative weight depends on which type of theory is being evaluated. And as we develop later, there are other types of relevant evidence for making causal inferences in case-based research.

One reason for the narrow definitions of CPOs is that many methodologists have linked their definitions to particular theoretical positions. For instance, Blatter and Haverland link their understanding of CPOs and the role they play in process-tracing to particular theoretical positions about the importance of time: "The new interest in case study methodology and especially in CPT [causal process tracing] has been triggered by theoretical developments in which temporality plays a major role" (2012: 110). Yet while temporal sequences might be relevant for assessing historical institutionalist theories (e.g., Pierson 2004), where temporality plays a key role, there are many other types of theories where temporality plays less of a role, if any. Should these theories that do not put emphasis on temporal factors then be evaluated empirically using sequences of events as evidence? This would be like empirically assessing a theory of a crime by looking for empirical finger-prints that the theory is unlikely to leave in the case.

As we develop later in this chapter, relevant mechanistic evidence for empirically assessing a theorized mechanism can take many forms in case study research; even statistical co-variation can be relevant evidence in cer-tain circumstances, although this would take a very different form than in variance-based designs, where it would be in the form of cross-case differ-ences in values of X and Y. In a case study, statistical information might inform our interpretation of what something means in a particular context, or it might be in the form of within-case evidence like whether there differ-ences in the lengths of the policy briefs possessed by different types of actors. But privileging particular types of empirical material over others results in methods that are biased toward (or against) particular theories.

In this book we prefer to use the term "mechanistic evidence" because it more clearly flags the link between empirical material and the type of causal relationship we are studying. Mechanistic evidence is similar to the evidence used in a court of law. In US evidence law there is a very helpful term—relevant evidence—which is an appropriate standard for defining which forms of empirical material can act as mechanistic evidence in case-based designs. In the Rule 401 of the Federal Rules of Evidence, relevant evidence is defined as "any evidence having any tendency to make the existence of any fact that is of consequence to the determination of the action more prob-able or less probable than it would be without evidence." This wide-ranging standard is therefore very appropriate for social science case studies, where we should not limit ourselves to searching for particular types of evidence, such as "sequences of events" (Mahoney 2012: 571) or "confessionals from participants" (Blatter and Haverland 2012). Instead, evidence can be *any* type of material that might be left by the workings of our theorized causal mechanisms that enables us to say something about whether the relationship was present or not in a case.

How Do CPOs Enable Inferences to Be Made?

The second problem with the term "CPOs" is that it masks what it is about mechanistic evidence that enables us to make causal inferences in case-based research. The result is the widespread practice in case studies of stating that

CPOs have been collected that provide evidence of a theory, but where the author does not discuss what a piece of evidence tells us in relation to the theory, or why we should trust the collected evidence. The scholar is implicitly saying, "Just trust me," which does not live up to emerging norms that state that scholars should make transparent how the empirical material is translated into evidence upon which inferences are made (Moravcsik 2014b).

In our framework, empirical material needs to be evaluated in a transparent fashion for (1) what it tells us in relation to a particular theoretical hypothesis and (2) whether we can trust it before it can be admitted as evidence. Unfortunately, the term *CPO* and the related methodological literature tells us little about *how* we should evaluate them to determine the inferential value of individual pieces of evidence.

In our reading, the key problem with the term *CPO* is that it conflates observations, understood as raw empirical material, with actual evidence upon which we can make inferences. An observation is a piece of empirical material collected from archival sources, interviews, newspapers, and the like. These observations first become evidence that we can use to make inferences only *after* being assessed in a transparent fashion for accuracy and interpreted for what they mean in their case specific context, assessing in particular what the material tells us in relation to a particular theoretical hypothesis.

Revealingly, when discussing how the researcher establishes that a given piece of evidence is "diagnostic," Collier writes, "Addressing this question raises issues about the logic of inquiry and the form of social scientific knowledge that are well beyond the scope of this discussion. Only a few basic points are addressed here that are salient for the accompanying exercises" (2010: 829n6).

One exception to this lack of focus on inferential logic in relation to CPOs might be Mahoney's (2012) work. However, his non-Bayesian foundations for how we can make inferences in case studies ends up depending on cross-case counterfactuals as evidence because he links empirical tests in case studies with comparative logics of inference suitable for assessing the necessity or sufficiency of conditions using difference-making evidence either by relying on cross-case patterns of covariation to eliminate conditions or through counterfactual reasoning, where the presence of a condition in a case is compared with a counterfactual "alternative universe" case where the condition is not present in order to evaluate whether it is logically necessary (for more on the two variants of comparative methods, see chapter 7).

For example, Mahoney describes a smoking-gun test as "identifying a mechanism that is necessary for the outcome. The analyst then determines whether the cause itself is necessary for this mechanism" (2012: 581). But what is doing the inferential heavy-lifting in enabling a claim that a cause is necessary for the mechanism in Mahoney's framework is *not* empirical material from the case itself, but whether there is *cross-case* evidence that enables us to either eliminate or substantiate the claim of a necessary relationship. The lack of any noticeable role for actual within-case empirical evidence in his framework is best illustrated in the appendix of his article, where he discusses how three classic works use empirical tests to make inferences. In the example of Downing, Mahoney claims that Downing's test involves claiming that a mechanism (M) that leads to the outcome (liberal democracy) is found to be necessary "using cross-case evidence" (Mahoney 2012: 592). This is followed by the claim that three causes (A, B, C) are each necessary for the M, substantiated by "the fact that A, B, and C are temporally proximate to M, such that it is easier to show that the counterfactual absence of any one of them would have eliminated M. Once [Downing] has persuaded us that A, B, and C are necessary for M, he then logically reasons that the three factors *must* also be necessary for Y, given that M is established to be necessary for Y" (Mahoney 2012: 592, italics in original). Note that within-case evidence, beyond the temporal sequence of occurrence of A, B, C, and M, is not utilized. Therefore, while logically clear, Mahoney's test types provide us only with a counterfactual-based framework based on evidence of difference-making, which we contend is not compatible with mechanism-based claims as developed in chapters 2 and 3.

In contrast, the recent incorporation of Bayesian logic into case study methodology has exposed the logical foundations for making non-variation-based inferences from mechanistic evidence (Rohlfing 2012; Beach and Pedersen 2013; Bennett 2008a, 2014). However, the existing literature has not developed a systematic framework for making inferences in case-based research in a transparent fashion, and in particular the existing literature has (1) neglected the use of Bayesian logic when making cross-case inferences using small-N comparative methods, (2) has focused only on theory-testing applications instead of discussing "empirics-first" research (where we attempt to interpret what found empirical material can tell us), (3) has not exposed that the evaluation of the probative value of actual empirical evidence has two steps (operationalization of predicted evidence in the form of propositions, and evaluation of what actual empirical material can act as evidence of in relation to the propositions), and (4) has overlooked the crucial role of measurement accuracy in Bayesian logic. We provide solutions to these deficiencies in our framework.

6.4. Informal Bayesian Logic and Case-Based Methods

At the core of Bayesian logic is the idea that science is about using new evidence to update our confidence in causal theories, either within a single case or across a bounded population.[11] Bayesians are intensely pragmatic about what type of empirical material can be used to make inferences, making the approach particularly well suited as a logical epistemological foundation for case-based research. Further, Bayesian empirical updating goes in both directions—confirmation and disconfirmation—which is a significant improvement on much existing Popper-inspired social science methodology, where falsification (disconfirmation) is claimed to be the only type of inference possible.

Before we turn to the presentation and discussion of the core elements of Bayesian logic, there are a few issues about how it can be applied to case-based research that have to be addressed in order to avoid misunderstandings.

As discussed in the previous sections, evidence in case-based research is either difference-making (cross-case) or mechanistic (within-case). In the latter, we are asking empirical questions such as, "Did we observe that a politician actually attempted to mobilize voters as our theory would predict?" This is a piece of evidence that contains *no* variation within a case because either it did or did not happen in any given case. However, this one piece of evidence (match or not match) still can enable inferences about causation. Making inferences using the correspondence between what we theoretically predict and what we actually find is how science is actually conducted in a large variety of fields where there is purely observational data with no meaningful variation present. For example, in 1975 the geologist Walter Alvarez found an unusually thick layer of ordinary-looking clay in rocks in the Apennine Mountains in Italy. From fossil records, he knew that the layer was dated to the time of a great extinction sixty-five million years ago. On further examination when testing whether the layer had been formed gradually or not, he found unusually high levels of iridium in the layer. After a theoretical evaluation of what this empirical finding could mean, he began to suspect that the found material might be evidence of a cataclysmic meteor impact, given that iridium does not naturally occur on Earth (Alvarez 2008). This preliminary evidence about a potential empirical fingerprint that can have been left by the operation of a part of a causal mechanism linking the meteor impact with dinosaur extinction—in which there is no variation present—encouraged a larger network of scholars to assess the causal relationship between a meteor impact and dinosaur extinction more systematically, which resulted after over a decade of research in a strong body of confirming evidence.

Another common point of misunderstanding arises when we utilize probabilistic language (Bayesianism) in case studies when making inferences based on empirical material while also claiming that case-based methods build on a deterministic ontological understanding of causation (see chapter 2). Yet confusion on this point typically arises because one does not distinguish between ontology and epistemology.

We claimed in chapter 2 that it is more analytically fruitful to talk about *deterministic ontology* as regards causal relationships at the case level because we can learn a lot by being wrong in a case. By putting forward deterministic claims that can be wrong in a case or small set of cases, we progressively refine our theories through repeated meetings with empirical reality. But at the same time, as discussed in chapter 2, our evidence-based knowledge about relationships in the real world will *always* be imperfect. Determinism at the ontological level does not logically imply that we can gain 100 percent certain empirical knowledge about why things occur. Bayesian logic is *epistemologically probabilistic*, where we can never absolutely confirm or disconfirm a theory because of the uncertainty of the empirical world, but instead we attach varying degrees of confidence in our theories based on the empirical evidence we find to confirm or disconfirm (Howson and Urbach 2006). We can never be 100 percent confident about any nontrivial causal relationship in the empirical world.

Epistemological probabilism does *not* mean that we cannot evaluate causal theories that are ontologically deterministic. It just means that there will always be a degree of uncertainty in our confidence in the inferences we make using empirical evidence. The useful of Bayesian logic is that this uncertainty is made explicit, giving us a language to express how confident we can be in a theory being valid based upon empirical evidence. In contrast, in the naive Popperian understanding widely used in political science, a theory is either "falsified" or not. Falsification here means that we are *100 percent confident* it is disconfirmed, which of course we never can be with nontrivial relationships because of the intrinsic messiness of empirical evidence. Even an empirical test like a DNA match is never 100 percent, especially when we have to interpret what finding a DNA match means in a particular context (for more, see section 6.7).

Therefore, when evaluating a deterministic claim empirically, when there is strong evidence suggesting that our theory does not hold in a case, we revise our theory. But we can naturally never be 100 percent confident that the theory did not hold; instead, we operate with degrees of confidence in a way similar to a court of law.

A final point of confusion is that the existing literature on test types in Bayesian terms focuses primarily on theory before empirics (e.g., Bennett 2014). Yet the reality of case study research is that the analyst usually has undertaken an empirical "soaking and probing" of the case *before* clear theoretical predictions of evidence are developed. In this exploration, scholars often find empirical material that they believe might be either confirming or disconfirming evidence of a given hypothesis. Yet in their published research they then present the material "as if" they had developed a test beforehand that was then employed on a case or set of cases, with the hypothesis, for instance, being confirmed because the predicted evidence was found in the case. However this "deductive myth" does not reflect how science is practiced in reality. Across science as a whole, many of the most interesting and important findings have not been the product of a preplanned theory test, but instead have been stumbled upon serendipitously. Yet just because we know what empirical material we will find before we evaluate the evidence does not mean we cannot use it as evidence to make inferences about theories.[12] Empirics-first research is also scientific in Bayesian logic. All that matters is that the evidence is new in relation to the existing body of knowledge, the empirical material gathered has a bearing on the merits of a theory *and* that we transparently evaluate what the found empirical material potentially can tell us in relation to the empirical record and whether we can trust what we found.

A Bayesian Framework for Making Inferences Using Evidence

Bayesian logic provides us with a set of logical tools for evaluating what finding particular pieces of evidence tells us about our theories. In Bayesian logic, empirical material acts as evidence that can either increase or decrease our confidence in a hypothesis being valid. Evidence in the form of difference-making enables cross-case inferences about causal relationships like necessity and/or sufficiency, whereas mechanistic evidence enables within-case inferences about causal mechanisms.

Updating our confidence in a hypothesis about a causal relationship being valid in a case or across a set of cases is a function of the following: (1) our prior confidence in a hypothesis, (2) the confirming or disconfirming power of a piece of empirical material as captured by the certainty and uniqueness of evidence when relating a proposition to a causal hypothesis (theoretical evaluation) and the relationship between a proposition about evidence and actual evidence (empirical evaluation) that together determine the probative value of evidence, and (3) our estimations of the probability of the accuracy of the evidence. After we have collected new evidence, we update our degree of confidence in the theory being valid, termed "posterior probability."

It is important to reiterate that we recommend the use of Bayesianism as an *informal* logic instead of its use more formally by estimating quantitative values for probabilities, as others have begun advocating (Bennett 2014; Humphreys and Jacobs 2013). There are several reasons not to assign numbers, in contrast to Bayesian statistical applications. First, if we want to quantify priors in relation to whether we should expect a causal relationship to hold in a particular case, our prior knowledge in a quantified form would typically be drawn from population-level variance-based research. Here, even if we ignore problems such as conflicting ontological foundations of the causal claims being made in case-based and variance-based designs that result in our evidence being of different things (probabilistic versus deterministic, symmetric versus asymmetric), population-level knowledge does not necessarily tell us anything about whether a relationship holds in a particular case, or whether it might work in a different fashion (Kaye 1986; Brilmayer 1986). In other words, the statistics-based, quantified prior (or lack thereof) that there is a relationship at the population level can be false for the chosen case. Using an analogy, in a criminal case, while we might possess population-based statistics on the propensity of particular ethnic or socioeconomic groups for committing particular types of crimes, this data would be relatively meaningless prior knowledge in relation to determining whether the suspect in a particular case actually committed the particular crime. If we know that low-income people have a higher propensity for robberies, would it help the judge to know that the suspect was poor? Indeed, in criminal trials this population-level data would usually be inadmissible because it is not relevant evidence in the case, as it tells us next to nothing, given the causal heterogeneity of the population. In other words, the population-level propensities would not tell us anything relevant about the guilt of the suspect in the actual case because there can be myriad reasons that the population-level trend does not hold in the case. More relevant priors would be whether the individual in the case had a prior criminal record, something that would be difficult to quantify in a meaningful fashion. While the prior record would not tell us that the person was guilty, it would at least make it more likely, other things equal. In the social sciences this form of case-specific prior knowledge is typically unavailable, and even if it were available in the form of existing case studies, it would not be quantifiable in any meaningful sense.

Second, at the case-level the probative value of empirical evidence is very difficult, if not impossible, to meaningfully quantify.[13] Here we typically have heavily contextualized empirical and theoretical knowledge that only enables us to make qualified guesses about ranges of values at best. Therefore, assigning numbers to the priors and certainty and uniqueness would be very arbitrary at best, misleading at worst. Even more damning is the argument that quantification leads to excessive simplification, given that the probative value of individual pieces of within-case evidence derives from complex interpretations of what evidence means in context. Charman and Fairfield (2015) work through an extended example of quantification of the probative value of evidence in an article, illustrating clearly that there is little analytical value-added in attempting to formalize qualitative interpretations of evidence. They write, "There is little productive middle ground between process tracing underpinned by informal Bayesian reasoning and full quantification to apply Bayes' theorem. . . . [T]he most probative pieces of evidence are precisely those for which quantification is least likely to provide added value. The author can explain why the evidence is highly decisive without the need to invent numbers" (2015: 31–32).

Another reason for the informal approach is that we strive to avoid creating an unnecessarily complex set of analytical techniques that risks overshadowing the case expertise that enables us to interpret what our data is telling us about the causal process we are studying. Finally, and more strategically, quantifying priors and probative value of evidence risks alienating many more qualitative-oriented scholars, in particular those with historical leanings who could utilize the framework to make their research more systematic and transparent, but who would be intensely skeptical of quantification.

One oft-heard critique of Bayesian logic is that it is too subjective, especially as regards setting prior confidence (Chalmers 1999: 177–81). However, the idea of purely objective "science" is a myth; scientists always bring some subjective biases to the table. Indeed, the Bayesian counterargument is that by placing subjective beliefs openly on the table, we are able to produce more objective research (Howson and Urbach 2006). A reason for this is that other scientists are able to evaluate better whether the conclusions of the research are justified given the arguments about prior confidence and why empirical material can be confirming or disconfirming evidence of a causal relationship. Further, laying one's cards on the table also encourages self-evaluation because they should enable us to detect better our own excessively subjective decisions about prior research and evidence evaluation.

Bayes's Theorem

The simplest version of Bayes's theorem is this: *posterior* α *prior* × *theoretical weight of evidence* × *accuracy of evidence.* This theorem states that the degree of confidence in the validity of a theory after collecting new evidence (posterior) is equal to the probability that a theory is true based upon our prior knowledge times the theoretical weight of the evidence (theoretical certainty and uniqueness) and the probability that our evidence is accurate.[14] In plain English, new empirical evidence updates our belief in the validity of the hypothesis, contingent upon (1) our prior confidence based on existing research, (2) the theoretical weight of the evidence in relation to the hypothesis, and (3) the amount of trust we can place in the evidence being accurate.

Bayesian logic suggests we must avoid cognitive biases that predispose the analyst to maintain confidence in a coveted hypothesis in the face of empirical evidence to the contrary. This is achieved in particular by the transparent evaluation of theoretical uniqueness, asking the question of whether we can account for the found evidence with *any* plausible alternative explanation (see section 6.6 for more).

We increase our confidence in a causal hypothesis being true when the posterior is greater than the prior, we disconfirm it to some degree when the posterior is less than the prior, and we learn nothing from our research when the posterior is equal to the prior. Note that confirmation never reaches 100 percent and disconfirmation never reaches zero, which is a logical impossibility in Bayesian logic (Howson and Urbach 2006: 103–5). This is the reason in law we speak of "beyond reasonable doubt" or the "preponderance of evidence," which expresses posteriors close to but not equal to 100 percent. In social science, we will never approach this standard of confirmation because of the nature of our sources, nor will we approach the falsification of a theory, which implies 100 percent disconfirmation.

One common misunderstanding in social science applications of Bayesian logic in case studies is that prior and posterior confidence in a hypothesis is relative to confidence in rival theories. This makes sense in fields like law and medicine, where hypotheses are typically binary. For example, a disease is either present or not, or the suspect is guilty or innocent. In both instances, the "rival" theory is simply that the hypothesis is not valid. In contrast, in social science our rival theories are typically drawn from broad theoretical approaches such as a constructivist or rationalism. But at the level of actual theoretical explanations, they are almost never mutually exclusive in either theoretical or empirical terms (Rohlfing 2014). For example, finding evidence that norms mattered (constructivist) in a case does not necessarily mean that cost-benefit calculations (rationalist) played no role.

Translated into social science case studies, Bayesian logic tells us that what we are assessing is whether there is evidence suggesting that a causal relationship is present or not in the studied case. We are *not* assessing whether rival theories are valid as explanations of the case, except in the relatively atypical situation where a rival hypothesis is mutually exclusive theoretically and empirically, *and* it is sufficient by itself (Eells and Fitelson 2000: 134; Rohlfing 2014). If we cannot make these demanding assumptions, high confidence in a causal hypothesis being valid in a given case does not rule out having high confidence in other theories (Eells and Fitelson 2000). At the theoretical level, multiple causes are usually present in any given case, meaning that just because we have found evidence that cause C_1 matters does not mean that other causes cannot be present also. Further, the empirical fingerprints various theories leave are often very different, meaning that just because we found evidence that suggests that cause C_1 matters, this does not thereby imply that other causes were not present because the evidence for other causes might be very different. For instances, a "norms matter" hypothesis would leave very different empirical fingerprints from a "cost-benefit calculations" hypothesis. Therefore, finding the empirical fingerprints of the norms-matter hypothesis would typically tell us nothing about whether "cost-benefit calculations" mattered or not.

Therefore, when we are speaking of priors and posteriors in case-based research, we should merely understand them as the confidence we can have in a causal hypothesis being valid based on the existing evidence from more general research on the topic and of the particular case, instead of treating the prior for a given cause as the inverse of the prior for "competing" theories.

Applied to case studies, we utilize empirical material as evidence to update our confidence in the validity of a causal relationship existing between a cause (C) and outcome (O) in the studied case, or across a bounded population of cases. As detailed in chapter 7, Mill's comparative methods utilize predictions of invariant membership patterns across cases (e.g., whether C is present in all cases of O) to make disconfirming inferences about cross-case causal relationships. In chapter 8 we develop the congruence method that enables the assessment of within-case causal relationships. Here we make multiple predictions about what within-case evidence the C → O relationship should leave in a given case that can be assessed empirically. If we find the evidence predicted by a strong test *and* we can trust it, we then make the inference that the relationship was present in the case with a level of confidence dependent on the weight of the evidence. In a process-tracing case study we are making inferences about a disaggregated causal mechanism existing in a case that links C and O together (see chapter 9). The mechanism between C and O is conceptually disaggregated into a series of parts composed of entities engaging in activities. Theoretical propositions about evidence of entities engaging in activities are made for each part and are then empirically assessed. If confirming evidence is found for each part, the inference can be made that the mechanism linking C and O as a whole was present in the case.

Given that we do not unpack the actual causal process, the type of mechanistic evidence produced by a congruence case study does not enable as much updating about causal relationships being present or not in a given case as process-tracing. But as discussed in chapter 3, this is a deliberate choice. We utilize a congruence case study in a situation where we have very low prior confidence in a causal relationship existing (e.g., because we only possess correlation-based evidence of cross-case variation). Here the congruence case study acts as a form of "plausibility probe" to update our low prior confidence. If the congruence case study finds some mechanistic evidence of a causal relationship, we can then employ a more robust but also more time-consuming process-tracing case study (either of the same case if new evidence is gathered that is independent of that used in the first congruence case study, or another similar case can be chosen) to further update our confidence in the *causal* relationship being present or not, as a process-tracing study provides stronger evidence of the existence of a causal process(es) linking C and O because evidence is provided for each part of the causal process.

Note that in both types of within-case studies, we are able to make evidence-based inferences only about C being *causally related* to O; we cannot utilize within-case mechanistic evidence to assess whether C is necessary or sufficient for O (Ragin 2000: 90). Regarding making inferences about necessity, as this type of causal claim builds on a counterfactual understanding of causation, we need to have counterfactual cases to compare it with. Basically, to assess counterfactual claims we need evidence of difference-making. Yet evidence of difference-making would require transforming the within-case study into a comparative cross-case analysis.[15] Similarly, evaluating sufficiency also requires some form of cross-case comparison that is not possible when we study only one case.

We now turn to a discussion of each of the elements of the Bayesian theorem as it applies to the theoretical evaluation of what particular pieces of empirical material can tell us about theoretical hypotheses in case-based research.

6.5. What Is Our Prior Confidence in the Theoretical Hypothesis?

Priors are among the most misunderstood aspects of Bayesian logic, particularly when applied to case study research. Prior confidence in a causal hypothesis combines our assessment of how confident we can be in its validity based upon existing research (at the population level and, if it exists, within the chosen case). In good Bayesian-inspired empirical research, different levels of prior confidence held by different scholars eventually wash out through repeated meetings of the theory with new empirical evidence.

The level of prior confidence in our hypothesis affects whether we should focus on collecting confirming (i.e., theoretically unique predictions) or disconfirming (i.e., theoretically certain predictions) evidence, along with the level of probative value of evidence required to update our confidence.[16] If our prior confidence is high, given that only very strong confirming evidence would further increase our confidence, it can be more productive to focus on disconfirming evidence in an attempt to potentially learn something new. In contrast, when we have low prior confidence, even relatively weak confirming evidence will update our confidence. Here a case study acts as a form of plausibility probe.

Prior confidence is determined by an assessment of the plausibility of a given theoretical hypothesis holding in a case, or in a bounded population if cross-case analysis is being done. When determining priors for within-case analysis, existing evidence from the particular case should trump knowledge from the cross-case level because it is a more proximate form of knowledge because there can be many reasons a population-level trend does not hold in a particular case.

Additionally, in the social sciences, our existing cross-case knowledge about relationships is often based upon variation-based analysis of observational evidence of difference-making instead of experimentally manipulated evidence. When using observational evidence of difference-making, we are actually just *assuming* causation based on covariation between X and Y, but we possess no actual evidence of causal processes working (i.e., correlation is not causation) (Holland 1986; King, Keohane, and Verba 1994).

Finally, if we can assume that the population is relatively causally homogeneous, evidence from experiments can inform priors at the population level. However, for many types of phenomena studied using case studies, the external validity of experimental findings is very low. Just because experiments conducted on political science undergraduates suggest that stress (X) tends to produce poor decision-making processes (Y), this does not mean that the elite decision-makers we are studying in an actual foreign policy crisis will be affected by stress in the same fashion.

The typical situation in which within-case studies are employed is where we have a low overall prior confidence in C being *causally* related to O in any given case, as we only have covariational evidence at the cross-case level gained from regression-based analysis using observational data (Lieberman 2005). Here a positive result from even a relatively weak within-case test would significantly update our confidence in a causal relationship existing in the case in hand. It does not necessarily tell us anything about whether the relationship exists in the population for the same reasons that going from population to case-level is problematic.

What our prior looks like depends on the type of case-based method being employed. As regards case-based comparative methods (chapter 7), we would want to assess what existing research tells us about the degree of confidence we reasonably can hold about C being necessary or sufficient for O in a bounded population of cases. Typically the prior knowledge we have about a causal relationship holding across cases comes from variance-based research, meaning that it tells us little about the types of deterministic and asymmetric causal claims investigated using case-based comparative methods. Further, it is also challenging to determine the appropriate bounds for the population, which has implications for the level of our prior confidence. If the bounds are set inappropriately, we might claim that existing research suggests we should have low prior confidence in a theory, whereas if we set the bounds to cases in which the relationship might actually hold, we might have much higher confidence. The more certain we are about the bounds being appropriate, the higher the prior confidence we can have in the relationship, other things equal.

In a congruence case study (chapter 8), our prior confidence would relate to how confident we are, based on existing research (in particular in the case in hand), that the hypothesized causal relationship would exist *in the case* being studied.

Setting priors is more complicated in process-tracing (chapter 9), in that we need to estimate prior confidence both for each part of the mechanism being studied and for the overall relationship. Given this, we will walk through how priors can be set in process-tracing by using an example of research on how ratification by referendum (C) might produce congruence between what voters want and governmental positions in negotiations (O) in EU treaty reforms (see Beach forthcoming). Figure 6.2 illustrates the relationship between priors for each part of the mechanism and the whole.

The theorized causal mechanism separates the causal relationship into

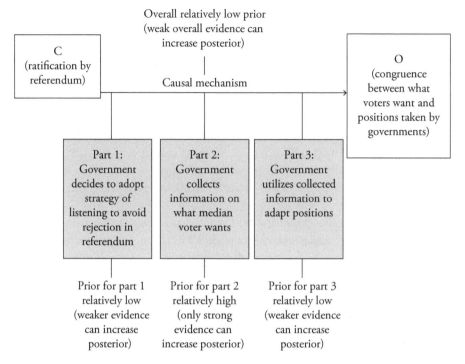

Fig. 6.2. A hypothesized causal mechanism and priors in process-tracing

three parts that work together to account for how C can hypothetically cause O. The first part contends that for referendums to matter, the government must initially make a decision, in light of the probable referendum, to actively *adopt* a strategy of ensuring that the final outcome can be ratified by deciding to listen to public opinion. The second and third parts detail how positions are adapted to voter views through the collection of data on voter views and the modification of positions on the basis of this information.

Given that existing findings are purely observational evidence of difference-making that do not enable causal claims to be made (e.g., Finke 2007; Hug and König 2002; Hug and Schultz 2007), we could set the overall prior for the causal relationship existing as being relatively low in any given case. Additionally, given that there are no case studies of the relationship, we would have a low relative prior confidence irrespective of which case we select to study. Overall, this low prior confidence means that even if our process-tracing case study can produce only relatively weak confirming evidence, it would still enable some updating to take place if we found the predicted evidence for each part of the mechanism in a case study.

The priors for each individual part determine the type and strength of evidence necessary to further update our confidence for each part of the mechanism existing in the case—what can be thought of as mini case studies embedded within the overall study of the mechanism in the case. This means that the prior for each part of the mechanism should be described. For example, the prior for part 2 (p_{h2}) is set relatively high, given what we know about modern representative governments in general. That is, it is almost self-evident that they would be monitoring public opinion in some fashion on important issues. Therefore, only very strong confirming evidence would increase our confidence further. In contrast, the low priors for parts 1 and 3 reflect our overall low confidence in the mechanism, given that these are the real "working parts" of the causal relationship, if it exists.

Taken together, new empirical evidence for each individual part then enables us to increase or decrease our confidence in the mechanism as a whole being present. The level of our posterior confidence in the whole mechanism reflects the lowest posterior level for each of the parts *after* we have done our empirical research. For example, after collecting new evidence, our posterior confidence for part 1 might be quite high and very high for part 2, but if we were not able to deploy a strong confirming test for part 3, the posterior might only be somewhat low, meaning that little updating took place. Given that each part of a mechanism has to be present for us to infer that the mechanism as a whole is present in a case,[17] our posterior confidence in the mechanism being present in the case would be only somewhat low—only as strong as the weakest test.

What Priors Look Like in Practice

How should we present priors in our research? Basically, one needs to present fairly what existing research tells us about the plausibility of the causal relationship being present in the chosen case, or in the bounded population when using comparative methods. This involves mustering existing theoretical and empirical research in a transparent fashion. Unfortunately, when we look at case study research, the evaluation of prior confidence is often quite superficial.

One exception is found in Janis's 1982 book on the groupthink hypothesis, which states that a cohesive small group (C) can result in flawed decision-making in foreign policy (O) in particular contexts through a groupthink causal mechanism. He starts by writing that we know little about social-psychological process in foreign policy decision-making, describing what was known from existing research using other types of small groups (1982: 3–6). He concludes this by stating that knowledge on "group dynamics is still in the early stages of scientific development, and much remains to be learned" (Janis 1982: 6). He then moves on to discuss the low prior confidence in the hypothesis in relation to a particular case (decision-making in the Bay of Pigs fiasco), where he assesses existing explanations for faulty decision in the case, claiming, "After studying Schlesinger's analysis of the Bay of Pigs fiasco and other authoritative accounts, I still felt that even all four factors operating at full force simultaneously could hardly have given rise to such a faulty decision. . . . Sensitized by my dissatisfaction with the four-factor explanation, I noticed in Schlesinger's account of what policy-makers said to each other during and after the crucial sessions. . . . Groupthink does not replace the four-factor explanation of the faulty decision; rather, it supplements the four factors and perhaps gives each of them added cogency in the light of group dynamics" (Janis 1982: 33–34). One can infer from his description of the state of the art of the theory and knowledge of the case that he believes that the prior confidence in the group dynamic (group-think) hypothesis is relatively low. Therefore, it makes sense when he then claims that plausibility probes with relatively weak evidence are sufficient to update prior low confidence in the hypothesis. He writes, "For purposes of *hypothesis construction*—which is the stage of inquiry with which this book is concerned—we must be willing to make some inferential leaps from whatever historical clues we can pick up" (1982: ix).

We suggest that scholars should be explicit about which forms of existing evidence they derive their estimation of prior confidence by answering three questions. First, at the most abstract level, is the postulated causal relationship plausible theoretically? Do we find plausible causal mechanisms linking C with O in the literature, or is it possible to derive these from existing research? Second, what does existing research tell us about the relationship at the cross-case level? Given that this evidence is typically of correlations across cases, it provides relatively weak evidence of a causal relationship, especially when applied to single cases. Additionally, why should we expect that the cross-case relationship might actually be present in the selected case? That is, you need to justify the assumption of causal homogeneity in the population.

Third, if we are doing within-case analysis, what does the evidence from existing research on the case tell us about the plausibility of the relationship? This will often be in the form of historical work on the case, which can shed light on the plausibility of the relationship in the particular case. Finally, if one is working with process-tracing, what is the plausibility of the theorized mechanism being present in a particular case, along with each of the individual parts?

6.6. The Theoretical Weight of Evidence

This section focuses on what new evidence *hypothetically* can tell us about the validity of theoretical claims in relation to underlying causal relationships, focusing on the disconfirming and confirming power of evidence. We use the term *proposition* for the crucial logical link between actual empirical material and a causal theory, with the proposition providing arguments for why the empirical material might be relevant evidence of the causal relationship. Here arguments are put forward about the hypothesized data-generating process of the causal relationship (or part of it, if we are studying disaggregated mechanisms), describing which observable manifestations it might leave in a given case if it is valid. We use the term *proposition* in the following to mean the same thing as hypotheses about observable manifestations, or "tests" of theories. We do not use the term *hypothesis* or *test* because it creates associations to theory-first, deductive research, whereas in reality we often engage in empirics-first research in case-based designs, where we find empirical material and *then* evaluate what it can potentially be evidence of.

Theoretical certainty relates to the disconfirming power of evidence. If it was theoretically very certain that we had to find the predicted evidence and we do not find it in the case or across cases despite a thorough search in the empirical record, we can significantly downgrade our confidence in the hypothesis. However, if we are engaging in an empirics-first study, we would not evaluate certainty of evidence in relation to a given proposition because we have already found the evidence!

Theoretical uniqueness describes the expected probability of finding the predicted evidence if the hypothesis is not true, telling us about the confirmatory power of evidence. In plain English, if the predicted evidence is found, can we plausibly account for it with any alternative plausible explanation? This means that we have to evaluate the plausibility of *all* alternative explanations for finding the evidence. If we find the predicted evidence and it was theoretically unique, we can make a strong confirming inference.

Despite what some scholars claim (e.g., Bennett 2010; Collier 2011), alternative explanations are typically not drawn from rival theoretical hypotheses, except in extremely rare situations where two theories are mutually exclusive at both the theoretical and the empirical level (Eells and Fitelson 2000: 134; Rohlfing 2014).[18] Therefore, what we should be assessing

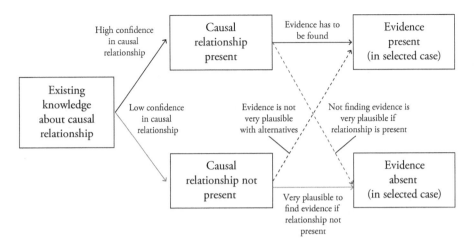

Fig. 6.3. Certainty and uniqueness of evidence in relation to a causal hypothesis
Source: Adapted from Friedman, 1986a.

is whether there are any plausible alternative explanations for finding the particular piece of evidence.

How, then, do we assess all plausible alternative explanations of the predicted evidence? While we can never assess all alternative explanations, the term "plausible" means that we focus our analytical attention on the most promising alternatives. These can come from rival theories, but only if they offer competing interpretations of the particular piece of evidence, that is, if the two rival theories have mutually exclusive predictions of evidence (Rohlfing 2014). However, alternative explanations more typically come from empirical knowledge of the context of the case itself or more ad hoc, case-specific theoretical hypotheses, as long as they are plausible.

The relationship among theoretical certainty and uniqueness, new evidence, and a causal hypothesis can depicted heuristically in diagram form, as in figure 6.3. Our prior confidence determines the degree to which we are confident that the hypothesis holds before we engage in our research (depicted as relative probability of the causal relationship being actually present or not). The arrows depict paths through which we might reach the found evidence or its absence.

What finding the predicted evidence or not hypothetically tells us about the existence of a hypothesis is then determined by the theoretically certainty and/or uniqueness of evidence.[19] In the figure, if we find evidence—and it is very implausible that we would find it with alternative explanations—the newly found evidence makes us more certain that we have "traveled" to the found evidence through the "causal relationship is present" node, meaning that the evidence strengthens our confidence in the causal relationship being valid, whereas it is not very plausible that we reached "found evidence" through the lower node (causal relationship not present). In contrast, if we had to find the evidence (high certainty) and we do not find it, then the absent evidence would make us more confident that the causal relationship does not hold. In the figure, this means that we are more confident that we reached absent evidence through "causal relationship not present" (i.e., the bottom pathway) instead of through the node "causal relationship is present."

Assessing theoretical certainty and uniqueness for each proposition involves providing reasoned theoretical arguments for why the data-generating processes of the causal relationship being studied would leave particular empirical fingerprints in the case (propositions about evidence). These justifications need to include theoretical arguments *and* case-specific arguments about what the postulated evidence would mean in a given context. It is important to be clear about where in the empirical record one would expect the evidence to be found and why the data-generating process of the causal relationship would leave these specific fingerprints.

What Does Evidence Look Like in Case-Based Research?

Answering the question of which empirical fingerprints a given theory might leave requires that we think carefully but also creatively about the data-generating processes that the operation of the theorized causal process will leave in a case. When thinking about which empirical evidence a causal relationship might leave, it is important to be cognizant about (1) whether one is talking about cross-case or within-case fingerprints, (2) the type of causal relationships (necessary, sufficient, contributing, or mechanisms), and (3) which kind of inference one intends to make (disconfirming, confirming). There is a large difference between making a disconfirming inference about a cross-case relationship of necessity and making a within-case confirming inference about parts of a causal mechanism being present. If we are engaging in a congruence case study, we ask ourselves, "Which empirical fingerprints would we expect the theorized causal process to leave in a specific case?" If process-tracing, "Which fingerprints would *each* part of the causal process be expected to leave?" In both within-case methods, mechanistic evidence, or within-case empirical fingerprints, should have probative value in relation to the causal process we are assessing in the selected case. In contrast, in Mill's comparative methods, we are assessing invariant patterns of membership across a bounded population of cases, for example, that all cases where C occurs, O also occurs if testing the sufficiency of C.

What Does Cross-Case Evidence of Difference-Making Look Like?

Comparative methods utilize evidence of cross-case difference-making as evidence for making disconfirming inferences about necessary or sufficient causal relationships within a bound population of cases based on difference-making evidence (for more, see chapter 7). However, comparative methods do not enable confirming inferences because of a lack of theoretical uniqueness of the evidence. For example, finding that all instances of O are in the set of C does not enable us to determine whether the found invariant pattern is just a correlation across a handful of cases or actually reflects causation. This is why comparative methods should always be combined with within-case case studies that provide mechanistic evidence that enables confirming causal inferences to be made.

A claim that C (or a set of causes) is necessary for an outcome means that all cases of the outcome should be in the set of the cause (see chapter 3). If this holds, we should expect to find this cross-case pattern in the population. This is a theoretically certain prediction, because logically if C is a necessary condition, it *always* has to be present for O to occur. If we then find that there are cases where O occurs and C is not present, we can disconfirm the hypothesis of necessity with a large degree of confidence, contingent on how confident we are that our measures of case scores are accurate (see below). In contrast, the theoretical uniqueness of the expected cross-case pattern is very low, which means that if the predicted evidence is found, little confirmation takes place. The reasoning for low theoretical uniqueness is that there are many different alternative explanations for finding that all cases of O are in the set of C. It could be that C is a trivially necessary case, although this could be relatively easily discounted if we find that C is present in almost all positive and negative cases (Braumoeller and Goertz 2000). More important, C might be a *spurious* necessary condition, with no causal relationship with O. While at the theoretical level we need to be able to flesh out a causal explanation for why C can be necessary for O, at the empirical level the *cross-case* test offers us no way to really assess whether C is actually causally related to O in any given case, meaning that we cannot conclude that the correlation is a causal relationship. To make a confirming causal inference, one would need to either utilize mechanistic evidence of a single case or change the focus of the research into an experimental design to produce evidence of difference-making that enables confirming causal inferences. Given that manipulating the presence or absence of causal conditions is near impossible for most of the research questions we are interested in studying using case-based methods, mechanistic, within-case evidence is usually required to make confirming causal inferences in case-based research.

Turning to propositions about evidence if a causal relationship is sufficient, here we would expect to find that O occurs *every time* that C is present. The confirmatory strength of finding this cross-case pattern of evidence is relatively low, whereas the disconfirmatory power is significantly greater. This is because the evidence is theoretically certain because we have to find the pattern if C is sufficient, but finding this pattern has a low level of theoretical uniqueness as there are many plausible alternative explanations for finding that C is a subset of O. One plausible explanation is that C is tautologically sufficient because the attributes included in C and O overlap. However, we can assess this by revisiting our conceptualization of C and O. More problematic is the fact that we really cannot know on the basis of the cross-case data that C is not a spurious cause.

What Does Within-Case Evidence Look Like?

The within-case, mechanistic evidence that a given theory will leave depends on the theory *and* the case being studied (Beach and Pedersen 2013). What we want to capture here depends on whether we are operating with a minimalist or systems understanding of mechanisms. In the minimalist understanding, propositions about evidence detail the empirical fingerprints a given causal process might have left in a given case. In contrast, in the systems understanding we dig deeper into the process by attempting to capture the activities of entities that transmit causal forces from one part to the next. A banal point is that different theories will leave different empirical fingerprints. More interesting is the claim that the same theory can leave different predicted evidence in different cases. The basic point is that theories and mechanisms often have slightly different empirical fingerprints, despite being the same theory. As an example, when testing whether a democratic peace causal mechanism is present, Owen (1994) presents quite different evidence for the presence of the same part of a causal mechanism in two different cases. For part 4 of the mechanism in the case of the 1796–98 Franco-American crisis, evidence includes actions by Jefferson-led Republicans in Congress against a war declaration, along with finding that "the Republic press shrieked in protest" (Owen 1994: 107). In contrast, the evidence produced in the Anglo-American crisis during the US Civil War includes stating that "the Proclamation energized evangelical Christian and other emancipation groups in Britain," and that there were mass rallies in Manchester at the end of 1862 and in London in spring 1863 agitating against British recognition of the Confederacy (Owen 1994: 112). Given the very case-specific nature of the evidence implied by the mechanism in the different cases, the empirical material that counts as evidence in one case is not necessarily evidence in the other. Developing empirical fingerprints that are sensitive to the particulars of individual cases requires considerable case-specific knowledge and expertise.

When developing predictions about which empirical fingerprints a causal relationship might leave in a case (theory-first) or evaluating what found empirical material potentially is evidence of (empirics-first), it is important to be as creative as possible. In the natural sciences, new types of empirical fingerprints are developed by creatively gaming through which types of clues causal relationships might leave. A good example of this creativity can be found in research about theories of human evolution. Before the 1990s, scientists utilized skull and teeth morphology or microscopic wear patterns in teeth as a form of crude evidence of evolution, but this evidence had a relatively low probative value, meaning that it told us little about the diet of early hominins. In the 1990s it was discovered that different types of plants leave different ratios of carbon-12 and carbon-13 in skeletal tissue (best preserved in dental enamel) and in soil samples in rocks (Klein 2013). Savanna grasses that thrive in a hot, dry climate leave a relatively high ratio of carbon-13 to carbon-12 because these plants use a photosynthetic pathway called C_4, whereas shrubs and woody plants in a wetter climate have a lower ratio of carbon-13 to carbon-12. Recently, a team of scientists used this technique to uncover what different species of hominins ate (Cerling et al. 2013). Notably, they found that as vegetation patterns shifted between three million and two million years ago toward more C_4 grasses, one hominin species (*Paranthropus bosei*) ate a narrow, grass-based diet, whereas early man (*Homo*) ate a more varied diet. This suggests that what marked us from our close ancestors was the ability to exploit and manipulate our relationship with the environment. Creatively exploiting different forms of empirical fingerprints as evidence has therefore resulted in new knowledge about early human evolution. We strongly recommend trying to be just as creative about developing propositions about empirical evidence in the social sciences in order to strengthen the conclusions we can make based on case study research.

We contend that there are four distinguishable types of mechanistic evidence: pattern, sequence, trace, and account (Beach and Pedersen 2013: 99–100). Pattern evidence relates to predictions of statistical patterns in the empirical record. For example, if we are testing a causal theory of racial discrimination in a case dealing with employment, then statistical differences in patterns of employment could actually be relevant evidence upon which we could make inferences. Sequence evidence deals with the temporal and spatial chronology of events that are predicted by a hypothesized causal mechanism. For example, if we are testing a causal theory about rational decision-making in a given case, we might predict that decision-makers would first collect all available information, then make an assessment of the information, and finally make a decision that maximizes their utility based on that assessment. If, in contrast, we found in the case that decision-makers first took a decision and then collected information, this would be disconfirming evidence in relation to the hypothesized rational decision-making model being valid in the case.

Trace evidence is evidence whose mere existence provides proof. For example, if we were testing a theory about lobbying, the existence of some record of a meeting being held between a decision-maker and a lobbyist would be proof that they had met. If this predicted evidence had to be found, and we did not find it despite having full access to the empirical record, we would then downgrade our confidence in the lobbying theory in the case. Finally, account evidence deals with the content of empirical material, be it meeting minutes that detail what was discussed in a meeting an oral account of what took place in a meeting, or in the form of a discourse present in speeches or other material.

When designing theory-first propositions, we need to state clearly which types of evidence the causal relationship should leave in the empirical record and what it potentially can tell us in relation to a given theory (theoretical certainty and uniqueness). The clearer we are in describing what we expect to find, the easier it is to determine whether we have actually found it in the case. When evaluating what evidence potentially can tell us, it is also important to provide contextual information that enables us to assess the probative value of evidence because of the importance of case-specific context (Kreuzer 2014).

6.7. Linking Propositions with Empirical Material

In Bayesian logic it is not enough to have strong propositions about the evidence that should be found in a case. What is overlooked in the existing literature is that the assessment of causal hypotheses using empirical evidence is actually a two-step process. We detailed earlier the theoretical evaluation of potential evidence through the development of propositions about the empirical fingerprints a causal relationship might have left. But once these propositions that operationalize the theoretical causal relationship are developed, we still need to assess the relationship between actual empirical material and the propositions. In many situations there might be multiple pieces of actual evidence attached to each proposition about evidence. For example, in the example of Tannenwald's 1999 article (discussed in more depth in section 6.9), she develops a proposition about within-case evidence in the form of "taboo talk." However, this is just an abstract proposition about potential empirical fingerprints of her causal theory that might be found in the case. To assess whether norms actually mattered, actual empirical material has to be collected to evaluate whether there is evidence that the proposition about taboo talk actually was present.

What makes the assessment of actual empirical evidence much more difficult than many acknowledge (e.g., Bennett 2014; Goertz and Mahoney 2012) is that each of the actual pieces of evidence also has to be evaluated in terms of both empirical certainty or uniqueness, depending on whether predicted evidence is found, and measurement accuracy, to conclude whether we have confirmed or disconfirmed a given theoretical proposition about evidence in relation to a causal hypothesis.

We discuss assessing measurement accuracy in the next section. Here we focus our attention on evaluating what found (or not found) empirical evidence tells us about the existence of the proposition in both theory-first and evidence-first research. In theory-first research, we first develop predictions about the empirical fingerprints our theory should leave in the form of propositions and supporting propositions. Depending on whether we find the predicted evidence or not, we then have to evaluate either empirical certainty (if not found) or uniqueness (if found). In empirics-first research, we have already found empirical material, meaning that assessing empirical certainty is not a concern. Here we only have to evaluate empirical uniqueness of found evidence.

If we find a piece of evidence that we think matches what our theory predicted, we have to assess the empirical uniqueness of the found piece evidence, assessing whether it enables us to confirm that the proposition actually existed in the case. In the Tannenwald (1999) example, one would ask whether a particular statement by an actor in a source actually is "taboo talk," whether finding it enables us to infer that taboo talk was actually present, and whether we can trust the source.

We therefore have to assess empirical uniqueness in terms of whether the piece of evidence enables us to confirm the existence of the proposition or whether it is just an empirical anomaly. There might be situations where one piece of found evidence is so definitive (high empirical uniqueness) that it is by itself enough to confirm that the proposition about evidence held in the case. If we are investigating a proposition dealing with the influence of lobbying activities upon politicians that expects to find politicians in accounts discussing how they were influenced by lobbyists' money, and we have an actual piece of evidence in the form of a confessional by a politician in a parliamentary hearing where she admits taking money for influence, then we could reasonably conclude that that one piece of evidence is enough to confirm the existence of the proposition in the case in hand.

However, the more typical situation is that multiple pieces are required to confirm that the proposition is present in the case. Therefore, it is important to situate a particular piece of evidence within the full body of potential evidence in a given case. This is important to avoid the cherry-picking of pieces of evidence that do not represent the broader pattern of what happened in a case (Kreuzer 2014). This danger is particularly acute when we do convenience sampling based on which types of sources are most accessible. In effect, what one is introducing is control on whether one is merely seeing what one wants to see, in order to avoid what Moore described as "too strong a devotion to theory always carries the danger that one may overemphasize the facts that fit a theory beyond their importance in the history of individual countries" (1966: xiii).

We recommend that the *representativeness of individual pieces of evidence* is evaluated explicitly when discussing uniqueness of pieces of evidence in relation to the predicted evidence (the proposition). For example, if we are testing a causal hypothesis relating to whether a decision-making process was "rational," we might have developed a proposition that states that we should expect to find evidence in the form of well-organized meetings in which there was a critical discourse between decision-makers evaluating the costs and benefits of different options. However, finding in the minutes of a *particular meeting* that the discussion was relatively well structured does not necessarily allow us to infer that the *proposition itself was actually present*. A plausible alternative explanation for finding this actual piece of evidence could be that the particular meeting was the exception that proved the rule, with later meetings being relatively unstructured and chaotic. However, if we found that in a majority of meetings in the process, and in particular the key ones where decisions were actually taken, that there was actual evidence demonstrating systematic cost-benefit reasoning, it would be much harder to claim that the proposition "well-organized meetings" was not present. Here finding multiple pieces of evidence would be required to assess whether the proposition was actually present in the empirical record in the case. This means however that we need to elaborate on how the found piece of evidence fits into the overall jigsaw of empirical evidence that the causal relationship is theorized to produce in the case.

If we do not find the expected evidence in the actual empirical record, we also have to evaluate whether there are any empirical reasons why we did not find the expected empirical fingerprints (i.e., the proposition). It can be that we simply were unable to gain access to empirical material that would enable us to evaluate the proposition, meaning that even if our proposition was theoretically certain, we have no empirical way of knowing whether the predicted evidence actually exists. We might be unable to interview participants in a negotiation, or we cannot gain access to archives to search for the minutes of meetings. In these circumstances, the empirical certainty of the evidence is low, meaning that little or no disconfirmation takes place despite the proposition itself being theoretically certain. In contrast, if we are able to gain nearly full access to the empirical record and we still do not find the predicted evidence, we can disconfirm that the proposition actually was present with considerable confidence.

Measurement Accuracy of Found (and Not Found) Evidence

The risk of measurement error is also crucial in determining the probative value of individual pieces of found or not found evidence (Howson and Urbach 2006). A piece of found empirical evidence that has a low probability of being accurate means that finding it does little to update our confidence in a causal relationship being present or that a given case is a member of a causal concept. Inaccurate pieces of evidence therefore have lower inferential weight, other things equal. Inaccurate measures can be the product of either nonsystematic or systematic errors in the source we use for evidence. Nonsystematic (or random) error is commonly termed "reliability," whereas systematic error is the level of bias in our source.

The relationship between uniqueness and accuracy in relation to confirmation is depicted in figure 6.4. If we find a highly unique piece of actual evidence, but it is highly questionable whether we can trust it because it is "too good to be true," little or no confirmation would be enabled. In contrast, if we have a high degree of trust in a source, but the evidence is not very unique, then only a small amount of confirmation would be enabled by

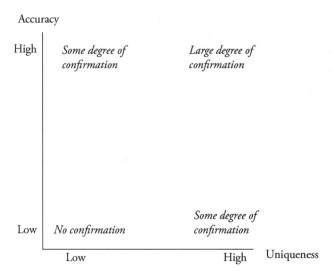

Fig. 6.4. Relationship between uniqueness and accuracy

finding the evidence. High degrees of confirmation based on actual evidence are possible only when we have high confidence in the accuracy of our evidence *and* it is highly unique.

The relationship between certainty and accuracy is similar, in that if we have not found the evidence but believe a given source might be withholding information from us, we would not be able to conclude definitely that we have not found the predicted evidence.

Some case study methodologists have acknowledged the importance of measurement accuracy but suggested that these considerations can be folded into our evaluation of theoretical uniqueness of evidence because they claim that error is always related to a causal hypothesis, meaning that an alternative explanation for finding the evidence when the causal relationship does not hold can be that an actor has motives for not telling the truth (e.g., Charman and Fairfield 2015: 37). However, we contend that measurement accuracy is *not* always hypothesis-dependent. In particular, reliability is usually not a function of a given hypothesis, but instead it often relates to factors like natural cognitive limitations in human memory when actors do not remember that something took place even though it did, or vice versa. But even validity concerns often are not always correlated with our hypotheses, meaning that it can be a good idea to evaluate both theoretical and empirical uniqueness or certainty and accuracy distinct from each other as much as possible.

One of the reasons for this conflation of certainty and uniqueness with accuracy concerns is that most existing presentations of Bayesian logic utilize very simple examples. For instance, a common example of certainty and uniqueness is using a DNA test to assess a hypothesis. Here the uniqueness of evidence such as a match in a DNA test is typically given as the rate of false positives in the test (the odds are roughly one in a million). But this is a good example of the peril of folding concerns about accuracy into uniqueness. In this example, what a DNA match can *hypothetically* can tell us (level of uniqueness) depends crucially on the *context* in which we are using the evidence, whereas the accuracy of the test does not vary across contexts if it is executed in the same manner. If we find a match of the suspect's DNA with that of a hair found in a heavily trafficked room, this has little confirming power in determining whether the suspect was guilty, because there were many other people in the room (low uniqueness). However, the same evidence (a DNA match) found in a context where the suspect's DNA matches bloody tissue found under the nails of the victim would have a much higher probative value because of high uniqueness. Crucially, the *accuracy* of the test is the *same*, but the *probative value* of the evidence *differs* because of different levels of uniqueness of what the evidence means in various contexts.

An additional reason to separate certainty and uniqueness from accuracy relates to different procedures by which we can increase the probative value of evidence by increasing certainty or uniqueness and accuracy. Theoretical uniqueness or certainty can be increased only by changing predictions about which evidence will be found or not found (e.g., uniqueness can be increased by making an expectation about evidence more specific, such as precisely described phrases in particular documents). Empirical uniqueness can be improved by searching for better sources that enable a more representative picture of the empirical record to be given. In contrast, improving accuracy relates to both asking critical questions in relation to particular sources (e.g., assessing potential motivations for distorting their account) *and* through corroboration with other independent sources.

Accuracy issues related to reliability are unavoidable (we are human after all), but they can be minimized in our research by carefully double-checking our sources and by documenting in online appendices the content of sources and the analytical procedures used to evaluate them. In contrast, validity problems stem most often from a partial reading of sources, from seeing what you want to see instead of examining each source critically using the questions we describe later in this section.

A rule of thumb is to be suspicious when evaluating the probability that evidence collected is accurate. Evidence that appears to be a definite smoking gun in favor of your theory is probably too good to be true either because of the inherent ambiguity and messiness of empirical fingerprints left by the operation of most social science hypotheses or because political and bureaucratic actors can have motivations to distort the truth.

We can attempt to estimate the degree of inaccuracy by critically evaluating its size and direction through triangulation of independent pieces of evidence, in particular by corroborating the use of other sources whose independence can be assessed (see the next section). This can be accomplished by both critically assessing the source of each piece of evidence and by comparing all the pieces with other relatively independent pieces in a triangulation process to assess the size and direction of bias contained in the sources. Particular focus should be on assessing the degree that the evidence either favors or disfavors the hypothesis more than seems reasonable in the given context. Finally, when actors have strong interests in a case, we should as a rule be more skeptical about measurement accuracy, other things equal.

For each of our empirical sources we therefore have to evaluate transparently the degree to which we trust it is actually measuring what we think it is measuring (measurement accuracy). The good news is that we can also use the Bayesian framework to improve our confidence in measurement accuracy by *corroborating* with other sources. Here independence between sources is crucial, in that if we find similar patterns we can make the Bayesian argument, "How probable is it that we would find similar patterns in the sources unless we are actually measuring what we wanted to measure?" If pieces of empirical material in different sources are truly independent, it is highly unlikely that the measures will result in the same evidence unless they are actually measuring what happened (Howson and Urbach 2006: 125).

But unless we explicitly discuss the confidence we have in a given source using questions that historians typically ask when they evaluate the veracity of sources, we should assume that the found piece of empirical evidence has little (if any) probative value.

What then are the questions we can ask of our sources of evidence to evaluate whether we can trust them or not?

I—Can the Source Have Known about the Events?

Can the source have known something firsthand about the events he or she describes? If we find through careful assessment of the position that a particular person held at the time of an event that he or she would not have been privy to key discussions, we would conclude that the source is not an eyewitness but instead heard the information from some other source. Furthermore, given that the source misled us about his or her role, should we really trust anything else this source says? In both instances our assessment of measurement accuracy of the source of evidence would fall.

2—How Many Steps Removed from the Events Is the Source?

Second, how many steps removed from the original data-generating process is the source of the found empirical evidence? We define primary sources as eyewitness accounts of a given process, for example by participants, or as documents produced by participants at the time an event occurred, whereas secondary sources are produced based on primary sources. For example, the work of a historian studying primary sources (e.g., the documentary record of a negotiation) is a secondary source.

Logically there are three ways that two sources can be related to events and each other (see figure 6.5). The first way is when source A has given source B information about events. Here source A is primary and source B is secondary in relation to the event(s). Second, sources A and B are reports drawn from a common source C, and C is either known or unknown to us. If C is unknown, then A and B are both primary to us, but if C is known, they are secondary. In both instances, A and B are not independent, even if we do not know the common source. Third, if parts of B draw on A, but B also reports something from C and C is unknown to us, then A is primary, the parts of B that draw on A are secondary, and those parts that rely on the unknown C are primary to us. However, if both C and A are known, then they are both primary sources and B is secondary (Erslev 1963: 44–45).

It can often be difficult to determine whether a source is primary or secondary. Figure 6.6 illustrates the number of steps removed from the actual event (the data-generating process) that our source potentially can be.

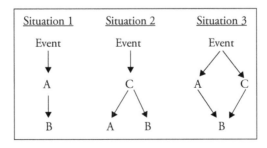

Fig. 6.5. Dependence between sources

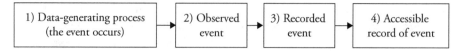

Fig. 6.6. Relation between sources and the data-generating process

Even though a participant took part in a particular event, he or she is still one step removed from the "objective" event. Given the limitations of human cognition, the objective external event is not always even accurately reflected in the subjective perception of what took place among participants. Common cognitive biases include the use of simple categorizations and stereotypes to understand events, the tendency to simplify causal inferences about what took place, the use of historical analogies to understand new situations, and the ignoring of information and avoidance of situations that produce dissonance with existing beliefs and images (Jervis 1976; Khong 1992). For example, the human mind tends to see the actions of others as intentional and planned, whereas there is a tendency to overemphasize the situational causes of one's own behavior. Actors also tend to over- or underemphasize their role in others' policies: "When the other behaves in accord with the actor's desires, he will overestimate the degree to which his policies are responsible for the outcome. . . . When the other's behavior is undesired, the actor is likely to see it as derived from internal sources rather than as being a response to his own actions" (Jervis 1976: 343).

But it is by no means certain that the original participants record the actual events. Instead, they might discuss what took place with colleagues or with an official record-maker after events, meaning that if we interview the colleagues and not the participant, the interview would be a secondary source, two steps removed from the original event. It is therefore vital to discuss with interviewees the sources of the information they provide to determine whether they are a primary source who took part in the event or are referring to official minutes of the meeting or discussions with actual participants, in which case the interviewee is a secondary source.

Finally, accessibility issues are endemic in the social sciences, especially for research questions like corruption or political violence in nondemocratic systems. Therefore, the record of events that is accessible is often even further removed from the original event. Often we do not even know about primary sources closer to events because they are classified or otherwise inaccessible to us, which forces us to rely on insiders or the information that public authorities decide to release.

We can use tools such as the dating of documents or text analysis to determine which sources are primary and secondary, as well as the number of steps removed from events that our source is (Milligan 1979). For example, if source A has the same linguistic phrasing as source B, *and* we can show that the production of source A preceded the production of source B, this suggests that source B should be treated as secondary material that builds on source A, as it is highly unlikely that they would have used the same phrasing unless source B draws on source A. This means the sources are dependent on each other.

Although the reasons for favoring closeness to events by historians is somewhat arbitrary, it does have merits, because for each step between an event and our source there are potential sources of error (either random or systematic). In Bayesian terms, the fewer the steps between a source and the data-generating process, the greater the probability of accuracy, other things equal. However, as we discuss later, there can be reasons to prefer a secondary source who has triangulated his or her findings across multiple independent sources over a "hard" primary source where we have no way of objectively controlling for the amount of error in the measure, or sometimes even knowing the size and direction of potential bias.

3—Is the Source Reliable?

Third, what are the reasons to trust a source in terms of it being reliable? Here we ask questions like, "Was the source competent to observe what took place and provide an accurate account of it?" For example, in interviews there is the core concern of whether the respondent can accurately recall complicated events that might have taken place several years ago. Additionally, was the source able to comprehend what was going on? For example, in a complicated legal negotiation in a subcommittee, did a particular politician possess the requisite knowledge to understand what was going on? If we are working with a document, we would ask ourselves what is normally included in the type of source (e.g., minutes from a cabinet meeting)? One way to test for reliability is to use our knowledge of the case to evaluate the reliability of a particular source in relation to what we know from other sources (in effect a form of triangulation with other sources to establish reliability). If we are dealing with trade statistics, in which multiple different indicators exist that are produced by different authorities, are there sources that appear to produce more reliable indicators when compared with other sources? In interviews, we can use questioning techniques used in criminal interrogations, where reliability is probed by asking similar but differently phrased questions at different times in an interview to assess whether we hear similar things. If a respondent has an unusually clear recollection of events, we can probe which factor has enabled the respondent to remember events so well. If we find that the events took place on the respondent's birthday or, for example, on the day the low-level civil servant met the US president in a later meeting, it would be more probable that the respondent actually recalled events than otherwise.

4—Does the Source Have Motives for Distorting Content?

Can we provide justifications for the claim that the source did not have any significant motives for distorting content? If bias exists (and it always does), the found evidence can be measuring something other than the predicted evidence, resulting in flawed inferences. In this section we discuss how we can evaluate measurement accuracy for sources taken by themselves, assessing with all available knowledge whether the source can have motivations for distorting content. This section builds on Beach and Pedersen (2013). In the next section we discuss how we can *compare* what we find in other sources to assess actual levels of bias.

Bias can express itself in many different forms depending on the type of source. For instance, if we are dealing with classified documents, there can be reasons particular documents are declassified and others withheld to remain classified, with actors wanting to release only documents that fit their interpretation of events (Trachtenberg 2006: 157). Here, if we study only the documents we have without taking into consideration what we might find in documents that we do not have, the result could be a skewed picture of what really took place. Further, bias can manifest itself in what the source tells us. If we go to a prison in a well-functioning legal system and ask the convicted criminals whether they actually committed the crime they are accused of, we might be amazed at the number of "innocent" people in prison.

Each collected piece of evidence should be evaluated relative to what is known about the actors, their possible intentions, their interactions, and the situation they found themselves in (Thies 2002:357). When analyzing documents, one has to ask what the purpose of the document was intended to serve and what agenda the author of the document might have. Is the document even authentic? This can be investigated by assessing whether there is anything wrong with the style, timing, genre, or origin of the document. Was the document produced at the time and place when an event occurred? How does the document fit into the political system, and what is the relation to the stream of other communications and activities within the policy-making process? Assessing this requires considerable background knowledge. For example, how does the given political system work? Is there anything amiss in the events that have been uncovered? What is normally included in the type of source (e.g., minutes of a cabinet meeting)?

Unfortunately, for most of the research questions we are studying as social scientists, actors often have strong incentives to distort content. Even seemingly innocuous sources of data on statistics like unemployment figures can be politically motivated to distort information, for example by excluding parts of the labor force from the statistics to produce lower unemployment figures. More insidious are the validity problems created by public authorities deliberately "cooking the books," as seen in the systematic underreporting of levels of political violence in authoritarian systems.

When our sources have strong interests in distorting content, it can be near impossible to evaluate with any degree of confidence the level of bias without extensive corroboration with other independent sources (see the next section). We should therefore, other things equal, assume a much lower probability that the measure is accurate when the political stakes are high unless we can provide strong justifications for why we can trust a particular source.

In general, open sources such as public statements contain more potential bias, given that there can be many reasons for strategic communication in public. This means that we should place greater trust in confidential records that will be made public only long after events have taken place, other things equal (Trachtenberg 2006: 151–53; Khong 1992). Further, we should trust accounts that go against the motives we would expect a given actor to have, although this can be very difficult to establish. Historians tend to trust interviews much less than archival documents, given that our respondents "have a real interest in getting you to see things in a certain light" (Trachtenberg 2006: 154). However, we should be skeptical of all sources per default, and we contend that any ranking is quite arbitrary. Wohlforth warns us, "Documentary records are ambiguous in their intrinsic meaning for many reasons, not least because the historical actors who created them were deliberately deceptive in their efforts to bring about desired results. Theories and interpretive debates focus on precisely the information that statesmen and diplomats face incentives to obscure" (1997: 229).

When assessing the potential incentives actors can have that would cause them to distort, we can ask ourselves whether, on the basis of what we know about the case, the particular source might have institutional or personal interests in skewing the account. As an example, if we are studying decision-making before the 2003 Iraq War, we might be very pleased with ourselves for securing an interview with such a central participant as former secretary of state Colin Powell. Yet if we assessed motives even superficially, we could seriously doubt the veracity of Powell as an accurate witness of events, as he has strong institutional and personal interests in producing an unflattering account of the Bush administration, and particularly figures like former vice president Cheney and former secretary of defense Rumsfeld. Powell "lost" the internal debates, and as a result he was publicly humiliated when he was forced to go to the UN Security Council before the invasion with dubious intelligence. His position finally became so untenable that he left office, meaning that his "revenge" motive is quite strong. Of course, if Powell were to give an account that ran against what we expected based on all available information of his potential motives, we would tend to trust it even more. Here the Bayesian reasoning is this: how probable is it that Powell would tell us an account that manifestly goes against everything we know about his potential motives unless it is actually a true account?

5—Cross-Check to Increase Our Confidence in Measurement Accuracy

We recommend that every source is vigorously cross-checked with independent sources when possible in an attempt to evaluate the measurement accuracy of each individual piece of evidence. This recommendation is often suggested as the best solution to the problem of inaccurate measures, and it is commonly referred to as triangulation. Triangulation can involve collecting observations either from different sources of the same type (e.g., interviewing different participants; collecting observations across different types of sources, such as archives and interviews) or different types of evidence, if available (i.e., pattern, sequence, account, trace). Another method is to utilize area experts to cross-check our measures, exploiting their contextual knowledge to evaluate the accuracy of particular sources (e.g., most experts might treat the work of a particular historian with extreme skepticism) and passing judgment on our evaluations of evidence (Bowman, Lehoucq, and Mahoney 2005: 940). However, this is by no means a panacea, as area experts often have a horse in the race, meaning we cannot treat them as "neutral," nonbiased sources for cross-checking information, because they are involved in academic debates about causes of important events.

6.8. The Collective Body of Evidence—Aggregating Individual Pieces of Evidence

Assessing individual pieces of evidence using the procedures described until now in this chapter only relates to establishing the probative value of individual pieces of evidence. In relation to assessing cross-case claims of necessity or sufficiency, we can stop here because the empirical evidence is simply the cross-case pattern of cases as members of C and O (see chapter 7). But when we are working with mechanistic, within-case evidence, we typically operate with many different pieces of evidence for the hypothesized causal process, or for each part of the causal mechanism as in process-tracing. Here we need to sum together the collective picture painted by multiple pieces of evidence.

The first step in aggregating mechanistic evidence in support of inferences about a causal relationship in a given case study is to map the structure of the arguments about the empirical fingerprints that a causal relationship might have left (propositions) and the actual evidence found (or not found) for each proposition. Some propositions might have the character of a smoking gun in relation to the overall causal relationship being studied because they are very theoretically unique (Van Evera 1997), where finding evidence of the proposition is highly confirming, but not finding it would do little to disconfirm the causal relationship. Other propositions can be more like hoops that have high theoretical certainty, where not finding evidence in support of it would be highly disconfirming but finding it tells us little (Van Evera 1997).

However, in most research there is a complex, multilayer structure in the collective body of evidence.[20] There might be multiple propositions related to each causal hypothesis, with several supporting propositions attached to each. Each proposition or supporting proposition is then usually bolstered by many different pieces of empirical evidence. Often we might find strongly confirming evidence of a supporting proposition, but the supporting proposition is only weakly confirming of a higher-level proposition, or vice versa. Therefore, when aggregating evidence we have to start at the lowest level, evaluating the evidence for each supporting proposition individually and what it can tell us about the existence of the supporting propositions before we move onto evaluating how the supporting propositions relate to overall propositions, and so on.

In the argument road map depicted in figure 6.7, we are testing a causal theory about a suspect who is hypothesized to have killed the victim in order to stop a pattern of physical abuse by the victim on the suspect. There are

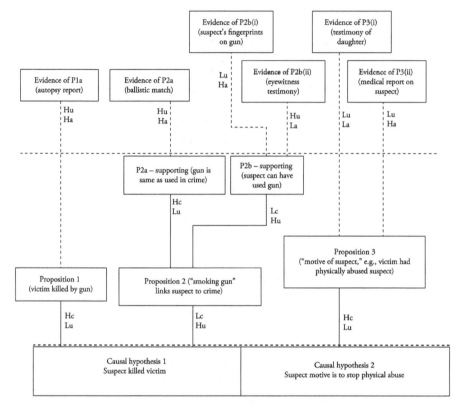

Fig. 6.7. The argument road map—mapping propositions, evidence, and the relationship with causal hypotheses

Note: Lines indicate theoretical relationship between propositions and supporting propositions; dotted lines indicate theoretical relationship between propositions and hypothesized evidence. For links between propositions and causal hypotheses, theoretical certainty (c) and uniqueness (u) are depicted. For the links between propositions and actual found evidence (or not found), the questions asked are whether the found or not found evidence is empirically unique (or certain) and whether we can trust the found evidence (accuracy).

two parts of the causal hypothesis, (1) the suspect killed the victim with a gun, and (2) the suspect had a motive.

Propositions 1 and 2 are predictions about evidence in relation to hypothesis 1, and proposition 3 relates to hypothesis 2. Proposition 1 states that there should be evidence that the victim was actually killed by a gun. This proposition is highly theoretically certain, for if they were killed by a gun it would leave clearly observable fingerprints. However, just because we find strong evidence that the victim was killed by a gun this does not mean that the suspect committed the crime (low theoretical uniqueness).

Proposition 2 states, "There is a smoking gun that links the suspect to the crime." In relation to the overall causal hypothesis of the suspect being guilty of murdering the victim, the smoking gun proposition is highly confirming if trustworthy evidence can be found (high theoretical uniqueness), but it tells us little if we do not find the smoking gun (low certainty). However, what has often been overlooked in the existing literature is that a smoking gun proposition is a set of supporting propositions that actually have different logical relationships with the smoking gun proposition, and that have different types of evidence that are relevant when making inferences.

For the sake of example, the smoking gun can be disaggregated into two supporting propositions: "the gun is the same as used in the crime" (P1b), and "the suspect can have used the gun to kill the victim" (P1c). Naturally more and other supporting propositions could be developed; here the point is simply that the many propositions require multiple supporting propositions that have different logical relationships with the overall proposition.

For the logical links between propositions and supporting propositions in the figure, levels of theoretical certainty and uniqueness are developed. For the links between actual pieces of found (or not found) empirical evidence and propositions and supporting propositions, the empirical uniqueness or certainty (for not found pieces) is assessed, along with the assessed measurement accuracy of the piece of evidence. In the latter, we ask ourselves whether we have actually found (or not found) a piece of evidence that matches the proposition, what it tells us about the proposition (is the one piece enough?), and whether we can trust it (accuracy).

Note that for each of these propositions or supporting propositions there is different evidence that might be relevant, and even more important, the inferential relationship in terms of empirical certainty or uniqueness between evidence and supporting propositions is not necessarily the same as the theoretical uniqueness and certainty between supporting propositions and higher-level propositions and causal hypotheses themselves. For instance, relevant confirming evidence for proposition 2 could be a forensic report that shows a ballistic match between the smoking gun and the crime. However, finding strong confirming evidence of P2a does not enable us to confirm the smoking gun proposition 2 by itself; it could be just as probable that someone else used the gun to kill the victim unless other evidence is put forward. In contrast, if we find a credible witness who testifies that he saw the suspect fire the gun at the victim (evidence of P2b), given that (1) the piece of found evidence is highly empirically unique, (2) proposition 2b is highly theoretically unique in relation to proposition 2, and (3) proposition 2 is theoretically unique in relation to hypothesis 1, we could on the basis of this one piece of evidence confirm the overall hypothesis 1 with a reasonable degree of confidence.

An additional consideration is whether the pieces of evidence supporting a particular proposition are independent of each other, in which case they can be summed together to enable more updating, or whether they have varying degrees of dependence, which lowers our ability to sum them together.

The argument road map can also be presented in table form—a more efficient presentation form when dealing with multilevel propositions and/or more pieces of evidence than can be easily managed in the visual road map. Presentation in table form also enables us to provide transparent justifications for why we believe, for example, that particular evidence is highly certain and/or unique in relation to a given proposition (see table 6.1). As in figure 6.7, the "lowest" level are the actual pieces of empirical evidence upon which inferences are based, followed by the logical links from empirical evidence to propositions and/or supporting propositions. One can decide to present one's case study in an analytical narrative form, but where key parts of the narrative should be explicitly linked to the underlying set of propositions and evidence and the justifications for why empirical material is evidence (theoretical and empirical certainty or uniqueness) and why we can trust evidence. The actual table can then be presented as an appendix (either printed or as an online archive).

At the end of the chapter we illustrate how the argument road map can be used in practice by applying it to systematize and make transparent the evidence mustered by Tannenwald (1999) in support of her argument in her case study of nuclear nonuse by the United States in the Korean War.

However, aggregating pieces of evidence is not just a simple additive process in most research situations. In particular, we often face situations where we find some pieces of confirmatory and some disconfirmatory pieces of evidence (a mixed picture) in relation to propositions, or alternatively, we find evidence only for some propositions but not for others in relation to the overall causal theory being assessed,

When aggregating, we therefore first need to map the structure of the propositions put forward and how they relate logically to the underlying hypothesized causal relationship—be it of a causal process, or to each of the parts of a causal mechanism. This takes the form of an assessment of theoretical certainty and uniqueness where justifications are provided for why the proposition could be evidence of the causal relationship. This should be followed by the evaluation of the pieces of found (or not found) evidence for each proposition or supporting proposition in terms of what the evi-

TABLE 6.1. Argument road map

Causal hypothesis 1: Suspect killed the victim		
Propositions linked to causal hypothesis 1		
1	**The victim was killed by a gun (Hc, Lu)**	
Evidence P1	Autopsy report found that documents that victim was killed by a gun.	
	• The report is quite unique evidence, for finding a bullet hole and the associated signs of death by gunshot are difficult to account for with alternative explanations (e.g., someone poisoned the victim but then reconstructed all of the forensic traces that would be produced by death by gunshot and masked the signs of poisoning).	
	• The report can be reasonably held to be accurate, for we would expect that in most legal systems an autopsy report would be both competent and independent of the suspect.	
2	**A smoking gun links the suspect to the crime (Lc, Hu)**	
Supporting proposition P2a	Gun same as used in crime (Hc, Lu) justifications for why high certainty, low uniqueness	
Evidence P2a	Ballistic match found in forensic test that documents that gun same as one that killed the victim.	
	• From forensic science we know that the ballistic match would be highly unique.	
	• As with the autopsy report, we would expect the forensic lab to be competent and independent, meaning it is highly accurate.	
Supporting proposition P2b	Suspect used gun to kill victim (Lc, Hu)	
Evidence P2b(i)	Suspect's fingerprints found on gun	
	• If found, it does not mean the suspect fired the gun, only that the suspect touched the gun at one point (Lu).	
	• We would expect the crime scene investigation and forensic lab to have collected and assessed the evidence in a competent manner and to be independent.	

(*continued*)

TABLE 6.1. Argument road map (continued)

Propositions linked to causal hypothesis 1

Evidence P2b(ii)	Testimony from eyewitness who claims to have seen suspect with gun in hand. • It would be difficult to account for the evidence with other explanations that the suspect had a gun in hand, although we might not be sure it was the same gun as used in the crime (Hu). • There can however be many reasons why we might not trust the witness, in particular we can never really know whether they are independent of the victim or suspect, but also the witness could have been far away and not really seen the suspect (and even worse, had poor vision) or the crime took place in a dark place (La).
Aggregation of evidence for supp. proposition P2b	Because both pieces of evidence are found, we can confirm the suspect used the gun. • If only P2b(i) is found, we cannot confirm, whereas if P2b(ii) is found, we might cautiously infer that P2b is present, although the low expected accuracy of the witness reduces the probative value of the evidence. • If neither is found only a slight disconfirmation occurs.

Causal hypothesis 2: suspect had motive (to stop physical abuse)

3	Motive—victim had been physically abused by suspect
Evidence P3(i)	Testimony of daughter that states that suspect had been abused by victim. • Very few alternative explanations for finding evidence (Hu), but there can be many reasons the daughter would exaggerate or lie to protect her mother (suspect) (La).
Evidence P3(ii)	Medical report of suspect that finds evidence of bruising. • There can be many plausible alternative explanations, like the suspect fell down the stairs (Lu). We would though expect the medical examiner, if independent of the victim and suspect, would be an accurate source (Ha).
Aggregation of evidence in support of proposition 3	• If both are found, we still cannot really confirm the proposition about a motive because of low uniqueness. • If either or both are not found, little disconfirmation occurs.

dence can tell us about the proposition (empirical certainty or uniqueness) and whether we can trust the sources of the evidence. Using the road map and the logical links between evidence and propositions, we then start the aggregation process at the lowest level of proposition, assessing in which direction the weight of evidence for each proposition or supporting proposition points. For example, if we have found multiple independent pieces of confirmatory evidence that we can trust for a given proposition, we would sum their probative value together. However, the picture is often murkier, with different pieces of evidence pointing in different directions. When we face this common situation, it is vital that the aggregation process is as transparent as possible, with our justifications made clearly and openly for why we conclude that the collective body of evidence points more in one direction than the other.

The following develops two sets of rules for aggregating evidence, enabling the systematic and transparent evaluation of what causal inferences and the degree of confidence in them that are warranted based on the collective body of empirical evidence. The first set of rules relates to summing evidence together at one level, after which we discuss how to move from lower to higher levels of proposition using the second rule.

I—The Additive Properties of Independent Evidence, but with Diminishing Returns

The basic rule for aggregating evidence is that two pieces of evidence that are independent of each other have an additive effect in terms of the amount of updating they enable (Good 1991: 89–90; Fitelson 2001: S125). This results in rule 1a, which states:

> Rule 1a—The <u>probative value of independent pieces of evidence should be summed together</u> unless the conditions for rules 1b and/or 1c hold.

The reasoning behind rule 1a relates to "sequential updating," where a piece of new (independent) evidence is used to update our posterior confidence, which then becomes the prior for the next round of "updating."[21] Following Good, evidence is taken in single bites, where the first bite updates our confidence and then informs the prior for the next bite of evidence (1991: 90). For the sake of example, we use quantified terms in the following, but as we stated earlier, we believe that numbers cannot meaningfully express the probative value of evidence in case-based research.

In simplified terms, if finding E_1 updates our prior confidence by 5 percent and E_2 also updates by 5 percent, then finding both would update our confidence with 10 percent when both are found, contingent on E_1 and E_2 being independent of each other (rule 1b).[22] In principle this means that adding more pieces of "weak" evidence will provide stronger evidence confirming or disconfirming a given proposition, contingent on rules 1b and 1d holding.[23] However, pragmatically there is also a limit to just adding more pieces of weak evidence. Rule 403 in US evidence law states, "The court may exclude relevant evidence if its probative value is substantially outweighed by a danger of one or more of the following: unfair prejudice, confusing the issues, misleading the jury, undue delay, *wasting time, or needlessly presenting cumulative evidence*" (italics added). When adding more pieces of evidence would be a "waste of time" because it would not tell us anything new because the small amount of additional updating new evidence would provide is outweighed by the boredom it would provoke in us, then no more additional evidence should be produced. In other words, when adding new pieces of evidence does not tell us anything new, we should stop.

If the evidence points in different directions in relation to a particular proposition, we use the direction they point and the relative probative value of individual pieces to determine the overall inference enabled by the evidence. If we find two pieces of confirming evidence that each enable 1 percent updating, but if we do not find a highly certain piece of evidence (disconfirming evidence) that reduces our confidence by 10 percent, the overall result might be a disconfirming inference where we are 8 percent less confident in a proposition holding based on the evidence. Rule 1b states:

Rule 1b—The <u>level of independence</u> of two pieces of evidence determines the <u>amount of updating that finding both enables.</u>

As a natural corollary to rule 1a, if two pieces of evidence are completely dependent on each other in relation to a particular proposition, finding both does not tell us anything more than finding either of the single pieces by itself. If E_1 and E_2 are completely dependent of each other, finding E_2 after we already know E_1 would not tell us anything new about the underlying proposition, given that any updating that E_2 could enable was already incorporated into our posterior confidence after finding E_1. For instance, if we know from the minutes of a meeting that actor A opposed an action (E_1), and if participants we later interviewed also tell us that actor A opposed an action (E_2), little additional updating would take place unless we could establish that the source for E_2 had not prepared for the interview with us by reading the minutes. If the source had read the minutes, E_1 and E_2 would be very dependent on each other because E_2 builds primarily on the information included in E_1 (E_1 is primary to us, and E_2 is a secondary source that builds on E_1), meaning that E_2 does not tell us anything new.

Given rule 1b, unless we can establish that sources are actually independent of each other, we should assume that there is a considerable degree of dependence of evidence on other evidence in relation to particular propositions. When we can demonstrate independence, we can sum pieces of evidence according to rule 1a. But in other situations when we cannot demonstrate full independence, we need to try to estimate the degree of independence of sources, which determines the amount of total updating that takes place with subsequent collection of evidence. The higher the level of dependence, the less additional weight per piece evidence has.

Establishing independence is often easier when we are dealing with very different types of evidence from very different sources—one of the reasons Bayesians favor evidential diversity (Fitelson 2001; Howson and Urbach 2006). A particularly important tool when determining the independence of sources is determining their relationship with each other, in particular whether they both are secondary sources building on the same primary source or whether they are, for instance, two independent primary sources. Determining independence between sources is what good journalists have to do when they attempt to get a story published by getting it past a critical editorial review process, where their editor will ask, "Why we should believe that the sources are truly independent of each other?" Before the story is printed, the reporter will have to provide extensive documentation to the editor that can make independence between sources plausible, with the result that the cross-confirmation across sources enables the editor to be more confident in the story being true.

This cross-checking should include information regarding (1) what the degree of "match" is between sources, ideally with full documentation of this in an online appendix, and (2) the extent to which we can document that the sources are actually independent of each other. Demonstrating independence is relatively easy in situations where there are two opposing sides in a negotiation and where they have self-evident motivations that are not correlated with each other. Yet there can be situations in which one actor might have incentives to downplay her role, even though she "won" in the negotiations. Here the "loser" and "winner" would both have incentives to portray the negotiations as an equitable 50-50 deal where no one "won" or "lost." The winner might want to avoid "gloating" about victory because he or she is engaged in a long-term, iterated game of repeated negotiations with the loser, whereas the loser might want to avoid being portrayed as the loser for domestic political reasons. Therefore, we cannot assume just because two actors are on opposing sides that they are independent; it must be empirically verified. And we will never be 100 percent confident, meaning that there will always be a degree of uncertainty about independence of our sources. Rule 1c says:

> Rule 1c—When *independent pieces of evidence* can be used to *corroborate* each other, the probative value of the found evidence increases even more because we become more confident about *measurement accuracy*, other things equal.

While Bayesian scholars have suggested that evidentiary diversity matters because it enables us to be confident that successive pieces of evidence are independent of each other (e.g., Fitelson 2001), another important but sometimes overlooked aspect of evidential diversity is that it also enables us to increase our estimation of the accuracy of individual measures when multiple pieces of evidence can be used to corroborate each other. If we have undertaken an interview with a lobbyist who tells us that she significantly influenced legislation in a given policy area (E_1), given that the lobbyist has strong motives for skewing the truth, we would not confirm a proposition about lobbyist influence merely based on finding E_1. However, if we were able to corroborate the evidence in E_1 by talking to informed neutrals who witnessed the process but did not have any stakes in the matter (E_2), finding similar things in E_1 and E_2 would enable more updating than merely summing each on its own because there can be reasons not to trust the veracity of what either E_1 or E_2 on its own tell us. For instance, E_1 might overstate her importance, whereas E_2 might actually not have been a witness but is merely passing on hearsay. Before we sum E_1 and E_2, the corroboration provided across the two (relatively) independent sources would increase the probative value of both E_1 and E_2 in and of themselves. Therefore, the probative value of both would increase even more than we would expect merely based on the simple additive rule 1a. Both E_1 and E_2 might have only enabled 2 percent updating on their own, but after corroboration the probative value of each might have increased to 5 percent. Therefore, the total increase in updating would be significantly more than it would have been if the two sources had not also enabled us to update our confidence in measurement accuracy.

Take a common example of conducting participant interviews to measure what happened in a political negotiation. If we interview three participants in the negotiations and find that their accounts are roughly similar, *and* if we can verify that the accounts are independent of each other, we would increase our confidence in the accuracy of the evidence of the account of the negotiations, given that it would be highly unlikely to find similar accounts unless the observed material is a true measure of what happened. However, finding similar accounts could also mean that the participants met afterward to agree upon a common account of the events or were just retelling the publicly available account of the event. And finding that the accounts are *too* similar should actually decrease our assessment of the accuracy of the measure quite dramatically, as it is highly unlikely that we would find close-to-perfect correspondence down to particular phrases in interviews unless the measure is not accurate. Here the collected evidence is too good to be true, meaning it is not plausible we would find such a close fit with what we expected to find, which results in a significantly downgrading of our confidence in the accuracy of our measures (Howson and Urbach 2006: 116–18). If we are using a secondary source and the collected evidence matches too closely, more than seems reasonable, this would suggest that we have selected a biased historical source whose implicit theories run in the same direction as our own (Lustick 1996: 608, 615). In this situation, we should significantly downgrade our assessment of accuracy, with the result that the collected evidence would not enable us to make inferences about the veracity of our hypothesis.

It cannot be overstressed that corroboration does not increase confidence in measurement accuracy unless we can substantiate that sources are actually independent of each other. Doing three interviews and postulating that you have triangulated sources is not enough—instead you need to provide proof that the interviews are actually independent of each other to corroborate accuracy across sources. And so rule 1d:

Rule 1d—*There are* <u>*diminishing returns from new evidence*</u> *as the level of our confident increase/decrease.*

A final well-known property of evidence in Bayesian logic is that there are diminishing returns on new evidence. Given the important role of the size of prior confidence in determining how much updating can take place based on new evidence, as we approach higher or lower degrees of confidence in a proposition existing (i.e., there is stronger evidence in support or not supporting), only increasingly strong confirmatory pieces of evidence (read: higher probative value) can increase or decrease our confidence even further (e.g., Howson and Urbach 2006; Friedman 1986b).

In practical terms, this means that there is a natural point at which collecting further evidence is no longer warranted unless it provides significant new evidence that would update our confidence significantly. However, as much case-based research starts in a situation similar to a plausibility probe, where our prior confidence in a causal theory actually working at the within-case level is relatively low, collecting pieces of confirmatory pieces that enable only a modest amount of updating still will enable us to make inferences. But we stop our evidence collection when additional pieces of evidence no longer tell us something new about the validity of a given proposition.

2—Using the Road Map to Evaluate the Inferences Enabled by Empirical Evidence

Rule 2a—Evidence-based inferences only travel up one level of proposition.

After the collected body of evidence in support of a given proposition is assessed following rules 1a–1d, we need to move from evidence in support of specific propositions to the overall inferences enabled by the evidence for all of the propositions. This is done by moving sequentially from the collected evidence for propositions at one level, then summing together the inferences enabled to the next level. The link between levels is forged by the logical arguments put forward in relation to whether a given proposition is theoretically certain and/or unique in relation to either higher-level propositions or the underlying causal hypothesis itself.

In the example provided in figure 6.7, there are two propositions made about the suspect having killed the victim: (1) the victim was killed by a gun, (2) there is a smoking gun linking the suspect to the victim, and a third proposition about the motive of the suspect. Propositions 1 and 3 are theoretically certain but not unique, whereas proposition 2 is theoretically unique but not certain. Proposition 2 does not stand on its own, but is composed of two supporting propositions, each of which has different evidence that is relevant for it.

A lower-level proposition that is theoretically certain and has strong disconfirming evidence backing it (evidence not found despite far-ranging search) enables us to disconfirm the proposition at the next level. This situation is depicted in figure 6.8, where evidence for supporting propositions

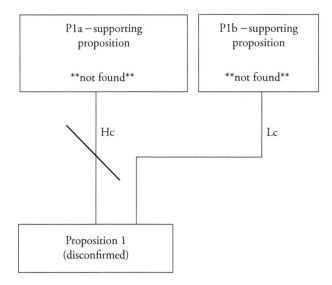

Fig. 6.8. Disconfirmation of higher-level propositions due to high certainty at a lower level

P1a and P1b are not found. Given that P1a is highly theoretically certain, we would disconfirm proposition 1 based on not finding support for P1a. This is marked in the figure as a slash over the line linking P1a with proposition 1.

Often there is a mixed picture. For instance, if we had found pieces of evidence confirming P1b, and assuming that it is theoretically unique, we would be in a situation where our overall inference about proposition 1 would be determined by the relative probative value of the disconfirming evidence of P1a in relation to the confirming evidence of P1b. If there was stronger disconfirming evidence, we would cautiously conclude that on balance there was more disconfirming than confirming evidence, and vice versa.

In the situation in figure 6.9, we have found confirming evidence of both P1a and P1b, but given that P1b is not theoretically unique, our confirmation of proposition 1 would be driven by the evidence that supports P1a. Confirmation is marked as a bold line linking P1a and proposition 1.

> *Rule 2b—Claims about higher-level propositions can never be stronger than the evidence upon which they rest.*

Claims about propositions can never be stronger than the actual pieces of evidence in support of them directly or through their supporting propositions. In figure 6.10 we illustrate a situation where there is a mixed evidential picture, but where we could reasonably conclude that there is support for

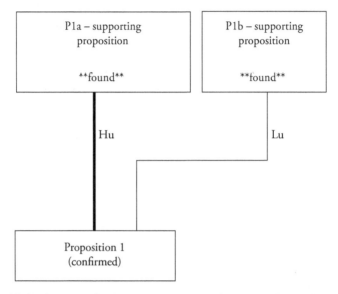

Fig. 6.9. Confirmation of higher-level propositions due to lower-level uniqueness

the overall hypothesis because the confirming evidence for proposition 1 is stronger than the disconfirming evidence for proposition 2. Here it would be the contrast in the amount of trust we would place in evidence for P1a(ii) and P2 respectively that would enable an overall (cautious) confirming inference to be made. In other words, confirmation or disconfirmation of propositions is only as strong as the weakest evidential link at the lowest level in the road map.

6.9. An Example of the Aggregation of Evidence in Practice— Tannenwald (1999)

We now illustrate the utility of our argument road map framework by reconstructing the arguments and evidence supporting them in a well-known article. The aim is not to discredit Tannenwald's (1999) research, but to illustrate the methodological point that a more systematic evaluation that asks what empirical material can be evidence of should be done to prevent us from claiming too much on the basis of weak empirical evidence. In the example, we show that she is actually justified in claiming that norms mattered based on the evidence provided in the case, but it paradoxically is not the evidence on which she claims to be basing her argument.

In the article, Tannenwald uses four parallel case studies to assess whether

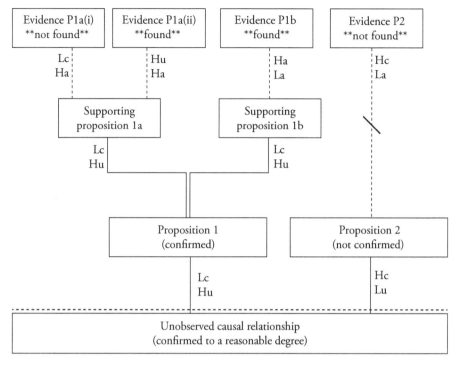

Fig. 6.10. Overall confirmation because of different levels of measurement accuracy

norms against the use of A-weapons (C) affected the US decision to not use them after 1945 (the outcome, O). Here we focus on reconstructing how she uses within-case evidence to assess whether C is causally related to O in the Korean War case (1999: 443–51).

While Tannenwald claims to only put forward one proposition about evidence in relation to the causal hypothesis norms→ non-use ("taboo talk"), when we carefully read the Korean War case study there are (at least) four propositions about evidence put forward. Interestingly, when we then aggregate the actual found evidence in support of the core propositions and supporting propositions, it appears that there is only very weak confirming evidence in favor of Tannenwald's core proposition (1—norms operating leave empirical fingerprints) (see table 6.2), mostly because we are unable to assess what finding "taboo talk" by a particular actor means in the context of the case (low empirical uniqueness), and because no arguments are produced for why we could trust the sources of evidence. In similar fashion, while she claims that norms against using nuclear weapons may have resulted in

TABLE 6.2. Aggregation of evidence in Tannenwald's 1999 study of the Korean War case

Causal hypothesis: Norms (C) resulted in US nonuse of nuclear weapons (O) in Korean War case

Proposition	
1	Norms operating leave empirical fingerprints (taboo talk)—Lc, Hu
	• Account evidence: "non-cost-benefit-type reasoning along the lines of 'this is simply wrong' in and of itself (because of who we are, what our values are, 'we just don't do things like this,' 'because it isn't done by anyone,' and so on)" (440).
	• Low certainty, as it does not describe whether it has to be found, only opening up the possibility that when norms really matter (more taken-for-granted), they do not manifest themselves openly (440).
	• Relatively high uniqueness. "Taboo talk [the predicted evidence] is not just 'cheap talk', as realists might imagine" (440). But Tannenwald only describes one alternative and does not explain whether the realist cheap talk is actually the most plausible alternative.
• Evidence P1(i)	"General Ridgway wrote later that using nuclear weapons in situations short of retaliation or survival of the homeland was 'the ultimate in immorality'" (445).
	• Lu, La: No information given about centrality of Ridgway in the decision-making process, meaning it is difficult for the reader to evaluate whether he might be so peripheral that finding "taboo talk" tells us little or nothing about the existence of the proposition. Given that the remark is found in an autobiography written twenty years later, we can assume both low uniqueness and low accuracy.
	• **Very weak confirmation of proposition 1**
• Evidence P1(ii)	"Paul Nitze, director of policy planning ... nevertheless found them [nuclear weapons] 'offensive to all morality'" (445).
	• Lu, La: We are not told about Nitze's role in the decision-making process, and no contextual information is given, meaning that the comments could have nothing to do with the Korean War case.
	• **Very weak confirmation of proposition 1**
• Evidence P1(iii)	"Dean Rusk, at the time assistant secretary of state for the Far East ... 'We would have worn the mark of Cain for generations to come'" (445).
	• Hu, La: Suggests taboo talk present, but only for a relatively minor official (at the time). Given that we do not know when the interview took place, we cannot evaluate its veracity. An autobiographical work should though be taken with a large grain of salt. Overall low measurement accuracy.
	• **Very weak confirmation of proposition 1**

- *Evidence P1(iii)*

"Truman later recalled his resistance to pressures of some of his generals . . . 'I could not bring myself to order the slaughter of 25,000,000 . . . I just could not make the order for a Third World War'" (446).

- **Lu, La:** Not really evidence of "taboo talk." Given that we do not know more about context, we cannot evaluate accuracy. However, given that Truman had strong interests in how history judged him, we should assume low measurement accuracy.
- **No confirmation of proposition 1**

- *Evidence P1(iii)*

"Truman's own personal post-Hiroshima abhorrence of atomic weapons appears to have been a crucial factor" (446).

- **Hu, La:** While the evidence is highly unique, we know nothing about the source of this evidence, therefore we should assume very low measurement accuracy.
  Very weak confirmation of proposition 1

- *Evidence P1(iii)*

"In Gavin's view [Army General who was member of Weapons System Evaluation Group], the United States had not pursued tactical nuclear options aggressively enough because of "old thinking" that nuclear weapons could only be used strategically and also because of moral qualms about nuclear weapons in general" (448).

- **Lu, La:** No information about relation of author to top officials. We do not know anything more about the context of the document other than it is a memoir, which should lead us to expect very low measurement accuracy.
- **Very weak confirmation of proposition 1**

- *Aggregation of evidence for proposition 1*

Tannenwald's conclusions: "In sum, the evidence suggests . . . the normative opprobrium that was already developing heightened the salience of moral and political concerns . . . Nuclear weapons were clearly acquiring a special status that encouraged political leaders to view them as weapons of last resort" (448).

- Sources of evidence appear to be relatively independent.
- **But overall only very weak confirmation possible** due to La of all of the sources and relatively low uniqueness of the actual pieces of evidence provided by Tannenwald. **Tannenwald's conclusions not warranted.**

(continued)

TABLE 6.2. Aggregation of evidence in Tannenwald's 1999 study of the Korean War case (*continued*)

Causal hypothesis: Norms (C) resulted in US nonuse of nuclear weapons (O) in Korean War case

2 "US and global public opinion was opposed to using atomic weapons" no information provided about certainty or uniqueness)
- Evidence expected not clearly described
- Certainty and uniqueness not discussed in case study.

- *Evidence P2(i)*

"An officer in the State Department's Bureau of Far East Affairs warned in November 1950 that even though 'the military results achieved by atomic bombardment may be *identical* to those attained by conventional weapons, the effect on world opinion would be vastly different'" (444).
- **Lu, La:** No information given about this secondary source, meaning that it is difficult to evaluate whether we can trust it. Additionally, there is low uniqueness because one could argue that the report does not reflect the overall empirical record but is an exception.
- **Very weak confirmation of proposition 2**

- *Evidence P2(ii)*

"British prime minister Clement Attlee rushed to Washington for anxious discussions on nuclear use policy" (444).
- **Lu, Ha:** We are not told anything about whether his trip was in reaction to moral abhorrence to nuclear weapons or strategic concerns about possible retaliation, meaning that uniqueness is relatively low.
- **No confirmation of proposition 2**

- *Evidence P2(iii)*

"At the end of November 1950 the Joint Chiefs advised using nuclear weapons was inappropriate except under the most compelling military circumstances, citing, in addition to battlefield factors, world opinion and the risk of escalation" (444).
- **Hu, La:** Little information is available about the source, which hinders a source-critical evaluation.
- **Weak confirmation of proposition 2**

- *Evidence P2(iv)*

"Secretary of State Dean Acheson thought that the Chinese might not act 'rationally' if atomic weapons were used" (444).
- **Not evidence as no relationship is established linking it with proposition 2**

- *Evidence P2(v)*

"Perceived public opprobrium against using atomic weapons on Chinese cities made it difficult to think about this option in any purely military fashion" (445).
- **Not evidence:** No information is given about the source of this statement, meaning that it is a postulate without any backing.
- **No confirmation of proposition 2**

- *Evidence P2(vi)*

"US leaders that using atomic weapons would destroy Asian and others' support for the United States in any future global war. . . . If the United States acted "immorally" (by using atomic weapons) it would sacrifice its ability to lead" (445).
- **Lu, La:** Little information is given about source other than that that it is a memorandum by Paul Nitze. We are given no information about why the memorandum enables the claim that US leaders worried about public opinion.
- **Very weak confirmation of proposition 2**

- *Evidence P2(vii)*

"State Department followed public opinion closely, reporting in the months after Truman's infamous press conference that European public opinion on atomic weapons was generally negative" (445).
- **Hu, Ha:** Given that the evidence relates to what the State Department officials who wrote the report believed about public opinion based on polling data, and not whether the questions used were of poor quality, the accuracy can be evaluated as relatively high. However, we are not told whether these reports from State were isolated instances or reflect a broader pattern in the case.
- **Some confirmation of proposition 2**

- *Aggregation of evidence for proposition 2*

Tannenwald's conclusions: "the public horror of atomic weapons presented a serious political obstacle" (444).
- Sources of evidence appear to be relatively independent.
- **Overall confirmation of proposition 2 warranted.**

3   "Inhibitions about nuclear weapons may have operated in more indirect ways as well, for example, by influencing perceptions about suitable targets and the state of readiness for tactical nuclear warfare" (446) (no information provided on certainty or uniqueness).
- Certainty and uniqueness not discussed explicitly in case study, meaning that we are not told how this claim relates to the underlying causal hypothesis.

(*continued*)

TABLE 6.2. Aggregation of evidence in Tannenwald's 1999 study of the Korean War case (*continued*)

Causal hypothesis: Norms (C) resulted in US nonuse of nuclear weapons (O) in Korean War case

• *Evidence P3(i)*	"In March 1951 a Johns Hopkins University research group working with the Far East Command informed MacArthur that many 'large targets of opportunity' existed for nuclear attack. But the group found U.S. forces ill-prepared for tactical nuclear warfare" (446).
	• **Lu, La:** No information given for whether this finding is linked to moral inhibitions or merely stating that the US was not ready (low uniqueness). We also do not have any information about the context of the remarks, preventing us from further evaluating why it could be evidence of P3.
	• **No confirmation of proposition 3**
• *Evidence P3(ii)*	"Truman's general reluctance to consider nuclear weapons as like any other weapon . . . must be taken into account. Because of this, as Rosenberg and others have documented, U.S. planning for nuclear warfare lagged in the years before Korea" (447).
	• **Hu, La:** Citing three historical works without discussion means that we cannot evaluate accuracy. The two other works could build upon Rosenberg's; but we have no information that would enable us to assess whether this is the case or not. Some historiographical source criticism is warranted.
	• **Weak confirmation of proposition 3**
• *Aggregation of evidence for proposition 3*	• Tannenwald's conclusions: "In short, inhibitions about using nuclear weapons in general may have delayed readiness and planning for tactical nuclear use" (447).
	• No information about independence of sources given (P3ii might have built on P3i).
	• **Overall confirmation not warranted,** given that P3i is not really evidence of the link between planning and readiness and norms, whereas P3ii is of questionable accuracy.
4	"US leaders perceived a taboo developing and sought to challenge it" (448) (no information provided on certainty and uniqueness).
	• Certainty and uniqueness not discussed explicitly in case study, although it is relatively obvious that if found it would be difficult to account for leaders challenging a taboo unless a taboo actually existed that might result in nonuse.

• *Evidence of P4(i)*	"General Nicholas . . . expressed his disappointment over the failure to use nuclear weapons in Korea . . . 'I knew that many individuals in the United States opposed such thinking for idealistic, moral, or other reasons'" (447).
	• **Hu, La:** While finding that the "principal Pentagon authority on, and promoter of, nuclear weapons" wrote this might be unique evidence, given that it is in an autobiography many years later, we cannot trust that it actually reflects what he felt at the time.
	• **Very weak confirmation of proposition 4**
• *Evidence of P4(ii)*	"In Gavin's view, the United States had not pursued tactical nuclear options aggressively enough because of 'old thinking'" (448).
	• **Lu, La:** Memoirs have low accuracy, other things equal.
	• **Very weak confirmation of proposition 4**
Supporting proposition 4a	"Both Eisenhower and Dulles sought to resist an emerging perception that nuclear weapons should not be used and appeared far more concerned with the constraints imposed by a perceived taboo on nuclear weapons and negative public opinion than with any fear of Soviet retaliation" (448).
• *Evidence of P4a(i)*	"This moral problem' as Dulles referred to it, could potentially be an obstacle" (448).
	• **Hu, Ha:** National Security Council meeting minutes used as a source. However, Dulles's pronouncement only took part in one meeting in the spring of 1953, making it more debatable about whether it was an exception that proves the rule or not.
	• **Relatively strong confirmation of proposition 4a**

(continued)

TABLE 6.2. Aggregation of evidence in Tannenwald's 1999 study of the Korean War case (continued)

Causal hypothesis: Norms (C) resulted in US nonuse of nuclear weapons (O) in Korean War case

- *Evidence of P4a(ii)*
  "Later in the spring Eisenhower asserted his complete agreement with Dulles that 'somehow or other the tabu which surrounds the use of atomic weapons would have to be destroyed'" (449).
  - **Hu, Ha:** National Security Council meeting minutes used as a source. Very doubtful that we would find the President himself stating this in the meeting unless it reflected his concerns. Tannenwald evaluates uniqueness of this evidence when she writes, "It is sometimes argued that Eisenhower, famous for his dissembling, merely talked a 'tough' line on tactical nuclear weapons in order to maximize 'deterrence.' But these discussions were internal policy deliberations at the highest level where the audience he was attempting to persuade were his own advisers, not foreign enemies. These were not statements for public consumption" (449).
  - **Strong confirmation of proposition 4a**

- *Evidence of P4a(iii)*
  "In his memoirs Eisenhower maintained he was ready to challenge it" (449).
  - **Lu, La:** Public memoirs of a President have questionable accuracy.
  - **Very weak confirmation of proposition 4a**

- *Aggregation of evidence for proposition 4a*
  - No conclusions made by Tannenwald.
  - We do not know whether P4ai and P4aii are independent of each other.
  - **Strong overall confirmation** of proposition because of strong confirming evidence, where either P4ai or P4aii by themselves would enable a confirming inference in relation to proposition 4.

a lack of planning and readiness (proposition 3: inhibitions about nuclear weapons may have operated in more indirect ways as well, for example, by influencing perceptions about suitable targets and the state of readiness for tactical nuclear warfare), there is precious little evidence that substantiates this proposition—making her use of the phrase "may have" warranted.

In contrast, there is stronger support for propositions 2 (US and global public opinion was opposed to using atomic weapons) and 4 (US leaders perceived a taboo developing and sought to challenge it), although confirming proposition 2 does not enable any overall inferences about whether C caused O, because the proposition is most likely neither theoretically certain nor unique in relation to the causal hypothesis—although she does not evaluate this explicitly. However, despite not being directly linked logically to Tannenwald's theory that norms matter, proposition 4 is manifestly a direct logical corollary to the causal hypothesis that emerging norms mattered. And as we argue in table 6.2, despite the risk that the pieces of evidence P4a(i) and P4a(ii) in support of supporting proposition 4a are not empirically independent, finding either would, given the centrality of the actors and the context in which the remarks fell, be enough to confirm proposition 4 (very empirically unique in the context).

Therefore, in aggregate Tannenwald is warranted in concluding that norms mattered in the case. However, the evidence does not support many of her conclusions. We comment on this in the bracketed text in the following, where we reproduce her conclusions. She writes, "In sum, during the Korean War, an emerging taboo shaped how U.S. leaders defined their interests [*no evidence is put forward that warrants concluding that the norm defined interests*]. In contrast to the moral opprobrium Truman personally felt [*weak confirming evidence of proposition 1 supports this*], the taboo operated mostly instrumentally for Eisenhower and Dulles, constraining a casual resort to tactical nuclear weapons [*not warranted—only evidence for their attempt to counter the emerging norm (proposition 4) is produced*]. The burden of proof for a decision to use such weapons had already begun to shift. For those who wanted to challenge the emerging taboo, the best way to do so would have been to actually use such weapons, but the political costs of doing so were already high [*confirmation of proposition 2 supports the last claim about political costs, but the first parts of the claim are speculative*]. . . . But the political debate over the categorization of nuclear weapons as "unordinary" weapons suggests the early development of constitutive effects [*evidence for proposition 1 suggests that this might be warranted, although evidence very weak—therefore using the term "suggest" is warranted*] (Tannenwald 1999: 451).

Taken overall, this example illustrates that it is very important when aggregating evidence to be careful in making explicit first how propositions and supporting propositions are logically linked to the overall causal hypothesis, detailing theoretical certainty and uniqueness. In Tannenwald's example, the uniqueness of her core proposition 1 is evaluated in only a few short sentences. The reader not convinced by the logical arguments put forward in claiming that the test is theoretically unique could actually be justified in deciding not to continue reading the article at this point because that reader would believe that he or she could just as plausibly account for any evidence put forward in the case study.

The links from propositions to actual empirical evidence then have to be detailed, focusing on providing clear justifications for levels of empirical certainty for not found evidence, uniqueness for found evidence, and the expected accuracy of particular sources of evidence. Once empirical material has been collected, we can then assess whether there is support for propositions or not by aggregating from lower to higher levels, enabling overall conclusions about whether the collective body of evidence supports an inference that a given causal relationship existed in a case or not. In the example of Tannenwald, the strongest evidence she puts forward is actually not for her main proposition 1, but instead for proposition 4, which should have been given a more prominent place in the development of her argument.

6.10. Conclusions

This chapter has fleshed out how new empirical evidence enables inferences using Bayesian logic. We developed a set of guidelines for assessing prior confidence in a causal relationship in a single case or population of cases, followed by a discussion of the probative value of evidence, where the logical link between empirical material and causal relationships is developed using the language of certainty and uniqueness, and each piece of empirical evidence is also assessed to determine whether we can trust it. We suggested a two-step procedure, where theoretical arguments are put forward that detail the relationship between the causal hypothesis being assessed and its data-generating processes, resulting in the development of propositions (and supporting propositions) about potential evidence. Here we are answering the question, "What empirical fingerprints will the theorized relationship leave and why would it be evidence?" In the Tannenwald example, her proposition about evidence was that the hypothesized norms → nonuse relationship should leave "taboo talk." She discusses why she did not have to find it (low theoretical certainty), but claims that if found, there are really no plausible alternative explanations ("it is not just cheap talk").

Propositions then have to be related to actual pieces of evidence, where we evaluate the empirical certainty for not found evidence (e.g., did we have access to the empirical record?), empirical uniqueness for found evidence (e.g., is the piece of found evidence an anomaly?), and reasons for why we can trust the found or not found evidence. In the Tannenwald example, this happened when she evaluates the empirical record to figure out whether the proposition was actually present, finding several pieces of evidence that she claims are taboo talk.

Whether theory or empirical material comes first depends on whether one is engaging in theory-first or empirics-first research, but the evaluations are the same in both, with the exception that in empirics-first there is no need to evaluate either theoretical or empirical certainty of pieces of evidence because we already know we have found them.

The chapter provided a set of Bayesian-inspired rules for aggregating evidence in order to achieve the transparent assessment of what types of inferences the empirical evidence enable. Our framework is compatible with both empirics-first and theory-first research; the only requirement for updating is that the evidence used to make inferences is "new," that is, it is not the same evidence upon which the original theory was developed.

The theoretical and empirical assessment of evidence relates to what has been termed "analytical and production transparency." Moravcsik defines analytical transparency as a process where "social scientists should publicize how they measure, interpret, and analyze data. . . . For readers to understand and engage in scholarship, they must be able to assess what the data measure, how descriptive and causal inferences are drawn from them, and how precise and unbiased they are" (2014b: 666). Production transparency "rests on the premise that social scientists should publicize the broader set of research design choices they make. . . . In qualitative political science, specific concerns include oversampling of confirming evidence ('cherry-picking'), unfair framing of alternative theories ('straw-manning'), conducting idiosyncratic and non-robust tests, and aggregating findings unfairly" (Moravcsik 2014b: 666). While some of the concerns about production transparency relate to broader design questions that are dealt with elsewhere in this book, concerns such as how evidence is selected to avoid cherry-picking are relevant for the assessment in the argument road map.

Justifications are vital. For example, without explicit justification for why a proposition about evidence is, for example, theoretically certain in relation

TABLE 6.3. A template for an argument road map

Causal hypothesis:

Propositions linked to causal hypothesis

1   What is proposition? Then describe level of theoretical certainty and uniqueness of proposition—that is, how is it theoretically related to causal relationship?

   Evidence P1   Describe piece of evidence found (or not found)
   - justifications for empirical certainty (if not found) or uniqueness (if found)
   - evaluation of expected accuracy of piece of evidence

to a theorized causal relationship, the proposition is just a postulate that does not enable strong disconfirming inferences to be made if we do not find predicted evidence. When presenting in an actual work, we suggest a bare minimum of presentation of the theoretical and empirical evaluation of evidence, linking to some form of appendix in the work or online using active citation techniques (Moravcsik 2010) that would provide much more thorough documentation of what sources tell us and our justifications for things like theoretical certainty or why we trust a given piece of evidence.

To make the assessment of evidence transparent, we suggested the use of an argument road map like that used in criminal trials, where propositions are first developed about the empirical fingerprints (observable manifestations) that the causal relationship might leave in a case (or across cases) (see table 6.3 for a template). Each proposition should describe the logical relationship between hypothetical observables and the causal theory in terms of theoretical certainty (only when theory-first) and uniqueness. Pieces of evidence are then put forward in connection with each proposition (or supporting proposition), with clear descriptions of the empirical certainty or uniqueness, along with the accuracy of each piece of evidence found or not found.

CHAPTER 7

Comparative Methods

with Jørgen Møller and Svend-Erik Skaaning

> That comparative analysis is no substitute for detailed investigation of specific cases is obvious.
>
> Barrington Moore (1966: xiv)

7.1. Introduction

Despite being widely used, comparative methods that involve a relatively small number of cases are largely viewed as flawed research tools. The most common critique is that they involve too many variables in a small number of cases, termed the "degrees of freedom" problem, where we cannot assess the mean causal effect of any individual variable because there are not enough cases to enable assessment of what a change in X means for values of Y, controlling for other potential causes (Lijphart 1971; Lieberson 1991; Campbell 1975; Gerring 2011).

However, we contend that this critique builds on a misunderstanding of the research purposes that classic, small-N comparative methods can be used for, where there is an unfortunate tendency to believe that small-N comparisons are used to make confirming causal inferences (Geddes 1990; King, Keohane, and Verba 1994; Lieberson 1991, 1994). Indeed, we agree that comparative methods are very weak if we understood them only as a type of empirical test to confirm causation. For instance, the method of difference (see section 7.4) is at best a very weak confirmatory test of causal relationships when using observational data from a handful of cases. The problems are twofold: (1) the evidence of difference-making utilized is observational instead of experimentally manipulated data, thus preventing us from making confirmatory inferences because we cannot assess whether the relationship is causal or spurious, and (2) even if we could accept the observational data as evidence of difference-making upon which we could make confirming *causal* inferences, the small number of cases prevents us from robustly assessing whether the relationship is the product of coincidence or reflects a causal relationship.

However, understood as a component of a research design that combines within-case and cross-case methods, comparisons can play a vital role in enabling us to make strong inferences about causal relationships within causally homogeneous, bounded populations of a given theoretical phenomenon (Goldthorpe 1997; Waldner 1999; Mahoney 1999; Brady and Collier 2004; Rohlfing 2012; Slater and Ziblatt 2012; Tarrow 2010). Unfortunately, there are few practical sets of guidelines for how to achieve this in the existing methodological literature. For instance, in Goertz and Mahoney's (2012) excellent book on qualitative methods, while they note the importance of within- and cross-case analysis, they focus in particular on the use of within-case methods for making causal inference. Unfortunately, they offer little guidance on how to combine within-case process-tracing and cross-case comparisons. In a similar fashion, Berg-Schlosser's 2012 book on qualitative mixed methods focuses almost completely on comparisons, with little guidance on within-case analysis. The next three chapters are therefore intended to provide more substantial guidelines for how to combine within- and cross-case methods, flagging the respective division of labor in the tasks of theory-building, building causally homogeneous populations, and theory confirmation and testing.

We recommend that comparative methods are used (1) to find potential causes of social phenomena, (2) to build causally homogenous populations of a given theoretical phenomenon that enable the selection of appropriate cases for within-case analysis as well as the findings of within-case analyses to be generalized to other causally similar cases, and (3) to engage in disconfirming empirical tests of hypothesized necessary or sufficient conditions using cross-case evidence. In contrast, we do not recommend using comparative methods as a tool for confirming tests of necessity or sufficiency, given the lack of theoretical uniqueness of comparisons of similarities or differences across a small set of cases.

Combining cross-case comparisons and within-case studies does raise some challenges because they build on different ontological foundations (see chapter 2). Whereas comparative methods build on counterfactual understandings that lead one to make theoretical claims about necessity and/or sufficiency, case study methods like process-tracing and congruence build on a mechanism-based understanding. This means that the cross-case and within-case analyses are employing ontologically different types of causal explanations, creating the requirement that we are careful in specifying what evidence supports which type of causal claim (see chapter 6).

This also means that the idea that Bayesian logic can act as a tool for neatly integrating cross and within-case methods does not hold in case-based research, in contrast to what is claimed in Humphreys and Jacobs (2015). There are several reasons for this. The first reason is that when combining comparative and within-case studies, we are making different types of inferences (confirming or disconfirming) about different types of causal explanations (counterfactual-based necessity and/or sufficiency, or mechanism-based claims of a relationship or mechanism linking C and O) based on different types of evidence (cross-case evidence of difference-making or within-case mechanistic evidence) that together reduce our ability to use the empirical evidence that we gathered using within-case analysis to update our confidence in cross-case relationships, and vice versa. This does not mean that cross-method updating cannot take place—just that it is not as easy as many scholars portray because we have evidence of very different things at the two levels.

Second, the model developed by Humphreys and Jacobs assumes relative causal homogeneity within a population as the baseline, which means that it is relatively easy to move back and forth from the case to the population level. However, they also suggest that in-depth case studies have relatively limited value because, "at least for estimating population-level quantities, relative numbers matter [and] even strong process-tracing evidence, gathered on a small number of cases, will have only a very modest impact on conclusions drawn from the quantitative analysis of a much larger sample" (Humphreys and Jacobs 2015: 667). If we take context seriously, as we do in case-based research, the resulting causal heterogeneity creates major problems for their model—something they admit later in their article. But their recommendation for dealing with heterogeneity is to spend less effort on case studies and instead concentrate on population-level effects. In contrast, we contend that in case-based research, the core of our research should be focused on individual cases, because this is the level at which causal relationships actually play out. But this also means that we can generalize only to smaller, bounded populations of causally homogeneous cases.

In this chapter we explore how we can combine within- and cross-case elements to make stronger inferences about causal relationships in the relevant population. It is important to note that we develop tools for small-*N* comparative methods that are applicable beyond the types of causal relationships analyzed in the comparative-historical tradition, where only a very small number of complex cases are compared (Mahoney 2004, 2007; Rohlfing 2012). Naturally, when the analysis is case-centric, comparison is not a goal because the analytical focus is on crafting comprehensive explanations of the single case (see chapters 8 and 9 for more on "explaining outcome" case studies).

We first discuss the assumptions underlying small-N comparative methods, then elaborate on what it actually means to compare. We then present the core comparative tools for assessing either patterns of similarity or differences, illustrating in the process why Mill's methods of agreement and difference are not the same as most-similar- and most-different-system designs.

We then expand on the use of comparative methods in three research situations: building theories, building populations, and testing and revising causal theories. We include the analysis of counterfactual alternatives as a form of comparative theory test, because it is essentially a form of most similar test that utilizes hypothetical data as a counterfactual "what if?" to assess claims of necessity. In all the comparative tests we discuss, we explore how Bayesian logic provides us with an inferential framework for making disconfirming inferences based on cross-case evidence.

7.2. The Assumptions of Comparative Methods

An interest in causation playing out in individual cases is what distinguishes small-N comparative methods from larger-n comparative designs. This does not mean that we have to adopt a heavily contextualized, interpretive understanding of cases, where comparison does not make sense because causes in individual cases only function in the context of the particular case—what we called case-centric research. As discussed in chapter 1, the guidelines in this book are with certain adaptations applicable across a range of philosophical positions. However, it does mean that because our focus is on causation at the case-level, concerns about context and achieving causal homogeneity in the selected population of cases become even more important. Given that causation occurs at the case level, the "workhorse" of making causal inferences in case-based methods is within-case analysis. To generalize from the studied case to other cases, we have to be able to demonstrate that the population to be inferred to is at least roughly causally similar to the studied case. This means that contextual conditions are very important in relation to within-case analysis because they determine whether a given cause is linked to a given outcome through a particular mechanism. To demonstrate causal homogeneity in a population of cases, comparative methods have to be used.

Comparative methods build on the understanding of causation as counterfactuals when dealing with individual cases (counterfactual comparative methods), and counterfactuals and regularity when dealing with cross-case patterns. As with the other case-based methods in this book, we contend that comparative methods build on a deterministic ontological understanding of causal claims. While some scholars have argued for an "almost" deterministic understanding in comparative methods (Mahoney 2008), we contend that accepting "almost" determinism would define away a core element of the analytical value-added of case-based methods. Naturally we can never know something with 100 percent confidence in the empirical world, which is why we advocate the adoption of a Bayesian, probabilistic epistemology. Yet this does not mean that when we find an empirical anomaly we should treat it as an outlier in an otherwise robust cross-case pattern. Instead, in case-based research we want to know what it is about deviant case 1 that makes it different. For example, assume that there is a sufficient relationship between $C_1{}^*C_2$ (i.e., C_1 AND C_2 produce the outcome) and O that holds in nineteen out of twenty cases, but O does not occur in deviant case 1, despite the presence of C_1 and C_2. Instead of accepting that case 1 is an exception that proves the rule, the case-based researcher would want to ask, "What is it about case 1 that is different? Is there an omitted scope or causal condition that has to be present in order for O to occur?" By answering these questions, better theoretical explanations result.

7.3. What Does It Mean to Compare?

One of the reasons for the unease felt by many social science methodologists about small-N comparative methods is that they are in many respects closer to historical methods than experimental variance-based methods. The field of comparative history, which includes historians, political scientists, and sociologists, typically employs complex, heavily contextualized causal explanations that extend to only a small, bounded population (Skocpol and Somers 1980; Ragin 1987; Rueschemeyer 2003; Collier and Mahoney 1996: 68–69; Mahoney 2004; Emmenegger and Petersen 2015; Mahoney and Thelen 2015).

This type of contextualized and bounded explanation can seem far from the twin ideals of parsimony and generalizability that pervade areas of the social sciences where positivist philosophic views are prevalent (Jackson 2011; Mahoney and Thelen 2015). Case-based comparativists would counter that parsimony makes sense only when it does not come at the price of explanatory accuracy. If causes work only as part of more complex conjunctions, or only within a particular bounded context, we need to capture that complexity in our causal explanations instead of aiming for parsimonious explanations that would be incorrect in many instances.

As developed in chapter 2, case-based comparativists are very concerned about causal homogeneity, spending considerable analytical effort in building and revising populations (Collier and Mahoney 1996; Mahoney 2004, 2007: 130–31; Rueschemeyer 2003; George and Bennett 2005: 164; Ragin 1987: 54–55; Skocpol and Somers 1980). Case-based comparativists are therefore usually comfortable making inferences only to relatively small, bounded populations, given their claims that different causal conditions can have very different effects in different contexts. When equifinality at the level of conditions exists, the same outcome can be the product of different causes in different contexts. Including equifinality at the level of mechanisms makes the assumption of causal homogeneity even more important. The core comparativist claim that we should operate only with populations of causally homogeneous cases is well captured in the following quote:

> In the preface to *Social Origins*, Barrington Moore likens the generalizations his study established to "a large-scale map of an extended terrain, such as an airplane pilot might use in crossing a continent." This is an appropriate metaphor. And the reflection it inspires in this context is that no matter how good the map were of, say, North America, the pilot could not use the same map to fly over other continents. (Skocpol and Somers 1980: 195)

Working with a small number of cases is a deliberate choice, in contrast to what Lieberson claims: "If data were available with the appropriate depth and detail for a large number of cases, obviously the researcher would not be working with these few cases" (1991: 308–9). Here he misses the value-added of small-N comparisons. Case-based comparativists would counter that when we have data at the "appropriate depth and detail," we will often learn that it makes sense to compare only within small, bounded populations in most instances (Collier and Mahoney 1996).

The detection of causal heterogeneity and conceptual stretching requires extensive familiarity with the complexity of the cases in the population. For example, when analyzing democratization, case-based comparativists might feel comfortable making claims within a given region in a particular time period (e.g., Central and Eastern Europe in the 1990s), but they would not attempt to make more universal claims about the causes of democratization writ large (e.g., Bunce 2000).

Where case-based comparativists differ from many historians is in the idea that social phenomena can be studied outside of their specific context in a case. This is captured in the phrase "a case of," where proper names like President Reagan are replaced by abstract concepts like head of state (Przeworski and Teune 1970: 24–30).[1] Sartori describes this in terms of focusing our attention on the narrower theoretical aspect of a case that is then comparable with other instances of a particular phenomenon, where we ask the question, "Comparable *in which respect?*" (1991: 247).

A historian or a case-centric social scientist would understand a case like the Cuban Missile Crisis as a holistic whole, meaning that it cannot be compared with other crises because it is unique. In contrast, in theory-centric research the Cuban Missile Crisis would be seen as "a case of" several different theoretical phenomena, ranging from being a case of deterrence bargaining to a case of crisis decision-making. Here the theory-centric social scientist would focus analytical attention on specific aspects of the case related to the narrower theoretical aspect of the case, although he or she would still pay close attention to the importance of the case-specific context, especially in evaluating what observations mean in a particular case. Treated in this fashion, the Cuban Missile Crisis could then be used in a comparison with other instances of crisis decision-making. At the same time, by being relatively close to the case, we would also be in a position to judge whether the dynamics of the Cuban Missile Crisis were so unique that we could not expect the causal processes at play in the case to be comparable to other cases. The justification for this might be that the costs of failure were many orders of magnitude greater than other interstate crises in the twentieth century, given that it was the only crisis in which the threat of nuclear annihilation was a serious possibility if military hostilities between the United States and Soviets were to erupt. If we believe the case to be unique, we would then cull it from the population to create a more causally homogenous population of comparable interstate crises.

Comparing cases requires that cases are relatively independent of each other and that the population is causally homogeneous (Ragin 1987: 48). Comparisons can be made by comparing the same spatial unit (e.g., a country) at two or more distinct times, utilizing a before-and-after type of comparison. However, as we discussed in chapter 6, comparing a case across time runs into serious problems of endogeneity in most instances, given that what happens at t_0 affects what is happening at t_1—and this means that the cases are not fully independent of each other.

More relevant are comparisons of two or more different units either across space (e.g., comparing two countries) or by levels (e.g., comparing state and country-levels). Comparisons across units naturally run into the problem of whether the units are actually causally homogeneous or whether what is going on in case 1 is causally different from case 2. It is therefore very important that one assesses whether the cases are as comparable as possible in relation to the causal theory being assessed. Rohlfing gives the example of the challenges one can face when comparing two states at the same time (2012: 129–33). If we are studying two developing states, we might decide to compare Sierra Leone and Mauritius at the same chronological time (e.g., 1970). One problem of this comparison might be that while Sierra Leone had been independent since 1961, Mauritius achieved this only in 1968, meaning that we could not meaningfully compare postcolonial development in the two countries without taking into consideration what Rohlfing refers to as theoretical time, defined as the time in which a causal theory can be expected to play out. Therefore, a comparison ten years after independence might be more relevant (Sierra Leone in 1971 and Mauritius in 1978). The problem here, however, is that important contextual conditions would be different across the two cases because of the oil crisis in 1973, meaning that the two cases would not be strictly comparable (Rohlfing 2012: 130). In most circumstances in the social world, there is no such thing as a perfect comparison, especially when comparing countries or other complex social entities.

In the following we discuss comparisons primarily across units in spatial and temporal terms. For example, we might compare policy-making dynamics in law-making in the European Parliament across issue areas like environmental legislation and consumer protection, or we might compare dynamics before and after the European Parliament was made a colegislature.

On a final note, some causes might be more important than others when determining whether cases are causally similar or dissimilar (Glynn and Ichino 2012). When examining whether two or more cases are similar, there can be situations where we have good theoretical reasons to weigh only one or two causal conditions as more important in determining whether the cases are similar. For example, when determining whether two cases are similar in all respects except a particular cause and outcome, we might find that there were other differences between the two cases. However, if we are able to justify that these other differences are less causally relevant in explaining differences, we can proceed "as if" the two cases were similar.

7.4. The Tools of Comparative Methods

The following presents the analytical tools utilized in comparative designs, distinguishing between comparisons that focus on similarities and differences. In the first, the basic logic is that "similarities explain similarities," whereas the second is that "differences explain differences." Comparisons of similarity include the philosopher John Stuart Mill's method of agreement (positive on outcome) and the more recent most-different-system comparisons, whereas comparisons of differences are Mill's method of differences (differences of cause) and the more recent most-similar-system comparisons. Mill's methods are at the heart of case-based comparative methods. However, he was himself quite skeptical about their utility outside of experimental settings, especially for theory-building. But this does not mean that we cannot draw on them in our comparative designs for different purposes, and we contend that they have a range of theory- and population-building uses (Mill 1843/2011; for similar claims, see Rohlfing 2012: 100; Ragin 1987, 2000).

The defining feature of Mill's (1843/2011) methods is that relevant cases are selected based on their membership in the set of the outcome, whereas the most-similar/most-different tools are based on membership in the set of the cause (Przeworski and Teune 1970). This means that Mill's methods and most-similar/most-different tools are *not* the same thing despite being widely understood in such terms (e.g., the Wikipedia entry treats them as the same).[2] Indeed, they also have different uses that will be explored in the following sections.

Comparisons of Similarity

The core logic of both Mill's method of agreement (termed here *positive on outcome*) and the most-different-system comparisons is that "similarities explain similarities." While variance-based designs focus on differences, many of the most important research puzzles in the social science relate to accounting for puzzling similarities (van Kersbergen 2010).

In the *positive-on-outcome* comparison, cases are selected that share the same outcome; for example, two or more cases of war outbreak are compared to determine whether they share a common causal condition that has been theorized to be necessary. The tool is clearly based on an asymmetric understanding of causation, with only positive cases of the outcome selected.

Ideally, all instances of the outcome should be assessed. In practice,

TABLE 7.1. Positive-on-outcome comparison—Mill's method-of-agreement

Case	C_1	C_2	O
1	+	+	+
2	+	+	+
3	−	+	+
4	−	+	+

positive-on-outcome comparisons often use a small number of very similar cases that are selected for comparison, as illustrated in table 7.1. There, four cases are selected that share the outcome. In this instance, C_1 can be disconfirmed as a necessary cause with some confidence because O occurs in cases where C_1 is not present. It might be that C_2 is a necessary cause, but we cannot confirm it because the cross-case evidence does *not* enable us to distinguish between spurious correlations and causal relationships.

One of the critiques of comparative methods, and the positive-on-outcome framework in particular, is that it is an invariant design where we have selected cases based on values of the outcome (or the *dependent variable* in variance-based language) (Geddes 1990; King, Keohane, and Verba 1994) (see the discussions in chapters 2 and 6). Yet while the selection of cases according to positive values of the outcome would prevent us from assessing the difference that values of X have upon values of Y using variance-based designs, this critique misses the point regarding case-based designs. There are no case-based comparativists who would make confirming inferences about a given condition being a necessary cause solely based on a comparative test like the positive-on-outcome comparison; instead, they would use it only to make negative inferences that disconfirm causes as necessary or sufficient to a significant degree. This is also why Mill talks of comparative methods as methods of "elimination" instead of confirmation. Positive inferences, understood as a confirmative empirical test that strengthens our confidence in a given condition being causally related to an outcome, are made by utilizing within-case tests in case-based research. Here, variance in values of O across cases does not enable inferences; instead, mechanistic within-case evidence is used to make confirming inferences about causation.

In the *most-different-system* comparison cases are selected that differ in as many respects as possible, with the exception of the hypothesized causal condition.[3] A most-different-system comparison is depicted in table 7.2, where we should expect that O will be present in all cases if C_1 is a cause of O.

The goal in a most-different-system is to assess whether the outcome

TABLE 7.2. Most-different-system comparison

Case	C_1	C_2	C_3	O
1	+	−	+	?
2	+	+	−	?
3	+	−	+	?
4	+	+	−	?

is positive when the cause is present while all other potential causes differ. Other potential causes are therefore disconfirmed to some degree (Przeworski and Teune 1970: 35; Collier 1991: 111). One particular strength of most-different-system comparisons is that they enable us to explore the bounds of our population by focusing our attention on similar causal relationships across a wide variety of cases, leading us to either expand or limit the scope conditions in which we expect a causal relationship to apply (McAdam, Tarrow, and Tilly 2001, chapter 10).

Comparisons of Difference

The basic logic of both Mill's method-of-difference and the most-similar-system comparison is that "differences are explained by differences."

Whereas the positive-on-outcome focuses on assessing similarities across cases, Mill's method-of-difference compares two or more cases with different outcomes. It can therefore also be termed a *different-outcomes* comparison. As with the positive-on-outcome comparison, cases are here selected *solely* on the basis of membership in the set of the outcome.

In a difference-of-outcome comparison, cases are selected that differ on the outcome, for example, a case of peace (O) with a war (~O).[4] Factors that are present both when the outcome is present and absent are disconfirmed as potentially sufficient causes. This is illustrated in table 7.3, where two cases where O is present are chosen, together with two cases where O is absent. Note here that we are focusing only on causes of O, with other cases simply being negative cases that we are not attempting to explain. In other words, we are making asymmetric causal claims that have implications for the types of empirical tests that are relevant.

If the different-outcomes framework is used in an exploratory, theory-building fashion, we might not know what C_2 is; therefore, the purpose of the comparative analysis is to find it. If we are engaging in theory-testing, the pattern across cases in table 7.2 would downgrade our confidence in C_1

TABLE 7.3. Different-outcomes comparison—Mill's method of difference

Case	C_1	C_2	O
1	+	+	+
2	+	+	+
3	+	−	−
4	+	−	−

being a sufficient condition, whereas C_2 is only very weakly confirmed as possibly sufficient.

The basic idea of a *most-similar-system* comparison is that we investigate whether O is present in cases where C_1 is present and absent, with other potential causes held equal (Przeworski and Teune 1970). As with the different-outcomes framework, the assumption is that similarities cannot explain differences. It can also be termed a difference-on-cause, or a most-similar-system dissimilar-outcome (MSDO) if used in a hybrid fashion where values of C and O are relevant. The crucial distinction between the most-similar and most-different is that the most-similar framework involves *minimizing* the differences between the cases being compared across a range of causal conditions, whereas the most-different framework involves *maximizing* differences.

The logic of a most-similar-system comparison is illustrated in table 7.4, where we select two (or more) cases on the basis of differences in a single causal condition (i.e., C_1), holding other potential causal conditions equal. We then investigate whether the presence or absence of the outcome follows the same pattern as the presence or absence of C_1. The outcome for cases is depicted as question marks in the figure because cases in the most similar comparison described by Przeworski and Teune are selected before our knowledge of whether the outcome is present. If we find that O is present when C_1 is present, and absent when C_1 is absent, the hypothesis that C_1 is individually sufficient would survive, whereas our confidence in it would be downgraded if we did not find this pattern.

TABLE 7.4. Most-similar-systems comparison

Case	C_1	C_2	C_3	O
1	+	−	+	?
2	+	−	+	?
3	−	−	+	?
4	−	−	+	?

At the ontological level, the most-similar-system comparison is close to the experimental ideal,[5] where the difference produced by varying one causal condition is assessed while keeping everything else constant (Lijphart 1975).[6] Control for other causes is therefore critical, enabling us to claim that because "everything else" is equal, the cause that differs in the same pattern as the outcome must be the cause.

However, case-based comparativists would contend that because of the lack of comparable cases in the social world where "everything else" is equal—given the complexity and diversity across cases—there always will be important contextual conditions that differ across *even the most similar cases* (e.g., Ragin 1987: 48). Indeed, the two researchers who first developed the most-similar-system method suggested that it is very weak because the "treatment" (the varied causal condition) cannot be isolated in most instances because other causally relevant conditions also are different across cases (Przeworski and Teune 1970: 34). The only exception to this would be if we engage in an actual experiment, where we manipulate the treatment across two randomly selected and relatively large subpopulations.[7]

Strictly speaking, given that the most-similar-system method only selects cases on membership of causal conditions, there are few theory-building applications. However, as we will discuss here, if we use a hybrid of the most-similar-system method and different-outcomes comparisons, we can select a range of cases that are similar across a range of potential causal conditions but differ on the outcome (Berg-Schlosser 2012). This can be termed a *most-similar-cause, most-dissimilar-on-outcome framework,* or MSDO (Berg-Schlosser 2012). We would then search for the causal condition that is present when O is present and absent when O is absent. Used in this fashion, the most-similar-system comparison is a very important tool in theory-building, enabling us to detect potential causes without expending large amounts of analytical resources.

Challenges and Problems of Small-N Comparisons

The most significant challenge with small-N comparisons is that they cannot stand alone when making confirming causal inferences. Instead, they should always be coupled with within-case studies. The requirements for using the four types of comparisons to make any form of causal inferences are quite restrictive, including that (1) *all* potential causal conditions must be identified prior to theory-testing, so there are no omitted causal conditions, (2) causes work individually instead of as parts of conjunctions, and (3) the population from which cases are drawn has to be causally homogeneous.

In all four types of comparison, we cannot make any inferences about conditions that are not included in the comparison. Indeed, a central criticism of many comparative analyses that attempt to make positive, confirmatory inferences is that important causal conditions are omitted. For example, Putnam, Leonardi, and Nanetti compared regions in northern and southern Italy in the 1993 book *Making Democracy Work*. They utilize a most-similar-system framework in their analysis, where they argue that despite possessing similar political institutions, the two regions responded in opposite ways to the same regional reform. They contend that the key difference in the otherwise similar system is the difference in the civil involvement and civil competence in regions. However, others have dismissed their findings, because many causal conditions were omitted that were just as plausible causes of differences as civil involvement and civic culture (Tarrow 2010: 238). But this critique is only applicable if we want to use comparisons to confirm theories, whereas in disconfirmation and in theory-building, all potential causes do not have to be known. For instance, if we find that C_1 might be a necessary condition based on a initial comparison, it does not matter whether there might be other causes present because we would not be confirming that C_1 is causal based on the comparison—this requires a within-case analysis using either congruence or process-tracing.

Second, all four types of comparisons assume that causes work individually (Lieberson 1991: 312–14). This means that they have difficulty dealing with different forms of interactions between causal conditions. There can be conjunctional causation, where two causes together produce an outcome, or there might be interaction between causes, meaning that the effects of each cause are magnified, diminished, or otherwise modified in the presence of other causes.

The inability to deal with conjunctional causation and interactions is particularly problematic in the social sciences, given that only rarely do we theorize that individual conditions are necessary or sufficient by themselves (George and Bennett 2005: 157; Ragin 2000). In the difference-on-outcome comparison described in table 7.3, C_1 might have been an INUS condition (individually necessary part of unnecessary but sufficient condition) that, together with an unknown, omitted C_3, is sufficient to produce O. Yet on the basis of the results, we might have disconfirmed C_1 as a potential sufficient cause, which is naturally correct when taken individually. But it would be incorrect to infer that C_1 is not causally related to O in any fashion. It is therefore vital when making disconfirmatory causal inferences that we are very precise about exactly what type of relationship we are downgrading our confidence in. Here the proper conclusion would be that "C_1 is most likely not individually a sufficient cause, but we cannot rule out that C_1 might have other types of causal relationships with the outcome." And as with the previous critique, when comparisons are used for theory-building, this only means that we might fail to detect conjunctional causation. Therefore, if there are good empirical or theoretical reasons to expect conjunctional causation, we suggest that one should utilize QCA (qualitative comparative analysis) techniques instead of the four simple types of comparisons developed here (see, e.g., Schneider and Wagemann 2012).

Another problem relates to overdetermination, which refers to the situation where more than one causal inference is plausible based on the cross-case patterns found. In table 7.1, if both C_1 and C_2 were always present when O is present, we would be unable to discriminate between the situation where both are necessary and where only one is, with the other being spurious. When we are unable to discriminate between two or more causal conditions, the disconfirmatory strength of the comparative tests is significantly weakened. The risk of this problem increases the further that the number of causal conditions included in either a framework exceeds the number of cases compared. It is, however, important to note that this is not the same thing as the "too many variables, too few cases" critique (Lieberson 1991), which relates to our ability to make positive inferences that strengthen our belief in a condition being causally related to the outcome. Here we are speaking about our inability to make negative inferences, referring to the disconfirmatory power of tests, whereas Lieberson's critique relates to making positive, confirmatory inferences. If we face overdetermined outcomes in comparative tests, we should then utilize within-case tests that allow us to assess whether one or both of the causal conditions are causally related to the outcome (see chapters 8 and 9).

Concluding, the significant weaknesses in using small-N comparisons for confirming causal inferences does not mean that they are not analytically useful as part of broader comparative designs that combine cross-case and within-case elements. It just means that we need to be very careful about what inferences we make, for example not ruling out potential conjunctional causation based on either framework.

7.5. Using Comparative Methods to Find Causes

There is a crucial distinction between developing theoretical hypotheses from scratch and revising existing theories. In the first instance, we are engaging in exploratory work where we use comparative frameworks that maximize the odds of finding causal relationships that are potentially valid. Comparative methods can also be used after failed within- or cross-case theory tests to revise hypotheses. We focus on exploratory work here, returning to theoretical revision in the next section.

Theory-building is a creative, investigative process that starts with an exploration of the empirical field (Swedberg 2012: 7). It resembles what crime investigators do when figuring out who should be arrested as a plausible suspect in a crime, whereas the "theory test" occurs when the suspect is being tried in court (Swedberg 2012: 6). Naturally, there will be very different evidential standards in the two situations; in the first we are probing to find plausible causes using relatively weak, preliminary evidence, whereas in the latter the theory is fully fleshed out, and strong evidence needs to be presented in a systematic fashion to convict a suspect.

Unfortunately, it is impossible to provide a systematic framework for how theories can be built. Theory-building is intrinsically a messy process but is often presented in published research "as if" the theory appeared as the logical result of the interrogation of the empirical record. In the words of Merton, existing research often has "an immaculate appearance which reproduces nothing of the intuitive leaps, false starts, mistakes, loose ends and happy accidents that actually cluttered up the inquiry" (1967: 4).

This said, we believe that we can increase the odds of finding interesting causal explanations by using comparisons. If we are in the situation where we know an outcome but not a cause, we can employ either a positive-on-outcome or different-outcomes comparison, or preferably both in a sequential fashion. All we know before we have done our research is whether cases are members of the set of the outcome or not. We then engage in a wide-ranging comparative probing to search for possible candidate causes, a process that often takes the form of a brainstorm where we cast our net widely for any plausible cause, drawing on our knowledge of specific cases and theories from related fields as a source of inspiration. Parallel to this, we can engage in the type of congruence exploratory case study.

When there is existing research in a field, we can also draw on existing studies to narrow the focus of our search for potential causes. Given that we then have some idea about potential causes, we can also deploy cause-centered methods like the most-similar- and most-different-system comparisons if we expand them to include values of the outcome (O).

The most-similar-system comparison is here a particularly useful tool if used in a hybrid fashion (an MSDO comparison, as mentioned earlier), where we hold as many plausible causes constant while at the same time ensuring difference on membership of O. This is depicted in table 7.5, where

TABLE 7.5. A theory-building hybrid most-similar systems comparison

Case	?	C_2	C_3	O
1	+	−	+	+
2	+	−	+	+
3	−	−	+	−
4	−	−	+	−

the goal is to identify the unknown C. One way this can be achieved is to engage in a more in-depth comparison in conjunction with exploratory case studies of both cases 2 and 3, asking which factor differs between the two otherwise similar cases (Tarrow 2010).

The most-different-system comparison is also useful, focusing our attention on commonalities across a range of otherwise different cases. For both comparisons, the findings of our theory-building should be treated in a very preliminary fashion. They are merely candidate causes that then can be tested in a more rigorous design (see the discussion here under theory-testing).

Both positive-on-outcome and different-outcomes comparisons can be used to detect possible causal conditions, but they can additionally help us detect the type of causal relationship that is present. When employing a positive-on-outcome comparison for finding causes, the question we ask is, "Which condition is shared by all the cases?" In the different-outcomes comparison we ask, "Which conditions are present when the outcome is present and absent when the outcome is absent?" In the positive-on-outcome comparison, if we find a causal condition that is present in all the selected cases of the outcome, this is potentially a necessary condition. The different-outcomes comparison would allow us, in contrast, to detect potentially sufficient conditions.

A single cause will almost never be sufficient individually. Therefore, we should look for conjunctions of causes that might be sufficient when employing a theory-building different-outcomes framework. This might look like table 7.6. Initially we might conclude that neither C_2 nor C_3 is causally related to O, as, for instance, C_2 is present in case 3 but O is not. However, C_2 and C_3 might be INUS conditions.

Together C_2 and C_3 are *potentially* sufficient to produce O, consistent with the pattern in table 7.7. Naturally this is a very weak positive inference, and we would want to test this hunch about the conjunction of C_2 and C_3 further using within-case tests. Therefore, if our comparison finds plausible candidate causal conditions, we need to proceed to the more rigorous

TABLE 7.6. C_2 and C_3—a conjunctional sufficient causal relationship?

Case	C_1	C_2	C_3	O
1	+	+	+	+
2	+	+	+	+
3	+	+	−	−
4	+	−	+	−

comparative testing that is discussed in the next section and in the following chapters.

In contrast, if we find no potential causal conditions with any of the four types of comparison, the most plausible explanations are (1) that we have tapped into a causally heterogeneous population, most likely due to omitted causal conditions; (2) there is significant measurement error, with cases mistakenly categorized as in or out; or (3) causes work together only in very complicated conjunctional patterns. If we are confident in our empirical measures, we would then probe further to detect whether there omitted causal conditions, for example by using a positive-on-outcome framework to detect omitted similarities. For example, if we are studying economic development, we might have selected countries both with and without a colonial past, which potentially might be a contextual factor that could influence how particular causal conditions operate. If we are not confident in our empirical measures, the solution would be to attempt to improve further the measures and to remove cases from the population assessed in which there is a substantial degree of empirical uncertainty about their correct categorization. The third problem is more difficult to deal with in classic small-N comparisons, whereas utilizing QCA techniques allows for the systematic probing of causes for more complicated conjunctional patterns.

When building theories using comparisons, we need to be cognizant of two challenges. First, we need to be aware that commonalities across cases that we detected with a positive-on-outcome or most different system might

TABLE 7.7. An omitted causal condition

Case	C_1	C_2 (omitted)	C_3	O
1	+	+	+	+
2	+	+	−	+
3	+	+	+	+
4	+	+	−	+

be trivially necessary causes. These are defined as causes that are present in all cases regardless of whether they are in the set of the outcome or not (Dion 1998; Braumoeller and Goertz 2000). For example, human beings are present in all wars that we know of, but this is because per definition human beings have to be present in any social phenomena (Mahoney 2004: 83).

Second, we have identified a tautological sufficient cause, usually produced when our conceptualization of a cause contains attributes that overlap with those of the outcome (Mahoney 2004: 83). For example, if we want to explain economic development, if we have included a causal condition like large-scale industrialization in our analysis, the condition would be tautologically sufficient because development is usually defined in a fashion where it contains attributes that overlap with those included in industrialization (Mahoney 2004). One way to assess whether there is overlap is to ask whether the cause came before the outcome. In this example, industrialization can occur at the same time, or in some instances it might occur only after a certain level of economic development is achieved. The solution to this problem would be to revise the conceptualization and operationalization of causal concepts to remove this problem.

7.6. Building Causally Homogeneous Populations

One of the most important uses of comparative methods is in finding sets of cases that are as causally similar to each other as possible, resulting in bounded populations of relatively causally homogeneous cases. It is important to recognize that populations in case-based research are not fixed but dependent on both theory and the subsequent empirical analysis that finds evidence of causal heterogeneity (Ragin 2000: 53). Therefore, the definition of a population should be seen as a continuing process, always contingent on the theories being investigated and subject to updating based on empirical research. The refinement of the population should continue until one is able to justify that one has a relatively causally homogeneous population of cases, with the most important contextual conditions mapped out. The context of the causal theory (i.e., the bounds of the population) will of course be subject to continual updating throughout the research process. Here it is the closeness that we have with cases that enables us to update the proper bounds of the population being studied. In connection with employing a within-case analysis in combination with a comparative design, we might discover that we have included a case that differs significantly from the other studied cases. For example, we might find that causal relationships found in the other cases do not apply in the anomalous case, suggesting that there might be omitted scope conditions for the theory that are present in all the cases except one. In this case, we would want to bound our population by excluding cases without the requisite scope conditions. The goal is to build causally homogeneous populations to ensure that our findings from within-case analysis can travel to the rest of the population.

The following section discusses two key challenges when building populations of causally similar cases in case-based research: (1) achieving causal homogeneity by delineating contextual conditions for causal claims and (2) avoiding omitted causal conditions. We then present a four-step procedure for building causally homogeneous populations in practice.

Achieving Causal Homogeneity by Delineating Contextual Conditions

Key to generalizing beyond the single case (external validity) is our ability to substantiate that we have a causally homogeneous population of the theoretical phenomenon we are investigating. If we find strong within-case evidence in case 1 that C is causally related to O, we can cautiously infer that we should expect to find the causal relationship in similar cases 2 and 3. Similarity, or comparable cases, is defined as cases that are causally homogeneous, where the same causes are expected to produce the same outcomes through the same causal mechanism(s) because the set of causally relevant contextual factors are similar, also referred to as scope conditions for a theory.

Unfortunately, causal theories are not like electronic products that come with clear recommendations for proper operating conditions for the product (e.g., not in water, not below or above a certain temperature). A causal theory that states that proportional representation (C) produces close congruence between what voters want and governmental policies (O) does not have written in the owner's manual the cases in which the theory might operate, or even the proper scope of a "case." Part of the challenge is created by the fact that the issue of causal homogeneity and the proper scope of populations relates to difficult philosophical issues about the ambition of "science" to generalize by creating universal, lawlike propositions, or at the other extreme, highly contextualized explanations that cannot travel beyond the single case (Jackson 2011; George and Bennett 2005: 127–35; Przeworski and Teune 1970; Lieberson 1991). While this philosophical debate is outside the bounds of this book, case-based researchers, when push becomes shove, tend more toward the contextualized pole, which is why causal homogeneity is viewed as so important in case-based research (e.g., Collier and Mahoney 1996; Skocpol and Summers 1980; Ragin 1987; George and Bennett 2005: 164).

A key reason for working with smaller, bounded populations of cases is because of deterministic understandings of causal relationships in case-based research. If we claim that C is necessary for O, we would not expect the relationship to hold for every case of O across space and time. Instead, we might claim that C is necessary for O under a set of causally relevant contextual conditions. For example, Theda Skocpol claims that external military threats (C_1) were necessary conditions for social revolutions (O) in France, Russia, and China (1979: 23). She carefully defines the bounds of the population by developing a set of causally relevant contextual conditions for when C_1 is necessary, including that it works only for wealthy, politically ambitious states that have not experienced colonial domination. Outside of this context, she expects that social revolutions might have very different causes, especially in Latin America. Therefore, the bounds of her population are deliberately kept very small because she is working with deterministic claims of necessity.

Claims of sufficiency are also typically made within small, bounded populations of cases. These types of bounded claims are best seen in research that builds on QCA techniques. For example, Hicks, Misra, and Ng (1995) investigated the causal conditions that were sufficient for the consolidation of welfare states (O). In a population of fifteen countries, they found that unitary systems with working-class mobilization were necessary across all states, whereas two more conditions were different across cases: (1) a Bismarckian combination of non-Catholic government and a patriarchal state in countries like Germany, (2) a liberal labor route composed of liberal government in a non-Catholic government in countries like the United Kingdom, and (3) a Catholic paternalistic combination of nonliberal state and Catholic government in southern Europe. Crafting causally homogeneous populations would then require dividing the population of fifteen consolidated welfare states into three distinct subpopulations: Bismarckian, liberal labor, and Catholic paternalistic, resulting in very small, bounded populations in which the different conjunctions of causal conditions are sufficient.

In contrast, if we are "merely" claiming that there is a causal relationship between C and O, we might operate with a slightly larger population of cases, contingent on causal homogeneity still being present. If we are also making causal claims about mechanisms linking C to O, then we would need to also ensure that the same mechanism links C and O across a set of cases. We return to the question of causal heterogeneity at the level of mechanisms in chapter 9.

Avoiding Omitted Causal Conditions

Avoiding omitting causal conditions when crafting populations is a requirement when using Mill's methods. At worst, omitted conditions can result in flawed inferences about causality. Table 7.8 later in this chapter depicts a situation where the causal claim is that C_1 is necessary for O. Using a positive-on-outcome selection of cases, C_1 is not disconfirmed as a necessary cause. However, if C_2 is an omitted cause, this could mean that in reality, C_1 *and* C_2 together are necessary, or that C_2 is the cause of C_1. In the first instance, it would be imprecise to claim that C_1 by itself was necessary given that C_2 also must be present. More problematic is the second instance, where it would be a flawed inference to claim that C_1 is a necessary cause because it is produced by C_2, as is the outcome.

However, the problem of omitted causes is not as serious as it might seem, given that we are not making positive, confirming causal inferences using comparative tools. While the claim "C_1 is necessary" might survive the comparative analysis to fight another day, the real battle for the causal claim would be the subsequent within-case analysis. In a properly conducted congruence or process-tracing analysis, we would quickly find that the expected empirical fingerprints of a theorized causal relationship between C_1 and O are not present, leading us to search for other causes that were mistakenly omitted from analysis.

A Four-Step Procedure for Building a Causally Homogeneous Population of Cases

How, then, do we produce a causally homogeneous population of cases that can be used for both cross-case and within-case analysis? We suggest a four-step procedure that can be adapted to situations where one knows the cause(s) and the outcome, or where one does not know either C or O.

Step 1—Getting to Know Both C and O.   The first step in building a causally homogeneous population of cases that can be used for comparative or within-case analysis is relevant only when we either do not know C or O. In both instances, we need to figure out what the unknown C or O is before we proceed to select cases, given that we do not know the relevant scope of the causal theory in question. Returning to the example of sports used in the introduction, if we do not know whether we are dealing with a game of baseball or football, we cannot select a relevant set of games (cases) to study.

There are two parallel ways to determine what C or O is. First, we should engage in a far-reaching survey of existing theoretical work for inspiration about either what a given C might produce or what the cause(s) of an outcome could be. If we want to explore what effects crisis-induced stress (C) have (Oneal 1988), but do not know what it could do, we could turn to the large cognitive psychological literature to ascertain whether others have studied what stress might do for decision-making. In surveying the literature, we would want to select an outcome where there is both relatively strong evidence suggesting a causal relationship between C and O, and that is relevant in the type of context we are interested in investigating. For instance, we might have found a large body of work suggesting that stress produces violent behavior among experiment subjects in controlled circumstances. However, we would probably not select this as a relevant outcome to investigate because we do not believe that elite decision-makers in democratic systems are very likely to attack each other physically during decision-making processes, although we can never rule it out. Instead, we would want to select an outcome that was causally possible in the type of context we are studying.

Second, exploratory case studies are a useful tool to find unknown causes or outcomes. As we develop in chapter 8, when used in a very pragmatic fashion we can probe in a case study what the causes of a particular outcome might be, or the outcome that plausibly could be produced by a given cause. It is vital to have some rough idea about what a cause or outcome might be though, because otherwise the case study might have an inappropriate scope, either temporally or spatially. For instance, if the exploratory case study attempts to figure out what shifts in relative power among great powers (C) does by focusing only a few years after a noticeable shift like in the 1880s, one might miss the important effects that would manifest only over a longer time period, such as the increase in great power rivalry that ultimately led to World War I. Therefore, surveying the theoretical literature and engaging in exploratory case studies should be done together, except in the rare situation where we are dealing with a completely novel theoretical phenomenon.

Once an idea about the unknown C or O is in hand, one can proceed to theorize more carefully about how to define the causal concept (chapters 3 and 4), along with gaming through what the relationship might actually be in terms of necessity, sufficiency, or merely a causal relationship (chapters 2 and 3).

Step 2—Explore the Potential Bounds of the Population.   Once both C (or a set of causes) and O are known,[8] then one can begin exploring the contextual conditions that determine the bounds of the population in which the theorized causal relationship is possible by (1) looking to the existing research on the causal relationship for inspiration and (2) engaging in exploratory case studies. The result of the exploration should be a set of potential contextual conditions that might affect how the causal relationship functions.

When reviewing the existing literature, it is important to make sure that the "lessons learned" from existing research actually map onto the causal claim being made. In particular, drawing on large-N, variance-based research that assesses mean causal effects within a very large population is often not relevant because of causal heterogeneity. For instance, if we are studying the causal relationship between two states being democratic (C) and peaceful relations (O), using quantitative research such as Oneal, Berbaum, and Russett (2003) as a source of inspiration would be less relevant given that they investigate covariation between almost ten thousand pairs of states (both democracies and nondemocracies) over a period spanning from 1885 to 1992. Other things equal, a case-based scholar would expect mutual democracy to have very different effects (or no effects) within such a broad population. For instance, would we even expect to see causal effects at all in most of the "cases," given that most of the "cases" are pairs of countries (dyads) with no serious conflicts of interest that potentially could produce armed conflict in the first place? At the even more basic level, a case-based scholar would question whether the definition of a "case" as a pair of states (democratic or not) during one year is the most appropriate for the theorized causal relationship. Instead of using the temporal scope of one year to define a case, should the scope not be the full duration of the conflict of interest that could have produced armed conflict, which might be one week or several years? The scope of the defined case needs to match the temporal and spatial scope of the theorized causal relationship.

In parallel, one can engage in some form of initial probing of contrasting cases to detect potentially relevant causal conditions for a relationship to function. Here one can select a case from the existing literature in which the relationship has been found and then compare it with another case where there is some evidence that the relationship was not present.

As an example, returning to the stress induced by crisis (C) → poor decision-making (O) theory, we might engage in an exploratory analysis of the cases of the Carter administration in the early phases of the Iranian hostage crisis in 1979 where C and O were present, and then compare the preliminary findings with another case like the Kennedy administration in the Cuban Missile Crisis in 1962, which was a case where C was present but O did not occur. Here we would engage in a rough comparing and contrasting of the cases to determine which conditions the two cases share and where they differ. We might find that there are important differences between the two cases because of the extreme stakes involved in the Cuban Missile Crisis (potential nuclear annihilation). This would suggest that "existential threat to state itself" might be an important contextual condition for the stress → poor decision-making theory to function. If present, extreme stress might actually produce better decision-making because the extreme stakes involved make participants extra vigilant, whereas the theorized C → O relationship works only when the stakes are lower than survival of the state itself. The Cuban Missile Crisis would therefore, in the interests of causal homogeneity, be excluded from the population where C could produce O.

Step 3—Select Initial Population Where the Number of Similarities Is Maximized.   Once an initial set of relevant contextual conditions is developed, the positive-on-outcome comparison can be used to map the overall population. All cases in the initial population should be members of C (or a set of causes) and O, after which membership on the list of contextual conditions is determined for each case.

Cases in the population should then be assessed for the number of contextual conditions that they share (Berg-Schlosser 2012). The goal is to select an initial small subset of positive cases where similarities are maximized to increase the chances that we have tapped into a causally homogeneous population (Ragin 2000: 59–62). The mapping of cases can be undertaken using simple procedures, like those depicted in table 7.8, if there are only a handful of cases and contextual conditions. In contrast, if more cases and more conditions are included, the more formal procedures described by

TABLE 7.8. Mapping cases for similarity

	C_1	C_2	C_3	C_4	C_5	# of similarities with case 1	O
1	+	+	−	−	+		+
2	+	+	−	−	+	5	+
3	+	+	−	−	−	4	+
4	+	+	+	−	−	3	+
5	+	+	+	+	−	2	+

Berg-Schlosser are well suited for this mapping exercise (2012: 111–59). This can be done in simple spreadsheets that compare the number of conditions shared across cases.

In table 7.8 the causal relationship being studied is between C_1 and O. In the table, a subset of cases of O is depicted. In principle, all cases of O should be utilized, but in practice one can utilize one's empirical and theoretical knowledge to reduce this to a subset of cases that we a priori expect to be causally homogeneous. For instance, we might decide to select only European countries if we are studying causes of welfare-state consolidation.

Within the set of positive cases of C_1 and O, we then can assess the number of similarities between cases. In the figure, cases 1 and 2 share C_1 and all four other conditions (C_2–C_5), whereas cases 1 and 5 only share one condition (C_2). In this example, the two cases of maximum similarities would be cases 1 and 2, which could constitute in the first instance an expected causally homogeneous population of cases, subject to further updating after empirical research. Case studies could then be done of either cases 1 or 2, or both, to determine whether the causal relationship between C_1 and O is actually causal, after which one can start to explore the outer bounds of the population.

Step 4—Expand Population Outward after Within-Case Analysis.   In later stages of research we can begin exploring the outer bounds of the population, if relevant in relation to the research question and in alignment with the underlying philosophical tradition within which one is working (Slater and Ziblatt 2013; Rohlfing 2012: 200–11). Pragmatic scholars working within the analyticism tradition are more interested in gaining a rich understanding of the causal factors at play in a single case, and therefore actively exploring the bounds of the population would not be as relevant.

In contrast, more positivist-oriented scholars would actively explore these outer bounds, testing whether what they found in the small bounded population also can travel to other contexts. This can be done by removing a single contextual condition and selecting a case in the new population to see whether what was found in the former population also holds in the broader population. In table 7.8 we could move on to study case 3, which shares three contextual conditions (C_2–C_4) with cases 1 and 2. If we then find the relationship in a within-case study of case 3, we can gradually expand outward to include ever more diverse cases. In contrast, if we do not find the relationship in further cases, we would expect that they are causally distinct subpopulations. In table 7.8, we might find that cases 1 to 3 are one population, and cases 4 and 5 are another causally distinct set of cases.

Returning to our example of the impact of stress on decision-making, one could investigate whether what one found for top-level elites also holds at lower, more bureaucratic levels of decision-making, a level at which one might otherwise expect that stress would have fewer effects because of more routinized decision-making processes (e.g., standard operating procedures and the like).

7.7. Disconfirming Theory Tests Using Comparative Methods

In this section we develop the argument that it is only the combination of within-case and cross-case tests that enable us to make confirmatory causal inferences that can be generalized across a population of cases. We differentiate between designs aimed at assessing whether a condition is necessary or sufficient. In both instances, while we speak of testing individual causes, there are no logical reasons we cannot substitute a single cause with multiple causes working in conjunction if they are theorized to be necessary and/ or sufficient. This is particularly relevant regarding sufficiency, given that individual causes are almost never theorized as being sufficient. Therefore, while the following discusses necessity and sufficiency in terms of a single condition, the guidelines are also applicable to conjunctions (e.g., C_1 AND C_2 together are sufficient to produce the outcome O).

Testing Necessary Conditions

If we are interested in testing whether a causal condition (or conjunction of conditions) is a necessary condition, we can start with a cross-case positive-on-outcome comparison (Dion 1998: 128; Ragin and Schneider 2008: 156–57).[9] The comparison can ignore cases where the outcome is absent. Basically, we are claiming that quadrant II in figure 7.1 should be empty if C_1 is an individually necessary condition. Cases within quadrant I are typical, whereas cases in quadrant II are deviant in relation to the theorized causal relationship. Cases where the outcome is not present are analytically irrelevant to assessing whether C is individually necessary (Ragin and Schneider 2008).

The comparison is depicted in figure 7.1. Here the Bayesian bet is that should always be present when we analyze all of the instances of O, C_1.[10] The predicted evidence is shown in figure 7.1, where quadrant II is predicted to be empty of cases. In Bayesian terms the test is theoretically certain but has a low theoretical uniqueness. The test is theoretically certain, because logically

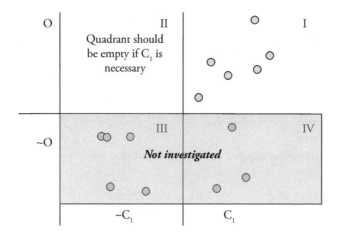

Fig. 7.1. Testing whether C_1 is an individually necessary condition with a positive-on-outcome test

if C_1 is an individually necessary condition, it always has to be present for O to occur. If we find that there are cases in quadrant II *and* we have good reasons to believe that the categorization of cases has a high degree of measurement accuracy, we can disconfirm the hypothesis that C_1 is individually necessary with a high degree of confidence.

In contrast, the theoretical uniqueness of the test is very low, which means that if the predicted evidence is found, very little confirmation takes place. The reasoning for low theoretical uniqueness is that there are many different alternative explanations for finding quadrant II empty. It could be that C_1 is a trivially necessary case, although this can be relatively easily checked by assessing whether it is present in almost all positive and negative cases (Braumoeller and Goertz 2000). In figure 7.1, this would involve a cursory investigation of whether there are cases in quadrant IV. If there also are many cases of C_1 here, it suggests that C_1 is trivial.

Alternatively, C_1 might be a spurious necessary condition, with no causal relationship to O. While at the theoretical level we need to be able to flesh out a causal explanation for why C_1 can be necessary for O, at the empirical level the *cross-case* evidence offers us no way to really assess whether C_1 is actually causally related to O in any given case because it is not evidence of difference-making derived from experimental manipulation, nor is it mechanistic within-case evidence (see chapter 6 for more on these two types of evidence). This is why we always follow-up a cross-case test with a within-case analysis. Therefore, in most situations we would assess theoretical uniqueness as being very low, given that the alternative explanation for finding the cross-case evidence (the pattern we found is a spurious relationship) is quite plausible.

It is important to note that in most situations our ability to update our confidence is further weakened because of inaccurate measures. If we find that quadrant II is empty, it might also be due to empirical inaccuracies, with some cases in quadrant II incorrectly categorized as members of C_1 and O. One way to assess measurement accuracy here is to investigate the differences that minor changes in measures produce, also termed calibration thresholds in the literature (Skaaning 2011). If minor tweaks of measures of C_1 and/or O result in major changes in patterns of case membership, then we should treat measurement accuracy as being quite low. In contrast, if our findings are robust across different calibrations of measures, we can then be relatively confident about measurement accuracy, meaning that more updating results from our tests, other things equal. However, combining a not theoretically unique cross-case test with low levels of measurement accuracy means that little, if any, updating of our confidence in C_1 being individually necessary occurs after passing a positive-on-outcome test.

Another form of cross-case comparison that also assesses other causal conditions for necessity would be a hybrid most-different system test, as illustrated in table 7.9. The reason it is referred to as hybrid is that cases are selected on values of causal conditions *and* the outcome. While a very weak confirmatory test of C_3, the test is a stronger disconfirming test of C_1 and C_2 as individually necessary conditions. While there might be case-specific reasons C_2 is not present when O is present, if C_2 is individually necessary we would not expect two exceptions, resulting in a significant downgrading of our confidence in C_2 being individually necessary for O.

If we then find the predicted evidence (quadrant II empty in figure 7.1), our confidence in C_1 being a potentially individually necessary causal condition would be only slightly increased. To make stronger confirming causal claims we have to supplement the cross-case test with within-case analysis and/or a counterfactual comparative comparisons. Here we would select a case that displays the hypothesized relationship of necessity, that is, any case

TABLE 7.9. Testing necessity with a hybrid most-different-systems test

Case	C_1	C_2	C_3	O
1	+	−	+	+
2	−	+	+	+
3	+	−	+	+
4	−	+	+	+

in table 7.9. or any case in quadrant II in figure 7.1 is relevant. However, we might want to select a case within a smaller subset where we maximize the chances of causal homogeneity to enable us to generalize from the within-case study to causally similar cases. This requires mapping the positive cases and selecting a case within a subpopulation where the similar contextual conditions are maximized (see discussion of building populations).

As we discuss in more detail below, the counterfactual comparative case study basically asks the question, "What if?" regarding what plausibly would have happened in the case had C_1 not been present. However, given that "evidence" on which we are basing our inferences is purely hypothetical, it does not enable us to make strong causal inferences. The advantage of applying either a congruence or process-tracing within-case theory test is that we are utilizing actual empirical material about what happened, and not what could have happened hypothetically, as evidence. The downside is that neither congruence nor process-tracing enables us to test directly whether a cause is necessary, which is what a counterfactual comparison enables. We would also only use process-tracing tests after the causal condition has first been tested in a more preliminary fashion using congruence, as we would not want to deploy a so demanding analytical tool to test a conjecture that we are not very sure about. For specific guidance on the application of these types of tests, see chapters 8 and 9.

If we do not find the expected cross-case evidence because there are cases in quadrant II (figure 7.1) or there are positive cases of the outcome in table 7.9 where the hypothesized necessary condition is not present, we would want to know why. The analytical goal is to empty quadrant II of cases (Ragin and Schneider 2011), either by finding omitted conditions or by redefining the outcome conditions by adding attributes in a concept PLUS attribute format—for example, developing subpopulations that would be treated as causally distinct outcomes (see chapter 4).

If there is one or a small number of cases that are deviant in relation to the otherwise robust pattern of necessity, we can choose to do an in-depth comparison of a deviant case in quadrant II with a typical case from quadrant I that is as different on other conditions as possible (approximating a most-different system) in an attempt to find a common omitted condition. For example, if we have theorized that a strong middle class (C) is an individually necessary condition for stable democracy (O) and we find a case where O is present but C is not, we can compare this deviant case with a typical case (both C and O are present) that is as different as possible from the deviant case in as many aspects as possible. We would then explore what causal conditions these two cases share. If we find that they share a high level of equality in society, we might revise our theory along the line of expecting that equality is a necessary condition instead of a strong middle class, a proposition that then can be tested further with in-depth and cross-case case studies. The cross-case element could involve using another positive-on-outcome test using the newly identified causal condition.

If there are many cases in quadrant II, and we can make plausible that their placement is not merely the product of inaccurate measures, we can disconfirm that the hypothesized individually necessary condition is actually necessary, at least for the population studied. We might then either return to the building population stage to create a more homogeneous population, or engage in a new round of theory-building.

Concluding, cross-case tests such as a positive-on-outcome comparison are useful disconfirmatory tests of the hypothesis that a given cause (or set of causes) is necessary for an outcome to occur. However the cross-case analysis is only a very weak confirmation of necessity (at best), and therefore it needs to be combined with either counterfactual single-case comparisons or within-case analysis (either congruence or process-tracing). Counterfactuals have the advantage that they are able to actually assess necessity in contrast to either congruence or process-tracing case studies, but the drawback is that they build on hypotheticals instead of actual empirical mechanistic evidence.

Testing Sufficient Conditions

The most straightforward cross-case test to assess whether a hypothesized cause is sufficient is a different-outcomes comparison, depicted in figure 7.2. Here we want to know whether quadrant IV is empty or not, with the predicted evidence of C_1 being sufficient being no cases found in quadrant IV.

As with the cross-case test of necessity, the confirmatory strength of the test is very low, whereas the disconfirmatory power is significantly greater. This is because the test is theoretically certain because we have to find quadrant IV empty if C_1 is sufficient, but the test has a low level of theoretical uniqueness, as there are many plausible alternative explanations of finding only positive cases of C_1 in quadrant I. One plausible explanation is that C_1 is tautologically sufficient because the attributes included in C_1 and O overlap. However, we can assess this by revisiting our conceptualization of C_1 and O. More problematic is the fact that we really cannot know based on the cross-case data that C_1 is not a spurious cause. To assess this we have to engage in within-case analysis to get mechanistic evidence of the actual causal process in-between, or we have to engage in a counterfactual single case comparison.

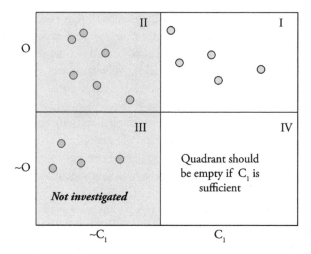

Fig. 7.2. Testing whether C_1 is a sufficient condition with a different-outcomes test

A most-similar-system comparison is also a weak confirmatory test, but it does have some uses as a disconfirmatory test. If we find the expected pattern (depicted in table 7.2), given that we have selected only a small number of cases, a very plausible alternative explanation for finding the evidence is that it is merely random and does not reflect a causal relationship. Therefore, if we find the predicted cross-case evidence we have not really increased our confidence in C_1 being sufficient. However, the test is stronger as a disconfirmatory test of both C_1 and other potential individually sufficient conditions. If we find that C_1 is present in a case where O is not present, this suggests that there is an omitted causal condition that has to be present for C_1 to be sufficient. Therefore, we would explore the possibility that C_1 might be an INUS condition. The most-similar-system test is also disconfirmatory as regards C_2 or C_3 being individually sufficient; however, here we cannot rule out them being part of a conjunction that together is sufficient with the data in table 7.10.

If we find the predicted evidence (quadrant IV is empty in figure 7.2, or the expected pattern is found in table 7.10), we would then want to deploy within-case tests to strengthen our causal inferences. We might select both cases 1 and 2 to detect whether there is within-case evidence of C_1 being causally related to O. If we do not find the predicted within-case evidence, the question becomes, "What explains the deviance in the findings between the within- and cross-case levels?"

TABLE 7.10. A most-similar-systems test for sufficiency

Case	C_1	C_2	C_3	O
1	+	−	+	+
2	+	−	+	+
3	−	−	+	−
4	−	−	+	−

If there are a large number of cases in quadrant IV, we can conclude that C_1 is not sufficient by itself, and we would then engage in a theoretical revision process to detect new causes.

If there are only a small number of cases in quadrant IV in figure 7.2, we can start by assessing one of the deviant cases. There can be two reasons for deviance: (1) there are omitted causal conditions from the model that have to be present for the mechanism to operate, and/or (2) there are omitted contextual conditions that have to be present for the mechanism to operate. The goal of this theoretical revision is to empty quadrant IV by detecting omitted causal and contextual conditions (Ragin and Schneider 2011).

Here we can engage in an analytical two-step procedure, where we use within-case analysis (either congruence or process-tracing) to assess where and why the relationship between C and O breaks down (for more on this, see chapter 9, under theoretical revision process-tracing). We then use these insights to inform our comparative analysis with a typical case in quadrant I to uncover omitted causal and/or contextual conditions. For example, if we are utilizing process-tracing, the within-case test of the deviant case involves tracing the theorized mechanism from C until it breaks down in the case (Andersen 2012; see also chapter 9). Using a theorized sufficient relationship between economic development (C) and democratization (O) as an example, we might find a case in which C is present but O does not occur. By tracing the mechanism between C and O, we might find that the part of the mechanism where the middle-class demands increased political participation was not actually present, with demands for democratization coming instead from elite actors, as happened in many transitions across Central, Eastern, and Southern Europe. We would then compare the single deviant case with what we know more broadly about typical cases in the population, where we know the theorized relationship functioned as expected to uncover whether there is a missing causal or scope condition in the deviant case that can explain why the causal condition did not work as predicted.

7.8. Single-Case, Counterfactual Comparisons

We conclude the chapter with a discussion of single-case, counterfactual comparisons. In contrast to the other methods in this book, single-case counterfactual comparisons build on hypothetical evidence about "what might have been" instead of providing empirical evidence about what actually took place in a case in order to update our confidence in causal relationships. The crucial distinction between counterfactual comparisons and other forms of comparisons is that hypothetical data is utilized, making our inferences dependent on our ability to substantiate our analysis of potential changes in the outcome produced by the absence of C with theoretical and empirical knowledge from similar cases.

Irrespective of how good the logical arguments presented, the conclusions can therefore always be dismissed as "parlor games." However, these counterfactuals can act as useful logical tools to discipline ourselves when engaging in causal research by shedding light on whether things might plausibly have been different if key events had not taken place.

Single-case, counterfactual comparisons involve comparing an existing real-world case with a hypothetical counterfactual case, where the logical argument is then made that if a particular C had not occurred, O would not have occurred (Goertz and Levy 2007; Tetlock and Belkin 1996; Lebow 2000; Levy 2014; Fearon 1991).

In effect, a single-case counterfactual comparison attempts to approximate a most-similar-system test, where a specified causal condition is hypothetically removed while keeping "everything else equal." To achieve an analysis as close to a most-similar-system test as possible, the most important criteria for selecting a causal condition to remove hypothetically is the "minimal-rewrite" rule, which states that a minor change in a causal condition that potentially can produce a major change in an outcome (Tetlock and Belkin 1996). For example, gaming through the consequences that Archduke Franz Ferdinand would not be assassinated in 1914 is an example of a minimal rewrite that potentially could have prevented the outcome (World War I) from occurring (see Lebow 2007 and Schroeder 2007 for a discussion).

Naturally, a minimal rewrite is a nonachievable ideal in most circumstances, as the absence of all but trivial conditions would have significant knock-on effects for other causal conditions, meaning that everything else would not be the same. In the words of one critic, "Though it is logically defensible to think up counterfactual questions with which to confront the historical record, the exercise seems pointless or at best of limited value from a practical standpoint because even so-called 'easily imagined variations' introduced into the complex matrix of historical developments can change so many variables [conditions] in so many unpredictable or incalculable ways, leading to so many varied and indeterminate consequences, that the procedure quickly becomes useless for helping us deduce or predict an alternative outcome" (Schroeder 2007: 149).

While this critique partially reflects a historian's skepticism of theory-driven social science research in general, it is important to acknowledge that it is almost impossible to minimize the scope of the rewrite. There can be, though, certain types of research questions that are more amenable to counterfactual comparisons than others.

Rewrites that involve the importance of changes in political leaders are good examples of minimal rewrites. For instance, Harvey (2012) games through whether the Iraq War would have occurred if Al Gore had been elected president in 2000 instead of George W. Bush, concluding that Gore most likely would have gone to war also. But even this minimal rewrite can be critiqued as involving more changes than just leader. If Gore had been elected, the argument can be made that the terrorist attacks of 9/11 would have potentially been prevented because of the amount of attention the Clinton-Gore administration was paying to the threat from al-Qaeda in the late 1990s (see, e.g., Clarke 2004). The incoming Bush administration chose instead to focus attention on more traditional, state-based threats such as China and Russia, with the result that despite strong signals that an attack was imminent, the Bush administration ignored that threat (Woodward 2004; 9/11 Commission Report).

Other types of research questions that can be used include the impact of changes in who won military battles or the options that leaders could have chosen but did not (Levy 2014; Cappoccia and Keleman 2007). In contrast, structural causal conditions like the economic or political system of a country, or the organizational culture of an institution, are more far-reaching changes that would have been produced by processes that also would have an impact on a range of other conditions, meaning the comparison would be far from the ideal "everything else equal" (Levy 2014: 13–14). Additionally, these other changes might also undercut the outcome itself (Lebow 2000: 582). For example, comparing a "Cuban Missile Crisis" in the absence of nuclear weapons would require comparing what actually happened with an almost unthinkable alternative universe where neither the United States, the Soviet Union, nor any other power developed nuclear weapons. In this nuclear-free world, it is for example plausible that the United States would *not* have been able to deter the Soviet Union from invading West Berlin in the late 1950s and early 1960s, with the result being a major conventional conflagration between the two powers *before* the Cuban Missile Crisis even occurred. Without the Berlin crisis and the Soviet concerns about the missile gap, it is highly unlikely the Cuban Missile Crisis would have even occurred. And even if the crisis actually occurred despite no nuclear weapons, would the Soviet Union and the United States have risked war over the placement of *conventional* missiles in Cuba?

When gaming through the hypothetical consequences of a minimal rewrite, there are several standards widely used in the literature. The causal condition that is hypothetically removed must be formulated in as clear and specific terms as possible. Further, it is important that well-established and relevant theories are used as the basis for reasoning when gaming through what consequences the rewrite could have had (Lebow 2000: 578). Another requirement is that the investigation of hypothetical consequences is as close to the removed condition as possible (proximity) (Fearon 1991; Levy 2014).

We are quite skeptical about the utility of counterfactual single-case comparisons because of the hypothetical nature of the empirical evidence. While the careful use of theory-grounded, minimal-rewrite counterfactuals can illuminate potential changes that could result from the absence of certain causal conditions, we cannot confirm or disconfirm that a cause was necessary on the basis of a counterfactual case study; we can only illuminate potentialities. Simply put, what we are engaging in here is a most-similar-system comparison with hypothetical data, and who would ever confirm a causal relationship solely based on either hypothetical data or a most-similar comparison?

Therefore, we recommend in most circumstances deploying within-case methods like congruence or process-tracing instead, enabling us to shed light on what actually happened in cases, enabling inferences about causal relationships in real-world cases. The exception is when we are strongly interested in determining whether a given cause can hypothetically be necessary for an outcome, with a counterfactual analysis offering a logical tool to make this relationship plausible theoretically.

7.9. An Example of Comparative Design

Schnyder (2011) uses a comparative design to explore whether the "party paradox" identified by other authors actually holds. The party paradox posits that center-left parties in several countries in the 1990s supported pro-shareholder corporate governance reforms, contrary to what we would expect these parties interests to be (Cioffi and Höpner 2006).

Schnyder employs a combination of a disconfirming most-similar-system test and three detailed case studies that he claims are process-tracing to test whether the causal condition of inclusion of labor in the postwar formation of corporate governance structures (C_1) can explain the party paradox.

He first puts forward a most-similar-system test of three countries (Switzerland, Sweden, and the Netherlands). He claims that the test makes it "possible to isolate the impact of the macro-level variable (left inclusion or exclusion) on the dependent variable (center-left support for proshareholder reform) as these are the only factors that vary between the three cases" (Schnyder 2011: 190). As can be seen in table 7.11, there is also a difference in C_7, but he claims that he can disconfirm its importance by linking with other studies that disconfirmed the importance of this condition because it was similar in their study and therefore could not explain differences, although he does not explicitly cite which studies he is referring to.

Unfortunately, he gives no information about how the causal conditions and outcome are actually defined and measured, making the categorization into present or absent in table 7.11 uncertain. Why should we trust the categorization of all cases as being members of causal condition C_4 just because Schnyder writes, "See Katzenstein 1985," (2011: 189) especially given that Katzenstein's work was published over fifteen years before the Dutch reforms discussed in the case study? Given that little information is provided about how these conditions and the outcome are defined and measured, we should be quite cautious about disconfirming on the basis of the results of the most-similar-system test. Further, he neglects to qualify the scope of disconfirming inferences possible, because he can only rule out that the conditions that are similar across cases can *individually* explain differences. They might be part of more complex conjunctions not captured in table 7.11. The methodological point here is that one must be very clear about how causes are defined and measured, and provide empirical justifications for why cases are categorized as in or out of the set of the concept.

He then claims that this most-similar-system test enables him to focus attention on the importance of C_1 for O, writing, "My study attempts to show precisely, based on a historical analysis of the role of labor in the establishment of the postwar corporate governance regime, that the macro-level factor explains the difference between the paradox case and the two non-paradox cases" (Schnyder 2011: 190).

TABLE 7.11. Schnyder's (2011) most-similar-systems test of explanations of center-left support for pro-shareholder reform

	C_1	C_2	C_3	C_4	C_5	C_6	C_7	O
	Inclusion of left in defining corporate governance	Economic structure (large # of MNC)	Consensual policy-making	Neocorporatist arrangements	Employee shareholding	Reduced managerial agency costs	Codetermination rights?	Center-left support for pro-shareholder reforms?
Switzerland	−	+	+	+	+	+	−	−
Sweden	+	+	+	+	+	+	+	+
Netherlands	+	+	+	+	+	+	+	+

To make positive, confirming inferences about the importance of C_1, he engages in what he calls a process-tracing case study. We are more skeptical about whether it is really process-tracing, because there is no development of a causal mechanism linking C_1 with O, instead a compelling narrative describing reform processes in the three countries is put forward. He is also not clear about what actually constitutes evidence of the $C_1 \rightarrow O$ relationship, or about whether there are any plausible alternative explanations for finding the empirical material other than that C_1 mattered. In this example we do not produce an argument road map to evaluate his three case studies, because the focus in this example is on the overall design of combining a most-similar-system design to make disconfirming inferences and case studies to make confirming inferences.

Based on the combination of the most-similar-system test and three case studies, Schnyder makes the inference that "the single most important determinant of center-left preferences in Sweden and the Netherlands is the influence of labor on the establishment of postwar corporate governance arrangements and a consequential preference alignment between labor and employees" (2011: 186), although he is more cautious in the conclusion by making inferences only within the bounded population. He writes, "Future research will have to test the general validity of this explanation by including new cases and by investigating the impact of additional factors. An important aspect that could not be discussed in this article relates to the question of interaction effects between different institutional spheres" (Schnyder 2011: 204). In his conclusions he also makes claims about the "lessons learned" that might have broader implications for theories, focusing attention on the equivalence of party preferences across countries because his study showed that "center-left parties are neither invariably a proreform force nor an antireform force" (Schnyder 2011: 203).

7.10. Concluding Guidelines

Comparative methods can be utilized for building populations of cases of a given causal relationship, for building causal theories (e.g., identifying new causes), and for assessing cross-case causal claims of necessity or sufficiency.

Building Theories

Comparative methods can be used to detect new causes. If we are in the situation where we know an outcome but not a cause, we can either:

1. Employ a positive-on-outcome or different-outcomes comparison, or preferably both in a sequential fashion; or
2. When there is existing research in a field, we can also draw on existing studies to narrow the focus of our search for potential causes. Given that we then have some idea about potential causes, we can also deploy cause-centered methods like the most-similar- and most-different-system comparisons if we expand them to include membership in the set of O.

If we find no potential causal conditions with any of the four types of comparisons, the most plausible explanations are (1) we have tapped into a causally heterogeneous population, most likely due to omitted causal conditions, (2) there is significant measurement error, with cases mistakenly categorized either in or out, or (3) more complex patterns of conjunctional causation are present that can be assessed using QCA.

Building Populations

Building (relatively) causally homogeneous populations enables proper case selection for within-case analysis and enables cross-case inferences to be made from cases studied to other similar cases of the causal relationship. If either causes or outcomes are not known, we should first engage in a far-reaching survey of existing literature and/or conduct an exploratory case study to identify potential causes of an outcome, or effects of causes. After C and O are known, we suggest a four-step procedure:

1. Get to know both C and O.
2. Explore potential contextual conditions that determine the bounds of the population by looking to the existing research on the causal relationship for inspiration and engaging in exploratory case studies.
3. Select a small subset of positive cases where the number of similarities of contextual conditions are maximized in order to achieve causal homogeneity.

4. Expand the population outward after initial case studies of positive cases to detect the outer bounds of causal homogeneity.

Testing Theories

Comparative methods can be used for making disconfirmatory inferences about the following types of causal relationships:

1. For testing necessary conditions:
   - Cross-case comparisons are strong disconfirmatory tests of necessity, but only very weak confirmations.
   - If a cause (or set of causes) survives as a plausible necessary cause, select one or more typical cases of the relationship (C and O are present) to assess whether there is evidence of a causal relationship, using either counterfactual single-case comparisons or within-case analysis.
   - Employ either positive-on-outcome or hybrid most-different-system comparisons. Positive-on-outcome comparisons are weak confirmations if the predicted cross-case evidence is found, but strong disconfirmation of C if not found. Most-different-system comparisons are even weaker confirmation if cross-case evidence found, but stronger disconfirmation of other causes predicts the cross-case evidence.
   - If confirmation of C in cross-case, employ confirmatory within-case tests—either counterfactual comparison, congruence, or process-tracing.
   - If small number of deviant cases (quadrant II), employ in-depth comparison of deviant with typical case (quadrant I) to revise theories of necessity.
2. For testing sufficient conditions:
   - Cross-case tests are strong disconfirmatory tests of sufficiency, but only very weak confirmations.
   - If a cause (or set of causes) survives as a plausible sufficient cause, select one or more typical cases of the relationship to investigate whether there is evidence of a causal relationship using within-case analysis.
   - Employ either a different-outcomes or a most-similar-system comparison for sufficiency. For the different-outcomes, quadrant IV (C, no O) should be empty. For the most-similar-system

comparison, other conditions that do not differ (see table 7.9) can be disconfirmed as sufficient.

- If small number of deviant cases (quadrant IV), employ in-depth comparison of deviant with typical case (quadrant I) to revise theories of sufficiency, detecting omitted contextual conditions that have to be present for causal relationship to function.

CHAPTER 8

Congruence Methods

To understand is to perceive patterns.
Isaiah Berlin

8.1. Introduction

Despite being the within-case study method most widely used by scholars in practice, the congruence method described by George and Bennett (2005) has all but disappeared from the recent methodological debate, eclipsed by the surge in popularity of process-tracing methods, and recent treatments of the method generally seem to conflate process-tracing and congruence methods (e.g., Goertz and Mahoney 2012; Collier 2011; Mahoney 2012; Bennett and Checkel 2014). But while they have important similarities, these two within-case methods also differ in ways that are overlooked in the existing literature, primarily because mechanisms are explicitly disaggregated in process-tracing, whereas congruence produces only within-case evidence, but there is no explicit mechanism being traced. For example, recent work by Goertz and Mahoney (2012) and Collier (2011) conflates the two methods. Goertz and Mahoney write that process-tracing is "built around two main kinds of tests: [h]oop tests and smoking gun tests" (2012: 93). Yet test types are not what define a method.

A core reason for this confusion is that recent case study methodological work does not define what causal mechanisms actually are, or if it does, it does so in a very minimalist fashion where the actual causal links in the process are black-boxed as arrows in a causal graph. For instance, the 2014 edited volume by Bennett and Checkel on process-tracing does not offer a clear definition of what mechanisms are, preventing us from knowing a theorized mechanism when we see it in practice. The result is that most chapters in the edited volume talk about studies that actually engage in congruence (e.g., Lyall 2014; Schimmelfennig 2014),[1] but where the actual causal process being traced is not unpacked. But if we are not told about what the process actually is, how can we claim that we have traced it empirically?

In reintroducing congruence case study methods, we go beyond George and Bennett's original formulation because we believe that the congruence they described was a very weak tool that provides evidence only of *correlations* across values of causes and outcomes (2005: 181–204). In their original formulation, they state, "The investigator begins with a theory and then attempts to assess its ability to explain or predict the outcome in a particular case. The theory posits a relation between variance in the independent variable and variance in the dependent variable. . . . The analyst first ascertains the value of the independent variable in the case at hand and then asks what prediction or expectation about the outcome of the dependent variable should follow from the theory. If the outcome of the case is consistent with the theory's prediction, the analyst can entertain the possibility that a causal relationship may exist" (George and Bennett 2005: 181). Yet do we actually learn anything by figuring out about a causal relationship when we learn about values of a cause and outcome in a particular case? Indeed, we would already know the value of cause (C) and outcome (O) to select an appropriate case for within-case analysis in the first place.

We contend that what scholars are actually doing when engaging in congruence is providing some form of within-case, mechanistic evidence, although because the actual causal mechanism producing the evidence is not explicitly theorized, the evidence for causality is not as strong as that produced in a process-tracing study. What differentiates congruence from process-tracing is therefore the understanding of causal mechanisms underlying the case study method (see chapter 2). The understanding of mechanisms in congruence is minimalistic, where the causal arrow between a cause and outcome is not explicitly unpacked theoretically. In contrast, in process-tracing the mechanism is unpacked into parts that are linked together in a system that transfers causal forces from causes to outcomes. The methodological implications of this difference is that process-tracing involves the detailed empirical investigation of disaggregated causal mechanisms in single case studies, producing detailed, step-by-step mechanistic evidence of the workings of the causal process, whereas the mechanistic evidence is quite weak in terms of enabling causal inferences to be made because the mechanism is not unpacked.

By not differentiating between the two methods, recent methodological work therefore produces confusing and often contradictory statements about what good process-tracing is. We suggest that one should not claim to be doing process-tracing when one is not actually tracing a causal process (e.g., an explicitly theorized causal mechanism). For example, Tannenwald's 1999 study discussed later in this chapter and in chapter 6 is often put forward as an example of good process-tracing (e.g., Goertz and Mahoney 2012: 91; Bennett and Checkel 2014). However, her study does not unpack causal mechanisms explicitly, meaning that she cannot claim that she is providing evidence of a causal process when she has not told us what the causal process actually is.

This chapter and the next clear up these common misconceptions by producing methodological guidelines for using congruence and process-tracing, illustrating when one should choose one or the other. We argue that the "weakness" of congruence case studies is actually a strength, given that there are more analytical situations where it can be used in comparison to the more specialized tool process-tracing.

In the following we further argue that it is useful to distinguish between four distinct variants of congruence: (1) explaining outcome congruence case studies that produce comprehensive explanations of particular historical outcomes, (2) theory-building congruence case studies, (3) theory-testing congruence studies, and (4) congruence case studies that refine causal theories. We also introduce two types of congruence tests: a singular test that details a single proposition about expected evidence that is then assessed multiple times in a case, and a cluster test in which a number of diverse propositions about possible evidence are developed and are then assessed collectively.

This chapter starts with a short exposition of the ontological assumptions that undergird the congruence method. We then discuss the type of causal inferences that we can make in congruence case studies in comparison to process-tracing. We then develop the four variants of congruence case studies, concluding with an example of congruence in a published study. In the article, the authors put forward multiple propositions about potential within-case (mechanistic) evidence that the theorized causal relationship. These propositions are then assessed using multiple pieces of empirical evidence, but in the study the underlying causal mechanism is not made explicit.

8.2. The Assumptions of Congruence Case Study Methods

We argue that because congruence is a within-case method, the goal is to produce some form of mechanistic evidence of a causal process in a case.

However, in congruence, the causal mechanisms linking causes and outcomes are not explicitly theorized, meaning that a minimalist understanding of mechanisms is adopted, where they are viewed as merely causal arrows in between causes and outcomes. The distinction between the system understanding and a minimalist understanding should realistically be thought of as a continuum, but there is a clear cutoff. On one side, process-tracing explicitly unpacks mechanisms, in particular detailing the dynamic, productive elements of the causal process that links parts together, whereas these elements are merely depicted as causal arrows in minimalist understandings as used in congruence case studies. This also means that many accounts in the methodological literature of process-tracing are in our terminology actually describing the congruence method (e.g., most chapters in Bennett and Checkel 2014; also Blatter and Haverland 2012).

In congruence, as in process-tracing, we are *not* engaging in a counterfactual-based comparison of an existing case with a hypothetical case in which the causal factor of interest is absent. The choice to engage in within-case analysis pushes us in a different direction, toward thinking more in terms of observable implications of hypothesized causal relationships because of our interest in capturing the complexity of what is going on in actual cases instead of cross-case patterns. The clearer the description of our expectations of what evidence we should find (propositions), the better we can assess whether there is a correspondence between what we found and what we expected. Other things equal, the more detailed our expectations of what evidence will look like, the easier it is to assess whether we have found it or not.

Congruence utilizes many of the same assumptions as process-tracing, including asymmetric and deterministic causal claims, coupled with Bayesian probabilistic epistemology when making inferences (see chapter 6).

We now turn to a discussion of what type of causal relationships we are making inferences about in congruence case studies, followed by a presentation of the four different variants of congruence methods in case-based research, starting with analysis of individual outcomes, and then moving to theory-building, theory-testing, and refining purposes.

8.3. What Are We Making Inferences About?

The inferences we make using congruence are either disconfirming or confirming claims about the existence or nonexistence of a plausible causal relationship. Congruence methods produce weaker mechanistic evidence than process-tracing, enabling us to make only tentative conclusions about a causal process that potentially links a given cause and outcome. Given that we cannot assess the necessity of causes in a single case unless we utilize hypothetical evidence from a counterfactual single-case comparison, congruence cannot be utilized to assess whether causes are necessary within a case. Additionally, sufficiency cannot be assessed within a case unless one adopts a more pragmatic understanding of science itself; an understanding that underpins what we term "explaining outcome" congruence and process-tracing methods (see also Beach and Pedersen 2013; Jackson 2011; Humphreys 2010).

However, while congruence case studies provides evidence that suggests there might be a causal process linking C and O, because mechanisms are not unpacked, the evidence behind this causal claim is relatively weak (see chapter 2 for more discussion). In process-tracing, if we can collect strong confirmatory evidence of each part of a mechanism that we can trust, we can make a relatively strong inference that C is causally related to O through a causal mechanism. In contrast, even if we find the predicted theoretically unique evidence in a congruence case study, because we have not actually traced the mechanism in an explicit fashion, we are able to make only a relatively weak inference about a causal relationship in the chosen case.

We distinguish two different types of congruence tests according to the depth of mechanistic evidence produced. In a singular test, a single proposition about potential evidence is assessed multiple times during a temporal process or across space (e.g., issues in a negotiation). In the cluster test, multiple non-overlapping propositions about evidence are assessed empirically. As can be seen in figure 8.1, in the singular test type, the mechanism is completely black-boxed, whereas in the cluster test it is plausible that when we are empirically assessing a set of diverse propositions, we will be getting closer to capturing what might be parts of a causal mechanism, thereby producing slightly stronger mechanistic evidence. However, because the mechanism is not explicitly theorized in either type of congruence test, the mechanistic evidence is *not* direct evidence of the workings of a causal process in the studied case. Unless we are told clearly what we are tracing in the form of an explicit theory of causal mechanism that details the parts of the causal process, the mechanistic evidence of the causal process will always be quite indirect. However, it is still mechanistic evidence because it provides indirect evidence of the causal mechanism.

While it might seem that it would be logical to always choose process-tracing if we are interested in studying causal relationships, there are many research situations where it is better to choose congruence case studies. Given that congruence case studies typically are less demanding in terms

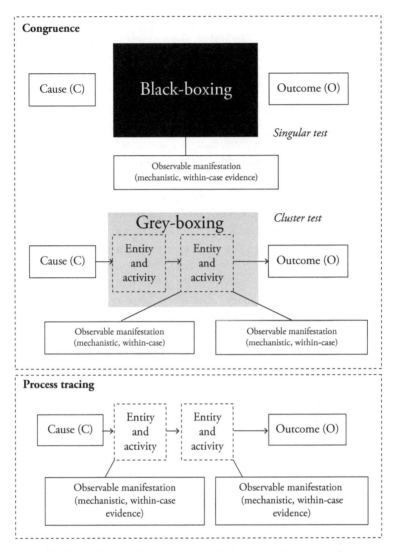

Fig. 8.1. Mechanisms in congruence and process-tracing case studies

of analytical resources, there is often a division of labor between the two case study methods. Our initial theoretical hypotheses are tested using congruence in the form of a plausibility probe. After this, the most promising causal conjectures that are confirmed can then be put to a more rigorous empirical test using process-tracing case studies.

It is also important to remember that because congruence is a within-case method, we are making claims only about plausible causal relationships within the studied case. To make inferences beyond the single case, we need to nest our congruence study in a broader, comparative design (see chapter 7 on comparative methods and sections 8.6 and 8.7 later in this chapter).

Finally, as we discussed in chapter 6, we are making inferences only about whether the expected empirical fingerprints of a causal hypothesis are present or not, in contrast to the way that Blatter and Haverland (2013) frame congruence as competitive theory tests. In Blatter and Haverland's presentation, congruence is usually a form of "three-way" fight between two different theories and empirical reality. However, this understanding is not compatible with a Bayesian-inspired logic of empirical testing as applied to mechanistic evidence because our theories are almost never mutually exclusive at both the theoretical and the empirical levels (Rohlfing 2014). We are only in the situation where we can make claims about competing theories based on our empirical tests when the tested theory and the alternative are mutually exclusive at the theoretical *and* empirical level (Rohlfing 2014).

8.4. Explaining Outcome Congruence Studies

Congruence can be used to assess causal relationships in particular cases *without* the ambition to generalize beyond the case itself, in particular when used in conjunction with a pragmatic or analyticist philosophical approach of case-centric research (see chapters 1 and 2; see also Jackson 2011). We term this "explaining outcome" congruence because the goal is to account for why a particular historical outcome occurred.[2]

In explaining outcome congruence, cases are understood in a more holistic fashion instead of being "cases of" a narrow theoretical relationship. In the words of one scholar, "Not all cases are equal. Some have greater visibility and impact because of their real-world or theoretical consequences. World War I is nonpareil in both respects. Its origins and consequences are also the basis for our major theories in domains as diverse as political psychology, war and peace, democratization, and state structure" (Lebow 2000–2001: 594). The case in explaining outcome congruence is therefore defined using a proper name like World War I instead of as a "case of" war.

Given that the ambition is to account for the "big and important" things going on in the case, multiple different causes are usually at play, many of which are case-specific. Evans writes, "Cases are always too complicated to vindicate a single theory, so scholars who work in this tradition are likely to draw on a mélange of theoretical traditions in hopes of gaining greater purchase on the cases they care about" (1995: 4).

Developing sufficient explanations of particular outcomes therefore requires a strategy of analytical eclecticism, defined as the pragmatic use of different causal theories in combination with each other to craft a sufficient explanation of a particular outcome (Sil and Katzenstein 2010). It "offers complex causal stories that incorporate different types of mechanisms as defined and used in diverse research traditions . . . [and] seeks to trace the problem-specific interactions among a wide range of mechanisms operating within or across different domains and levels of social reality" (Sil and Katzenstein 2010: 419).

Given that there are so many causal conditions involved, and the outcomes are so complex, case-centric scholars question the usefulness of generalizing from the studied case to other cases. This means that the ambition of eclectic theorization is not to create synthetic grand theories, but instead it is a more pragmatic strategy to capture the multiplicity of causes linking them to outcomes that produce particular historical outcomes. This is also why eclectic theorization is also termed "problem-oriented research."

Theories are used here in a much more pragmatic fashion, as heuristic instruments that have analytical utility in providing the best possible explanation of a given phenomenon (Peirce 1955). Instead of being parsimonious theories that can be tested systematically, case-centric research scholars contend that it makes little sense to distinguish between systematic and case-specific theories, given the difficulties of generalization in the complex social world. Further, theories that are developed are typically more complex, often including conglomerates of different causes, along with more case-specific causes. The ambition is not to prove that a theory is correct; instead, the goal is to show that it has utility by providing the best possible explanation. Explanations are case-specific and cannot be detached from the particular case (Humphreys 2010: 269–70).

Pragmatism is not an "anything goes" excuse for sloppy empirical analysis but instead relates to how theories are understood and used as heuristic vehicles instead of as parsimonious and generalizable explanatory devices. The types of empirical tests used in explaining outcome congruence case studies should therefore be just as rigorous empirically, clearly defining theoretically why empirical material can be evidence and what it tells us if found or not found, along with careful source criticism to determine how much we can trust found evidence.

While causal theories from different research traditions are often combined in case-centric studies, it is also important to make sure that key concepts and theoretical assumptions are compatible with one another (Sil and

Katzenstein 2010: 414–15). For example, one cannot combine an ideational theory that contends that subjective beliefs drive actor behavior with an institutionalist theory where behavior is driven purely by the rational maximization of material interests. These two theories would be mutually exclusive at the theoretical level, meaning they should not be combined without developing some form of bridging theory that explains interaction between norms and rational interests.

The first stage of explaining outcome congruence involves examining existing scholarship for potential causes that can explain the particular outcome. If one was trying to account for the big and important things going on in the Cuban Missile Crisis, one can ask what the crisis was potentially a "case of," drawing on a range of different answers to the question to identify relevant theories. Empirical tests can then be developed for the different theoretical answers that are then assessed in the case to determine whether the theory mattered, and if so, whether it was sufficient to account for the outcome.

However, given that existing theorization usually will not be able to provide a sufficient explanation of the "big and important" things going on in a complex historical outcome, the second stage of explaining outcome congruence involves combining and revising existing theories to achieve a better account of what is going on in the case. The final explanation is therefore typically a combination of existing theories used in a complementary fashion to explain key aspects of the case outcome, supplemented with more case-specific explanations.

For example, Jervis's (2010) analysis of intelligence failures by the US national intelligence community attempts to build sufficient explanations of failure in two cases: the failure to detect the coup against the Shah of Iran in 1979 and the belief that weapons of mass destruction were present in Iraq in 2003 when they were not. While the explanations are complex, involving many different causes interacting with each other, the conclusions of the book do discuss the lessons that are potentially applicable to other comparable cases of intelligence-failure lessons that can be understood as causal explanations that potentially are present in other cases that can be investigated in further research (Jervis 2010).

Therefore, we should not draw the line between explaining outcome and theory-testing and building congruence too sharply. Explaining outcome congruence case studies often point to causal explanations that in principle can travel and be tested in other cases, or that can act as building blocks for future attempts to build generalizable causal theories that can explain outcomes across the population of relevant cases.

An Example of Explaining Outcome Congruence

Perhaps the best example of explaining outcome congruence analysis is Allison's classic study of the Cuban Missile Crisis, one of the most cited works in the social sciences (Allison 1971; Allison and Zellikow 1999). Bendor and Hammond, in a withering critique of Allison's original 1971 model of bureaucratic politics (which has become even more complex in the 1999 revision), state that the analysis "is simply too thick. It incorporates so many variables that it is an analytical kitchen sink. Nothing of possible relevance appears to be excluded" (1992: 318). Yet this critique misses the point, in that what Allison (and later Allison and Zellikow) was attempting to do was craft a comprehensive explanation of the "big and important things" in the case itself. Naturally, this requires multiple theories (or theoretical lenses in Allison's terminology) to capture.

In their joint work, Allison and Zellikow start by examining how far a "rational actor" explanation (model I) gets them in accounting for the case, assessing why the Soviets decided to send nuclear missiles to Cuba, why the United States responded with a blockade, and why the Soviet Union withdrew the missiles. They find that there were curious aspects of the Soviet deployment that could not be accounted for in the rational actor model, including why camouflage was not used to hide the missiles. These puzzling aspects of the case led them to supplement model I with an organizational theory explanation (model II) that sheds light on the importance of organizational standard operating procedures and the like—factors that produced puzzling things like the lack of camouflage. However, they contend that while model II does explain these things, there are still important aspects of the complex case that are unaccounted for, leading Allison and Zellikow to introduce in a supplementary fashion a third explanation— governmental politics (model III) that focuses analytic attention on the "politics of choice" and the bargaining between different government actors. They conclude, "The need for all three lenses is evident when one considers the causal bottom line. The painful 'but for which' test demands that one identify major factors, but for which the outcome would not have occurred, or would have been materially different" (Allison and Zellikow 1999: 383).

However, in many research situations single cases are studied because they represent "cases of" a broader causal relationship, where what is learned about the relationship by engaging in within-case analysis is generalized to other cases. It is to this task that we now turn.

8.5. Theory-Building—Exploratory Case Studies

A rigorous congruence case study requires some idea about cause (or causes) and outcome for the analyst to develop empirical tests about the empirical fingerprints the relationship might have in a given case. That said, congruence methods can be applied in a more pragmatic fashion to build theories, searching for unknown causes or outcomes.

Unfortunately, while the methodological literature is full of recommendations for how to engage in theory-testing, there are fewer guidelines for building theories using case studies.[3] Here we develop a set of steps that can be used in an iterative fashion in the search for unknown causes or outcomes.

First, existing theorization is a useful source of inspiration for what to look for. As also discussed in chapter 7, here one engages in a far-reaching survey of the existing literature, probing in different subdisciplines for ideas about which effects a given cause has been theorized to have or what could have caused a given outcome.

Second, ideas about what common building blocks different types of theoretical explanations share can be good to focus your analytical attention (see chapter 3). What overall type of causal explanation are you building—structural, institutional, ideational, or psychological (Parsons 2007)? For example, if we are searching for structural causes, we would focus our analytical attention on the potential impact of exogenous constraints and opportunities for political action created by the material surroundings of actors (Parsons 2007: 49–52).

Third, the actual case "study" involves a multistep procedure that can be started by producing a rough empirical narrative about what "happened" in a case. Doing this requires at least a preliminary idea about what a cause or outcome might be on the basis of the type of explanation being utilized. Otherwise, the case study might have an inappropriate scope, either temporally or spatially.

After a rough empirical narrative has been produced that categorizes who did what and when, more systematic empirical probing of the case can proceed. Given that we do not yet know the precise scope of the case, the probing should be quite open and far-reaching. This process resembles what an investigator does when building a theory of a crime. After a rough description of the case is developed, the investigator then probes the empirical record to determine whether there are any clues that can shed light on why things happened. One often stumbles on surprising or unexpected pieces of empirical material, which then are assessed using the two-step procedure for what the empirical material can potentially be evidence of using the Bayesian framework of chapter 6. For instance, the investigator, after finding a set of tire tracks in the mud leading away from the scene of the crime, would ask whether the found clue could be evidence linking the suspect's car to the crime, assessing whether there is any plausible theoretical link between the clue and the crime and whether this proposition about evidence matches what has been found empirically. By itself the clue would be only a weak piece of evidence in support of a proposition that a person who might be a suspect was present, but if combined with other pieces of evidence, like footprints of a person at the crime scene that are roughly the size of the owner of the car, the evidence would be stronger confirmation of the theory.

Empirical probing is an iterative process in which hunches about potential clues are explored to determine what they can tell us about the newly found candidate cause or outcome. If our initial hunch holds empirically and theoretically, we could then engage in more focused testing, exploring whether there are any other independent observable manifestations of the theorized relationship in the case. Returning to the previously mentioned crime scene, we could then investigate whether the suspect's footprints or other forms of forensic evidence are present at the scene of the crime. If we find the evidence, and if it is relatively unique (e.g., there is no evidence of other people being at the scene of the crime), we would be more confident that our theory holds empirically. Once we are relatively confident about the newly identified cause or outcome, we can then engage in more systematic and robust case studies, which are described in the following sections.

8.6. Testing—Plausibility Probes and Robust Congruence Case Studies

As we explore in the following, congruence case studies together with cross-case comparative methods can be used to test and refine hypotheses about causal relationships between causes and outcomes. The first step is to define in more detail both cause and outcome, specifying in particular the causal theory linking the two using the procedures described in chapters 3 and 4 (i.e., making theoretically plausible that a cause, or a set of causes, can be a cause of an outcome). The second step involves developing clear measurement procedures for both C and O as discussed in chapter 5. If the analysis has no ambition to generalize beyond the bounds of the single case, then the population of cases does not necessarily need to be mapped (chapter 7). However, in most circumstances, the next step is to use comparative methods to build a causally homogeneous population of cases to enable inferences from the analyzed cases to the rest of the population.

Mapping the Population of Cases—Typical, Deviant, and Irrelevant Cases

To select appropriate cases and to generalize from single cases studied using congruence (or process-tracing) to the rest of the bounded population of cases, it is first vital to map a causally homogeneous population of cases. This can be depicted graphically in figure 8.2, enabling us to distinguish between typical, deviant, and analytically irrelevant cases. Note that the placement of the cases within quadrants merely depicts how confident we are empirically that a given case is a member of C and/or O, and the contextual conditions that are theorized to be important for the relationship to work.

All cases in quadrant III are analytical irrelevant when assessing asymmetric causal claims, in that studying them does not shed any light on why the outcome in focus occurs because neither C nor O is present (Goertz and Mahoney 2004). If we are interested in studying the causal relationship between mutual democracy (C) and peace between states (O), studying why nondemocratic dyads (~C) go to war with each other (~O) tells us nothing.

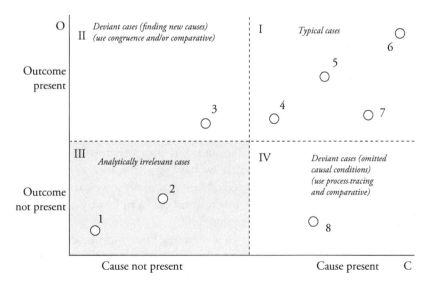

Fig. 8.2. Mapping the population of cases and different analytical purposes of congruence case studies

We would therefore not analyze these cases using within-case methods like congruence or process-tracing.

In contrast, cases in quadrants II and IV are deviant cases that can help us refine our causal theories, although in both instances within-case analysis will not stand alone. Deviant cases in quadrant II can be used to search for potential new causes, whereas deviant cases in quadrant IV can be used to search for omitted causal conditions when C (or a set of causes) is theorized to be sufficient. Quadrant II cases are ones where congruence is applicable, whereas process-tracing is best for deviant cases in quadrant IV. We return to these types of case when discussing refining theories using congruence analysis.

Typical cases of a given causal relationship are those where both C, O, and the requisite contextual conditions are present, depicted as all the cases in quadrant I. Note that we do not distinguish between most- and least-likely typical cases because we contend that this case selection practice is a vestige of variance-based thinking that is incompatible with the deterministic ontological understanding of causation in case-based research (see chapter 2).

When selecting typical cases, if there is evidence that suggests that the population is causally homogeneous, *any* of the cases in quadrant I are good candidates for congruence (cases 4–7 in figure 8.2). However, there are two additional criteria: (1) avoid cases where there is residual empirical uncertainty about membership in C and/or O, and (2) choose cases where you will have access to as rich an empirical record as possible.

First, there is often a considerable degree of ambiguity about whether cases that sit close to the border of set membership actually are in or out (see chapter 5). There can be theoretical ambiguity, where borderline cases might be in or out depending on how we conceptualize and operationalize our theoretical concepts. Additionally, there is often empirical uncertainty created by inevitable measurement error. Therefore, if we want to test whether there is within-case evidence of a causal relationship using congruence or process-tracing, we should select cases where we have good empirical evidence that can be used to justify that the selected case is actually a typical case of the relationship. This means that we might avoid case 4 in figure 8.2 because it is relatively close to the qualitative threshold.

Second, as discussed already, when selecting cases within a causally homogenous population, we might as well select a case where we have access to as rich an empirical record as possible, as this will enable us to actually learn something from our empirical research. If we have only patchy access, or the empirics to which we have access are of questionable accuracy, little actual updating will be possible on the basis of empirical research. Just having strong theoretical tests (propositions) does not mean that one can actually collect the evidence that would enable one to infer whether the relationship was present or not. In the words of Sherlock Holmes, "'Data! Data! Data!' he cried impatiently. 'I can't make bricks without clay'" (Doyle 1892: 343).

We do not have to select cases in which other potential causes are not present (Beach and Pedersen 2016). Variance-based scholars question whether we can make within-case inferences about mechanisms when we do not control for other causes by selecting cases in which only one potential cause is present. Gerring and Seawright write, "Researchers are well advised to focus on a case where the causal effect of one factor can be isolated from other potentially confounding factors" (2007: 122). They term this type of case a "pathway case." Schneider and Rohlfing draw on this guidance in their discussion of case selection for process-tracing when they state that we should choose "unique set" cases, where we "focus on one term . . . to unravel the mechanism through which it contributes to the outcome in the case under study" (2013: 566–67). Goertz writes that one should avoid cases that exemplify multiple causal mechanisms (2012: 18).

Our argument is that while the logic of controlling for other potential causal conditions is relevant for variance-based designs that aim to assess probabilistic claims about the mean causal effects of individual causes at the population level (i.e., evidence of difference-making), it is not relevant for the study of mechanisms in case-based research because congruence and process-tracing offer us analytical tools that can enable us to control for other causes working at the empirical level. When evaluating empirical evidence of mechanisms (be they disaggregated or not), we assess whether the particular piece of found evidence is empirically unique, or whether finding the evidence is just as plausible with other explanations of the evidence (be they competing theories or case-specific factors). If finding the evidence is just as plausible with alternative explanations, then no confirming causal inferences based on the piece of mechanistic evidence are possible. Control for other causes therefore does occur in within-case studies, but it happens at the level of mechanistic evidence *within* a case, which matches with the level of our causal inferences being made (within-case).

The difference between case-based and variance-based principles of case selection is most pronounced when dealing with potential overdetermination, defined as multiple sufficient causes being present in a case. If there is overdetermination in a given case, variance-based designs are unable to disentangle which cause actually produced the outcome because there is more than one possible cause of difference, making control for other causes through case selection even more important. However, overdetermination is not a serious problem when studying mechanisms because we can isolate the workings of individual mechanisms from each other empirically through our evaluation of the theoretical and empirical uniqueness of mechanistic evidence, asking whether finding the evidence can be accounted for with any other plausible explanation (see chapter 3). Basically, we should expect to find when we operate at the level of within-case mechanistic evidence that different causes will be linked to outcomes through different mechanisms that would leave empirical fingerprints that can be distinguished from each other empirically. Therefore, choosing a case where both C_1 and another potentially sufficient cause C_2 are both present should not matter because we can distinguish empirically the workings of the two causes and their mechanisms from each other.

Furthermore, selecting only pathway cases where C_1 is present also has the downside that it reduces even further the population of potential cases that can be inferred to afterward. Given the sensitivity of mechanisms to context, there is a risk that C_1 is linked to O through CM_1 in cases where only C_1 is present, whereas in cases where C_1 and C_2 are both present, C_1 might be linked to O through CM_2. This situation is depicted in figure 8.3. Yet if we follow Gerring and Seawright's advice, after studying a pathway case (C_1, O, ~ C_2), we would be able to infer only to other cases where only C_1 and O are present instead of the full population. We suggest if there are significant concerns about the potential impact of C_2 on which mechanism is working that we engage in a two-step process where we first select two cases for tracing mechanisms where C_1 and O are present but not C_2, followed by two cases where C_1 and C_2 are present to assess whether the presence of other causes affects which mechanism works.

Theory-Testing in Typical Cases

A within-case congruence theory-test should be used only in cases where the hypothesized causal relationship can actually be present. This means that we select typical cases where both C and O are present in the case, or at least theoretically can be possible in the case. After selecting a case that we are reasonably confident is typical, and where we have access to as rich an empirical record as possible, the next step is to evaluate the prior probability of theory being present in case based on existing research (see chapter 6 for more on case-specific priors).

If we have a strong prior confidence in the relationship being present

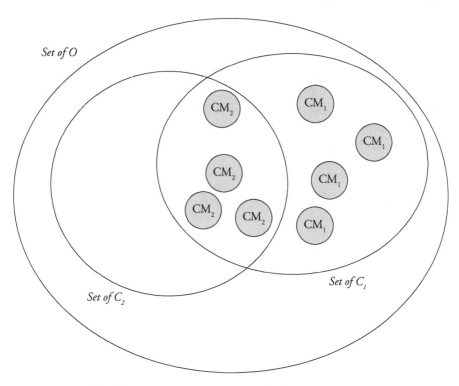

Fig. 8.3. Pathway cases reduce the bounds of the population

in both the chosen case and across the population, we should engage in stronger congruence empirical case studies, termed robust congruence case studies in the following, typically using a cluster of tests. In contrast, if there is a low prior plausibility because existing research has not studied the topic or existing studies of the case are very poor, then one can engage in plausibility probe, which is a type of "quick and dirty" congruence case study that employs relatively weak empirical tests (low certainty and uniqueness) to determine whether there is any empirical basis for proceeding further with more robust empirical case studies (either congruence or process-tracing). Here we typically utilize more singular empirical propositions about evidence deployed repeatedly over time or space in a case.

After both types of congruence case studies, we typically follow up the first case study with additional case studies of other typical cases, using either congruence or process-tracing, to update our confidence in both within-case causation and strengthen our cross-case inferences because we have found the relationship in more cases across the population.

Two Types of Congruence Tests—Singular and Cluster

We argue that there are two distinct types of congruence tests that can be distinguished according to whether one single proposition about empirical evidence is put forward or a series of propositions is put forward to capture a predicted cluster of evidence in the case. After we review these types of tests, we turn to how they are employed in plausibility probes and robust congruence case studies respectively.

The Singular Type of Congruence Tests

While there are exceptions, a singular test usually employs a single, theoretically unique but not certain proposition about the evidence that will be found (also termed a "smoking gun test" in the literature; see Van Evera 1997). This means that if the predicted evidence is found there is relatively strong confirmation, whereas if the evidence is not found, we do not disconfirm the proposition very much, if at all. The proposition is assessed either at different moments over time during a temporal process, or across spatial units (e.g., across issue areas within negotiation).

An example of the singular type of congruence test is found in Tannenwald's description of her methodology in her 1999 article, where she puts forward the proposition that she should find evidence of "taboo talk," which is then assessed at multiple times throughout the US decision-making process in the cases investigated (t_0, t_1, . . . t_n) among different actors (see chapter 6). She does not unpack theoretically the causal mechanism linking norms (C) and decisions for nonuse (O), meaning that she engages in congruence. She then claims she is testing the same simple proposition about evidence of the presence of norms at different points in time and for different actors in the cases.[4] Her claim about her design is depicted in figure 8.4, where the "taboo talk" proposition is tested empirically multiple times during the temporal process.

As discussed in chapter 6, the proposition about taboo talk has some degree of theoretical uniqueness but little theoretical certainty. In the singular proposition, the more times we find actual evidence of the proposition, the more confident we are that the collected evidence is an accurate representation of the empirical record that enables us to trust the found evidence. Finding it multiple times also increases the empirical uniqueness of the evidence because we can rule out the alternative empirical explanations of the evidence, for example that taboo talk took place only in one meeting or that

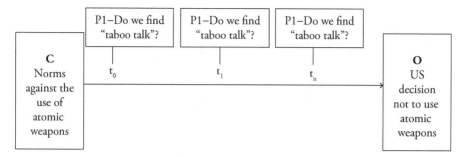

Fig. 8.4. Tannenwald's use of congruence—the singular proposition

it was expressed by only peripheral participants. The exception to this "more is better" logic would be if the found piece of evidence itself was highly empirically unique, meaning that because it is a particularly central actor or a particularly critical juncture in a causal process we can be more confident that taboo talk was present.

Cluster Congruence Tests

Compared to the singular version, the cluster type of congruence test employs a battery of non-overlapping propositions to assess the causal hypothesis. These propositions about evidence often are theoretically certain but not very unique (also termed "hoop tests" in the literature; Van Evera 1997). These are disconfirming when taken individually, but if we find evidence for each of the propositions and it is independent evidence, the small probative value of each individual proposition is summed together, enabling a relatively strong overall confirmation of the theory.

For example, our propositions might make predictions about evidence in the form of the timing and nature of decisions that we should find in the case if our theory is valid. In the evaluation literature on case studies, inspired by criminal science, Scriven (2011) develops what he terms "modus operandi" clusters that incorporate a range of different propositions of what we should find if a theory is valid. In the criminal sciences, modus operandi relates to clusters of traces left by a particular criminal. If the crime is a burglary, a criminal might leave signature traces that are similar across different cases, such as going in through basements, carefully taking windows out of their panes instead of breaking the glass, and stealing only jewelry. The logic is then is that, given that we know burglar X's modus operandi from other instances, if we find a crime that follows this pattern we are more confident that burglar X perpetrated it. Taken individually, each part of the cluster is a weak confirming test, but together the tests have a degree of confirmatory power based on the Bayesian argument "how probable is it that other burglars would do each of these steps in exactly the same fashion as the modus operandi of burglar X?" We return to an extended example of a cluster test later in the chapter.

Plausibility Probes

A plausibility probe case study requires fewer analytical resources because the propositions are typically "easy" to test, meaning that empirical material is usually easier to collect because they are not very certain and/or unique. Additionally, less time and effort is typically spent on evaluating the accuracy of the evidence. Taken together, this means that the combination of weak tests and lower-quality evidence results in only very tentative and cautious inferences, with little updating taking place. However, employing weak tests is a deliberate choice. What we are seeking to do is to explore whether it makes sense to deploy more extensive analytical resources in testing and refining a causal theory further. Using an analogy, this is similar to a pharmaceutical company doing a small trial before engaging in a much more costly, full-scale test of their product.

Plausibility probe case studies are typically done either very early or very late in a research project. Early in our research, we have only initial hunches about causal relationships based on the existing literature and preliminary descriptive case studies. Here it is a good idea to get our hands dirty to gain a better understanding of what is going on in a case before we employ more robust (and costly) congruence case studies. Plausibility probes can also be used late in a research process, where after we have refined existing theories based on extensive theory-testing, we want to investigate whether our new theory actually works in other cases.

Plausibility probes are typically singular propositions, given that developing a series of non-overlapping predictions (cluster) requires stronger theory, and in particular better knowledge of the data-generating processes, along with extensive empirical knowledge of the case or similar cases to develop theoretically certain propositions about the evidence we should find in the case. A simple empirical prediction is developed by asking, "If C (or a set of causes) is actually a cause of the outcome, what is the fingerprint that this relationship should leave in the empirical record?"

For instance, if we are studying judicial decision-making in international courts and have the theoretical hunch that powerful states (C) influence judicial decision-making to make it more in line with their own preferences (O), an initial proposition could be that we should expect to see that the legal reasoning in judgments in such cases is sparse in comparison to normal cases. This analysis would have the character of a plausibility probe, with the test being relatively weak, with low theoretical certainty and uniqueness. We do not have to find this fingerprint for the court to have deferred to what powerful states want, in that the judges might have been able to hide their concessions to states behind extensive legal reasoning. Further, the prediction is not very theoretically unique, in that there can be numerous plausible reasons for why a particular judgment lacks extensive legal reasoning—for example, the case is relatively straightforward, meaning that extensive use of precedent or other forms of legal reasoning is not necessary. Additionally, even if the analyst believes they have found a piece of evidence that matches what the proposition expected to find, this conclusion might have been reached because the analyst did not have the requisite legal knowledge to be able to interpret the actual judgment properly. This is often a problem when political scientists move into a field of research that requires extensive technical knowledge to interpret what actual empirical evidence means in the context, like law or climate policy.

However, even though we are employing weak tests in a plausibility probe, the analysis offers important insights that enable us to refine theories and/or choose to deploy stronger empirical tests. If we do not find the predicted evidence of our propositions, we would want to engage in a more comprehensive assessment of why. Was the lack of finding the evidence because we deployed a theoretically uncertain test? To assess whether the negative finding was because of the weak test, we should repeat the plausibility probe with one or more different tests, to be able to conclude more confidently that there is or is not a causal relationship.

If we can cautiously conclude that there was no causal relationship in the case, was this because the case was idiosyncratic, meaning that the relationship might be present in other typical cases? Here we can compare the chosen case with another typical case for their membership of a range of potentially relevant causal conditions, attempting to see whether there are important conditions that are different between the chosen case and the rest of the population (see chapter 7 on building homogeneous populations).

If, in contrast, we find the predicted empirical evidence, we can then proceed to a stronger case study test of the theory using either congruence theory tests or process-tracing.

Robust Congruence Case Studies

If we have higher prior confidence in a theoretical relationship being present in a case because of either existing research or our own plausibility probe, we can then proceed to deploy stronger congruence case studies. Here we typically deploy a cluster of empirical tests, using a set of non-overlapping, theoretically certain propositions that individually are theoretically certain but not unique. If the propositions are independent of each other, they can be summed together, meaning they would achieve a degree of theoretical uniqueness that enables relatively strong confirming inferences to be made if the predicted evidence is found. However, if the analysis finds that all or some of the tests were not passed, relatively strong disconfirming inferences can be made.

Given that we have discussed what empirical fingerprints look like in both variants of congruence tests, and we discussed theoretical and empirical evaluation of empirical material in detail in chapter 6, we now turn to the question of how we should proceed after negative and positive findings. If we do not find the predicted evidence, we want to diagnose why. Was our proposition merely a smoking gun, where not finding the predicted evidence tells us little or nothing about whether the causal relationship is present or not (see chapter 6)? Can we trust the empirical evidence collected? Or is there no causal relationship? If we are not very confident in the answers to these questions, we can first refine our empirical tests to be able to conclude with more confidence whether there is a causal relationship or not, using our case-specific knowledge to craft stronger propositions, often in the form of a set of non-overlapping, theoretically certain propositions that together would be able to confirm or disconfirm to a stronger degree than the first proposition(s). For example, assume we are studying the importance of norms in high-level political decision-making. If we do not find the predicted taboo talk in the empirical record, one reason for the negative finding could be that we simply did not have access to the minutes of meetings in which the evidence might be found. Another reason could be that the minutes did not record the arguments put forward by actors. In both instances, taboo talk might have occurred, but we simply were unable to observe it in the empirical record. In these circumstances, the analyst could employ different tests with a focus on theoretical certainty. For example, the analyst might make predictions about finding taboo talk in interviews with participants, or might predict that norms leave fingerprints that affect the form the final decisions take If after employing the new, more certain proposition we are still unable to find taboo talk, we would downgrade our confidence in the impact of norms in the case significantly—although following Bayesian logic, we would never falsify the hypothesis in the particular case with 100 percent confidence given the uncertainties involved in empirical research in the real world.

If we can trust the disconfirming evidence, another explanation for disconfirmation is that we might have chosen an idiosyncratic case. We can assess whether the chosen case was idiosyncratic using comparative methods, assessing whether there are causally relevant differences between the selected and other typical cases in quadrant I (see chapter 7). If we find that it was idiosyncratic, we can then select another typical case for analysis. If again we do not find the predicted evidence, we can cautiously conclude that the causal relationship is not present in the bounded population.

If we find the predicted evidence in the chosen case, the strength of our confirming conclusions is a function of the theoretical uniqueness of our proposition and the empirical uniqueness and accuracy of the found pieces of evidence. A singular proposition that is a strong smoking gun would significantly increase our confidence in a hypothesis holding in the case, whereas a positive finding in a single theoretically certain but not unique proposition does little, if anything. However, when employed in a cluster *and* we have positive findings for all or most of the propositions, we can also infer with a reasonable degree of confidence that C is causally related to O in the chosen case (see chapter 6).

Given that we can only make inferences to the case at hand using congruence, we should then repeat the case study on another typical case using either congruence or process-tracing methods to gain greater confidence in the cross-case inference that what we found in the chosen cases should also be present in the other causally similar cases in the bounded population. If possible, we should select another typical case that differs in as many conditions as possible. The reasoning behind this recommendation is that there will be some difference across cases even within what we claimed was a causally homogeneous population. In Skocpol's 1980 book on social revolutions, there are of course a number of conditions that differ between the French, Russian, and Chinese revolutions despite the claim that the same theory functions in the same fashion across the cases. Therefore, mapping the different cases on a number of other conditions enables us to select another typical case that differs most from the originally chosen one while remaining within the "relatively" causally homogeneous, bounded population. By selecting two as different-as-possible cases, one can conclude with somewhat more confidence that what was found in the two chosen cases should also be found in the other cases.

There is always a trade-off between the level of empirical rigor of individual case studies that enable stronger within-case inferences to be made, and the number of cases within the population studied, where the more cases we study within a population, the better we are able to infer what was found in the chosen cases should also be present in other typical cases throughout the population (Rohlfing 2012). While enabling more updating to be made about causal relations within a case, other things equal, more rigorous studies of individual cases require significant analytical resources, meaning that in most research situations we can never aspire to more than two or three rigorous case studies. An additional challenge is more practical, in that presenting the results of rigorous case studies in a transparent fashion requires significant space, ruling out more than one or two case studies in article-length work. Yet if we study only one or two cases in a bounded population of a dozen or more cases, our cross-case inferences are very weak at best. The trade-off is between being more confident about a few cases and saying something about a greater number of cases. One cannot have one's cake and eat it too.

8.7. Refining Theories Using Congruence

In figure 8.2 there are two types of deviant cases that are analytically useful for revising our causal theories once we are relatively confident about causal relationships within the set of typical cases. As discussed earlier, congruence methods can be applied, strictly speaking, only when we know both C and O. However, used in a pragmatic fashion together with comparative methods, they can help shed light on new causes and be used to discover omitted causal conditions. We are more hesitant about using congruence when investigating omitted conditions in quadrant IV, instead recommending the use of process-tracing combined with comparative methods. In contrast, we suggest that one use congruence and not process-tracing only for finding new causes (quadrant II cases). We develop the reasoning behind these recommendations in the following discussion and in chapter 9.

Choosing case 8 for an explorative congruence case study can in principle shed light on other causal conditions that have to be present for C to be sufficient to produce O. These can take the form of contextual conditions that enable C to be sufficient, or causal conditions that act together with C to produce the outcome (conjunctions of causes). Here congruence can be utilized in a pragmatic fashion together with a focused comparison of a typical case where we are confident the causal relationship is present. However, we believe that it is more analytically useful to utilize process-tracing here, tracing a mechanism until it breaks down in the case, with this information then shedding light on potentially omitted contextual or causal conditions.

Congruence can also be used to uncover new causes (quadrant II cases), as we discussed under theory-building. For this type of deviant case, we do *not* recommend process-tracing because the combination of congruence and comparison are easier to utilize for searching for new causes than tracing an unknown mechanism backward from a known outcome.

Given that we already know about one $C \to O$ relationship, we can compare a typical case like 5 with deviant case 3 to detect the differences between the two cases, supplemented with a probing congruence study of case 3 that sheds light on clues about new causes that might account for the outcome. If we find a new cause, we can then search for other cases where it is present where the new theory can be tested. In terms of figure, this would involve bringing in new cases using the building-population tools described in chapter 7, and then deploying a congruence or process-tracing test on a typical case of this newly found relationship.

8.8. An Extended Example—Brooks and Wohlforth's Congruence Analysis

What was the impact of the material constraints imposed by relative Soviet economic decline (C_1) on the decisions of the Soviet leadership to engage in a major strategic shift of policy (O) that resulted in the end of the Cold War? Brooks and Wohlforth (2000–2001) assess this research question using a form of robust congruence case study, developing a cluster of propositions about predicted evidence of the $C_1 \to O$ causal relationship that they test empirically in the case study. In the following we describe how they used congruence, and we offer friendly suggestions for how the analysis could be improved to enable stronger inferences because more updating could take place if it was more transparent, thus enabling other researchers to better evaluate the inferential claims made.

While the article primarily aims to make inferences about this particular historical outcome, the case is explicitly framed as a "case of" major shift in great-power strategic policies in the modern era, with another case explicitly mentioned being the shifts in strategic policies of the United Kingdom in response to the rise of Germany in the late 1800s (Brooks and Wohlforth 2000–2001: 21–27). The work does mention contextual differences between the Soviet case and other cases, including bipolarity instead of earlier multipolar great-power balances and the extent of Soviet imperial overstretch in contrast to earlier declining great powers, which might affect our ability to infer from the chosen case to the rest of the population. Therefore, the conclusions also only make cautious inferences about what happened in the end of the Cold War case, with no mention of "lessons learned" for other cases.

The authors claim they are engaging in a competitive theory test between the impact of neorealist-inspired theories that focus on the importance of material constraints due to relative economic decline (C_1) and constructivist theories related to the importance of ideas and norms (C_2). They claim that C_1 is not sufficient, and that ideas always also matter (Brooks and Wohlforth 2000–2001: 11). However, the rest of the article focuses on testing whether material constraints mattered by deploying a cluster test of three distinct predictions of evidence of a relationship between C_1 and O. At points the C_2 → O relationship implicitly forms the "alternative explanation" part of the evaluation of theoretical uniqueness, whereas ideational factors completely disappears at other points. Therefore, one can read the article as mostly enabling updating of confidence of the relationship between economic constraints (C_1) and shifts in great-power strategic policies in the case. It is also this relationship and their congruence tests of it that we focus on in here.

The description of their propositions, in the form of the evidence that the authors "predict" to find in the case and why finding it would be confirming evidence, are not as explicitly developed as they could be. Indeed, the analysis reads as if the authors first engaged in a far-reaching empirical probing before explicit tests were put forward and then afterward framed the analysis as having been a testing exercise, where they use phrases like "we would expect" or the evidence is "strongly consistent" with tests. One indication that the analysis was empirics-first is that they repeatedly claim that "the evidence suggests" before they describe the logical links with theory. However, as discussed in chapter 6, empirics-first research also enables updating, but it does require that the empirical material is explicitly evaluated in a transparent fashion for what it can logically can tell us about a causal theory (theoretical uniqueness) and what the actual piece of evidence tells us about the existence of the proposition (empirical uniqueness) and whether we can trust the found piece of evidence.

While the propositions are not put explicitly forward, we can discern (at least) three predictions of evidence that can be understood as nonoverlapping, theoretically certain propositions (cluster variant of congruence testing). We describe them briefly here, discussing them and suggesting improvements in more detail in the argument road map in table 8.1 later in this chapter. We then present two of the empirical sources of evidence for illustrative purposes, showing that clearer empirical evaluation of the sources should have been undertaken. It is actually surprising that they do not do this given the richness of archival material that they are able to muster; doing so would enable them to highlight a key strength of the article.

Prior Confidence

Before we describe the propositions linking theory with evidence, we look at the level of prior confidence the authors had in their causal theory. The prior confidence in the importance of material constraints is discussed by juxtaposing the dearth of research on this causal condition to the "large literature" on how ideas influenced Soviet changes in policy (Brooks and Wohlforth 2000–2001: 50). The article should have engaged in a farther-reaching review of what we know from the existing literature on the impact of material constraints in the case (especially more historical works on the end of the Cold War), along with the broader literature on great-power strategic shifts. While the authors' comments on the dearth of research suggest that they view their study as a plausibility probe-type situation, they should have given more justification for why even weak confirming evidence can strengthen our confidence in the material-constraint explanation.

Propositions and Predicted Evidence

The first proposition about predicted evidence that they assess empirically is whether there is a lag in perceptions of decline among elites and actual economic decline. They frame this proposition as a competitive test between C_1 and C_2, putting forward the claim that if there is little lag between perceptions and actual decline, it would be evidence in favor of the impact of material factors (C_1) (Brooks and Wohlforth 2000–2001: 27–29). However, they are not explicit about why this is confirming evidence of C_1 and disconfirming for C_2, stating only that the "finding [of little lag] calls into question ideational models of Soviet foreign policy" (Brooks and Wohlforth 2000–2001: 27).

Another proposition implicitly put forward is that the timing of strategic shifts should map closely with the relative economic decline of the Soviet economy, with major changes only coming after there was "mounting evidence of further decline" that would suggest that material factors were driving the strategic shift instead of new ideas (Brooks and Wohlforth 2000–2001: 30). As with the first proposition, they do not explicitly evaluate theoretical certainty or uniqueness; both should be evaluated transparently to increase the persuasiveness of either positive or negative findings.

The third, and most explicit, proposition they put forward is that there should not be large differences between perceptions of the "old" and "new" thinkers regarding the crisis and the need for change (Brooks and Wohlforth 2000–2001: 44). Again, the theoretical reasoning for why finding this evidence would be evidence of their theory is not clearly described. The authors do postulate that the body of found evidence is relatively empirically unique—"overall pattern of evidence . . . can be explained only in light of the material trends" (Brooks and Wohlforth 2000–2001: 49)—but no justification for this is put forward.

Evidence Supplied for the Three Propositions

While the three propositions did not clearly describe exactly what the empirical fingerprints (observables) would look like, or where they should be found, for all three propositions it was not difficult to see where and what would be relevant evidence. They do provide a number of pieces of actual evidence for each proposition that suggests that the propositions about evidence were actually present. Despite not engaging in explicit source criticism, the breadth of different sources consulted and the number of pieces of evidence leave us with a good degree of confidence that the actual evidence mustered is relatively accurate. In the argument road map in table 8.1, we discuss for illustrative purposes only three pieces of evidence from their article. A full road map should transparently present and evaluate each piece of evidence, which in the Brooks and Wohlforth's work would run close to one hundred distinct pieces. While this requires investing substantial analytical resources, the payoffs in terms of more persuasive conclusions are greater (Moravcsik 2014a, 2014b).

Does the Inferential Weight of the Evidence Match the Conclusions?

Brooks and Wohlforth write, "In reviewing this evidence, our general finding is that material conditions undermined old Soviet ways of doing things to a much greater extent than scholars have recognized . . . If our research withstands the test of further releases of new evidence" (2000–2001: 50). They

TABLE 8.1. Argument road map for Brooks and Wohlforth (2000–2001)

Causal relationship
- Impact of the material constraints imposed by Soviet relative economic decline (C_1) upon the decisions of the Soviet leadership to engage in a major strategic shift of policy (O)

Prior relatively low
- "Large literature that examines how ideas influenced the Cold War's end is that it has developed in the absence of an accurate understanding of the material constraints facing Soviet policymakers in the 1980s" (50)
- Suggested improvement: much clearer review of existing literature of impact of material constraints in case (especially more historical works), along with the broader literature on great power strategic shifts.

Proposition

1   Lag in perceptions of decline amongst elites and actual economic decline (Hc, Lu)
- Pattern and account evidence: "The question . . . is how large that lag must be to present a puzzle for models based on material incentives . . . we would expect that Soviet policy-makers would have been cognizant of some profound, systemic shift for the worse . . . expect that perceptions of decline would grow steadily in the first half of the decade" (27–28).
- Soviet economic decline measured using quantitative indicators. Perceptions of Soviet elites measured using wide range of sources, including Politburo meeting transcripts, internal assessments, participant accounts (e.g., Gorbachev).
- Suggested improvements: test is framed as test of ideational models (C_2), but has implications for C_1 also given that they are framed as mutually exclusive at theoretical level. The test could be clearer regarding how much of a "lag" would be evidence in favor of C_1 or C_2, and what sources to be used for the evidence.
- Relatively high certainty: Little explicit discussion, although claims that disconfirming for C_2.
- Suggested improvement: much clearer reasoning required for why fingerprint is theoretically certain for either C_1 or C_2. Disconfirming for C_2 (42).
- Low uniqueness: no discussion of whether finding could be accounted for with other plausible explanations (either theoretical or case-specific).
- Suggested improvement: are there any alternative explanations of finding little lag? One can find little lag, but still contend that ideational factors mattered more in explaining the overall shift.
- Evidence P1 (i)   "Declassified transcripts of CPSU Politburo meetings from 1980, 1981, and 1982 . . . are full of apprehensive comments about the Soviet Union's [declining] relative power" (28) - clear measure of lack of "lag," with leaders perceiving problems already in early 1980s. (Source: Kramer 1999)
  - **Hu, Ha.** Quite self-evident that uniqueness is relatively high. Relatively high accuracy. Despite no *explicit* evaluation of accuracy, given historian's reputation we would give it higher probability of being accurate, other things equal. Cross-checked though with a number of other sources in article (e.g. other historical works and Gorbachev's recollections show similar accounts (28)).

(continued)

2 Timing and form of strategic shifts should map closely with the relative economic decline of economy (Hc, Lu)

- Account and sequence evidence: expect to find that leaders "cling to status quo" (30), with major policy shifts only when no other choice.
- Suggested improvement: relatively clear predictions, although more information could be provided on what it would look like in practice, and the types of sources that would be used.
- Relatively high theoretical certainty: no real discussion of prediction in relation to C_1, although the link is very clear to see. Disconfirming for C_2 (42).
- Suggested improvement: much clearer reasoning required to enable inferences.
- Low theoretical uniqueness: no discussion of whether finding could be accounted for with other plausible explanations (either theoretical or case-specific).
- Suggested improvement: much clearer reasoning required to enable inferences.

• Evidence P2 (i)	"And only in this later period did he begin privately to rely on the more radical intellectual proponents of new thinking and publicly to start a serious effort to radically redefine Soviet foreign policy practices and the country's international role" (31) - clear measure of P2, but no sources are given.
	• **Lu, Ha.** On its own, this piece of evidence is neither certain nor unique (it gains probative value in combination with a series of other pieces of evidence). Given that the source is not given, we are unable to evaluate whether we can trust the evidence of his "private thinking." However, the next sentence in the next paragraph does list a series of sources, including diaries and historical accounts that bolsters our confidence in the accuracy of the evidence.

3 No difference in perceptions of decline among old and new thinkers (Hc, Lu)

- Account evidence: "If the meaning and consequences of the material pressures facing the Soviet Union depended on ideational shifts, then people with different ideas should have had dramatically different strategic reactions to observable indications of material change." (44)
- Suggested improvement relatively clear predictions, although more information could be provided on what it would look like in practice, and the types of sources that would be used.
- Relatively high theoretical certainty: no reasoning given for claim of high certainty.
- Suggested improvement: much clearer reasoning required to enable inferences.
- Low theoretical uniqueness: no discussion of whether finding proposition could be accounted for with other plausible explanations (either theoretical or case-specific), although they claim that "overall pattern of evidence . . . can be explained only in light of the material trends" (49)
- Suggested improvement: much clearer reasoning required to enable inferences. It is not enough to postulate that the evidence cannot be explained with other theories, one has to demonstrate this by providing arguments.

TABLE 8.1. Argument road map for Brooks and Wohlforth (2000–2001) *(continued)*

- • Evidence P3 (i)   Marshall Yazov (key participant in 1991 anti-Gorbachev putsch) "Absolutely. . . . We simply lacked the power to oppose the USA, England, Germany, France, Italy—all the flourishing states that were united in the NATO bloc. We had to seek a dénouement . . . . We had to find an alternative to the arms race . . . . We had to continually negotiate, and reduce, reduce, reduce—especially the most expensive weaponry" (48) (Source: Interview by Skvortsov—not discussed who this is)
  - • **Lu, Ha.** No discussion of whether Yazow might have other motives in making the statement. No explicit evaluation of whether we can trust this interview from 1999, many years after the events, conducted by a person who we are not told anything about, but cross-checked though with a number of other interviews and secondary sources (e.g., a letter from another old thinker made similar claims (46)).
- • <u>Inferences made:</u> Evidence that material conditions (C_1) mattered in case—only within-case inferences made. "In reviewing this evidence, our general finding is that material conditions undermined old Soviet ways of doing things to a much greater extent than scholars have recognized. . . . If our research withstands the test of further releases of new evidence" (50). Careful setting of scope of inferences, stating that new evidence could undermine inferences, and that more research might show that C_2 (ideational factors) were more important at a finer level of decisions.

<u>Discussion of whether inferences warranted:</u>
- • Given that they did not evaluate theoretical uniqueness explicitly except in connection with juxtaposition with claims that ideas matter, one can question whether the degree of confirmation that they suggest the evidence merits is justifiable. We would recommend that the article had more explicitly evaluated theoretical uniqueness of the tests by openly discussing whether there were any plausible alternative explanations for finding evidence of propositions 1, 2, and 3 are beyond C_2 (ideational factors). Despite the lack of source criticism, the breadth of different types of sources that show similar accounts suggests the evidence can be trusted.
- • Inferences about causal theory framed relatively cautiously, with clear indications for the limits of their claims, as we would recommend given the inherent ambiguity of all empirical research in relation to causal theories. We commend in particular the following statement, "In particular, future research may reveal that ideational factors are very important in explaining more finely grained decisions. . . . We do not claim—no responsible analyst can—to account for each microanalytical decision or bargaining position adopted during the Cold War endgame" (50).

do not make inferences beyond the case, and they are cautious about the exact scope of their inferences: "In particular, future research may reveal that ideational factors are very important in explaining more finely grained decisions. . . . We do not claim—no responsible analyst can—to account for each microanalytical decision or bargaining position adopted during the Cold War endgame" (Brooks and Wohlforth 2000–2001: 50). We commend this careful setting of the scope of the inferences being made.

However, given that they did not evaluate theoretical uniqueness of the propositions explicitly, one can question whether the degree of confirmation that they suggest the evidence merits is justifiable. We would recommend that the article had more explicitly evaluated uniqueness of the propositions and the evidence for them by openly discussing whether there were any plausible alternative explanations for finding evidence of the propositions beyond C_2 (ideational factors). Despite the lack of source criticism, the breadth of different types of sources that show similar accounts suggests the evidence can be trusted.

8.9. Concluding Recommendations

This chapter developed congruence case studies, illustrating the types of inferences made possible (within-case, causal relationship confirmed or disconfirmed to some degree). We conclude with a description of the steps involved when employing congruence case study methods.

When we are interested only in explaining the "big and important" things going on in a particular historical outcome, we can utilize explaining outcome congruence. Here theories are used in a pragmatic, heuristic fashion to develop a set of questions that we ask of our case. The goal is to craft a sufficient explanation of the outcome, understood as a holistic whole. The steps involved include the following:

- Examine existing scholarship for inspiration for potential causes that can explain the particular outcome. Asking what the case is potentially a "case of" enables one to identify relevant literatures— naturally the case is a case of many different things, because one wants to develop a comprehensive explanation that includes case-specific elements.
- Develop empirical tests for theories and employ the tests to see how much of the case they can account for.
- Continue until one has crafted a sufficient explanation, often combining several different theories in an eclectic fashion, along with incorporating case-specific factors.

Building theories with congruence involves the following steps:

- Review existing theories for inspiration for potential clues of potential causes or outcomes.

- Decide what "type" of theoretical explanation you are working with (structural, institutional, ideational or psychological) and focus your attention on the common building blocks that this type of explanation would include,
- Produce a rough empirical narrative of what happened in the case.
- Select a typical case after a causally homogeneous population is mapped.
- Engage in a creative probing of the case, searching for "clues" that can suggest a theoretical explanation.
- Once you are relatively confident about the newly identified cause or outcome, move forward to theory-testing.

Finally, congruence theory-testing involves first selecting an appropriate case, followed by the development of empirical tests (either singular or clusters). The guidelines we propose for case selection in theory-testing congruence involve the following:

- Map the population of cases of the causal relationship into typical, deviant and irrelevant cases.
- Select typical cases for congruence testing of theories, ensuring that there is no ambiguity about whether it actually is a typical case and that there is access to enough empirical material to enable in-depth case study.
- Avoid using most-likely/least-likely logic when selecting cases.

If we have strong prior confidence in a causal relationship being present in a given case, we should employ robust congruence tests (often in the form of a cluster of certain propositions). When we have low prior confidence, we can employ plausibility-probe congruence (usually singular proposition).

If confirming evidence is found in the selected case, follow up on the case study (if possible) by selecting another typical case to investigate using either congruence or process-tracing.

If disconfirming evidence is found in the selected case, investigate whether the chosen typical case was idiosyncratic by comparing it with another typical case. If there is not a significant difference, we can cautiously conclude that there is not a causal relationship. If there is a difference, proceed to select another typical case.

CHAPTER 9

Process-Tracing Methods

This is your last chance. After this, there is no turning back. You take the blue pill—the story ends, you wake up in your bed and believe whatever you want to believe. You take the red pill—you stay in Wonderland and I show you how deep the rabbit-hole goes.

Morpheus, in *The Matrix* (1999)

9.1. Introduction

Process-tracing has become a buzzword in recent years, but until recently there has been little agreement about what we actually are tracing or how to conduct this tracing properly. We contend that in comparison to congruence case studies, the defining feature of process-tracing is the unpacking of causal mechanisms into their constituent parts, which are then traced using in-depth case studies. The focus on causal mechanisms understood as a theoretical system in process-tracing provides stronger mechanistic evidence of causal relationships between causes and outcomes because the activities associated with each part of the mechanism are traced empirically.[1] At the same time, tracing mechanisms in a case also sheds light on *how* a given theoretical cause (or set of causes) produces an outcome. The drawbacks of process-tracing include the large amount of analytical resources required to conduct it properly and, as with congruence studies, the inability to infer beyond the single case unless coupled with comparative methods that map causally homogeneous populations of cases to which inferences can be made.

This chapter builds on our previous work on process-tracing (Beach and Pedersen 2013) but also brings in more recent innovations and developments to produce a set of guidelines for using process-tracing methods to analyze causal mechanisms using in-depth single case studies. The chapter proceeds in five steps. After we briefly discuss the debate on what process-tracing actually is tracing, we then develop the assumptions underlying process-tracing methods. This is followed by a section discussing the types of inferences that process-tracing methods enables, after which we present four different variants of process-tracing: outcome-explaining, theory-building, theory-testing, and theory-refining. We conclude with an extended example of a process-tracing research design (Brast 2015), illustrating how Brast attempts to trace something a causal mechanism linking regional interventions (C) with the ability of a state to gain a monopoly on violence that can stop a civil war (O).

The Debate about What Process-Tracing Is Actually Tracing

Many scholars use the term *process-tracing* to refer to forms of descriptive narratives that trace empirical events between the occurrence of a cause and an outcome (Abell 2004; Roberts 1996: 16; Suganami 1996: 164–68; Evangelista 2014). However, this is a form of descriptive inference that demonstrates historical continuities, but we do not gain any insight into the causal mechanism that links cause and outcome together, which prevents us from making strong inferences about causal processes. Other scholars contend that what we are tracing are intervening variables between causes and outcomes (King, Keohane, and Verba 1994: 85–87; Gerring 2007: 172–85). Yet this understanding implies that we have some form of meaningful variation that can produce difference-making evidence that, when coupled with the ability to control for other causes, enables us to make causal inferences. However, we believe that causal inferences are possible only when we have either mechanistic within-case evidence or the manipulated, experimental evidence of difference-making (Russo and Williamson 2007); designing process-tracing in KKV's terms would not enable us to infer causation because the types of evidence they describe are observational data of difference-making. This problem can be clearly seen in Gerring's (2007) description of process-tracing as a method. Gerring follows KKV by suggesting that we first need to disaggregate the single case into multiple subcases that can be compared to measure variation in intervening variables, holding other independent variables constant. This can occur either by disaggregating a decision-making process over time (before and after) or by cutting it up into subissues or other relevant distinctions. However, as discussed in chapter 6, the problem here is that these subcases are not independent of each other, making assessment of mean causal effects problematic at best. Further, by focusing on cross-case variation, we lose a focus on the causal process itself, particularly how it unfolds in cases. We contend that thinking of process-tracing in terms of producing mechanistic within-case evidence better captures the analytical advantages of the method.

Recently a consensus has begun developing that sees the tracing of causal mechanisms as the core of process-tracing (Bennett and Checkel 2014; George and Bennett 2005; Checkel 2008; Waldner 2012; Bennett 2008a; Beach and Pedersen 2013; Rohlfing 2012; Beach and Rohlfing 2016). However, even in the 2014 edited volume by Bennett and Checkel, there is little discussion of what mechanisms actually are, preventing us from knowing good process-tracing when we see it because we do not know what scholars actually claim to be tracing.

The reasons for the confusion about the nature of process-tracing are manifold. One reason is that some scholars interpret process-tracing case studies in light of ontological assumptions about causation used in variance-based research (King, Keohane, and Verba 1994; Gerring 2007). For example, Lyall (2014) interprets process-tracing in counterfactual terms when he attempts to reconstruct the method within a potential outcome framework that builds on counterfactuals. The result is that process-tracing as a method becomes a poor way to produce evidence of difference-making. It would be third-best because it is inferior to both actual experiments and large-N observational studies. In relation to experiments, process-tracing lacks the experimental manipulation required to make causal inferences using difference-making evidence. Compared to large-N studies, using only a small number of cases makes our research more vulnerable to measurement error and other forms or error that tend to wash out across a large number of cases.

Another reason for the confusion is that many scholars wed process-tracing as a method to a particular theoretical approach (e.g., Mahoney 2012; Blatter and Haverland 2012). As discussed in chapter 3, many scholars infuse their recommendations for good process-tracing of causal mechanisms with theoretical ideas when discussing how to test whether mechanisms are present or when defining the levels at which mechanisms function. For instance, Mahoney (2012) focuses on temporal sequences as evidence in process-tracing, which is consistent with testing of historical institutionalist theories but not necessarily other types of theoretical explanation.

A final reason for the confusion is that many scholars attempt to define process-tracing as a *single* research method. We argue that a lot of the murkiness about what process-tracing actually is and how it should be used in practice can be cleared up by differentiating it into four distinct variants determined by the research purposes and philosophical position of the researcher. We first differentiate process-tracing into two overall types of research: theory-centric and case-centric. In theory-centric work, the goal of research is to contribute to broader theoretical debates by tracing mechanisms in single cases in order to generalize to small, bounded populations, whereas in case-centric work the goal is to craft comprehensive explanations of individual historical cases, drawing on arguments found in the burgeoning literature on topics such as eclectic theorization (where the case is front and center) (Sil and Katzenstein 2010) and pragmatism as a research strategy (Friedrichs and Kratochwill 2009). This distinction reflects the case-centric ambitions of many qualitative scholars who use case study methods to better understand particular historical outcomes instead of attempting to generalize to a broader population of cases.

Within theory-centric work, we contend that process-tracing can be used for building and testing theories about causal mechanisms and for revising theories in combination with focused comparisons, uncovering omitted causal or contextual conditions that are required for a set of causes to produce a given outcome. Theory-testing process-tracing conceptualizes a theory based on existing literature and then tests whether there is evidence that a hypothesized causal mechanism is actually present in the selected case. After developing propositions that operationalize clear empirical observables for each of the parts of the mechanism, the research evaluates whether the predicted evidence was actually found in the case and whether it can be trusted. Theory-building process-tracing aims to infer that a more general causal mechanism exists from the "facts" of a particular case. Theoretical revision involves tracing a mechanism, which has been found in other cases, in a deviant case and then using the evidence gained about where the mechanism broke down in the deviant case to inform a focused comparison with a typical case to detect omitted causal or contextual conditions required for the mechanism to function.

The differentiation of process-tracing into four variants has important implications for how and when we use process-tracing methods, in particular between the case-centric and theory-centric variants that we explore in the rest of the chapter.

9.2. The Assumptions of Process-Tracing Methods

As presented in chapter 2, causality is understood in process-tracing in terms of mechanisms as a system that transfer causal forces from C to O.

Mechanisms as a system are often described as comprising a series of parts that themselves comprise entities engaging in activities (Machamer, Darden, and Craver 2000; Machamer 2004). Entities are what engage in activities (the parts of the mechanism, the toothed wheels in a machine), where the activities are the producers of change or what transmits causal forces through a mechanism (the movement of the wheels transferring causal forces from one part to the next) (Machamer, Darden, and Craver 2000; Machamer 2004). Parts have no independent existence (i.e., they are not considered variables) in relation to producing an outcome; instead, they are integral parts of a system that transmits causal forces to the outcome. As discussed in chapter 3, we are fleshing out the causal story that links a given cause (or set of causes) together with an outcome, unpacking the causal arrow(s) linking cause and outcome into a series of interlocking and interacting parts. This does not necessarily mean that all parts of the mechanism can be understood as only embedded in a particular mechanism. Within families of theories, there can be certain modules or building blocks that are shared (see chapter 3 for more on modularity).

In contrast to symmetric causal claims about covariation between values of X and Y, process-tracing follows other case-based methods in making asymmetric causal claims (Beach and Pedersen 2013; Waldner 2012). Theorizing that developed countries (C) are a subset of democratic countries (O) makes no claims about whether less developed countries (~C) are not democratic (~O). The causes of a given outcome (O) are often very different from the causes of the outcome's conceptual negation. It can be argued that this asymmetry is even stronger in process-tracing, given that we are focusing on what links C and O together. Without C, there is nothing to trigger the subsequent mechanism. Additionally, we should not expect that the mechanisms linking causes and an outcome (O) will be the same as those that link other causes with the absence of the outcome (~O). Therefore, it makes little sense to compare the mechanisms that produce an outcome with those that produce its negation (~O), given that they are expected to be different at both the theoretical level and in their empirical manifestations. For example, if we are studying a theory that claims that strong interest-group demands for more spending on an issue area (C) results in disproportionate public spending in the issue area (O) through a mechanism involving the activities of lobbyists using campaign contributions, the claim is asymmetric because we would not be making any claims about what happens when there are not strong interest-group demands—nor are we making any claims about other causes of proportionate public spending. We are therefore only focusing on positive cases of both the cause (or set of causes) and the outcome.

9.3. What Are We Making Inferences about in Process-Tracing?

Process-tracing case studies in their case-centric variant enable us to craft sufficient explanations of particular historical cases, using a combination of systematic and case-specific mechanisms to produce a comprehensive explanation of the "big and important" things going on in a case. Naturally, these findings are case-specific, although some of the findings might be "lessons learned" that can be used as inspiration in the search for generalizable but narrower causal explanations in other cases.

Theory-centric variants of process-tracing enable inferences about mechanisms linking causes with outcomes through the collection of mechanistic evidence of the operation of each of the parts of a causal mechanism in a case study. By tracing mechanisms explicitly, the causal inferences that can be made are arguably much stronger than in congruence studies.

Theory-centric variants of process-tracing do not enable cross-case inferences about the presence of mechanisms linking C with O across a population to be made—to do so requires that they are combined with comparative methods for mapping causally homogeneous populations (see chapter 7). However, mechanisms are often very sensitive to contextual conditions (see chapters 2 and 3). This requires that when mapping a population of cases using comparative methods, we also are sensitive to the problem of equifinality at the level of mechanisms. This was defined as the situation where the same cause is linked to the same outcome through different causal mechanisms depending on the contextual conditions present. This problem reduces our ability to infer across cases that the mechanism found in the chosen case should also be present in the other typical cases of the causal relationship. For example, in the theoretical relationship between economic development (C) and democratization (O), there might be a number different plausible mechanisms linking the two, depending on the contextual conditions (Gerring 2010). Hypothetically, economic development might be linked with democratization through some form of middle-class growth mechanism in Southeast Asia, whereas the same cause might be linked to democratization through pressures from industries in Latin American cases.

Given that we almost never have complete knowledge of contextual conditions that enable or prevent particular mechanisms from being triggered, there is a very real risk of making flawed cross-case inferences about mechanisms being present in a bounded population if we assume that a mechanism found in one case is present in other cases, unless we have actually studied some of the other cases, at least in a cursory fashion. The implication of the problem of equifinality at the level of mechanisms is that inferences from a single case to the rest of the population are more difficult when they involve tracing mechanisms, as they require that we expend even more effort in justifying that we have built a causally homogeneous population of cases by discussing in detail whether there are any noticeable differences in contextual conditions that might result in equifinality at the level of mechanisms.

Process-tracing does *not* enable inferences about necessity or sufficiency to be made within the studied case unless we adopt the assumptions about science itself underlying the case-centric, pragmatic tradition (see chapter 1 and discussion later here). Why, then, can we not claim that mechanisms are sufficient when operating within a neopositivist or critical realist tradition? The claim that mechanisms have to be sufficient to produce an outcome is otherwise found widely in the literature (Mahoney 2001: 580; Mayntz 2004: 241–53; Andersen 2012: 416; Waskan 2011: 403; Waldner 2014). However, unless the cause that triggers the mechanism is also theorized to be a sufficient cause, requiring that mechanisms are sufficient would result in the causal mechanism being more influential than the actual cause. A mechanism cannot be anything "more" in terms of sufficiency than the cause that triggers it. And given that we cannot assess sufficiency empirically within a single case because we lack a counterfactual comparison, requiring mechanisms to be sufficient would result in an assumption about the nature of causal relationships to be put forward that cannot be assessed empirically.

In conclusion, it is important to be very clear about the scope and types of inferences one is making when employing process-tracing, either alone as in the case-centric variant or together with comparative methods and congruence case studies. Theory-centric process-tracing case studies enable inferences only about mechanisms in the studied case and not claims about causes being necessary or sufficient in the studied case. The cross-case claims enabled by combining a mapping of a causally homogeneous population using comparative methods and process-tracing case studies are even more restricted than when using congruence, given the problem of equifinality at the level of mechanisms and the importance of contextual conditions for which mechanisms link a given cause with an outcome.

9.4. Explaining Outcome Process-Tracing

As with explaining outcome congruence, case selection in explaining outcome process-tracing is driven by a strong interest in accounting for a particular interesting and/or historically important outcome. The outcome is not viewed as a "case of" something, but instead is a particular event that is expressed as a proper name. Explaining outcome process-tracing can therefore be thought of as a single-outcome study, defined as seeking the causes of a specific outcome in a single case (Gerring 2006). Examples of this type of study in the literature include Layne's (1996) study of US grand strategy toward Western Europe after World War II and Schiff's (2008) analysis of the creation of the International Criminal Court.

While case selection in explaining outcome process-tracing can resemble the selection of extreme cases (Gerring and Seawright 2007), it is vital to emphasize that a case like the Holocaust, when understood in a more holistic fashion as in explaining outcome process-tracing, is not just a case of a theoretical concept like genocide. In explaining outcome process-tracing, the goal is to craft a sufficient explanation that captures the unique character of a specific (horrific) historical event like *the* Holocaust. We choose the case because it is the Holocaust or the Cuban Missile Crisis—cases that in and of themselves are historically important to understand the causes of.

The findings of explaining outcome process-tracing cannot be generalized to other cases for two reasons. First, the case itself is unique given our broader conceptualization of outcomes (*the* Cuban Missile Crisis instead of a narrower theoretical phenomenon like a case of deterrence bargaining). Second, given the inclusion of nonsystematic parts and case-specific combinations of mechanisms in our explanations, the actual explanation is also case-specific.

It is vital to first note that the term *causal mechanism* is used in a much broader sense in explaining outcome process-tracing than in theory-centric variants. First, whereas theory-testing and building variants aim to test or build mechanisms that are applicable across a bounded population of cases, to craft a sufficient explanation we almost always need to combine mechanisms into an eclectic conglomerate mechanism to account for a historical outcome, incorporating also case-specific factors into the conglomerate causal mechanism. While some scholars like Elster contend that mechanisms always have to be at level of generality that transcends a particular spatio-temporal context (i.e., they are systematic mechanisms) (1998: 45), thereby excluding the use of case-specific elements in mechanisms, other scholars have more pragmatically argued that mechanisms that are unique to a particular time and place also can be defined as mechanisms. Wight for instance has defined mechanisms as the "sequence of events and processes (the causal complex) that lead to the event" (2004: 290). Case-specific, or nonsystematic, mechanisms and their parts can be distinguished from systematic ones by asking whether we should expect the mechanism or their parts to play a role in other cases.

The importance of nonsystematic elements in explaining a particular outcome makes explaining outcome process-tracing sometimes more analogous to the historical interpretation of events (Roberts 1996). However, these nonsystematic factors will almost never stand alone, given that social reality is not just a "random" hodgepodge of events but includes mechanisms that operate more generally across a range of cases within a bounded population.

At the same time, the inclusion of nonsystematic mechanisms that are often depicted as events has an important advantage: it enables us to capture actor choice and the contingency of historical events that pervade historical events, thus immunizing our research from the criticisms of political science from historical scholars (Gaddis 1992–93; Rueschemeyer 2003; Roberts 1996; Schroeder 1994). In the words of Lebow, "Underlying causes, no matter how numerous or deep-seated, do not make an event inevitable. Their consequences may depend on fortuitous coincidences in timing and on the presence of catalysts that are independent of any of the underlying causes" (2000–2001: 591–92). This does not mean that we have to adopt probabilism at the ontological level, because this would imply that things "just happened" in the case. Events in a case happened for a reason, but the reasons might be complex and case-specific, including explanations related to case-specific factors such as critical junctures in a particular case that help account for the particular outcome. And our empirical knowledge of why things happen might be very poor, but this is an epistemological question instead of an ontological debate about the nature of causation.

The admission of case-specific causes does not mean that case-specific factors are preferable: "To clarify, single-outcome research designs are open to idiographic explanation in a way that case study research is not. But single-outcome researchers should not assume, *ex ante*, that the truth about their case is contained in factors that are specific to that case" (Gerring 2006: 717). What differentiates explaining outcome process-tracing from historical research is both the causal-explanatory focus—where the analysis is theory-guided—and the goal to go beyond the single case in some instances (Hall 2003; Gerring 2006). As regards the ambition to go beyond the single case, this involves attempts to identify which mechanisms are systematic and nonsystematic in the specific case study. This is typically done in book-length works, where lessons for other cases are developed in the conclusions. For example, which factors do we believe can potentially be systematic based on the findings of our study and in light of what we know from other research? Which findings can potentially be "generalized" to other cases, and to what extent are they unique to the case? Individual causal mechanisms can potentially be generalized, but the *case-specific composite* cannot.

Conducting an Explaining Outcome Process-Tracing Case Study

Explaining outcome process-tracing is an iterative research strategy that aims to trace causal mechanisms defined in the broader and more pragmatic sense discussed earlier. In many respects, it resembles the method of abduction, where there is a continual and creative juxtaposition of empirical material to theories. Claims about sufficiency are made once one pragmatically has accounted for the big and important things in the case. Using abduction, the interaction of theory and empirics enable us to converge on the "best explanation" in the particular case (Day and Kincaid 1994; Peirce 1955; Timmermans and Tavory 2012).

There are two different starting points—theory or empirics—depicted in figure 9.1. The theory-first path follows the steps described in the discussion of theory-testing, where an existing mechanism is tested to determine whether it can account for the outcome. In most explaining outcome studies, a single existing mechanism cannot provide a sufficient explanation, which results in a second stage of research where either a testing or building path can be chosen, informed by the results of the first empirical analysis. If the testing path is chosen again, this would involve testing another theorized mechanism as a supplemental explanation to see whether together they can account for the big and important things going on in the case. Alternatively, the theory-building path can be chosen in the second iteration, using empirical evidence to build a new mechanism that can account for the elements of the outcome that were unaccounted for using the first mechanism, following the steps discussed later here under theory-building. In both paths, theorized mechanisms and empirical tests are treated more pragmatically as heuristic devices to understand important events (for more on this type of research, see Humphreys 2010).

The building path is often used when we are researching a little-studied phenomenon. Here the analyst can proceed in a manner more analogous with historical methodology (Roberts 1996), for example, working backward from the outcome by sifting through the empirical record in an attempt to uncover a plausible causal mechanism that can have produced the outcome; in many ways, this is analogous to classic detective work. This is a bottom-up type of analysis, using empirical material as the basis for building a plausible explanation of causal mechanisms whereby C (or multiple causes) produced O.

The important question, then, is when should we stop this process (i.e., how do we know a sufficient explanation when we see it)? There is no foolproof answer to this question in the pragmatic understanding of research;

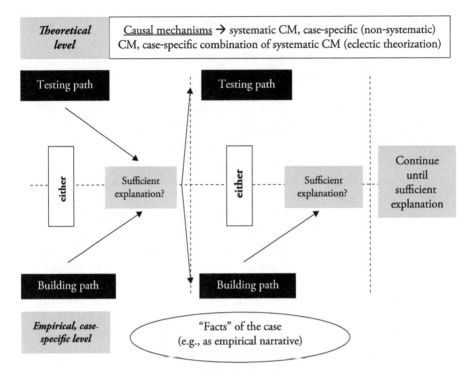

Fig. 9.1. Explaining outcome process-tracing

instead, the decision that we have a sufficient explanation is based on a relatively subjective assessment of whether all the relevant facets of the outcome
have been accounted for adequately, while at the same time ensuring that
the evidence is best explained by the developed explanation instead of plausible alternative explanations (Peirce 1955). We can never confirm a theory
with 100 percent confidence; instead, we stop when we are satisfied that the
found explanation is able to account for the most important aspects of the
outcome.

An Example—Schimmelfennig's Explaining Outcome Process-Tracing

A good example of explaining outcome process-tracing can be seen Schimmelfennig's (2001) article on the eastern enlargement of the European
Union. The article attempts to explain a particular case—the eastern enlargement of the European Union, focusing on three subquestions related
to this larger outcome, particularly on why countries like France that were

opposed to enlargement of the EU ended up not opposing it (Schimmelfennig 2001: 49).

The case study proceeds using three iterations of the testing path to account for each of these subquestions (see figure 9.1). He takes as his point of departure two competing theorized causal mechanisms from "rationalist" and "sociological" theories of international cooperation to explain the existing EU member states' positions toward eastern enlargement. He first tests a rationalist mechanism and finds it can account for national preferences but not for the final decision to enlarge. Informed by the findings of his first empirical analysis, he undertakes a second round of tests to determine whether a sociological mechanism can account for the question of why the opponents accepted enlargement when they could have blocked it as a result of unanimous decision-making rules. He finds that it can account for the final decision of France to accept enlargement, but it cannot account for the negotiating process.

Not surprisingly, however, Schimmelfennig finds that neither mechanism can fully explain the outcome (neither is sufficient), finding them both "wanting in the 'pure' form" (2001: 76). In response he uses the empirical results of the first to iterations to formulate an eclectic combination of the two mechanisms that attempts to "provide the missing link between egoistic preferences and a norm-conforming outcome" by developing the idea of "rhetorical action" (the strategic use of norm-based arguments).

In the third iteration of the case study he tests this eclectic conglomerate mechanism, finding that, together with the first two causes, that it provides a sufficient explanation of the historical outcome. He provides relatively strong evidence suggesting that the more complex mechanism is actually present in the case and that it is sufficient to account for the outcome. Sufficiency is confirmed when it can be substantiated that there are no important aspects of the outcome that are unaccounted for by the explanation.

In all three iterations, Schimmelfennig is tracing causal mechanisms by testing them to see what they can account for in relation to the particular case. However, in the first two iterations, the theoretical rationalist and sociological causal mechanisms are more generally applicable, whereas the eclectic combination is much more case-specific, thus limiting the ability to make generalizations based on the findings of the study.

9.5. Theory-Building Process-Tracing

In its purest form, theory-building process tracing starts with empirical material and uses a structured analysis of this material to build a plausible hypothetical causal mechanism whereby C is linked with O that can be present in multiple cases, meaning that it can be generalized beyond the single case. In effect, it involves using empirical material to answer the question, "How did we get here?" (Friedman 1986a: 582; Swedberg 2012: 6–7). Theory-building process-tracing is utilized primarily when we know that there might be a relationship between C and O, but we are in the dark regarding potential mechanisms linking the two. We contend that if we do not know C, we should first engage in theory-building using either congruence or comparative methods such as a most-similar-systems comparison to identify a candidate cause (see chapters 7 and 8).

All variants of theory-centric process-tracing require the mapping of the population of the C → O relationship to select an appropriate case to either build or test theories of causal mechanisms or to trace mechanisms in deviant cases as a tool to refine causal theories. As in chapter 8, we present this mapping using the following figure (figure 9.2). In both building and testing mechanisms, we select cases in which C and O, along with the requisite contextual conditions, are present, meaning that typical cases in quadrant I are always selected in the first instance. The argument behind only selecting typical cases is that if we want to build a theory about a mechanism linking C and O together, we probably should select a case in which the mechanism can at least in principle be present (see Beach and Pedersen 2016). As discussed in chapter 8, for both theory-building and theory-testing purposes, we do *not* need to select typical cases where other potential causes are not present, because we can isolate the workings of particular mechanisms empirically through evaluating the uniqueness of empirical evidence. In other words, control for other causes is at the level that is more appropriate when working with mechanistic evidence: the empirical level within the case.

Given that we do not know what the mechanism binding the two is when using theory-building process-tracing, nor do we know anything about the contextual conditions that have to be present for the mechanism to function properly, we select cases solely based on membership in C and O. In contrast, when testing a mechanism we will have some idea about contextual conditions, meaning that these also need to be mapped to enable us to select a typical case in which a mechanism might be present. We naturally do not know a priori whether the mechanism is actually present in a case or whether there is enough evidence to update our confidence in the existence of the mechanism in the particular case. But by selecting a case where the mechanism can hypothetically be present, we are able to either test whether a hypothesized mechanism linking C and O is present or to build a theory about which mechanism(s) link C and O.

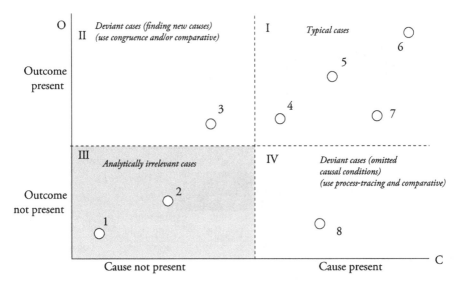

Fig. 9.2. Mapping the population for theory-centric variants of process-tracing

Conducting Theory-Building Process-Tracing

The basic framework for building theories of mechanisms is illustrated in figure 9.3. After the key theoretical concepts (C and O) are defined and operationalized using the procedures discussed in chapters 4 and 5, theory-building proceeds to investigate the empirical material in the case (step 1), using empirical material as clues about the possible empirical manifestations of an underlying causal mechanism between C and O that fulfills the guidelines for a properly conceptualized causal mechanism. This involves an intensive and wide-ranging search of the empirical record. Here it can be helpful to first develop a descriptive narrative of what happened in the case to shed light on potential mechanisms. For instance, by crafting this narrative, we might find that what took place was a period of slow institutional change, which would suggest that we should look for mechanisms incorporating structural or institutional theoretical elements that could account for the institutional stickiness in the face of massive pressures for change (Grzymala-Busse 2011: 1272).

Figure 9.3 illustrates that an underlying theoretical causal mechanism is what is being traced in theory-building process-tracing (C, causal mechanism, O). In contrast to theory-testing, the empirical analysis itself, understood as the collection of the "facts" of the case, is two inferential leaps

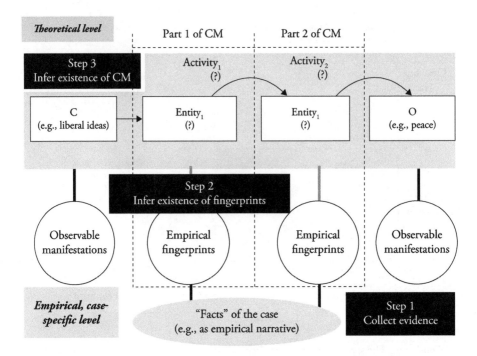

Fig. 9.3. Theory-building process-tracing

Note: Bold lines = primary inferences; shaded lines = secondary inferences; shaded area = what is being traced.

removed from the theorized causal mechanism. This is illustrated by the bold lines linking the "facts" with found evidence (primary inferences) and the subsequent inferential leap from these pieces of evidence to the idea that the found pieces of evidence tap into a proposition about the observables that the operation of a part of a causal mechanism left in the case.

Evidence does not speak for itself. Often theory-building does have a testing element, in that scholars seek inspiration from existing theoretical work and previous observations for what to look for. For example, an analyst investigating socialization of international administrative officials within international organizations could seek inspiration in theories of domestic public administration or in psychological theories of small-group dynamics, while also reading more descriptive accounts of the workings of international organizations as sources of inspiration for plausible causal mechanisms. Here existing theory can be thought of as a form of grid to detect systematic patterns in empirical material, enabling inferences about predicted evidence to be made. In addition, one can look to research on mechanisms on similar research topics for inspiration for what parts of the mechanism might look like. As discussed in chapter 3, there are parts of mechanisms that might have a modular character, meaning that we should expect that families of theories should share certain parts. Any rational institutional explanation will have a part of the mechanism that details how institutional constraints create opportunity structures for actors. If we are building a theorized rational institutionalist mechanism, we can seek inspiration from existing research for what it might look like theoretically and what observables we might expect it to leave.

In other situations the search for mechanisms is based on hunches drawn from puzzles that are unaccountable for in existing work. In step 3 the secondary inferential leap is made from found evidence to infer that they reflect an underlying causal mechanism.

In reality, theory-building process-tracing is usually an iterative and creative process. Hunches of what to look for that are inspired by existing theoretical and empirical work are investigated systematically, with the results of this search then forming the background for further searches. This means that steps 1 and 2 are often repeated before step 3 is reached.

An Example—Janis's Theory-Building Process-Tracing

An example of a theory-building process-tracing work is Janis's (1982) book on groupthink. In the book he attempts to build a causal mechanism that details how conformity pressures in small groups can have an adverse impact on foreign policy decisions, using a selection of case studies of policy fiascoes that were the result of poor decision-making practices by small group of policy-makers who constituted a cohesive group. He uses the term *groupthink* to describe the causal mechanism whereby conformity pressures in small groups produce poor decisions.

The first exploratory case that he uses in the book is an analysis of the Bay of Pigs Invasion fiasco. He notes first that groupthink was by no means the sole cause of fiasco (Janis 1982: 32), but at the same time, he notes a puzzle that existing explanations are unable to account for: why the "best and the brightest" policy-making group in the Kennedy administration did not pick to pieces the faulty assumptions underlying the decision to support the intervention by a group of Cuban exiles. He writes, "Because of a sense of incompleteness about the explanation, I looked for other causal factors in the sphere of group dynamics" (Janis 1982: 32–33). He suggests that the groupthink mechanism is a part of the explanation but not sufficient to explain the outcome (Janis 1982: 34).

The starting point of each of his case studies is to draw on psychological theories of group dynamics and relevant political science theories, such as Allison's (1971) organizational model, and own previous research as an inspiration for his search through empirical record for systematic factors that form part of possible groupthink causal mechanism. His search for parts of the mechanism is also informed by empirical works on the Bay of Pigs decision. For example, he writes, "When I reread Schlesinger's account, I was struck by some observations that earlier had escaped my notice. These observations began to fit a specific pattern of concurrence-seeking behavior that had impressed me time and again in my research on other kinds of face-to-face groups. . . . Additional accounts of the Bay of Pigs yielded more such observations, leading me to conclude that group processes had been subtly at work" (Janis 1982: vii). Here we see the importance that imagination and intuition play in devising a theory from empirical evidence, while at the same time Janis is informed by theoretical research.

Step 1, then, involves collecting empirical material to detect potential evidence of underlying causal mechanisms. Inferences are then made from empirical material that evidence of the part of the mechanism existed (step 2), which results in the secondary inference that an underlying mechanism was present in step 3. He writes, "For purposes of *hypothesis construction*—which is the stage of inquiry with which this book is concerned—we must be willing to make some inferential leaps from whatever historical clues we can pick up. But I have tried to start off on solid ground by selecting the best available historical writings and to use as my springboard those specific observations that appear to be solid facts in the light of what is now known about the deliberations of the policy-making groups" (Janis 1982: ix). Further, "What I try to do is to show how the evidence at hand can be viewed as forming a consistent psychological pattern, in the light of what is known about group dynamics" (Janis 1982: viii).

The presentation of the empirical evidence is not in the form of an analytical narrative describing events or causal steps between C and O. Instead, he writes, "Since my purpose is to describe and explain the psychological processes at work, rather than to establish historical continuities, I do not present the case studies in chronological order. The sequence I use was chosen to convey step-by-step the implications of group dynamics hypotheses" (Janis 1982: viii–ix). He describes four different "symptoms" of groupthink that can be understood as evidence of the parts of a groupthink mechanism, including the illusion of invulnerability held in the group, the illusion of unanimity in the group, the suppression of personal doubts, and the presence of self-appointed "mind guards" in the group. For example, the shared illusions of invulnerability and unanimity helped members of the group maintain a sense of group solidarity, resulting in a lack of critical appraisal and debate that produced a dangerous level of complacent overconfidence.

He concludes, "The failure of Kennedy's inner circle to detect any of the false assumptions behind the Bay of Pigs invasion plan can be at least partially accounted for by the group's tendency to seek concurrence at the expense of seeking information, critical appraisal, and debate. The concurrence-seeking tendency was manifested by shared illusions and other symptoms, which helped the members to maintain a sense of group solidarity. Most crucial were the symptoms that contributed to complacent overconfidence in the face of vague uncertainties and explicit warnings that should have alerted the members to the risks of the clandestine military operation—an operation so ill-conceived that among literate people all over the world the name of the invasion site has become the very symbol of perfect failure" (Janis 1982: 47).

9.6. Theory-Testing Process-Tracing

Theory-testing process-tracing involves assessing whether a hypothesized causal mechanism exists in a single case by exploring whether the predicted evidence of a hypothesized causal mechanism exist in reality. This variant of process-tracing is often used when previous case studies (e.g., congruence) have suggested that there might be a causal relationship between C and O, but we are still unsure whether there is an actual causal relationship or not. By providing evidence of a disaggregated mechanism linking C and O, stronger claims of causation can be made within the studied case. At the same time, by tracing disaggregated mechanisms we gain a greater understanding of *how* C causes O. Causal mechanisms are treated as middle-range theories in theory-testing process-tracing, and they are expected to be present in a bounded population of cases when the cause that triggers the mechanism and the contextual conditions that allow it to operate are present (Falleti and Lynch 2009).

In theory-testing process-tracing we know both C and O and either we have existing conjectures about a plausible mechanism or are able to deduce one from existing theorization relatively easily. We would always select typical cases in figure 9.2 when testing theories of mechanisms, given that we already know that in cases in the other quadrants that either there is no mechanism linking C with O because C is not present (quadrants II and III), or that it does not work properly because C does not result in O (quadrant IV).

While not depicted in figure 9.2, all cases in quadrant I are theorized to be in the set of relevant contextual conditions. When we are uncertain about which contextual conditions have to be present for a given mechanism, we should start by selecting a case in which almost any thinkable contextual condition is present. If we then find the mechanism in this case, we cannot automatically infer to other cases where fewer of the potential contextual conditions are present.[2] To do so requires that we investigate mechanisms in another case with fewer contextual conditions present. In a perfect world, one would gradually whittle the number of contextual conditions down to the bare minimum for the mechanism to work. However, this would require repeating stepwise for a range of conditions—something that cannot be done because of the amount of analytical resources that proper process-tracing takes. Therefore, we recommend carefully mapping the population for differences across potentially causally relevant contextual conditions, and then probing using two or three process-tracing case studies toward a "bare minimum" of contextual conditions that have to be present for a given mechanism to function in the same manner. These cases can be selected on the basis of a principle of maximizing differences within the set of causally homogeneous cases (see also chapter 8 for similar recommendations in congruence case studies). One can also do only one or two process-tracing studies, followed by one or more congruence case studies of other typical cases that focus on assessing whether a "core" observable of the causal mechanism found in the first process-tracing case is also present in other cases.

While there are large differences in how the natural and social sciences conduct within-case analysis that produces mechanistic evidence, there can be research situations where it makes sense to focus our analytical attention on the workings of a particular part of a mechanism by studying its workings in a more conducive context for research (where there is a large amount of available data), and then using that evidence to infer that we should expect similar processes in other contexts. This is referred to as extrapolation of findings from one context to another; a practice widely used in the natural sciences (Steel 2008).[3] Extrapolation requires that the part or parts of the theorized mechanism we are studying exhibit "modularity," meaning that they have a degree of interchangeability with similar mechanisms in other contexts (see chapter 3).

When we are particularly interested in understanding the workings of a particular part, we can potentially study it in a more conducive context (e.g., a historical case for which there is a richer archival record). This is not done for reasons of isolating the workings of the part from other potential causes because in a system understanding we view mechanisms in holistic terms, where the whole is more than the sum of the parts. Instead, we do it to move our research to a context in which it is actually possible to observe the workings of the part of the mechanism in far greater empirical detail. In the natural sciences, researchers who decide to focus on a particular part of a mechanism might investigate its workings in a setting where they can gain richer observational evidence, such as by substituting laboratory animals for human subjects, for obvious reasons (Steel 2008). For example, in research on the causal mechanism linking smoking and lung cancer, researchers investigated how smoke is absorbed into the lungs of rats. The researchers would then evaluate whether it is reasonable to extrapolate from the mechanistic evidence for the operation of parts of a causal mechanism found in rats, enabling us to expect that the part of the mechanism would function in a similar fashion in humans. We would need to ask ourselves whether there could be relevant differences across the two contexts, such as metabolism differences in rats and humans, that would hinder the extrapolation of findings from one setting to another (Steel 2008: 88–99).

In the social sciences, we might want to focus our attention on a part of an ideational theory that details how shared norms restrain decision-makers. If we want to say something about the workings of this part of the mechanisms in cases of modern US presidential decision-making (e.g., in the past two decades), we might decide to go back and select a historical case for which there is a much richer empirical material available instead of attempting to rely solely on biased empirical material from recent cases, such as memoirs by participants or elite interviews. If we find strong evidence of the part of the mechanism operating in the historical record, we would then have to evaluate whether there are theoretical and/or empirical reasons to expect that what we found in the earlier case would not also hold in a recent case.

This said, extrapolation of findings about parts of mechanisms studied in different contexts is very difficult, if not impossible, for most social mechanisms. One reason for this is that our knowledge of social science mechanisms is much shallower than what we possess in many natural sciences, where we have a good understanding of many of the core mechanisms such as natural selection, enabling us to compare well-known contexts with new contexts for similar mechanisms to extrapolate findings. Another reason is that social mechanisms are arguably even more sensitive to context because of the self-awareness of social actors. This is not the time or place to delve into the classic sociological question of how self-awareness affects our ability to understand social scientific questions, but suffice it to say, it adds an additional level of contextual factors into the equation that makes it very difficult to assume that what we found in the context of presidential decision-making in the 1960s would also be relevant today. This means that one should be extremely cautious when attempting to extrapolate findings about the operation of parts of mechanisms gained in different contexts. However, the information gained from studying a part of a mechanism in a more conducive context can be helpful in focusing our attention on developing better theories of parts of mechanisms and better empirical "tests" of them in other contexts.

Conducting Theory-Testing Process-Tracing

Figure 9.4 illustrates the three steps involved in theory-testing process-tracing using a simple abstract example. The first step in testing whether a hypothesized causal mechanism was actually present in the case is to conceptualize a causal mechanism between C and O based on existing theorization along with making explicit the context within which it functions (see chapter 3 for more on conceptualizing mechanisms). In this example a two part mechanism between C and O is developed, with each part composed of entities engaging in activities. Conceptualization involves using logical reasoning and existing theoretical and empirical literature to formulate a plausible causal mechanism whereby C produces O, along with the contextual conditions that can be expected to affect the functioning of the mechanism. It is important to note that the theoretical conceptualization of the entities includes *nouns* and the activities include *verbs* that are the "transmitters" of causality through the mechanism. In social science terms, social entities have causal powers, which can be understood as "a capacity to produce a certain kind of outcome in the presence of appropriate antecedent conditions" (Little 1996: 37). The theorized causal mechanism is *not* a causal graph where the causal links are black-boxed. Indeed, a good theorized mechanism should clearly describe what it is that links each of the parts together, ideally resulting in productive continuity between cause and outcome in a seamless causal story.

The amount of logical work necessary to flesh out a causal mechanism and the context in which it is expected to function depends on whether existing theories are formulated in terms of mere correlations, as plausible causal links between C and O (e.g., intervening variables), or as full-fledged causal mechanisms. Most common is the situation where we know C and

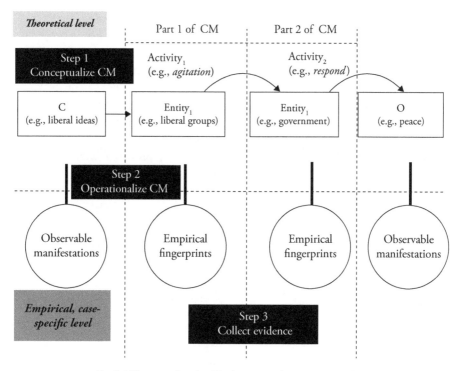

Fig. 9.4. The steps involved in theory-testing process-tracing

O but where the process (i.e., causal mechanism) by which C causes O has not been explicitly conceptualized. If a detailed causal mechanism has not already been formulated, the first step of theory-testing process-tracing is to conceptualize a plausible and generalizable causal mechanism, focusing on the parts of the mechanism that are theorized to be necessary for the mechanism to produce an outcome. In Owen's 1994 article on democratic peace, he spends almost twenty pages discussing the existing theoretical and empirical literature as a means to flesh out a plausible causal mechanism linking mutual democracy with peaceful relations. Chapter 3 also includes several examples of what conceptualized mechanisms can look like in practice, along with examples of what they should not look like. Additionally, the prior confidence we can hold in the causal mechanism being present in a given case also need to be developed, as this determines the strength and type of empirical tests that should be utilized (see chapter 6).

The theorized causal mechanism then needs to be operationalized in step 2, translating theoretical expectations into case-specific propositions about what evidence each of the parts of the mechanism should have left if they are actually operating as theorized in the case (see chapter 5). There can be multiple propositions about observables for each part or only one proposition if it is relatively theoretically unique.

At the core of theory-testing process-tracing is a structured empirical test of whether a hypothesized causal mechanism is actually present in the evidence of a given case. Empirical material is gathered to see whether the predicted evidence (proposition) was present or not, and then evaluated in context to determine whether the predicted evidence for each part was actually found, and whether it can be trusted (for more on this, see chapter 6). If we can claim that the actual evidence found or not found for each of the parts of the mechanism matched what our propositions about evidence were, and we can trust it, we can then infer that the hypothesized causal mechanism is present in the case on the basis of Bayesian logic. The bold lines in figure 9.4 illustrate the inferences made in theory-testing process-tracing, where we infer from the empirical evidence collected that a causal mechanism was present in the case.

Note that the empirical analysis in step 3 proceeds stepwise, testing whether there is evidence in the case that enables us to infer whether each part of the mechanism was present or not. Most important, the evidence to test whether the different parts are present can be very different, making evidence for the different parts not comparable with each other. In this respect, a theory test does *not* necessarily read like an analytical narrative, contrary to what scholars like Büthe (2002) and Rubach (2010) claim. We present and discuss an extended example of a theory-testing process-tracing case study at the end of this chapter.

What is the scope of inferences that can be made after we have found evidence of a mechanism in a typical case selected from quadrant I? If evidence of a causal mechanism is found in a particular case, we then need to decide whether we want to know whether the causal relationship is also present in other typical cases or whether we also want to infer not only that the relationship is present but also that the same mechanism is present in other cases. In the former, we can deploy a theory-testing congruence case study of another typical case. If we find confirming evidence in the second case, we can cautiously infer to the rest of the typical cases that C is causally related to O, contingent on the population being relatively causally homogeneous.

If we also want to know whether the same mechanism links C and O in the other cases, we would engage in a second theory-testing process-tracing case study. If we then find that the mechanism is also present in another typical case, we can make the cautious inference that the causal mechanism is probably also present in the rest of the bounded population (quadrant I) if we can assume a degree of causal homogeneity across the selected population. Given the sensitivity of mechanisms to contextual conditions, it is best if these two studies were done on cases that are maximally different within the set of typical cases (see chapter 7). Our confidence in the cross-case validity of our findings is a function of our confidence in the degree of causal homogeneity of the bounded population, in particular whether there are similar contextual conditions.

If we are not able to detect a causal mechanism between C and O in a typical case after numerous repeated attempts, there can be two reasons for this: (1) the case is idiosyncratic, or (2) there is no causal relationship. To determine which of the two is correct requires comparing the chosen case with what we know about other typical cases, assessing whether there are any important differences between them that could potentially prevent the mechanism from working. In particular, this comparison can shed light on the contextual conditions for the proper functioning of the mechanism, enabling us to assess whether the bounds of the population have been set properly. This procedure is the same as used when comparing deviant cases in quadrant IV with typical cases to detect omitted conditions (we discuss this more in relation to revising theory process-tracing studies). However, if we cannot detect any significant differences between the chosen case and other typical cases in the population, we can make the cautious inference that there is not a causal relationship between C and O. We would conclude that while there is a correlation between C and O, there is no underlying causal mechanism linking the two, meaning that the postulated causal relationship is spurious.

Finally, we might have found evidence for some of the parts of the mechanism but not for others. This would suggest that we should revise our theorized mechanism, using the insights gained from the empirical analysis as inspiration for new parts of the mechanism. Here the procedure becomes theory-building using the same case (see section 9.4). However, the revised mechanism that results from the theory-building process-tracing can actually be tested again on the same case, contingent on our ability to develop new empirical tests that result in new evidence being produced (i.e., the new tests are empirically independent of the ones used to build the revised mechanism).

9.7. Revising Theories with Process-Tracing

In revising theories with process-tracing our analytical focus is more on revising causal *theories* (C → O), and tracing mechanisms are an adjunct analytical tool to probe the contextual conditions in which a causal relationship functions. Here we select cases for tracing mechanisms that are deviant in relation to an existing theoretical understanding, usually based on previous research on typical cases that found the relationship. By studying mechanism breakdown in these deviant cases in quadrant IV (see figure 9.2), we gain information about omitted contextual or causal conditions that can be used to build better causal theories. It is, however, important to note that tracing mechanisms do not stand alone in this type of design; indeed, the analytical heavy-lifting in revising theories is done by systematically comparing a deviant with a typical case (see later discussion on deviant cases in quadrant IV) in what can be thought of as a "paired comparison."[4]

In revising theory process-tracing, we select only deviant cases in quadrant IV. Cases in quadrant II are also deviant cases where an existing known cause (C) is unable to account for the outcome (O is present). Quadrant II deviant cases can be used to find new causes of the outcome; however, as discussed in chapters 7 and 8, we are skeptical about whether process-tracing is the most efficient methodological tool for these purposes, in contrast to the arguments otherwise found in the existing literature.[5]

The basic idea for using process-tracing of deviant cases in quadrant IV is that one traces back from the occurrence of the outcome to find a new cause. But what one is actually tracing under these circumstances is far from straightforward. The existing literature suggests that we engage in backward tracing using case studies, but this advice only works when we utilize an understanding of mechanisms where they are viewed merely as series of events. Yet tracing "events" is not the same thing as tracing mechanisms, which involves tracing a theorized system linking C with O. However, if we have no idea about the cause, we also have no clue about the mechanism(s) linking the mystery cause with the outcome, meaning that we are in effect blindly groping in the dark after a cause. We therefore claim that a most-similar-system comparison or a congruence case study would be much more efficient analytical first steps in detecting new causes. For instance, we could compare systematically two cases that are similar in all aspects except the occurrence of the outcome (O, ~O) using a most-similar-system comparison. We would then want to know what new, undiscovered C is different between the two cases. After having found this using a paired comparison, it would be possible to engage in a form of in-depth case study that focuses on this new candidate of a cause, attempting to discern whether the new condition is causally related to O.

Deviant cases in quadrant IV have two different purposes depending on whether one is theorizing that C is a sufficient cause for O or that C is merely a contributing cause. The following offers the first set of comprehensive guidelines that illustrate how we combine comparative and within-case methods to uncover omitted causal or contextual conditions.[6]

If we theorize that C is a *sufficient* cause of O, deviant cases where C is present but where O is not present are useful to investigate the *contextual conditions* that have to be present to trigger the mechanism that will produce O. If C is *not* theorized as a sufficient cause, deviant cases in quadrant IV can be used to detect omitted *causal conditions* that together with C would be sufficient to produce O.

In both instances we employ this type of design only *after* we have positive results when tracing a mechanism in one or several typical cases within quadrant I. The argument here is that there is no reason to investigate mechanism breakdown before we are more confident about the actual existence of a mechanism linking C and O in one or more typical cases.

The process-tracing component involves tracing a mechanism in a deviant case until it breaks down. Here we want to uncover when and why the mechanism failed (Anderson 2011: 421–22). Existing theories of causal mechanisms that were either built or tested on typical cases within quadrant I provide the foundation for the tracing in deviant cases until mechanism breakdown. Finding out when and why a mechanism breaks down gives us clues about omitted contextual or causal conditions, although to repeat, the process-tracing component here is auxiliary, and the main analytical method is a systematic paired comparison of the deviant case with a typical case. Using an example of tracing mechanisms linking smoking and cancer, this type of hybrid design would involve tracing mechanisms linking C and O in a heavy smoker who does *not* get cancer (deviant case) to shed light on an omitted condition that can have inhibited the carcinogenic effects of smoke. We might, for instance, find that in the deviant case there was a particular gene that suppressed the carcinogenic effects of smoking in lung cells, resulting in mechanism breakdown. This would suggest that the absence of the particular gene is a scope condition for C to produce O.

A revising theory process-tracing design therefore relies on a two-step analysis, where we use a deviant case first to trace where and why the theorized mechanism breaks down. We then use these insights to inform our pairwise comparison of the deviant and typical case to uncover omitted causal and/or contextual conditions.

Using as a hypothetical example research focused on studying links between economic development (C) and democratization (O) through some form of "middle-class" mechanism that details a causal mechanism whereby the growth of the middle class spurs democratization, we might find in a deviant case like Poland that while a middle class was produced by C, the next part of the mechanism was not present, with demands for democratization instead coming from elite actors. We would then compare the single deviant case (Poland) with what we know more broadly about other typical cases in the population where we know the middle-class mechanism functioned as expected (e.g., South Korea) to uncover whether there is a missing causal or contextual condition that can explain why the mechanism did not work as predicted in the deviant case. Here we might find that when parallel state-building processes are under way, as in Poland post-1989, the middle-class mechanism does not produce the same demands that mobilized citizens in South Korea to demand democratic reforms. This finding suggests that the absence of parallel state-building processes could be an important contextual condition in which economic development (C) is linked to democratization (O) through a middle-class causal mechanism. Poland would then be reclassified as a case outside of the relevant contextual conditions that define the causally homogeneous population of cases where C is linked to O through the middle-class mechanism.

After we have found an omitted contextual or causal condition, we would have to reclassify our cases, with previously deviant cases becoming irrelevant (moved to quadrant III), as they lack a causal condition that has to be present for O to occur (sufficiency) or a contextual condition that enables the mechanism to function properly.

9.8. An Example—Brast's Study of State-Building Interventions

Brast in a 2015 article uses process-tracing to explain why some liberal state building interventions succeed. He claims that when intervening actors cooperate with regional security organizations (C), this triggers a causal mechanism that produces a monopoly on violence in the state that means the intervention succeeded (O). The mechanism he develops can be divided into three parts, each of which is linked to propositions about evidence (see table 9.1).

Brast argues that the causal mechanism is triggered by the cooperation between the key regional states and the intervening actors, under the contextual conditions that require that a liberal state-building intervention occur. This cooperation makes it possible to enforce borders, thereby denying armed groups access to transnational spaces. Brast suggests that without these zones of retreat and devoid of access to transnational markets, armed groups will not be able to resist monopolization efforts and will agree to disarm.

TABLE 9.1. A causal mechanism linking regional cooperation and monopoly on violence

	Contextual condition: Liberal state-building intervention occurring				
	Cause (C)	Part 1	Part 2	Part 3	Outcome (O)
Theory	Regional cooperation →	Enforcement of border regime disarms nonstate groups →	Disarming of nonstate groups →	Allows for buildup of sustainable armed forces that enables →	Monopoly on violence
Proposi- tions about evidence in the case (ob- servable manifes- tations)	Key regional actors sup- port the state- building intervention	Neighboring states secure their borders against trans- national rebel- lion, either voluntarily or through regional pres- sure	Armed groups are either militarily defeated, or weakened enough to agree to a DDR process	With exter- nal assistance, government builds armed forces that are propor- tional in size, politi- cally control- lable and economically sustainable	Interna- tional actors withdraw. Government is the only actor who controls the means of organized violence

Source: Adapted from Brast 2015: 89.

This leads to the expectation of the military defeat of the rebel groups that allows the government to benefit from international technical assistance in building a professional security force that will be both effective and politi- cally controllable. The outcome of this mechanism is the establishment of a state monopoly on violence (Brast 2015: 88).

Brast then tests the mechanism empirically in a typical case in which C, O, and the requisite contextual conditions are present to see whether there is evidence that regional cooperation actually produced the mechanism theo- rized to be linked with the monopoly on violence. The typical case chosen was the civil war in Sierra Leone, which ended in 2002. Brast finds mecha- nistic evidence that suggests that regional cooperation did contribute to the successful conclusion of the civil war through the proposed mechanism.

Propositions and Predicted Evidence

The three propositions about predicted evidence are depicted in table 9.1. We suggest that he could be more explicit regarding what type of evidence we should expect to see, why this material can act as evidence, and what sources of evidence will be utilized, although to be fair there are practical limits to how thorough one can be when working with word limits for articles. The result of the lack of reasoning about theoretical certainty and uniqueness—basically answering the question of why empirical material can be evidence—reduces our ability to update our confidence in the existence of parts of the mechanism. To alleviate this problem, we suggest that this should be done to make the argument and the evidence supporting it in the article more persuasive, presenting it as an online appendix that is cited using active citation (Moravcsik 2010).

Prior Confidence

Brast argues that he has a relatively high prior confidence in the presence of the causal relationship between C and O based on his reading of the existing literature, arguing that "statebuilding interventions will succeed in establishing a monopoly on large-scale violence if they enjoy the support of key regional actors" (2015: 81). He also notes, "While the existing theory has provided arguments that support the idea that the ability of armed groups to challenge a government's claim to the monopoly on violence strongly depends on external assistance has already been articulated . . . the causal mechanisms that show how regional politics affect statebuilding outcomes remain unclear" (2015: 87). This suggests that he believes that the prior confidence in the mechanism itself is relatively low, meaning that he is in a plausibility-probe situation, where any evidence of a mechanism updates our confidence. Therefore, it can be justified not to develop "stronger" reasoned propositions that are tested using stronger empirical evidence. When we have low prior confidence, even relatively weak confirming evidence can be enough to update our confidence (see chapter 6 for more on this logic).

Brast briefly discusses case selection, arguing first for Sierra Leone as being a typical case, but he later frames it as a least-likely case. He claims, "Sierra Leone is selected as a crucial case, because the intervention was successful despite the presence of many unfavorable conditions. At the domestic level, the country had a history of weak statehood, was poor and torn by a decade of civil war" (2015: 82). This argument resembles the logic of the least-likely case, which we argued is not compatible with the deterministic assumptions underlying case-based methods. In relation to the Sierra Leone case, either the causal relationship between C and O through the theorized causal mechanism is possible or not. It cannot be least or most likely (see chapter 2 for more on why most-likely/least-likely case selection practices do not make sense in case-based research).

Evidence Supplied for the Propositions

In his article Brast does not engage in a thorough theoretical evaluation of why empirical material might act as evidence (propositions), nor does he engage in an evaluation of the individual pieces of actual found evidence in terms of empirical uniqueness or accuracy. For sake of brevity, we focus only on the evidence produced in relation to proposition 1 in table 9.2, describing propositions 2 and 3 without discussing the evidence in support of them provided in the article.

TABLE 9.2. Argument road map of Brast's 2015 process-tracing case study

Causal relationship
Causal mechanism linking liberal regional cooperation and state building (see table 9.1).
Prior relatively low
• Existing research has only focused on causes and outcomes but has not unpacked the mechanisms in-between.

Proposition	
1	Neighboring states secure their borders against transnational rebellion, either voluntarily or through regional pressure (?c, ?u)
	• Type of evidence unclear, making it difficult to evaluate what type of evidence is relevant, and its logical relationship with the theoretical claim of part 1 of the mechanism.
	Suggested improvements: Discussion needed for proposition about observable evidence that supplies a description of what types of observable manifestations the part will have if present, and the expected certainty and uniqueness of the observables.
Evidence of P1 (i)	"UNAMSIL began to switch to 'progressive deployment' across Sierra Leonean territory in mid-2000. While this put increasing military pressure on the RUF, the rebels were still able to control wide areas of the countryside as well as their traditional stronghold close to the Liberian border in the East of the country. The UN forces were backed up by the UK, which however limited its military operation to the Freetown area. Military resistance was fierce, and overall the UN suffered 192 casualties. Additionally, the UN started to organize economic sanctions against Liberia" (90).
	- not directly evidence of neighboring states securing their borders either voluntarily or through regional pressure.
	Source: UN, "Sierra Leone—UNAMSIL—Facts and Figures" 2005.
	• **Lu, Ha.** Difficult to evaluate exactly why this is evidence, but it does suggest that the UN intervention assisted in putting pressure on the rebel group RUF. Accuracy probably high for this statement, especially for the number of casualties suffered by the UN.

(continued)

Evidence of P1 (ii)	"Already during the formation stages of UNAMSIL, Nigeria had tried to convince the UN that Taylor's supplies were crucial for the RUF" (90). - potentially evidence for P1, as it focuses on regional pressure. Source: Olonisakin 2008. *Peacekeeping in Sierra Leone: The Story of UNAMSIL*. Boulder, CO: Lynne Rienner. • **Lu, La.** Difficult to evaluate whether this was unique evidence. Additionally, no information is given about the source, thereby weakening our ability to make confirming inferences based on evidence found.
Evidence of P1 (iii)	"In July 2000, the UN put a ban on trade with diamonds from Sierra Leone. More importantly, in March 2001 it also placed an embargo on Liberia, thereby diminishing the ability of the Taylor regime to deal with diamonds sold by the RUF" (90). - not directly evidence of neighboring states securing their borders either voluntarily or through regional pressure. Source: UNSC "Ninth Report of the Secretary-General on the United Nations Mission in Sierra Leone," Document No. S/2001/228, New York, UNSC, 2001, §58. • **Lu, Ha.** Difficult to evaluate because not direct evidence of P1, but it does suggest that the UN intervention assisted in putting pressure on the rebel group RUF. Accuracy probably high for this statement.
Evidence of P1 (iv)	"The Guinean government intensified its involvement in the conflict in Liberia. Having tolerated the formation of the Liberians United for Reconciliation and Democracy (LURD) rebel movement on Guinean territory, the Conté administration allowed LURD to start an offensive against the Liberian Taylor regime in July 2000" (91). - Not directly evidence of P1. Source: ICG, "Liberia: The Key to Ending Regional Instability," No. 43, Freetown/Brussels: ICG, 2002, 4. • **?u, ?a.** Not evidence of P1, but contextual evidence of what led to crackdown by Guinea. Impossible to assess uniqueness or accuracy here.
Evidence of P1 (v)	"In return, Guinea orchestrated an offensive against the Liberian armed forces and the RUF which involved regular Guinean troops, Sierra Leonean militias and LURD rebels. From late 2000 on, the fighting made diamond smuggling much more difficult for the RUF. . . . Guinea kept up its support for LURD, which increasingly threatened the Taylor regime in Monrovia" (91). - evidence of P1 Source: Hazen 2013. *What Rebels Want: Resources and Supply Networks in Wartime*. Ithaca: Cornell University Press, 99–101. • **?u, ?a.** Relatively clear evidence of P1, but we are unable to evaluate uniqueness because it is not apparent that the Guinean offensive was for the reasons posited by the causal theory. Additionally, no information is given about the secondary source.

Evidence of P1 (vi)	"Eventually, LURD conquered the border region in early 2002 and, thereby, cut off the remaining RUF supply network" (91). - not evidence of P1 because it deals with a non-state rebel movement (LURD) and not a neighboring state. Source: Hazen 2013. *What Rebels Want: Resources and Supply Networks in Wartime.* Ithaca: Cornell University Press, 130. • **?u, ?a.** No discussion of why evidence, nor any evaluation of secondary source.
Evidence of P1 (vii)	"ECOWAS did not simply support Liberian rebels, but it eventually intervened in Liberia in 2003. The following statebuilding mission has transformed Liberia into a state that respects its neighbors' sovereignty" (91). - evidence of P1. Source: Gerdes 2013. *Civil War and State Formation: The Political Economy of War and Peace in Liberia.* Frankfurt: Campus Verlag, 167–68. • **Hu, ?a.** Relatively self-evident that this is relatively unique evidence, although the secondary source is not discussed, preventing us from trusting it too much.
Evidence P1 (viii)	"Nigeria has fostered the development of ECOWAS from a project of economic integration into a security community. ECOWAS goals today are the mutual support of governments and a commitment to liberal democracy. . . . Regional cooperation was not a one-off event, but was sustained and increased over the course of the statebuilding intervention" (91). - evidence of P1. Source: Rashid 2013. "The Sierra Leone Civil War and the Remaking of ECOWAS," *Research in Sierra Leone Studies* (RISLS): 1 (1): 6–7. • **Hu, ?a.** Relatively self-evident that evidence, but no discussion of secondary source.

2   <u>Armed groups are either militarily defeated, or weakened enough to agree to a DDR process (?c, ?u)</u>
- <u>Type of evidence unclear, making it difficult to evaluate what type of evidence is relevant, and its logical relationship with the theoretical claim of part 2 of the mechanism.</u>

Suggested improvements: Discussion needed for proposition about observable evidence that supplies a description of what types of observable manifestations the part will have if present, and the expected certainty and uniqueness of the observables.

Not reproduced

3   <u>With external assistance, government builds armed forces that are proportional in size, politically controllable and economically sustainable (?c, ?u)</u>

(*continued*)

TABLE 9.2. Argument road map of Brast's 2015 process-tracing case study (*continued*)

> • Type of evidence unclear, making it difficult to evaluate what type of evidence is relevant, and its logical relationship with the theoretical claim of part 3 of the mechanism.
>
> Suggested improvements: Discussion needed for proposition about observable evidence that supplies a description of what types of observable manifestations the part will have if present, and the expected certainty and uniqueness of the observables.
>
> Not reproduced

Inferences made:
"The evidence strongly suggests that the expected causal mechanism was present in the case of Sierra Leone" (94).
Discussion of whether inferences warranted:
More discussion needed of why empirical material is evidence, first by developing more clearly the logical relationship between the propositions about observables and the parts of the causal mechanism, and then discussions of why actual empirical material is evidence for each of the propositions. Little or no source criticism, although the breadth of sources and multiple pieces of evidence utilized increases our confidence in measurement accuracy. Given these weaknesses, it is difficult to claim that the evidence "strongly suggests" that the mechanism was present.

As can be seen in the argument road map, he provides (at least) eight pieces of evidence. We argue that each of the different pieces of evidence only provides relatively weak updating in the confidence of the presence of part one in the mechanism, but this is OK when there is a relatively low initial prior confidence in the hypothesized theory.

Does the Inferential Weight of the Evidence Match the Conclusions?

Taken together, the empirical evidence for each individual part should enable us to increase or decrease our confidence in the mechanism as a whole being present. The level of our posterior confidence in the whole mechanism reflects the lowest posterior level for each of the parts after we have done our empirical research. And our inferences about the causal mechanism as a whole being present are only as strong as the weakest test. We conclude that Brast's analysis, despite its innovations regarding its theoretical clarity about the causal mechanism, only provides evidence that slightly increases our confidence in the causal mechanism he has theorized. However, this use of "weak evidence" is warranted in the research situation he faced, given that one can frame the study as a plausibility probe where even weak evidence of the disaggregated causal mechanism is better than no evidence.

9.9. Concluding Guidelines

Process-tracing is chosen when you want to study causal mechanisms using in-depth case studies, with a particular focus on empirically assessing whether the theorized activities of entities in each part of a hypothesized mechanism were actually present. The variant of process-tracing that one chooses depends on the research situation.

If one wants to build a comprehensive explanation of a particular historical outcome and the goal is to gain a greater understanding of the processes that produced the outcome, then one chooses explaining outcome process-tracing. The core difference with explaining outcome congruence is that causal mechanisms are disaggregated and investigated empirically; that is, what is going on in between C and O is fleshed out to some degree, whereas in congruence the focus is merely on C $\rightarrow$ O causal relations. The analysis is undertaken in an iterative fashion until a sufficient explanation of the outcome is produced, using either a theory-first or empirics-first path:

- Start with existing theories as inspiration, defining potential causal mechanisms to account for the outcome that are then tested in the case to see whether they provide a satisfactory account of the outcome
- Or use an empirics-first, theory-building style of research attempt to probe the empirics of the case for clues about potential mechanisms.

If one has a good idea about causal relationships (known causes and an outcome), but what connects causes and outcomes are unknown and cannot be deduced from existing theorization, one can employ theory-building process-tracing. The steps involved include the following:

- Select typical cases where C, O, and the requisite contextual conditions are present.
- Develop a detailed empirical narrative of the case, engaging in an intensive, wide-ranging search for clues that might be more systematic empirical fingerprints of a part of an underlying causal mechanism.
- Assess whether the found empirical clues actually are empirical fingerprints of the mechanism. Important here is a theoretical evaluation of what the found empirical material can be evidence of, enabling inferences from the empirical material to update confidence in the existence of an underlying mechanism.

Theory-testing process-tracing is used when it is possible to theorize a mechanism linking a cause or causes with an outcome. The steps involved include the following:

- Select typical cases.
- Conceptualize and operationalize a causal mechanism in the form of the development of clear predictions in the form of propositions about what observable manifestations that the operation of each of the parts of the mechanism should have left in the selected case.
- Collect empirical material to evaluate whether the predicted evidence was actually found, and evaluate it in a source-critical fashion to determine whether we can trust it.
- If evidence is found for each part of the mechanism, employ additional case studies, either using congruence or process-tracing to enable inferences across cases. If one is to infer not only that there is a causal relationship in similar cases but also that it is the *same mechanism*, one has to be very careful in evaluating the causal homogeneity of the population with regard to any potential contextual condition that might result in C and O being linked with other mechanisms than the one found in the studied case.
- If evidence is not found for the mechanism as a whole, one should investigate whether the chosen case was idiosyncratic by comparing it with other typical cases. If it is not idiosyncratic, disconfirming inferences can be generalized to the rest of the population.
- If evidence is not found for a part of a mechanism, engage in theory-building to revise the theorized causal mechanism.

Process-tracing can also be used to refine existing causal theories, focused on tracing mechanisms until they break down in deviant cases where C is present but O is not present. Information about when and why the mechanism breaks down informs a comparative analysis of the most similar typical case to detect potential omitted contextual or causal conditions.

CHAPTER 10

Bringing It All Together

10.1. Introduction

This book was written especially for the post-KKV generation of scholars who have begun asking the "and now what" question regarding case-based methods. In this book, we have attempted to shift the focus of methodological work toward defining the nature and uses of different causal case study methods on their own terms instead of living in the shadow of quantitative, variance-based designs. Despite pledging to be something different, much existing case-based methodological guidance still retains many practices that are more appropriate for use when assessing population-based, probabilistic claims.

While we acknowledge that many scholars have contributed to the process of building up a new set of methodological guidelines that are appropriate for causal case study research, we have taken what we believe are a number of important steps. We first developed a coherent set of ontological foundations upon which case-based research logically can rest, delineating the nature of causal claims made by different case-based methods. The rest of the book then fleshed out the methodological implications of these ontological positions, developing a set of methodological guidelines in alignment with the ontological foundations. This includes guidelines for concept definition and measurement, making causal inferences using mechanistic within-case evidence or cross-case evidence of difference-making, along with more precise guidelines for using the three case-based methods developed in this book: comparative methods, as well as congruence and process-tracing methods.

This conclusion chapter first discusses the methodological contributions of the book, followed by discussion and preemptive rebuttal of a common critique of our case-based approach. The chapter then points toward areas where we need more methodological exploration, including on the nature of mechanistic theories in the social sciences and the need for better guidelines to generalize findings from individual cases within causally heterogeneous populations.

10.2. Our Contribution

This book has gamed through the implications of taking cases as our analytical point of departure. We argued first that if we take causation at the case-level seriously—which is what we should be doing if we treat cases as something more than just illustrative exemplars of postulated mean effects of causes within a population—we should acknowledge that it only makes sense to make ontologically deterministic and asymmetric causal claims.

Beyond this, we contend that there are two key ontological choices one can make in case-based research: whether causation is understood in counterfactual or mechanistic terms, and whether singular causation is viewed as possible or not. If one chooses to make counterfactual-based claims, this leads one down the path of comparative methods. In contrast, if one is interested in probing causal relationships in cases, this involves mechanism-based causal claims unless one is content with utilizing hypothetical "what if" data as in counterfactual single-case studies. These differences in foundations also make it difficult to communicate across the two types of methods, although we have tried to develop suggestions for a productive division of labor between the two, with comparative used for building theories and populations and within-case studies for confirming causal inferences.

Taking different ontological positions as the starting point, the book gamed through their methodological implications for how we define causal relationships (chapter 3), concept formation (chapter 4), measurement of causal concepts (chapter 5), and how and which types of causal inferences are possible on the basis of different types of evidence that were relevant to the type of causal claim being made (chapter 6).

In gaming through these implications, we found the following:

- The widespread use of most-likely/least-likely cases is not in alignment with deterministic ontological causal claims (chapter 2). Put simply, a causal relationship is either possible or not in a case, making within-case likelihoods meaningless. We should therefore think of cases as possible or not possible. There can be cases that we are unsure about whether the relationship might be possible or not because of contextual conditions, but finding a relationship in an adverse context does not necessarily tell us anything about how relationships work in other cases in the population, and there is the risk that the findings from an "adverse context" case (i.e., quite different from the rest of the population) will have different mechanisms linking the same cause with the same outcome (i.e., equifinality at the level of mechanisms).

- Causal homogeneity is even more important for case-based research than is widely recognized because of the assumption of ontological determinism, especially when working with theories of causal mechanisms in process-tracing. In case-based research, we take the case as the analytical point of departure, but we cannot infer from what we found in the single case to other cases unless we can demonstrate that the cases to be inferred to are causally similar to the studied case. Generalizations are about trends in population-based research on mean causal effects, whereas in case-based research we are making determinate claims that C is causally related to O through mechanism CM_1 under specified contextual conditions. In case-based research, we would not be comfortable inferring from the studied case to all cases where C and O are present because there could be important contextual conditions that might have an impact on the relationship in different ways (e.g., same cause, same outcome, but linked with different mechanism).

- Causal concepts in case-based research should *only define the positive pole* of concepts. Most important, though, the theoretical concepts we are working with in causal case study research are not just "inanimate" definitions where we can work isolated from the causal relationship in which our concept is theorized to work. A complex concept like democracy can both be a cause of many different outcomes and produced by many different causes. It is therefore meaningless to define a concept like democracy isolated from the causal context in which we are working; instead, our definitions should capture, for example, the attributes of democracy that can produce peace between two countries that otherwise might have gone to war. Therefore, causal concepts should be defined and measured in a way that captures what it is about a concept that can be a cause or outcome. Finally, when defining concepts, we should also concentrate on differences in kind, because degree differences are at best irrelevant and at worst produce flawed generalizations in case-based research because of the asymmetric nature of the causal claims we are making.

- Strong confirming causal inferences are possible only using either evidence of difference-making gained from experiments in variance-based research or within-case mechanistic evidence gained from congruence or process-tracing case studies. Comparative methods using observational data do not enable confirming inferences, but only disconfirming inferences about necessity or sufficiency.

- When using *Bayesian logic* as applied to within-case, mechanistic evidence, we are able to control empirically for other potential causes at the level of individual pieces of evidence, eliminating the need for controlling for other causes through case selection. When we select cases where C_1 is present but all other causes are not, we unnecessarily bound our population, meaning that we cannot generalize to the other cases where other causes are present because the other causes might affect the relationship between C_1 and the outcome. This would be like testing a medicine only in isolation from other medicines, whereas in reality many sick patients take a cocktail of different drugs that might have strong effects upon each other. Therefore, we need to assess cases where only C_1 is present and cases across the full bounded population to assess whether it is actually a causally homogenous population or not.

The book developed guidelines for the use of comparative methods and case studies (congruence and process-tracing) for a variety of different research purposes. In aggregate, we believe that the comparative methods developed in this book are best applied when searching for unknown causes and when mapping cases to build bounded populations of causally similar cases (causal homogeneity). Congruence case studies, a method that can also be thought of as a form of process-tracing "lite," are particularly useful as plausibility probes in research situations where we are unsure, on the basis of existing research, whether there is a causal relationship. Here even relatively weak confirming within-case evidence updates our confidence in the relationship. In contrast, process-tracing is particularly strong when we are relatively confident that some form of causal relationship is present but we want to make stronger confirming or disconfirming inferences, and/or we want to gain a greater understanding of *how* a cause (or set of causes) produces an outcome through a causal mechanism.

Finding Causes and Building Theories

When searching for causes of outcomes, we contended that a hybrid most-similar-systems design is a good analytical starting point (chapter 7), attempting to find what difference across cases might account for different outcomes in otherwise similar cases. Once a cause is found, the analysis can then move on to a within-case plausibility probe of one of the positive cases where the newly found C (or set of causes) and O are present, using congruence to confirm or disconfirm that the found cause (or set of causes) is actually causally related to the outcome (chapter 8).

If one is building theories of what links a known cause and outcome together, theory-building process-tracing should be employed. This involves starting with a thorough "soaking and probing" of the empirical record in the case, attempting to detect whether there are any systematic patterns in the evidence that might be the observable manifestations of an underlying causal mechanism. Once an initial hunch about the mechanism is developed, the analyst can proceed to a more robust empirical assessment in the case (if new, independent evidence can be collected) or in another case.

Testing Theoretical Claims

In chapter 7 we explored several different comparative designs for testing necessity and sufficiency claims, both of which can be followed up by case studies if there are deviant cases in the bounded population. For instance, if a test of sufficiency finds a deviant case where C is present but O is not present, theoretical revision process-tracing can be employed to trace where the mechanism broke down, shedding light on which aspect of the case should be exposed to systematic comparisons with one or more typical cases.

Finally, when testing theories using case studies, whether one chooses congruence or process-tracing depends on the level of prior plausibility of the theorized causal relationship in the case, and whether more detailed theoretical knowledge of the working of the mechanism are relevant for one's research question. In both forms of theory tests, typical cases are selected where C, O, and the requisite contextual conditions are present. Often the empirical results suggest that one or more parts of the mechanism did not work as theorized, which should result in a theoretical revision process to be less and less wrong about the conditions under which causal relationships play out, and the mechanism(s) linking causes and outcomes.

10.3. Possible Critique and Responses

The most common critique of our framework for case-based research that we have faced is that we are just as monist as the scholars whose frameworks we criticize. We suggested in chapters 1 and 2 that we take a pluralist position, where case-based research is perceived to differ on a variety of parameters from both variance-based and interpretivist research designs. We argued that there is not "one logic of inference," but many different logics of inference and proper research design. The consequence of a unified logic is, in our opinion, that scholars elevate one methodological position above others, relegating other positions to second-best status.

Experiments are great designs for providing evidence of difference-making upon which causal inferences can be made, but in the social sciences we are typically only able to engage in the manipulation of relatively trivial causes (in contrast to medicine, where treatments can save lives). And there are many research situations where a quasi-experimental design will shed little, if any, light on a causal relationship. And if we want to understand *how* a cause produces an outcome, an experiment leaves us in the dark, meaning that we need to observe closely the mechanisms linking the two as they operate in real-world cases using mechanistic, within-case evidence.

In contrast, case-based research focuses on providing within-case, mechanistic evidence of causal relationships that can be generalized in certain situations within small, bounded populations of causally homogeneous cases. Case-based researchers opt to keep populations smaller than in variance-based designs that assess probabilistic claims to ensure that the cases being compared are as causally similar to each other as possible. However, case-based research has difficulties in generalizing to larger populations, as we discuss in the final section.

We are also pluralist regarding differences between case-based methods, arguing that there are several distinct methodological positions depending on the stand one takes on the foundational questions of counterfactuals versus mechanisms and regular versus singular causation. We contend that comparisons make sense only when one builds on a counterfactual understanding of causation, whereas within-case analysis is compatible with mechanism-based understandings only if one accepts hypothetical "what ifs" as evidence. We respected differences in this book by showing that particular case-based methods have distinct comparative advantages when used in appropriate research situations.

But as we argued in chapters 1 and 2, pluralism does not in our opinion mean that "anything goes." There are certain ontological assumptions that are difficult to reconcile with case-based research, in particular ontological probabilism. If we believe that all causal claims involve trends or mean causal effects at the population level, it is difficult to see what purpose case studies actually have beyond providing anecdotal exemplars of trends. Regardless of whether we find or do not find evidence of the expected relationship in the exemplar case, if our theory deals with trends, the single case will tell us nothing about whether the trend *actually* reflects a causal relationship or not within the population. Therefore, we contend in this book that the only logical ontological assumption that can be taken when cases are the analytical point of departure is a deterministic one. In any given case, a causal relationship either has played out or not.

Additionally, it is difficult to see other epistemological frameworks for making causal inferences using empirical evidence in case-based research other than a Bayesian-inspired framework. Indeed, here it is useful to look toward legal studies, which have a long tradition of using Bayesian-inspired logic as the inferential framework for asking the right questions when assessing what empirical material can act as evidence of (Friedman 1986a, 1986b; Cohen 1986; Good 1991).

10.4. Directions for Future Methodological Research

Despite the confidence we hold in the set of methodological guidelines we have put forward, there is much work still to be done. In particular, we suggest further research and development on the following issues.

Building Theories of Mechanisms

First, while we have put forward some suggestions for how theories of mechanisms can be developed from empirics, we acknowledge that they are very provisional. Further work is needed to develop a framework that can assist scholars in their search for mechanisms in cases. At the same time, we believe that it is not possible to develop a firm set of guidelines for theory-building process-tracing because it would be like trying to develop a formula for creativity. However, what we can do is maximize the chances we have to be creative in theory development by coming up with further suggestions for how empirics and existing theorization can inform theory-development of mechanisms.

Learning from Single Cases

Second, the literature on how we can generalize from single cases to populations is still in its infancy as regards case-based research. We take individual
cases as the analytical point of departure either to understand the complexi-
ties of the individual case (explaining outcome-type research) or to shed
light on more general relationships within a population.

In the latter, existing guidelines still boil down to basically this: Study
one case. If you find a relationship, investigate whether it holds in a causally similar case. If you still find it, study it again in another case that is
not as similar (fewer shared contextual conditions), attempting to snowball
outward until one finds the bounds of the population in which the inference holds. However, we still lack good case-based methodological tools for
generalizing.

Qualitative comparative analysis (QCA) gets us some way toward systematizing our ability to infer to causally homogeneous subpopulations,
with an analysis of sufficiency typically returning two or more conjunctions
of causes, each of which can be thought of as a bounded population of causally homogeneous cases.

However, how do we know the proper bounds of generalizing from a
single case? For example, let us say that we want to study the motivations
of an Islamic militant group like al-Qaeda using a detailed case study. But
could we generalize what we learn from studying al-Qaeda to other cases of
Islamist militancy? Would studying al-Qaeda's motivations tell us anything
about groups such as Hamas or ISIS? Here recent research has suggested
that the population of cases of the relationship motivations → types of Islamic militancy is very causally heterogeneous. One way of splitting up the
population could be to disaggregate it into a theoretical typology of several
distinct causally similar bounded populations. Hegghammer (2009), for instance, distinguishes five different types of motivations (in our terminology
this can be understood as C_1 to C_5) for violent or nonviolent Islamic activism
(see table 10.1).

Focusing on the violent type of activism in this example, Hegghammer
suggests that "umma-oriented" groups engage in either classical (neighbor-
ing enemies) or global jihadism struggles (2009: 259).[1] Al-Qaeda is here depicted as a case of an umma-oriented → global jihadist relationship, meaning that we could not necessarily learn anything about other groups like
Hamas from it because Hamas is a case of nation orientation → violent
irredentism. Despite similarities, it can also be argued that ISIS as a case is
outside of this typology. While it is an umma-oriented group, it differs from

TABLE 10.1. Typology of Islamist Activism

| Motivation | Nonviolent | | Violent | |
	Type of activism	Potential cases	Type of activism	Potential cases
State-oriented	Reformism	MB (Muslim Brother-hood), Saudi Sawha	Socio-revolutionary activism	GIA (Armed Islamic Group), GSPC (Salafist Group for Preaching and Combat), EIJ (Egyptian Islam Jihad)
Nation-oriented	Nationalism		Violent ir-redentism	Hamas, Chechen Mujahideen, Islamic army (Iraq)
Umma-oriented	Pan-Islamism	MWL (Muslim World League)	Classical / global jihad-ism	QAP (Arabs in al-Qaeda)
Morality-oriented	Pietism	Tagligh, Madkalis	Vigilantism	Unorganized hisha
Sectarian	Sectarianism		Violent sec-tarianism	Lashkar e Janghvi, Iraqi militias

Source: Hagghammer 2009: 259.

al-Qaeda in that ISIS has put chosen to create a caliphate-state before the "struggle" is completed, whereas al-Qaeda views the creation of an Islamist state as something to be done in the future.[2]

Typological theorization is therefore one useful tool for engaging in a focused investigation of causal heterogeneity and the probing of the bounds of generalizations from single cases. However, this type of methodology is still in its infancy (see Møller and Skaaning [2015] for a recent attempt to develop this type of methodology). Further work is therefore needed in case-based research, developing procedures for mapping causally homogeneous populations in a way that takes seriously the individual cases as the point of departure, and that enables us to proceed in a more systematic fashion when generalizing from the single case.

Causes Working Together

Finally, further work is needed on how we can theorize causal mechanisms in ways that fit with the types of causal relationships we study in the social sciences. Much of the existing literature on causal mechanisms stems from the natural sciences, in particular fields like medicine and biology (e.g., Machamer 2004; Machamer, Darden, and Craver 2000; Waskan 2011; Glennan 1996). We have suggested in this book that the language of mechanisms as a system (parts with productive continuity in relation to each other, each composed of entities engaging in activities) is particularly useful, but further work is needed on several issues, including the degree to which particular parts of social science mechanisms exhibit "modularity" and how mechanisms can be theorized and studied empirically when they take more complex forms. Given that the first issue has already been discussed in chapters 3 and 9, we focus here on the second issue.

While the theorized mechanisms we have discussed in this book take the form of relatively simple, linear processes, there is nothing that prevents more complicated, nonlinear mechanisms from being formulated. However, things begin to become very complicated when we begin working with multiple causes triggering different mechanisms, and the same cause potentially triggering multiple mechanisms (for a longer discussion, see Beach and Rohlfing 2016). In the first instance, if causes C_1 and C_2 are together sufficient to produce an outcome, they might together produce a single mechanism (CM_1). But they might also act in sequence, where $C_1 \rightarrow CM_1 \rightarrow C_2 \rightarrow CM_2 \rightarrow O$, a relationship that would pose considerable difficulties for us when attempting to assess whether the observable manifestations of mechanisms are present. A cause might also trigger more than one mechanism, which would further increase the difficulties in tracing mechanisms.

Conclusion

Methods is all about trade-offs, and case-based methods are by no means the only way to provide evidence of causal relationships in the social sciences, nor are they necessarily the best way. The appropriateness of a given method or set of methods depends on the research question being analyzed. But we hope that this book proves useful to scholars attempting to leverage case-based methods in relation to their own research questions.

Notes

Chapter 1

1. This book concentrates on causal case study methods, thereby excluding other qualitative methods such as interpretive and reflectivist methodologies. Causal case studies can be treated together, as they share similar understandings about a focus on causal relations (deterministic, asymmetry, and counterfactuals or mechanisms), whereas there are huge divides on these questions when we move toward more interpretive and reflectivist methodologies (see Jackson 2011). While variance-based methods and causal case studies can be understood as being two different "cultures" (Goertz and Mahoney 2012), the divide between causal case studies and qualitative interpretive and reflectivist methods is perhaps better understood as life on two different planets.

2. *Critical realism* is the term for philosophical realism within the social sciences.

Chapter 2

1. In real-world research, description and causal explanation often cannot be strictly separated, with descriptions of events often melding together with causal explanations. For a good discussion, see Kreuzer (2014).

2. The term "mechanistic evidence" is used in the philosophy of science, for example by Russo and Williamson (2007, 2011) and Illari (2001).

3. For a good recent example of analysis that conflates ontological debates about which types of causal claims we can make (e.g., the nature of causation) and epistemological debates of how we can make inferences about our causal claims, see Lucas and Szatrowski (2014: 8–10). In the same section where they quote (and critique) Mahoney for ontologically deterministic arguments (8–9), they also discuss measurement error and other epistemological challenges in a way that suggests that they are speaking about the same thing. Yet ontological claims about the nature of the world do not necessarily have anything to do with epistemological claims about how we can learn something about the world empirically.

4. For a clear example of the variance-based argument, see Gerring (2005). He argues that more cases are almost always better, as it enables us to better detect (statistically) patterns of covariation across cases. He writes, "The more comparative reference points one has at one's disposal, the better one can test the veracity of a given proposition. . . . [T]he more cases one has to demonstrate a posited causal relationship, the more confidence one is likely to place in the truth of that proposition" (Gerring 2005: 182–83).

5. Laplace discussed this in relation to his famous "Demon." He posited that an infinite intellectual capacity (the Demon) that had *perfect* knowledge of both present conditions and the laws that govern the universe could in principle predict the future perfectly. This is an ontologically deterministic statement, but note that *perfect* knowledge of both the present conditions and the laws governing nature is required, neither of which we would realistically ever have. In response, Laplace developed an epistemologically probabilistic approach to account for empirical uncertainty.

6. These relate in particular to the indeterminacy of properties, the nonlocalizability of quantum objects, and the nonseparability of quantum states as a result of entanglement (Kuhlmann and Glennan 2014).

7. Complexity does not mean that one has to adopt probabilistic ontological assumptions. The branch of mathematics known as "chaos theory" attempts to model deterministically what might appear to be probabilistic systems using more complex, nonlinear mathematical theories. For a good introduction, see Stewart (2002).

8. Note that we use the terms *contextual* and *scope* conditions to refer to the same thing: contextual factors that must be present for a causal relationship to work as theorized.

9. In this book we use the notation C for cause and O for outcome when referring to asymmetric causal relationships. We use the standard X/Y notation when speaking about symmetric claims of causal relationships between independent and dependent variables.

10. Deviant cases where C is present but O does not occur can however be relevant when studying when and why causal mechanisms break down. For more, see chapters 8 and 9.

11. A logically similar but weaker claim is that one form of causation is perceived to be superior, with other understandings second-best alternatives. We see this in Lebow's use of the Aristotelian term "inefficient causation" in relation to qualitative methods, where causation in understood to be "those processes and mechanisms that might be responsible for the outcomes they seek to explain" (2014: 44). In his account, this is viewed as a second-best to what he terms "efficient" causation, which he claims exists when we have experimental manipulation (Lebow 2014: 148).

12. We suggest that investigating whether predispositions toward feeling more comfortable with either counterfactuals or mechanism-based explanations varies depending on cognitive factors or formative experiences is a very interesting avenue for further research. In developmental psychology there is evidence that even relatively young children engage in mechanism-based explanations (e.g., Schlottmann 1999).

13. This does not mean that multivariate causal claims are not possible, only that the core of counterfactual logic is the isolation of the difference that individual causes make (Morgan and Winship 2007; Woodward 2003).

14. Bunge (1997: 428).

15. Applications of quantum theory to psychology, biology, and even social science have begun appearing in recent years (Shrapnel 2014; Atmanspacher 2015; Wendt 2015). It can be argued that quantum theories about the nonlocalizability of quantum objects and the indeterminacy of properties might wreak havoc on mechanism-based explanations based on entities engaging in activities in a causal process, for how can we theorize entities placement if they are nonlocalizable? However, given that theories of causal mechanism focus on providing explanations about macroscopic processes that are embedded in local environments, the quantum-level indeterminacy washes out, with the result that what we are analyzing behaves in classical fashion; that is, it is amenable to theorization as causal mechanisms (Kuhlmann and Glennan 2014).

16. While the mechanism understanding has typically been associated with philosophical or critical realism (Kurki 2008), one can also study mechanisms when one adopts different philosophical positions by slightly modifying how one theorizes mechanisms. In chapter 9, we contend that a pragmatic philosophical position can be coupled with the study of mechanisms, assessing how an eclectic combination of causes and mechanisms together produce a particular historical outcome.

17. Eckstein (1975).

18. We discuss the relationship between degree of empirical confidence based on within-case and cross-case evidence in Bayesian logic in chapter 6.

19. Variance-based methods utilize the term "contrast space" to refer to the appropriate frame of comparison (Collier and Mahoney 1996: 67). We prefer the term "causally homogeneous population." In variance-based designs, causal claims deal with the mean causal effects of values of X for values of Y. Given this, the appropriate population to assess a variance-based causal claim is one where there are differences in values of Y, often over a large number of cases in order to utilize statistical techniques. If the causal claim does not match the cases studied because there are only positive cases of Y in the population, this would be an inappropriate contrast space. However, given the type of asymmetric causal claims being made in case-based research, contrasting positive and negative cases of an outcome is often not relevant.

20. Causal homogeneity is typically termed "stable unit treatment effect" in variance-based research (Morgan and Winship 2007: 37–40; Rubin 1980: 961).

21. Asymmetry can also be used to refer to different causal effects of directions of change in values of causal conditions (e.g., moving from low to high values of C affects O differently than moving from high to low values), or in the magnitude of causal effects across values of C (e.g., a negative relationship in low values of C, a positive relationship at medium-values, and no relationship at high values) (Steel 2008: 22–27).

22. Note that many scholars who work with fuzzy-set analysis do not acknowledge the distinction between differences of kind and difference of degree, with subset relations determined fully by differences between degrees of membership (e.g., Eliason and Stryker 2009: 105–6).

Chapter 3

1. As discussed in chapter 2, a deterministic ontology does not mean that the world works in a highly predictable, clockwork fashion. Instead, it means that things do not

just happen by chance, and that through careful study we can gain greater understanding of how things work. As we explore further in chapter 6, we advocate a probabilistic epistemology (Bayesian updating) that we believe is the only logical foundation for making the type of non-variance-based inferences that we want to make in causal case study research.

2. On scope (contextual) conditions, see section 3.4.

3. The * symbol represents logical AND, whereas the + symbol represents logical OR. They can also be represented using the & symbol for AND and v for OR.

4. For more on theoretical and empirical exclusivity, see Rohlfing (2014).

5. For good introductions to set theory, see Ragin (2008); Schneider and Wagemann (2012); Rohlfing (2012).

6. For more on this type of research situation, see chapters 6 and 8.

7. For example, see Bennett (2014) and the introductory chapter in Bennett and Checkel (2014).

Chapter 4

1. Other terms in the literature for abstract concepts include "background concepts" (Adcock and Collier 2001) and the "basic level" of concepts (Goertz 2006).

2. The same arguments can be made for Coppedge (2012). Additionally, he focuses primarily on operationalization and measurement, with no real guidance on how to define concepts.

3. There are parallels to this in the quantitative culture when categorical variables are used. These are typically used in the form of dummy variables, with the term "dummy" referring to the fact that they are very indirect proxies for what is actually causally important. For example, one could introduce dummy variables such as region (e.g., Northeast, Southwest) into a model of voting behavior. Yet it would not be the dummy variable (region) that would be producing differences; instead, it is just a crude indirect proxy for some unknown factor that is causally relevant. The value-added of qualitative case-based research is that we would conceptualize what is actually producing these differences instead of using indirect proxies.

4. Another term used for this position is "ontological." See Goertz (2006).

5. Sarkees and Wayman (2010).

6. In variance-based research there are other forms of relationship that only make sense using when ordinal or higher scales are used to measure attributes. These relationships include taking the mean of attribute scores and multiplying the product of scores on individual attributes. For more, see Munck (2009: 71).

7. We prefer using the logical terms. Using the terms "necessary" and "sufficiency" both to relate to the relationship of attributes to each other and for the type of causal relationship between a condition and an outcome can result in confusing pronouncements, such as "Attribute 1 and 2 are necessary and sufficient parts of the causal condition which is necessary but not sufficient to produce an outcome." Therefore, we reserve the terms "necessary" and "sufficiency" for causal claims between conditions or between parts of a mechanism.

8. The AND relationship can be considered a weakest-link definition, in that a case only a member when all attributes are present (Goertz 2006: 111–14).

9. Collier and colleagues utilize the term "kind of" to denote the overarching theoretical concept (Collier, LaPorte, and Seawright 2012). Given that this can be confused with the differences in kind that are captured by the different subtypes, we suggest reserving the term "kind" to causally relevant distinctions captured by subtypes.

10. See the following central works: Hintze (1975 [1931]); Bendix (1962 [1946]: 366–68); Bloch (1971a [1939]: 228); Ganshof (1952 [1944]: 154); Strayer (1987 [1965]: 29); Anderson (1974); Poggi (1978, 1991); Møller (2015).

Chapter 5

1. Furthermore, when we speak of moving from one phase to the next (see figure 5.1), it is important to note that moving from the abstract to concrete is not same as talking about mechanisms as postulated by Goertz and Mahoney (2006: 239). In our understanding, mechanisms are what links causal concepts together, whereas moving across levels of concepts deals with defining and measuring concepts (see chapters 2 and 3 for more on mechanisms).

2. Ragin (2000: 225) makes a similar argument, contending that when we know our measures are imprecise we should only analyze cases that are clearly in or out of the set (depending on the type of comparative or within-case analysis).

3. We do not enter into the broader philosophical debate about whether theoretical constructs can actually be measured empirically or not. Here we adopt a pragmatic approach that is most in line with a realist understanding of science, but we do not rule out that there might be some causal concepts that can actually be directly observed empirically.

Chapter 6

1. Interestingly, in legal studies a similar debate on formalizing Bayesian logic using numbers took place in the mid-1980s (e.g., Kaye 1986, Brillmayer 1986). The non-quantification camp clearly won the debate as regards employing Bayesian logic within individual cases, given the importance of qualitative interpretations of what empirical material means in particular contexts that cannot be quantified in a meaningful fashion. We return to this point later.

2. See, for instance, Bennett (2014); Beach and Pedersen (2013); Rohlfing (2012).

3. See Van Evera (1997); Bennett (2010); Collier (2011).

4. See Collier, Brady, and Seawright (2010); Mahoney (2012).

5. The analogy should of course not be taken too far, since the standard of proof (beyond reasonable doubt in the US context) in criminal proceedings is realistically never achieved in case study research and because of the nature of the "theories" being tested using legal reasoning. More relevant for our purposes are the standards for proof in civil law proceedings, for instance the preponderance of the evidence in the US

context that merely claims that the evidence has made it more likely than not that something happened in a particular fashion.

6. In fields like medicine, mechanistic evidence is collected by tracing mechanisms using detailed observations of actual processes (often in animals for obvious ethical reasons). For instance, the mechanism linking smoking to cancer involves a "physiological mechanism [that] operates in the lungs. The hair-like cilia in the lungs, which beat rhythmically to remove inhaled particles, are destroyed by smoke inhalation; thus the lung cannot cleanse itself effectively. Cancer-producing agents in cigarette smoke are therefore trapped in the mucus. Cancer then develops when these chemical agents alter the cells, in particular, cell division" (Russo and Williamson 2007: 162). Our knowledge of this process derives from mechanistic evidence produced by numerous observational studies of parts of the mechanism linking C with O, such as how smoke enters lung tissue (Illari and Russo 2014).

7. They offer two additional suggestions, but both involve shifting the causal claim being assessed (e.g., by changing the outcome being explained). We believe that this advice basically boils down to creating variation by comparing apples and oranges.

8. Note that they use the term "observation" in the same way that we use the term "case" in this chapter, defined as one measure of one dependent variable on one unit.

9. If we have many units, the unit homogeneity assumption logically becomes less necessary as long as cases are independent of each other (ensured for example through randomization in experiments) (Brady 2008: 261–66). However, it is still important to note that this is a second-best strategy. See the excellent discussion in Gerring (2011: 246–55).

10. They use the term "process tracing observation" instead of "CPO," but the meaning is the same.

11. For good popular science introductions to the Bayesian approach, see Mcgrayne (2012) and Silver (2012).

12. This can also be interpreted as the "old evidence problem." For a more technical discussion of the topic, see Wagner (2001).

13. Charman and Fairfield (2015) attempted to quantify likelihoods for evidence using the propositions proposed in Fairfield's 2013 article on tax reform, illustrating the practical infeasibility of translating qualitative interpretations of evidence into quantified ratios.

14. The probative value of evidence is often depicted as the likelihood ratio. To keep matters nontechnical, we use the more commonsense terms in this chapter. For more technical introductions, see the appendix in Bennett and Checkel (2014) and good shorter expositions by Good (1968, 1991) and Friedman (1986a, 1986b). The best book-length introduction is Howson and Urbach (2006).

15. Alternatively one can utilize hypothetical counterfactuals, but this also transforms the case study into a comparative analysis. For more, see Goertz and Starr (2003); Goertz and Levy (2007).

16. For the Bayesian logic behind this, see Howson and Urbach (2006); Bennett (2014).

17. For the reasoning behind this, see chapter 9.

18. This situation is termed hypothesis symmetry by Eells and Fitelson (2000).

19. What evidence can actually tell us is also a function of the probability that the measures of the evidence being accurate, as will be developed further. This could be incorporated into figure 6.3, but it would make the figure much more complicated.

20. While Roberts (1996) presents a similar, multilayer diagram, he only uses it to *trace the course of events* that lead up to the explanandum event, whereas our framework focuses more explicitly on mapping the underlying nature of the *causal* arguments put forward and the *evidence* used in support of these claims.

21. There is some debate on this issue of "old" evidence and sequential updating (see, e.g., Eells and Fitelson 2000; Weisberg 2009; Gallow 2014).

22. Note this is a simplification, given that the subsequent test should actually provide a bit less updating, which is also contingent on how close our prior confidence approaches either 0 percent or 100 percent (see rule 1d on the declining marginal effects of adding more pieces of evidence).

23. Bennett (2014) talks about adding multiple straw-in-the-wind pieces of evidence to paint a more compelling overall picture. We agree with this, though with the caveat that we should avoid a more-is-always-better logic, where the analyst attempts to mask the poor quality of the evidence (i.e., low probative value) with a deluge of evidence.

Chapter 7

1. Przeworski and Teune talk about substituting proper names with variables, but this means basically the same thing as an abstract concept in our terminology.

2. See the Wikipedia entry "Comparative Politics," at https://en.wikipedia.org/wiki/Comparative_politics (accessed June 23, 2016).

3. Note that we are utilizing the most-different-system method in the manner adopted by case-based researchers such as Ragin (1987). Przeworski and Teune defined it as a tool for survey research, one where differences at a lower level were investigated by disaggregating into subgroups of a whole population. If there were no significant differences across subgroups, then differences across groups were not important.

4. The symbol ~ refers to logical NOT, so ~O should be read as "the outcome is not present."

5. Or more correct, a natural experiment given that we are not actively manipulating values of the treatment but instead using observations.

6. There is disagreement in the literature regarding whether all control conditions (everything else) actually have to be measured or not. For example, Gerring claims it is not necessary to measure them all (2007: 133), whereas Glynn and Ichino claim that they should all be listed (2014: 17). Our answer to this question is that if we are using a most similar system to make a positive, confirming inference, we would need to list as many plausible control conditions as possible. However, it is not strictly necessary if we are using the comparison for theory-building purposes, given that the comparison will be followed up by more intensive within-case analysis to make positive inferences.

7. For more on experimental design, see Morton and Williams (2010).

8. If negative cases are relevant to the research question, when building populations with negative cases we have to ensure that the outcome could actually have taken

place in the negative cases (Goertz and Mahoney 2004; Mikkelsen 2015). If we are investigating the causes of war, we would want to select cases in which war is at least theoretically possible (Goertz and Mahoney 2004).

9. Seawright (2002) suggests that we should utilize an all-cell framework to assess necessary conditions. We follow the Bayesian-inspired recommendations of Clarke (2002) in suggesting instead a positive-on-outcome test, because only positive cases of O are informative in relation to an asymmetric claim of necessity. See also Braumoeller and Goertz (2002) for theoretical justifications for ignoring negative-on-outcome cases.

10. As discussed in chapter 6, we will never actually utilize the Bayesian formula, although we can use things like prior confidence and plausibility of alternative explanations for finding evidence. Further, we will never quantify these values when engaging in qualitative case-based research because of the importance of interpreting what evidence means in a given context.

Chapter 8

1. Lyall's chapter develops a counterfactual-based account of process-tracing where the workings of mechanisms are completely black-boxed. Schimmelfennig does talk about causal mechanisms, but with the exception of his own work, the studies that he reviews do not unpack mechanisms.

2. This overlaps with explaining outcome process-tracing, with the difference being that when using explaining outcome congruence one does not unpack mechanisms, whereas in explaining outcome process-tracing mechanisms are in focus.

3. We recommended using a most similar systems comparison for searching for unknown causes or outcomes in chapter 7, although exploratory congruence case studies can also be used to search for unknown causes or outcomes.

4. As discussed in our reconstruction of her Korean War case study in chapter 6, in practice she puts forward four different propositions in the course of her case study, although only one is mentioned when describing her empirical test. This means that while Tannenwald claims that she is only engaging in a singular test, she is in reality putting forward a cluster of tests. Here we utilize her proposed design merely as an example of what the singular variant can look like methodologically.

Chapter 9

1. See the discussion in chapter 3 regarding whether causal mechanisms are actually existing phenomena, or whether they are analytical constructs whose observable manifestations are being traced.

2. While this guidance is similar to what Tarrow terms "progressively testing scope conditions" (2010: 251), here we are talking about within-case analysis that trace mechanisms instead of using paired comparisons as a research strategy.

3. Note that we do not follow Steel's (2008) approach fully because he does not distinguish between evidence of difference-making and mechanistic evidence. The

result is that process-tracing becomes an adjunct method in his framework, whereas we follow philosophers of science who contend that mechanistic evidence gained from process-tracing is just as strong evidence of causation as the evidence of difference-making gained from experiments (Russo and Williamson 2007).

4. Tarrow (2010). In contrast to Tarrow, we detail in the following the role that process-tracing plays in conjunction with a systematic paired comparison.

5. E.g., Lieberman (2005: 443); Rohlfing (2008: 1510); Schneider and Rohlfing (2013).

6. While Schneider and Rohlfing (2013) do discuss designs that compare a typical case and a deviant case in quadrant IV, they do not offer guidance on how the comparative and within-case methods are combined, nor do they offer any guidance when we do not theorize that C is necessary or sufficient, but is just causally related to O. Tarrow (2010) offers no guidance on how to combine paired comparisons and within-case tracing of mechanisms.

Chapter 10

1. This means groups that are motivated to protect the Islamic world from perceived external (non-Muslim) threats.

2. We thank our colleague Morten Valbjørn for this point.

References

Abell, Peter. 2004. Narrative explanation: An alternative to variable-centered explanation? *Annual Review of Sociology* 30 (1): 287–310.

Adcock, Robert. 2007. Who's afraid of determinism? The ambivalence of macrohistorical inquiry. *Journal of the Philosophy of History* 1 (2007): 346–64.

Adcock, Robert, and David Collier. 2001. Measurement validity: A shared standard for qualitative and quantitative research. *American Political Science Review* 95 (3): 529–46.

Allison, Graham. 1971. *Essence of decision: Explaining the Cuban Missile Crisis*. Boston: Little, Brown.

Allison, Graham, and Phillip Zellikow. 1999. *Essence of decision explaining the Cuban Missile Crisis*. New York: Longman.

Alvarez, Walter. 2008. *"T. rex" and the crater of doom*. Princeton: Princeton University Press.

Andersen, Holly. 2012. The case for regularity in mechanistic causal explanation. *Synthese* 189 (2012): 415–32.

Anderson, Perry. 1974. *Lineages of the absolutist state*. London: Verso.

Archer, Margaret. 2000. *Being human: The problem of agency*. Cambridge: Cambridge University Press.

Atmanspacher, Harald. 2015. Quantum approaches to consciousness. In *The Stanford encyclopedia of philosophy* (Summer 2015), edited by Edward N. Zalta, http://plato.stanford.edu/archives/sum2015/entries/qt-consciousness/.

Axelrod, Robert. 1984. *The evolution of cooperation*. New York: Basic Books.

Bacciagaluppi, Guido. 2012. The role of decoherence in quantum mechanics. In *The Stanford encyclopedia of philosophy* (Winter 2012), edited by Edward N. Zalta, http://plato.stanford.edu/archives/win2012/entries/qm-decoherence/.

Bartusevičius, Henrikas. 2014. The inequality-conflict nexus re-examined: Income, education and popular rebellions. *Journal of Peace Research* 51 (1): 35–50.

Beach, Derek. Forthcoming. Achieving methodological alignment when combining QCA and PT in practice. *Sociological Methods and Research*.

Beach, Derek, and Rasmus Brun Pedersen. 2013. *Process-tracing methods: Foundations and guidelines*. Ann Arbor: University of Michigan Press.

Beach, Derek, and Rasmus Brun Pedersen. 2016. Selecting appropriate cases when tracing causal mechanisms. *Sociological Methods and Research*. Advance online publication.

Beach, Derek, and Ingo Rohlfing. 2016. Integrating cross-case analyses and process tracing in set theoretic research: Strategies and parameters of debate. *Sociological Methods and Research*. Advance online publication.

Beck, Nathaniel. 2006. Is causal-process observation an oxymoron? *Political Analysis* 14 (2): 347–52.

Behrman, Jere Richard, and Mark R. Rosenzweig. 1994. Caveat emptor: Cross-country data on education and the labor force. *Journal of Development Economics* 44: 147–71.

Bendix, Reinhard. 1962 [1946]. *Max Weber: An intellectual portrait*. New York: Anchor Books.

Bennett, Andrew. 2006. Stirring the frequentist pot with a dash of Bayes. *Political Analysis* 14 (2): 339–44.

Bennett, Andrew. 2008a. Process-tracing: A Bayesian perspective. In *The Oxford handbook of political methodology*, edited by Janet M. Box-Steffensmeier, Henry E. Brady, and David Collier, 702–21. Oxford: Oxford University Press.

Bennett, Andrew. 2008b. The mother of all "isms": Organizing political science around causal mechanisms. In *Revitalizing causality: Realism about causality in philosophy and social science*, edited by Ruth Groff, 205–19. London: Routledge.

Bennett, Andrew. 2010. Process tracing and causal inference. In *Rethinking social inquiry: Diverse tools, shared standards*, edited by Henry E. Brady and David Collier, 207–20. 2nd ed. Lanham, MD: Rowman and Littlefield.

Bennett, Andrew. 2014. Appendix: Disciplining our conjectures: Systematizing process tracing with Bayesian analysis. In *Process tracing: From metaphor to analytic tool*, edited by Andrew Bennett and Jeffrey Checkel, 276–98. Cambridge: Cambridge University Press.

Bennett, Andrew, and Jeffrey Checkel. 2014. *Process tracing: From metaphor to analytic tool*. Cambridge: Cambridge University Press.

Besancon, Marie. 2005. Relative resources: Inequality in ethnic wars, revolutions, and genocides. *Journal of Peace Research* 42 (4): 393–415.

Bhaskar, Roy. 1978. *A realist theory of science*. Brighton: Harvester.

Bisson, Thomas. N. 2010. *The crisis of the twelfth century: Power, lordship, and the origins of European government*. Princeton: Princeton University Press.

Blalock, Hubert. 1982. *Conceptualization and measurement in the social sciences*. London: Sage Publications.

Blatter, Joachim. 2009. Performing symbolic politics and international environmental regulation: Tracing and theorizing a causal mechanism beyond regime theory. *Global Environmental Politics* 9 (4): 81–110.

Blatter, Joachim, and Markus Haverland. 2012. *Designing case studies: Explanatory approaches in small-N research*. Houndmills: Palgrave Macmillan.

Blaydes, Lisa, and Eric Chaney. 2012. The feudal revolution and Europe's rise: Political divergence of the Christian West and the Muslim world before 1500 CE. *American Political Science Review* 107: 1–19.

Bloch, Marc. 1971a [1939]. *Feudal society, volume I: The growth of ties of dependence.* Translated from the French by L. A. Manyon. London: Routledge and Kegan Paul.

Bloch, Marc. 1971b [1939]. *Feudal society, volume II: Social classes and political organization.* Translated from the French by L. A. Manyon. London: Routledge and Kegan Paul.

Bogaards, Matthijs. 2012. Where to draw the line? From degree to dichotomy in measures of democracy. *Democratization* 19 (4): 690–712.

Bogen, Jim. 2005. Regularities and causality; generalizations and causal explanations. *Studies in History and Philosophy of Biological and Biomedical Sciences* 36: 397–420.

Bogen, Jim, and Peter Machamer. 2013. Mechanistic information and causal continuity. Paper downloaded from http://www.hf.uio.no/csmn/english/research/news-and-events/events/archive/2008/machamer_docs/bogen_machamer.pdf.

Boix, Carles. 2003. *Democracy and redistribution.* Cambridge: Cambridge University Press.

Bollen, Kenneth A. 1989. *Structural equations with latent variables.* New York: John Wiley and Sons.

Borsboom, Denny. 2005. *Measuring the mind: Conceptual issues in contemporary psychometrics.* Cambridge: Cambridge University Press.

Borsboom, Denny. 2008. Latent variable theory. *Measurement* 6 (1): 25–53.

Bowman, Kirk, Fabrice Lehoucq, and James Mahoney. 2005. Measuring political democracy: case expertise, data adequacy, and Central America. *Comparative Political Studies* 38 (8): 939–70.

Brady, Henry. 2008. Causation and explanation in social science. In *The Oxford handbook of political methodology*, edited by Janet M. Box-Steffensmeier, Henry E. Brady, and David Collier, 217–70. Oxford: Oxford University Press.

Brady, Henry E., and David Collier, eds. 2004. *Rethinking social inquiry: Diverse tools shared standards.* Lanham, MD: Rowman Littlefield.

Brady, Henry E., and David Collier, eds. 2011. *Rethinking social inquiry: Diverse tools shared standards.* 2nd ed. Lanham, MD: Rowman Littlefield.

Brady, Henry E., David Collier, and Jason Seawright. 2006. Towards a pluralistic vision of methodology. *Political Analysis* 14 (2): 353–68.

Brast, Benjamin. 2015. The regional dimension of statebuilding interventions. *International Peacekeeping* 22 (1): 81–99.

Braumoeller, Bear F., and Gary Goertz. 2000. The methodology of necessary conditions. *American Journal of Political Science* 44 (4): 844–58.

Brecher, Michael. 1980. *Decisions in crisis: Israel, 1969 and 1973.* Berkeley: University of California Press.

Brilmayer, Lea. 1986. The role of evidential weight in criminal proof. *Boston University Law Review* 66 (4): 673–91.

Brooks, Stephen G., and William Wohlforth. 2000–2001. The end of the Cold War: Reevaluating a landmark case for ideas. *International Security* 25 (3, Winter): 5–53.

Brooks, Stephen G., and William Wohlforth. 2002. From old thinking to new thinking in qualitative research. *International Security* 26 (4, Spring): 93–111.

Brown, E. A. R. 1974. The tyranny of a construct: Feudalism and historians of medieval Europe. *American Historical Review* 79 (4): 1063–88.

Bunge, Mario. 1997. Mechanism and explanation. *Philosophy of the Social Sciences* 27 (4): 410–65.

Bunge, Mario. 2004. How does it work? The search for explanatory mechanisms. *Philosophy of the Social Sciences* 34 (2): 182–210.

Büthe, Tim. 2002. Taking temporality seriously: Modeling history and the use of narratives as evidence. *American Political Science Review* 96 (3): 481–93.

Cartwright, Nancy. 2007. *Hunting causes and using them: Approaches in philosophy and economics.* Cambridge: Cambridge University Press.

Cerling, Thure E., Fredrick Kyalo Manthi, Emma N. Mbua, Louise N. Leakey, Meave G. Leakey, Richard E. Leakey, Francis H. Brown, Frederick E. Grine, John A. Hart, Prince Kaleme, Hélène Roche, Kevin T. Uno, and Bernard A. Wood. 2013. Stable isotope-based diet reconstructions of Turkana Basin hominins. *Proceedings of the National Academy of Science in the USA* 26 (June 25): 10501–6.

Chalmers, Allen F. 1999. *What is this thing called Science?* Buckingham: Open University Press.

Chamie, Joseph. 1994. Population databases in development analysis. *Journal of Development Economics* 44: 131–46.

Charman, Andrew, and Tasha Fairfield. 2015. Applying formal Bayesian analysis to qualitative case research: An empirical example, implications, and caveats. Unpublished paper.

Chatterjee, Partha. 2011. *Lineages of political society: Studies in postcolonial democracy.* New York: Columbia University Press.

Checkel, Jeffrey T. 2008. Tracing causal mechanisms. *International Studies Review* 8 (2): 362–70.

Choi, Ajin. 2004. Democratic synergy and victory in war: 1816–1992. *International Studies Quarterly* 48 (3): 663–82.

Clarke, Kevin A. 2002. The reverend and the ravens: Comment on Seawright. *Political Analysis* 10 (2): 194–97.

Clarke, Richard A. 2004. *Against all enemies: Inside America's War on Terror.* New York: Free Press.

Cohen, L. Jonathan. 1986. The role of evidential weight in criminal proof. *Boston University Law Review* 66 (4): 635–49.

Coleman, J. S. 1990. *Foundations of social theory.* Cambridge, MA: Harvard University Press.

Collier, David. 2011. Understanding process tracing. *PS: Political Science and Politics* 44 (4): 823–30.

Collier, David, Henry E. Brady, and Jason Seawright. 2010. Sources of leverage in causal inference: Toward an alternative view of methodology. In *Rethinking social inquiry: Diverse tools, shared standards*, edited by Henry E. Brady and David Collier, 161–200. 2nd ed. Lanham, MD: Rowman and Littlefield.

Collier, David, Jody LaPorte, and Jason Seawright. 2012. Putting typologies to work: Concept formation, measurement, and analytical rigor. *Political Research Quarterly* 65 (1): 217–32.

Collier, David, and Steven Levitsky. 1997. Democracy with adjectives: Conceptual innovation in comparative research. *World Politics* 49 (3): 430–51.

Collier, David, and James Mahoney. 1996. Research note: Insights and pitfalls: Selection bias in qualitative research. *World Politics* 49 (1): 56–91.

Coppedge, Michael. 2012. *Democratization and research methods*. Cambridge: Cambridge University Press.

Coppedge, Michael, John Gerring, Staffan I. Lindberg, Jan Teorell, David Altman, Michael Bernhard, M. Steven Fish, Adam Glynn, Allen Hicken, Carl Henrik Knutsen, Matthew Kroenig, Kelly McMann, Daniel Pemstein, Megan Reif, Svend-Erik Skaaning, Jeffrey Staton, Eitan Tzelgov, Yi-ting Wang. 2014. *V-Dem codebook v2*. Unpublished manuscript.

Dahl, Robert. 1971. *Polyarchy: Participation and opposition*. New Haven: Yale University Press.

Dahl, Robert. 1998. *On democracy*. New Haven: Yale University Press.

Darden, Lindley. 2002. Strategies for discovering mechanisms: Schema instantiation, modular subassembly, forward/backward chaining. *Philosophy of Science* (Supplement PSA 2000 Part II) 69: S354–65.

Dion, Douglas. 1998. Evidence and inference in the comparative case study. *Comparative Politics* 30 (2): 127–45.

Dion, Douglas. 2003. Evidence and inference in the comparative case study. In *Necessary conditions: Theory, methodology, and applications*, edited by Gary Goertz and H. Starr, 95–112. Oxford: Rowman and Littlefield.

Dowe, Phil. 2011. The causal-process-model theory of mechanisms. In *Causality in the sciences*, edited by Phyllis McKay Illari, Federica Russo, and Jon Williamson, 865–79. Oxford: Oxford University Press.

Eells, Ellery, and Brandon Fitelson. 2000. Measuring confirmation and evidence. *Journal of Philosophy* 97 (12): 663–72.

Eliason, Scott R., and Robin Stryker. 2009. Goodness-of-fit tests and descriptive measures in fuzzy-set analysis. *Sociological Methods and Research* 38 (1): 102–46.

Elman, Colin, and Miriam Fendius Elman. 1997. Diplomatic history and international relations theory: Respecting difference and crossing boundaries. *International Security* 22 (1): 5–21.

Elman, Colin, and Miriam Fendius Elman. 2001. Introduction: Negotiating international history and politics. In *Bridges and boundaries: Historians, political scientists and the study of international relations*, edited by Colin Elman and Miriam Fendius Elman, 1–36. Cambridge: MIT Press.

Elman, Colin, and Diana Kapiszewski. 2014. Data access and research transparency in the qualitative tradition. *PS: Political Science and Politics* 47 (1): 43–47.

Elster, Jon. 1998. A plea for mechanisms. In *Social mechanisms*, edited by P. Hedström and R. Swedberg, 45–73. Cambridge: Cambridge University Press.

Emirbayer, Mustafa, and Ann Mische. 1998. What is agency? *American Journal of Sociology* 103 (4): 962–1023.

Emmenegger, Patrick, and Klaus Petersen. 2015. Taking history seriously in comparative research: The case of electoral system choice, 1890–1939. *Comparative European Politics*. Advance online publication, February 9. doi:10.1057/cep.2015.2.

Erslev, Kristian R. 1963. *Historisk Teknik: Den Historiske Undersøgelse Fremstillet I sine Grundlinier*. Copenhagen: Gyldendalske Boghandel.

Evangelista, Mathew. 2014. Explaining the Cold War's end: Process tracing all the way down? In *Process tracing: From metaphor to analytic tool*, edited by Andrew Bennett and Jeff Checkel, 153–85. Cambridge: Cambridge University Press.

Evans, Peter. 1995. Contribution to symposium "The Role of Theory in Comparative Politics." *World Politics* 48 (1): 3–10.

Fair, Ray. 2012. *Predicting presidential elections and other things*. 2nd ed. Stanford: Stanford University Press.

Fairfield, Tasha. 2013. Going where the money is: Strategies for taxing economic elites in unequal democracies. *World Development* 47 (1): 42–57.

Falleti, Tulia G., and Julia F. Lynch. 2009. Context and causal mechanisms in political analysis. *Comparative Political Studies*, 42 (9): 1143–66.

Fearon, James. 1991. Counterfactuals and hypothesis testing in political science. *World Politics* 43 (2): 169–95.

Finer, Samuel E. 1997. *The history of government II*. Oxford: Oxford University Press.

Freedman, David A. 1991. Statistical models and shoe leather. *Sociological Methodology* 21: 291–313.

Friedman, Richard D. 1986a. A diagrammatic approach to evidence. *Boston University Law Review* 66 (4): 571–620.

Friedman, Richard D. 1986b. A close look at probative value. *Boston University Law Review* 66 (4): 733–59.

Friedrichs, Jörg, and Friedrich Kratochwill. 2009. On acting and knowing: How pragmatism can advance international relations research and methodology. *International Organization* 63 (4): 701–31.

Fuchs, Christopher. 2010. QBism, the perimeter of quantum Bayesianism. *arXiv*: 1003.5209v1, March 26.

Gaddis, John Lewis. 1992–93. International relations theory and the end of the Cold War. *International Security* 17 (3): 5–58.

Gallow, J. Dimitri. 2014. How to learn from theory-dependent evidence; or, Commutativity and holism: A solution for conditionalizers. *British Journal of the Philosophy of Science* 65: 493–519.

Ganshof, François-Louis. 1952 [1944]. *Feudalism*. Translated by Philip Grierson. London: Longmans.

Geddes, Barbara. 1990. How the cases you choose affect the answers you get: Selection bias in comparative politics. *Political Analysis* 2 (1): 131–50.

George, Alexander L. 1997. Knowledge for statecraft: The challenge for political science and history. *International Security* 22 (1): 44–52.

George, Alexander L., and Andrew Bennett. 2005. *Case studies and theory development in the social sciences*. Cambridge: MIT Press.

Gerring, John. 1999. What makes a concept good? A criterial framework for understanding concept formation in the social sciences. *Polity* 31 (3): 357–93.

Gerring, John. 2005. Causation: A unified framework for the social sciences. *Journal of Theoretical Politics* 17 (2): 163–98.

Gerring, John. 2006. Single-outcome studies: A methodological primer. *International Sociology* 21 (5): 707–34.

Gerring, John. 2007. *Case study research*. Cambridge: Cambridge University Press.

Gerring, John. 2011. *Social science methodology—A unified framework*. Cambridge: Cambridge University Press.

Gerring, John, and Jason Seawright. 2007. Techniques for choosing cases. In *Case study research*. Cambridge: Cambridge University Press, pp. 86–150.

Giddens, Anthony. 1984. *The constitution of society: Outline of the theory of structuration*. Cambridge: Polity Press.

Gilpin, Robert. 1987. *The political economy of international relations*. Princeton: Princeton University Press.

Glennan, Stuart S. 1996. Mechanisms and the nature of causation. *Erkenntnis* 44 (1): 49–71.

Glennan, Stuart S. 2002. Rethinking mechanistic explanation. *Philosophy of Science* 69: 342–53.

Glennan, Stuart S. 2011. Singular and general causal relations: A mechanist perspective. In *Causality in the sciences*, edited by Phyllis McKay Illari, Federica Russo, and Jon Williamson, 789–817. Oxford: Oxford University Press.

Glynn, Adam N., and Nahomi Ichino. 2014. Increasing inferential leverage in the comparative method: Placebo tests in small-N research. *Sociological Methods and Research*. Published online May 2.

Goertz, Gary. 2003. The substantive importance of necessary condition hypotheses. In *Necessary conditions: Theory, methodology, and applications*, edited by G. Goertz and H. Starr, 65–94. Oxford: Rowman and Littlefield.

Goertz, Gary. 2006. *Social science concepts: A user's guide*. Princeton: Princeton University Press.

Goertz, Gary, and Jack S. Levy, eds. 2007. *Explaining war and peace: Case studies and necessary condition counterfactuals*. London: Routledge.

Goertz, Gary, and James Mahoney. 2012. *A tale of two cultures—Qualitative and quantitative research in the social sciences*. Princeton: Princeton University Press.

Goertz, Gary, and H. Starr, eds. 2003. *Necessary conditions: Theory, methodology, and applications*. Oxford: Rowman and Littlefield.

Goldberg, Jeffrey. 2007. The usual suspect. *New Republic*, October 7, 2007. https://newrepublic.com/article/63500/the-usual-suspect.

Goldthorpe, John. 1997. Methodological issues in comparative macrosociology. *Comparative Social Research* 16: 107–20.

Good, L. J. 1968. Corroboration, explanation, evolving probability, simplicity and a sharpened razor. *British Journal of Philosophy* 19: 123–43.

Good, L. J. 1991. Weight of evidence and the Bayesian likelihood ratio. In *Use of statistics in forensic science*, edited by C. G. Aitken and D. A. Stoney, 85–106. London: CRC.

Groff, Ruth. 2011. Getting past Hume in the philosophy of social science. In *Causality in the sciences*, edited by Phyllis McKay Illari, Federica Russo, and Jon Williamson, 296–316. Oxford: Oxford University Press.

Gross, Neil. 2009. A pragmatist theory of social mechanisms. *American Sociological Review* 74 (3): 358–79.

Grzymala-Busse, Anna. 2011. Time will tell? Temporality and the analysis of causal mechanisms and processes. *Comparative Political Studies* 44 (9): 1267–97.

Hall, Peter A. 2003. Aligning ontology and methodology in comparative politics. In *Comparative historical analysis in the social sciences*, edited by J. Mahoney and D. Rueschemeyer, 373–404. New York: Cambridge University Press.

Hawkins, D., D. Lake, D. Nielson, and M. Tierney. 2006. Delegation under anarchy: States, international organizations and principal agent theory. In *Delegation and agency in international organizations*, edited by D. Hawkins et al., 3–38. Cambridge: Cambridge University Press.

Hedström, Peter, and Richard Swedberg, eds. 1998. *Social mechanisms an analytical approach to social theory*. Cambridge: Cambridge University Press.

Hedström, Peter, and Petri Ylikoski. 2010. Causal mechanisms in the social sciences. *Annual Review of Sociology* 36: 49–67.

Hegghammer, Thomas. 2009. Jihadi-Salafis or revolutionaries? On religion and politics in the study of militant jihadism. In *Global Salafism: Islam's new religious movement*, edited by Roel Meijer, 244–65. London: Hurst and Company.

Hempel, Carl. 1965. The function of general laws in history. In *Aspects of scientific explanation and other essays*, 231–44. New York: Free Press.

Hermann, Charles. 1969. *Crises in foreign policy*. New York: Free Press.

Hernes, Gudmund. 1998. Real virtuality. In *Social mechanisms: An analytical approach to social theory*, edited by Peter Hedström and Richard Swedberg, 74–101. Cambridge: Cambridge University Press.

Hicks, Alexander, Joya Misra, and Tang Nah Ng. 1995. The programmatic emergence of the Social Security state. *American Sociological Review* 60 (3): 329–49.

Hintze, Otto. 1975 [1931]. The preconditions of representative government in the context of world history. In *The historical essays of Otto Hintze*. New York: Oxford University Press.

Holland, Paul W. 1986. Statistics and causal inference. *Journal of the American Statistical Association* 81 (396): 945–60.

Howson, Colin, and Peter Urbach. 2006. *Scientific reasoning: The Bayesian approach*. 3rd ed. La Salle, IL: Open Court.

Hug, Simon, and Thomas Schultz. 2007. Referendums in the EU's constitution building process. *Review of International Organizations* 2: 177–218.

Hui, Victoria Tin-bor. 2005. *War and state formation in ancient China and early modern Europe*. Cambridge: Cambridge University Press.

Hume, David. 1927. *Hume—Selections*. Edited by Charles W. Hendel Jr. New York: Charles Scribner's Sons.

Humphreys, Adam R. C. 2010. The heuristic explanation of explanatory theories in international relations. *European Journal of International Relations* 17 (2): 257–77.

Humphreys, Macartan, and Alan Jacobs. 2013. Mixing methods: A Bayesian unification of qualitative and quantitative approaches. Paper presented at the American Political Science Association annual conference, Chicago, IL, September.

Huntington, Samuel P. 1991. Democracy's third wave. *Journal of Democracy* 2 (2): 12–34.

Illari, Phyllis McKay. 2011. Mechanistic evidence: Disambiguating the Russo-Williamson thesis. *International Studies in the Philosophy of Science* 25 (2): 139–57.

Illari, Phyllis, and Federica Russo. 2014. *Causality: Philosophical theory meets scientific practice*. Oxford: Oxford University Press.

Illari, Phyllis McKay, and Jon Williamson. 2011. Mechanisms are real and local. In *Causality in the sciences*, edited by Phyllis McKay Illari, Federica Russo, and Jon Williamson, 818–44. Oxford: Oxford University Press.

Illari, Phyllis, and Jon Williamson. 2013. In defense of activities. *Journal for General Philosophy of Science* 44 (1): 69–83.

Jackson, Patrick T. 2011. *The conduct of inquiry in international relations*. London: Routledge.

Janis, Irving L. 1982. *Groupthink: Psychological studies of policy decisions and fiascoes*. Boston: Houghton Mifflin.

Jervis, Robert. 2010. Why intelligence and policymakers clash. *Political Science Quarterly* 125 (2): 185–204.

Joos, Erich, H. Dieter Zeh, Claus Kiefer, Domenico J. W. Giulini, Joachim Kupsch, and Ion-Olimpiu Stamatescu. 2003. *Decoherence and the appearance of a classical world in quantum theory*. Berlin: Springer-Verlag.

Kaplan, Abraham. 1964. *The conduct of inquiry—Methodology for behavioral science*. San Francisco: Chandler Publishing.

Kaye, David H. 1986. Comment: Quantifying probative value. *Boston University Law Review* 66 (4): 761–66.

Khong, Yuen Foong. 1992. *Analogies at war: Korea, Munich, Dien Bien Phu and the Vietnam decisions of 1965*. Princeton: Princeton University Press.

Kiewiet, D. Roderick, and Mathew McCubbins. 1991. *The logic of delegation*. Chicago: University of Chicago Press.

Kincaid, Harold. 1996. *Philosophical foundations of the social sciences*. Cambridge: Cambridge University Press.

King, Gary, Robert O. Keohane, and Sidney Verba. 1994. *Designing social inquiry: Scientific inference in qualitative research*. Princeton: Princeton University Press.

Klein, Richard G. 2013. Comments: Stable isotope-based diet reconstructions of Turkana Basin hominins. *Proceedings of the National Academy of Science in the USA* 26 (June 25): 10470–72.

Kramer, Mark. 1990. Remembering the Cuban Missile Crisis: Should we swallow oral history? *International Security* 15 (1): 212–16.

Kreuzer, Markus. 2010. Historical knowledge and quantitative analysis: The case of the origins of proportional representation. *American Political Science Review* 104 (2): 369–92.

Kuhlmann, Meinard, and Stuart Glennan. 2014. On the relation between quantum mechanical and neo-mechanistic ontologies and explanatory strategies. *European Journal of the Philosophy of Science* 4 (3): 337–59.

Kuhn, Thomas. 1977. *The essential tension: Selected studies in scientific tradition and change*. Chicago: University of Chicago Press.

Kurki, Milja. 2008. *Causation in international relations: Reclaiming causal analysis*. Cambridge: Cambridge University Press.

Larson, Deborah Welch. 2001. Sources and methods in Cold War history: The need for a new theory-based archival approach. In *Bridges and boundaries: Historians, political scientists, and the study of international relations*, edited by Colin Elman and Miriam Fendius Elman, 327–50. Cambridge: MIT Press.

Lebow, Richard Ned. 2001. Social science and history: Ranchers versus farmers? In *Bridges and boundaries: Historians, political scientists and the study of international relations*, edited by Colin Elman and Miriam Fendius Elman, 111–36. Cambridge: MIT Press.

Lebow, Richard Ned. 2007. Contingency, catalysts and nonlinear change: The origins of World War I. In *Explaining war and peace: Case studies and necessary condition counterfactuals*, edited by Gary Goertz and Jack S. Levy, 85–112. London: Routledge.

Leuffen, Dirk, Susumu Shikano, and Stefanie Walter. 2013. Measurement and data aggregation in small-N social science research. *European Political Science* 12 (1): 40–51.

Levy, Jack. 2007. The role of necessary conditions in the outbreak of World War I. In *Explaining war and peace: Case studies and necessary condition counterfactuals*, edited by Gary Goertz and Jack S. Levy, 47–84. London: Routledge.

Levy, Jack. 2008. Case studies: Types, designs, and logics of inference. *Conflict Management and Peace Science* 25 (1): 1–18.

Levy, Jack. 2014. Counterfactuals, causal inference, and historical analysis. Paper presented at the 2014 Annual Meeting of the American Political Science Association, Washington DC, August 28–31.

Lewis, D. 1986. *Causation: Postcripts to "Causation."* Vol. 2 of *Philosophical papers*. Oxford: Oxford University Press.

Lieberman, Evan S. 2005. Nested analysis as a mixed-method strategy for comparative research. *American Political Science Review* 99 (3): 435–51.

Lieberman, Robert. 2009. The "Israel lobby" and American politics. *Perspective on Politics* 7 (2): 235–57.

Lieberson, Stanley. 1991. Small N's and big conclusions: An examination of the reasoning in comparative studies based on a small number of cases. *Social Forces* 70 (2): 307–20.

Lijphart, Arend. 1971. Comparative politics and the comparative method. *American Political Science Review* 65 (3): 682–93.

Lijphart, Arend. 1975. *Democracy in plural societies: A comparative exploration*. New Haven: Yale University Press.

Lindberg, Staffan I., Michael Coppedge, John Gerring, and Jan Teorell. 2014. V-DEM: A new way to measure democracy. *Journal of Democracy* 25 (3): 159–69.

Little, Daniel. 1996. Causal explanation in the social sciences. *Southern Journal of Philosophy* 34: 31–56.

Lucas, Samuel R., and Alisa Szatrowski. 2014. Qualitative comparative analysis in critical perspective. *Sociological Methodology* 44 (1): 1–79.

Lupia, Arthur, and Colin Elman. 2014. Openness in political science. *Data Access and Research Transparency* 47 (1): 19–37.

Lyall, Jason. 2014. Process tracing, causal inference, and civil war. In *Process tracing: From metaphor to analytic tool*, edited by Andrew Bennett and Jeffrey Checkel, 186–208. Cambridge: Cambridge University Press.

Machamer, Peter. 2004. Activities and causation: The metaphysics and epistemology of mechanisms. *International Studies in the Philosophy of Science* 18 (1): 27–39.

Machamer, Peter, Lindley Darden, and Carl F. Craver. 2000. Thinking about mechanisms. *Philosophy of Science* 67 (1): 1–25.

Mackie, John L. 1965. Causes and conditions. *American Philosophical Quarterly* 2 (2): 245–64.

Madea, Burkhard, and Dirk W. Lachenmeier. 2005. Postmortem diagnosis of hypertonic dehydration. *Forensic Science International* 155 (2005): 1–6.

Mahoney, James. 1999. Nominal, ordinal, and narrative appraisal in macrocausal analysis. *American Journal of Sociology* 104 (4): 1154–96.

Mahoney, James. 2000. Strategies of causal inference in small-N analysis. *Sociological Methods Research* 28 (4): 387–424.

Mahoney, James. 2001. Beyond correlational analysis: Recent innovations in theory and method. *Sociological Forum* 16 (3): 575–93.

Mahoney, James. 2004. Comparative-historical methodology. *Annual Review of Sociology* 30: 81–101.

Mahoney, James. 2008. Toward a unified theory of causality. *Comparative Political Studies* 41 (4–5): 412–36.

Mahoney, James. 2012. The logic of process tracing tests in the social sciences. *Sociological Methods and Research* 41 (4): 570–97.

Mahoney, James. 2015. Process tracing and historical explanation. *Security Studies* 24 (2): 200–218.

Mahoney, James, and Gary Goertz. 2004. The possibility principle: Choosing negative cases in comparative research. *American Political Science Review* 98 (4): 653–69.

Mahoney, James, and Kathleen Thelen, eds. 2015. *Advances in comparative-historical analysis*. Cambridge: Cambridge University Press.

Mansfield, Edward D., and Jack Snyder. 2002. Democratic transitions, institutional strength, and war. *International Organization* 56 (2): 297–337.

March, James G., and Johann P. Olsen. 1989. *Rediscovering institutions: The organizational basis of politics*. New York: Free Press.

Marini, Margaret Mooney, and Burton Singer. 1988. Causality in the social sciences. *Sociological Methodology* 18: 347–409.

Marshall, Monty G., and Keith Jaggers. 2001. Polity IV project: Political regime characteristics and transitions, 1800–1999. Data set user's manual, Center for Systemic Peace. Online at http://www.systemicpeace.org.

Mayntz, Renate. 2004. Mechanisms in the analysis of social macro-phenomena. *Philosophy of the Social Sciences* 34 (2): 237–59.

McAdam, Doug, Sidney Tarrow, and Charles Tilly. 2008. Methods for measuring mechanisms of contention. *Qualitative Sociology* 31 (4): 307–31.

Mcgrayne, Sharon Bertsch. 2011. *The theory that would not die: How Bayes' rule cracked the Enigma Code, hunted down Russian submarines, and emerged triumphant from two centuries of controversy*. New Haven: Yale University Press.

Mearsheimer, John J., and Stephen Walt. 2007. *The Israel lobby and US foreign policy*. London: Penguin Books.

Merton, Robert K. 1967. *On theoretical sociology*. New York: Free Press.

Michell, Joel. 1999. *Measurement in psychology: A critical history of a methodological concept*. Cambridge: Cambridge University Press.

Michell, Joel. 2008. Is psychometrics pathological science? *Measurement* 6 (1): 7–24.

Michell, Joel. 2011. Qualitative research meets the ghost of Pythagoras. *Theory and Psychology* 21 (2): 241–59.

Mikkelsen, Kim Sass. 2015. Negative case selection: Justifications and consequences for set-theoretic MMR. *Sociological Methods and Research*. doi:10.1177/0049124115591015.

Mill, John Stuart. 2011. *A system of logic: Ratiocinative and inductive*. 7th ed. http://www.gutenberg.org/files/35420/35420-h/35420-h.htm.

Miller, Arthur H. 1978. Partisanship reinstated? A comparison of the 1972 and 1976 U.S. presidential elections. *British Journal of Political Science* 8 (2): 129–52.

Miller, Gary, and Norman Schofield. 2008. The transformation of the Republican and Democratic Party coalitions in the U.S. *Perspectives on Politics* 6 (3): 433–50.

Milligan, John D. 1979. The treatment of a historical source. *History and Theory* 18 (2): 177–96.

Møller, Jørgen. 2014. Composite concepts and historical analogies: Some considerations about the logic of control in comparative historical analysis. Unpublished manuscript.

Møller, Jørgen. 2015. *Mapping definitions of feudalism: A conceptual analysis—Party politics and democracy in Europe: Essays in honor of Peter Mair*. Abingdon: Routledge.

Møller, Jørgen, and Svend-Erik Skaaning. 2015. Explanatory typologies as a nested strategy of inquiry: Combining cross-case and within-case analysis. *Sociological Methods and Research*. Advance online publication.

Moore, Barrington. 1991 [1966]. *Social origins of dictatorship and democracy: Lord and peasant in the making of the modern world*. London: Penguin.

Moravcsik, Andrew. 2010. Active citation: A precondition for replicable qualitative research. *PS: Political Science and Politics* 43 (1): 29–35.

Moravcsik, Andrew. 2013. Did power politics cause European integration? Realist theory meets qualitative methods. *Security Studies* 22 (4): 773–90.

Moravcsik, Andrew. 2014a. Transparency: The revolution in qualitative research. *PS: Political Science and Politics* 47 (1): 48–53.

Moravcsik, Andrew. 2014b. Trust, but verify: The transparency revolution and qualitative international relations. *Security Studies* 23 (4): 663–88.

Morgan, Stephen L., and Christopher Winship. 2007. *Counterfactuals and causal inference: Methods and principles for social research*. Cambridge: Cambridge University Press.

Morton, Rebecca, and Kenneth C. Williams. 2010. *Experimental political science and the study of causality: From nature to the lab*. Cambridge: Cambridge University Press.

Munck, Gerardo. 2005. Drawing boundaries: How to craft intermediate regime categories. Committee on Concepts and Methods Working Paper Series No. 4.

Munck, Gerardo. 2009. *Measuring democracy: A bridge between scholarship and politics*. Baltimore: Johns Hopkins University Press.

Munck, Gerardo L., and Jay Verkuilen. 2002. Conceptualizing and measuring democracy: Evaluating alternative indices. *Comparative Political Studies* 35 (1): 5–34.

Musshoff, Frank, Peter M. D. Schmidt, Thomas Daldrup, and Burkhard Madea. 2002. Cyanide fatalities: Case studies of four suicides and one homicide. *American Journal of Forensic Medicine & Pathology* 23 (4): 315–20.

Nadeau, Richard, and Michael S. Lewis-Beck. 2001. National economic voting in U.S. presidential elections. *Journal of Politics* 63 (1): 159–81.

Nie, Norman, G. Bingham Powell, and Kenneth Prewitt. 1969. Social structure and political participation: Developmental relationships. *American Political Science Review* 63 (2): 361–78 (Part 1) and 63 (4): 808–32 (Part 2).

9/11 Commission Report. http://www.9-11commission.gov/report/911Report.pdf.

Oneal, John R. 1988. The rationality of decision making during international crises. *Polity* 20 (4): 598–622.

Oneal, John R., Bruce Russett, and Michael L. Berbaum. 2003. Causes of peace: Democracy: interdependence, and international organizations, 1885–1992. *International Studies Quarterly* 47 (3): 371–93.

Owen, John M. 1994. How liberalism produces democratic peace. *International Security* 19 (2): 87–125.

Owen, John M. 1997. *Liberal peace, liberal war: American politics and international security.* Ithaca: Cornell University Press.

Parsons, Craig. 2007. *How to map arguments in political science.* Oxford: Oxford University Press.

Patomäki, Heikki. 2002. *After international relations: Critical realism and the (re)construction of world politics.* New York: Routledge.

Peirce, C. S. 1955. *Philosophical writings of Peirce.* Edited by J. Buchler. New York: Dover Publications.

Pierson, Paul. 2004. *Politics in time: History, institutions, and social analysis.* Princeton: Princeton University Press.

Poggi, Gianfranco. 1978. *The development of the modern state: A sociological introduction,* Stanford: Stanford University Press.

Poggi, Gianfranco. 1991. Max Weber's conceptual portrait of feudalism. In *Max Weber: Critical assessments 1,* vol. 3, edited by P. Hamilton. London: Routledge.

Przeworski, Adam, and Henry Teune. 1966. Equivalence in cross-national research. *Public Opinion Quarterly* 30 (4): 551–68.

Przeworski, Adam, and Henry Teune. 1970. *The logic of comparative social inquiry.* New York: Wiley-Interscience.

Putnam, R. D., R. Leonardi, and R. Nanetti. 1993. *Making democracy work: Civil traditions in modern Italy.* Princeton, NJ: Princeton University Press.

Ragin, Charles C. 1987. *The comparative method: Moving beyond qualitative and quantitative strategies.* Berkeley: University of California Press.

Ragin, Charles C. 2000. *Fuzzy-set social science.* Chicago: University of Chicago Press.

Ragin, Charles C. 2008. *Redesigning social inquiry: Fuzzy sets and beyond.* Chicago: University of Chicago Press.

Ragin, Charles, and Garrett Andrew Schneider. 2011. Case-oriented theory building and theory testing. In *Sage handbook of innovation in social research methods,* edited by Malcolm Williams and W. Paul Vogt, 150–66. London: Sage.

Reiss, Julian. 2011. Third time's a charm: Causation, science and Wittgensteinian pluralism. In *Causality in the sciences,* edited by Phyllis McKay Illari, Federica Russo, and Jon Williamson, 907–28. Oxford: Oxford University Press.

Reynolds, Susan. 1994. *Fiefs and vassals.* Oxford: Clarendon Press.

Rhodes, William. 2010. Heterogeneous treatment effects: What does a regression estimate? *Evaluation Review* 34 (4): 334–61.

Roberts, Clayton. 1996. *The logic of historical explanation*. University Park: Pennsylvania State University Press.

Rohlfing, Ingo. 2012. *Case studies and causal inference: An integrative framework*. Houndmills: Palgrave Macmillan.

Rohlfing, Ingo. 2014. Comparative hypothesis testing via process tracing. *Sociological Methods and Research* 43 (4): 606–42.

Rosato, Sebastian. 2011. *Europe united: Power politics and the making of the European Community*. Ithaca: Cornell University Press.

Rozanski, Jerzi, and Alexander, Alexander. 1994. On the (in)accuracy of economic observations: An assessment of trends in the reliability of international trade statistics. *Journal of Development Economics* 44: 103–30.

Rubach, Timothy J. 2010. "Let me tell the story straight on": Middlemarch, process-tracing methods, and the politics of the narrative. *British Journal of Politics and International Relations* 12 (4): 477–97.

Rubin, Donald B. 1974. Estimating causal effects of treatments in randomized and nonrandomized studies. *Journal of Educational Psychology* 66 (5): 688–701.

Rueschemeyer, Dietrich. 2003. Can one or a few cases yield theoretical gains? In *Comparative historical analysis in the social sciences*, edited by James Mahoney and D. Rueschemeyer, 305–37. Cambridge: Cambridge University Press.

Runhardt, Rosa W. 2015. Evidence for causal mechanisms in social science: Recommendations from Woodward's manipulability theory of causation. *Philosophy of Science* 82 (5): 1296–1307.

Russo, Federica, and Jon Williamson. 2007. Interpreting causality in the health science. *International Studies in the Philosophy of Science* 21 (2): 157–70.

Russo, Federica, and Jon Williamson. 2011. Generic versus single-case causality: The case of autopsy. *European Journal of the Philosophy of Science* 1 (1): 47–69.

Sabetti, Filippo. 2004. Local roots of constitutionalism. *Perspectives on Political Science* 33 (2): 70–78.

Salmon, Wesley. 1998. *Causality and explanation*. Oxford: Oxford University Press.

Sambanis, Nicholas. 2001. Do ethnic and nonethnic civil wars have the same causes? A theoretical and empirical inquiry. *Journal of Conflict Resolution* 45 (3): 259–82.

Sarkees, Meredith Reid, and Frank Wayman. 2010. *Resort to war: 1816–2007*. Washington, DC: CQ Press.

Sartori, Giovanni. 1970. Concept misformation in comparative politics. *American Political Science Review* 64 (4): 1033–53.

Sartori, Giovanni. 1984. Guidelines for concept analysis. In *Social science concepts: A systematic analysis*, edited by in Giovanni Sartori, 15–85. Beverly Hills: Sage.

Sartori, Giovanni. 1991. Comparing and miscomparing. *Journal of Theoretical Politics* 3: 243–57.

Sartori, Giovanni. 2009. Guidelines for concept analysis. In *Concepts and methods in social science: The tradition of Giovanni Sartori*, edited by David Collier and John Gerring, 97–150. London: Routledge.

Sawyer, R. Keith. 2004. The mechanisms of emergence. *Philosophy of the Social Science* 34 (2): 260–82.

Schedler, Andreas. 2012. Judgment and measurement in political science. *Perspectives on Politics* 10 (1): 21–36.

Schimmelfennig, Frank. 2001. The community trap: Liberal norms, rhetorical action, and the eastern enlargement of the European Union. *International Organization* 55 (1): 47–80.

Schlottmann, Anne. 1999. Seeing it happen and knowing how it works: How children understand the relation between perceptual causality and underlying mechanism. *Developmental Psychology* 35 (1): 303–17.

Schmitter, Philippe C. 1979. Still the century of corporatism? In *Trends towards corporatism intermediation*, edited by P. Schmitter and G. Lehmbruch, 7–49. London: Sage.

Schneider, Carsten, and Ingo Rohlfing. 2013. Combining QCA and process tracing in set-theoretical multi-method research. *Sociological Methods and Research* 42 (4): 559–97.

Schneider, Carsten, and Claudius Wagemann. 2012. *Set-theoretic methods for the social sciences—A guide to qualitative comparative analysis*. Cambridge: Cambridge University Press.

Schroeder, Paul. 1994. Historical reality vs. neo-realist theory. *International Security* 19 (1): 108–48.

Schroeder, Paul. 1997. History and international relations theory: Not use or abuse, but fit or misfit. *International Security* 22 (1): 64–74.

Schwartz-Shea, Peregrine, and Dvora Yanow. 2011. *Interpretive research design*. London: Routledge.

Scriven, Michael. 2011. Evaluation, bias and its control. *Journal of Multidisciplinary Evaluation* 7 (15): 79–98.

Seawright, Jason. 2002. Testing for necessary and/or sufficient causation: Which cases are relevant? *Political Analysis* 10 (2): 178–93.

Shrapnel, Sally. 2014. Quantum causal explanation; or, Why birds fly south. *European Journal of the Philosophy of Science* 4 (3): 409–23.

Sil, Rudra, and Peter J. Katzenstein. 2010. *Beyond paradigms: Analytical eclecticism in the study of world politics*. Basingstoke: Palgrave Macmillan.

Silver, Nate. 2013. *The signal and the noise*. New York: Penguin Books.

Skaaning, Svend-Erik. 2011. Assessing the robustness of crisp-set and fuzzy-set QCA results. *Sociological Methods and Research* 40 (2): 391–408.

Skocpol, Theda. 1979. *States and social revolutions: A comparative analysis of France, Russia and China*. Cambridge: Cambridge University Press.

Skocpol, Theda, and Margaret Somers. 1980. The uses of comparative history in macrosocial inquiry. *Comparative Studies in Society and History* 22 (2): 174–97.

Sober, Elliot. 2009. Absence of evidence and evidence of absence: Evidential transitivity in connection with fossils, fishing, fine-tuning, and firing squads. *Philosophical Studies* 143 (1): 63–90.

Stasavage, David. 2010. When distance mattered: Geographic scale and the development of European representative assemblies. *American Political Science Review* 104 (4): 625–43.

Stasavage, David. 2011. *States of credit: Size, power, and the development of European polities*. Princeton: Princeton University Press.

Stasavage, David. 2014. Was Weber right? City autonomy, political oligarchy, and the rise of Europe. *American Political Science Review* 108 (2): 337–54.

Steel, Daniel. 2004. Social mechanisms and causal inference. *Philosophy of the Social Sciences* 34 (1): 55–78.

Steel, Daniel. 2008. *Across the boundaries: Extrapolation in biology and social science.* Oxford: Oxford University Press.

Stephenson, Carl. 1942. *Mediaeval feudalism.* Ithaca: Cornell University Press.

Stevens, Stanley Smith. 1946. On the theory of scales of measurement. *Science,* n.s., 103 (2684): 677–80.

Stinchcombe, Arthur L. 1991. The conditions of fruitfulness of theorizing about mechanisms in social science. *Philosophy of the Social Sciences* 21 (3): 367–88.

Strayer, Joseph R. 1975. Feudalism in Western Europe. In *Lordship and community in medieval Europe: Selected readings,* edited by F. L. Cheyette. New York: Huntingdon.

Strayer, Joseph R. 1987 [1965]. *Feudalism.* Malabar: Krieger Company.

Streeck, Wolfgang, and Kathleen Thelen, eds. 2005. *Beyond continuity: Institutional change in advanced political economies.* Oxford: Oxford University Press.

Suganami, Hidemi. 1996. *On the causes of war.* Oxford: Clarendon Press.

Swedberg, Richard. 2012. Theorizing in sociology and social science: turning to the context of discovery. *Theoretical Sociology* 41 (1): 1–40.

Tallberg, Jonas. 2006. *Leadership and negotiation in the European Union.* Cambridge University Press.

Tannenwald, Nina. 1999. The nuclear taboo: The United States and the normative basis of nuclear non-use. *International Organization* 53 (3): 433–68.

Tarrow, Sidney. 2010. The strategy of paired comparisons: Toward a theory of practice. *Comparative Political Studies* 43 (2): 230–59.

Tetlock, Philip E., and Aaron Belkin, eds. 1996. *Counterfactual thought experiments in world politics: Logical, methodological, and psychological perspectives.* Princeton: Princeton University Press.

Teune, Henry. 1990. Comparing countries: Lessons learned. In *Comparative methodology: Theory and practice in international social research,* edited by E. Fyen, 38–62. London: Sage.

Thies, Cameron G. 2002. A pragmatic guide to qualitative historical analysis and the study of international relations. *International Studies Perspectives* 3: 351–72.

Timmermans, Stefan, and Iddo Tavory. 2012. Theory construction in qualitative research: From grounded theory to abductive analysis. *Sociological Theory* 30 (3): 167–86.

Trachtenberg, Marc. 2006. *The craft of international history.* Princeton: Princeton University Press.

Valenzuela, J. Samuel. 1985. *Democratización vía reforma: La expansión del sufragio en Chile.* Buenos Aires: Ediciones del IDES.

Van Deth, Jan W. 2013. Equivalence in comparative political research. In *Comparative politics: The problem of equivalence,* edited by J. W. van Deth, 1–19. Colchester: ECPR Press.

Van Evera, Stephen. 1997. *Guide to methods for students of political science.* Ithaca: Cornell University Press.

Vanhanen, T., ed. 1997. *Prospects of democracy: A study of 172 countries.* New York: Routledge.

Van Kersbergen, Kees. 2010. Comparative politics: Some points for discussion. *European Political Science* 9: 49–61.

Van Zanden, Jan Luiten, Eltjo Buringh, and Maarten Bosker. 2012. The rise and decline of European parliaments, 1188–1789. *Economic History Review* 65 (3): 835–61.

Verkuilen, Jay. 2005. Assigning membership in a fuzzy set analysis. *Sociological Methods and Research* 33 (4): 462–96.

Von Baeyer, Hans Christian. 2013. Quantum weirdness: It's all in your mind. *Scientific American* 308 (6): 46–51.

Vu, Tuong. 2010. Studying the state through state formation. *World Politics* 62: 148–75.

Wagenaar, Hendrik. 2011. *Meaning in action.* Armonk, NY: M. E. Sharpe.

Wagner, Carl. G. 2001. Old evidence and new explanation III. *Philosophy of Science* 68 (3): S165–75.

Waldner, David. 1999. *State building and late development.* Ithaca: Cornell University Press.

Waldner, David. 2012. Process tracing and causal mechanisms. In *Oxford handbook of the philosophy of social science,* edited by H. Kincaid, 65–84. Oxford: Oxford University Press.

Waldner, David. 2014. What makes process tracing good? Causal mechanisms, causal inference, and the completeness standard in comparative politics. In *Process tracing: From metaphor to analytic tool,* edited by Andrew Bennett and Jeffrey Checkel, 126–52. Cambridge: Cambridge University Press.

Walker, Vern. 2007. Discovering the logic of legal reasoning. *Hofstra Law Review* 35: 1687–1708.

Ward, John O. 1985. Feudalism: Interpretative category or framework of life in the medieval West? In *Feudalism: Comparative studies,* edited by E. Leach, S. N. Mukherjee, and J. Ward. Sydney: Sydney Association for Studies in Society and Culture.

Waskan, Jonathan. 2008. Knowledge of counterfactual interventions through cognitive models of mechanisms. *International Studies in the Philosophy of Science* 22 (3): 259–75.

Waskan, Jonathan. 2011. Mechanistic explanation at the limit. *Synthese* (183): 389–408.

Weisberg, Jonathan. 2009. Commutativity or holism? A dilemma for conditionalizers. *British Journal of the Philosophy of Science* 60: 793–812.

Wendt, Alexander. 1999. *Social theory of international politics.* Cambridge: Cambridge University Press.

Wendt, Alexander. 2015. *Quantum mind and social science: Unifying physical and social ontology.* Cambridge: Cambridge University Press.

Wight, Colin. 2004. Theorizing the mechanisms of conceptual and semiotic space. *Philosophy of the Social Sciences* 34 (2): 283–99.

Williams, Malcolm, and Wendy Dyer. 2009. Single-case probabilities. In *The Sage handbook of case-based methods,* edited by David Byrne and Charles C. Ragin, 84–100. London: Sage.

Wohlforth, William C. 1997. New evidence on Moscow's Cold War: Ambiguity in search of theory. *Diplomatic History* 21 (2): 229–57.

Wohlforth, William C. 2001. Postscript: Historical science and Cold War scholarship. In *Bridges and boundaries: Historians political scientists and the study of international relations*, edited by Colin Elman and Miriam Fendius Elman, 351–58. Cambridge: MIT Press.

Woodward, Bob. 2004. *Plan of attack*. New York: Simon & Schuster.

Woodward, James. 2003. *Making things happen: A theory of causal explanation*. Oxford: Oxford University Press.

Woodward, James. 2004. Counterfactuals and causal explanation. *International Studies in the Philosophy of Science* 18: 41–72.

Ziblatt, Daniel. 2009. Shaping democratic practice and the causes of electoral fraud: The case of nineteenth-century Germany. *American Political Science Review* 103 (1): 1–21.

Ziblatt, Daniel, and Dan Slater. 2013. The enduring indispensability of the controlled comparison. *Comparative Political Studies* 46 (10): 1301–27.

Index

Page numbers in italics refer to tables and figures.